Thomas Jefferson
& the Stony Mountains

From this point Mount Hood is seen 20 leagues
distant, which is probably a dependence of the
Stony mountains . . . and the source of the
Missouri is probably in the Stony Mountains.

Jefferson to Meriwether Lewis, 15 July 1803

Thomas Jefferson
& the Stony Mountains

Exploring the West
from Monticello

DONALD *Dean* JACKSON

UNIVERSITY OF ILLINOIS PRESS

Urbana · Chicago · London

BY DONALD JACKSON

Black Hawk: An Autobiography (Urbana, 1955).

The Journals of Zebulon Montgomery Pike: With Letters and Related Documents. 2 vols. (editor, Norman, Okla., 1966).

Custer's Gold: The U.S. Cavalry Expedition of 1874 (New Haven, 1966).

The Expeditions of John Charles Frémont. 2 vols. (editor, with Mary Lee Spence, Urbana, 1970–73).

George Washington and the War of Independence (Richmond, 1976).

The Diaries of George Washington. 6 vols. (editor, with Dorothy Twohig, Charlottesville, 1976–79).

Letters of the Lewis and Clark Expedition: With Related Documents, 1783–1854. 2 vols. (editor, Urbana, 1978; first ed., 1962).

© 1981 by the Board of Trustees of the University of Illinois
Manufactured in the United States of America

Library of Congress Cataloging in Publication Data

Jackson, Donald Dean, 1919–
Thomas Jefferson & the Stony Mountains.

Bibliography: p.
Includes index.
1. Jefferson, Thomas, Pres. U. S., 1743–1826—
Views on the West. 2. Jefferson, Thomas, Pres.
U.S., 1743–1826—Books and reading. 3. The West—
Description and travel—To 1848. I. Title.
E332.2.J32 973.4′6′0924 80-10546
ISBN 0-252-00823-5

FOR ROBERT WOODS JACKSON AND

MARK RICHARD JACKSON

CONTENTS

MAPS

PREFACE

While they acknowledge his role in the Louisiana Purchase, and are aware that he sponsored Lewis and Clark, the American people have never thought of Jefferson as a man of the West. Among the folk heroes and demigods who inhabit that illusory land of gallant memories, Jefferson would seem to modern Americans rather out of place. He is their revered founding father and author of their Declaration, not one who belongs in the tumultuous world of Zebulon Pike, Kit Carson, Jim Bridger, Red Cloud, General George Custer, and the thousands of dusty travelers whose spirits crowd the Oregon trail.

But during four decades, while the future of the Trans-Mississippi West was being decided, Jefferson was the most towering westerner of them all. In the 1780s and 1790s, when American possession of the West seemed incredibly far in the future, he taught himself more about the plains and the Rockies than anyone else, as if preparing unconsciously to govern those vast spaces one day. During his presidency in 1801–9, he responded brilliantly to unexpected events in foreign affairs, using his knowledge and insight to project vital explorations and organize the newly acquired Territory of Louisiana. Then, as a senior statesman until his death in 1826, he was the counselor of men whose hopes for the future of the West were Jeffersonian in essence. The western policies of Madison, Monroe, and John Quincy Adams were a part of his legacy.

And so, incredibly, there is still a place in the historical literature for another book on Jefferson. I have not attempted a study of the whole man, for we are richly fitted out with such books. This is what must be called an "aspect" book, and we have plenty of those also: Jefferson the philosopher, the architect, the scientist, the book collector, the tourist. We happen not to have a work on the aspect of Jefferson's career which gave Americans a place they call Out West.

The writer of an aspect book has at first glance made things easier for himself by choosing not to rework the entire corpus of information on Jefferson. He finds, however, that the lives of great men do not easily come asunder. Still, if one historian can produce a study of Jefferson without mentioning the Columbia River, the Pacific Ocean, William Clark, Alexander Mackenzie, William Henry Harrison, or the Loyal Land Company, then another may feel justified in attempting an appraisal that does not touch upon such subjects as Maria Cosway and Sally Hemings, or go extensively into Jefferson's enigmatic attitude toward slavery, his views on theology, or the workings of his mind as he penned the Declaration of Independence.

My intention has been to devote this work to Jefferson's interest in the Trans-Mississippi West and its exploration, confining the material where I can to his preoccupation with tangibles: the mountains and watercourses, the plants and animals, the Indians. But almost everything that Jefferson did as a public man had some effect on the American West, so there are elements here besides the land and its biota. There is some foreign policy, there is some domestic politics, and there is always the personality of Jefferson bringing us back again and again to the whole man.

The writer of a special biographical study soon begins to make arbitrary decisions. When I deal with the Louisiana Purchase I choose not to dwell upon the familiar story of the negotiations, but rather upon Jefferson's later work in learning about what the nation had bought—the boundaries, the inhabitants, the potential of the country. I do not wade into the old Aaron Burr mysteries, but instead discuss Jefferson's perplexing relationship with James Wilkinson, Burr's "accomplice," who was involved in frontier intrigues during most of Jefferson's public life. In western matters, Wilkinson seemed forever on the scene, at least in the background.

Jefferson collected the greatest library in America on the geography, cartography, natural history, and ethnology of the New

World. Yet so little was known of that awesome *terra incognita* that he entered into the presidential years believing these things: that the Blue Ridge Mountains of Virginia might be the highest on the continent; that the mammoth, the giant ground sloth, and other prehistoric creatures would be found along the upper Missouri; that a mountain of pure salt a mile long lay somewhere on the Great Plains; that volcanoes might still be erupting in the Badlands of the upper Missouri; that all the great rivers of the West—the Missouri, Columbia, Colorado, and Rio Grande— rose from a single "height of land" and flowed off in their several directions to the seas of the hemisphere. Most important, he believed there might be a water connection, linked by a low portage across the mountains, that would lead to the Pacific.

The Lewis and Clark expedition—the exploring venture nearest his heart—quieted his myths but diminished his expectations. There was no water passage across the continent, nor any passage at all that was without suffering and incredible toil. But, as Lewis and Clark were returning down the Missouri in the summer of 1806, they met American traders rowing against the stubborn current with cargoes of Indian goods. While Jefferson still lived, a trail was opened to Santa Fe. Soon after his death there were trails to Oregon and then to California; the cargo in the wagons had changed from trade goods to plows and kitchenware. The prairie mornings rang with the eager chatter of westering settlers, and every turn of the wheel broadened a roadway that began at Monticello in Virginia.

• Acknowledgments •

My research before 1977 was done mainly at the University of Virginia Libraries, and after that at the Charles Leaming Tutt Library, Colorado College. I am grateful to librarians Ray W. Frantz, Jr., in Charlottesville, and Colonel George V. Fagan, in Colorado Springs, for the splendid assistance which they and their staffs provided. Members of the Library of Congress and National Archives staffs were predictably cooperative. At the American Philosophical Society, I could always count upon ready counsel from Whitfield J. Bell, Jr., and Murphy D. Smith.

To Dumas Malone and Merrill D. Peterson, my former associates at the University of Virginia, go my thanks for listening and for making fine suggestions.

A draft of the manuscript was read perceptively by Lester J. Cappon and Savoie Lottinville, whom I have long known as respected scholars and friends.

Finally, I elect the following persons to represent the many colleagues and even a few strangers who have given willing and essential aid: Irving W. Anderson, Harold B. Billian, Philander D. Chase, Paul R. Cutright, Robert B. Fisher, Stephen H. Hochman, Oliver W. Holmes, Robert E. Lange, Emily Miles, Nancy Morris, Joyce Price, Francis Paul Prucha, Frances H. Stadler, Richard W. Stephenson, and George Tweney. Were I to go back twenty-five years and acknowledge those peers who have been so generous in helping me to learn more about the westward movement, the list would be untenably long. And my wife, Mary Catherine Jackson, would have a listing of her own.

Colorado Springs   Donald Jackson
October 1979

Thomas Jefferson
& the Stony Mountains

CHAPTER ONE

A Gap in the Cumberlands

wo French explorers had come south from their trading
post on the Assiniboine River, in Canada, to travel in the
country of the Mandans and other tribes of the upper
Missouri. In the region that is now North and South Dakota,
they were pursuing the eternal French dream of finding a route
across the continent to the Pacific. The year was 1742, and the
brothers—Louis-Joseph and François de La Vérendrye—were the
sons of a man who had himself trod the high plains in the same
quest. They had been sent by the Sieur de La Vérendrye, who
ranks with Champlain and La Salle in the annals of French
exploration.

The wanderings of the La Vérendrye sons in 1742–43 cannot
be traced with certainty, for the record they left is vague. We do
not even know which Indians they met, but they probably encountered or traveled with the Arapaho, Cheyenne, Pawnee,
Kiowa, Arikara, and Mandan tribes. Some of their actions, of
which we know for sure, still excite the imagination. They
buried a crudely inscribed lead plate on a hill at the mouth of the
Bad River—to be found nearly two centuries later—and they
journeyed far enough to the west to observe a new range of
mountains. Although this undetermined range was possibly the
Black Hills of South Dakota, the brothers may have gone far
enough to see the Big Horns of Wyoming. In either case they
found snowy crests that fueled their dream, for there was said to
be a range called the Shining or Stony Mountains, from the
Western slopes of which a great river ran on to the sea. Fear of
hostile Indians forced the La Vérendryes to turn back, convinced
that they were near the Pacific or South Sea. Their real location is
less important than where they *thought* they were; the maps that

men draw in their minds, before the actual ones are made, are powerful documents that tempt the curious and the ambitious always farther afield.

After returning from the mountains, Louis-Joseph and François spent the winter with the Arikaras in their earth lodges along the Missouri. In the early spring, when cold rains were beginning to replace the snows and ice was stirring in the river, they reluctantly left their hosts and turned toward home. In their report they wrote, "Nous partîmes le 2 Avril bien regrettes de toute la nation."[1]

On the day the brothers urged their horses into the face of the north wind and headed homeward, Thomas Jefferson was born half a continent away in the colony of Virginia. He would probably never hear of the La Vérendryes, but some day the Arikaras and Mandans would call him their Great Father. He would never see the western mountains, but his interest in the unexplored parts of North America and the authority he bore as president of a restless, moving nation would make him the single most important figure in the early development of the American West.

· Growing Up with Geographers ·

The frontier of Jefferson's boyhood was not much older than that of the Frenchmen in the north. Born just a few days' ride from the Virginia Capes on the Atlantic shore, he lived less than twenty miles from the western edge of his world. The Blue Ridge, a mountain range lying dark and low on the horizon and looking, at times, much like the Black Hills so far away, was still a barrier to Virginians. There were gaps aplenty that made pathways through the mountains: Rockfish Gap, Jarman's Gap, and the rest. But in the 1740s not many wanderers were interested in those passages. Jefferson was born at Shadwell in the valley of the Rivanna. When his father, Peter, had settled in that part of the Piedmont, only a scattering of families had lived in the area.[2] Although some Virginians had long been crossing the Alleghenies, of which the Blue Ridge was a part, and knew the waters of the upper Ohio long before the French had any knowledge of its courses, there were few such adventurers.[3]

Jefferson's father, and a small group with whom he associated, were westbound men in their hearts. Some only thought of the rich lands beyond the Blue Ridge, some talked heartily of going there, and some went. Of these, four men can be said to have shaped by work and action the view of the West that prevailed in Jefferson's household and neighborhood. They are Peter Jefferson, Joshua Fry, Thomas Walker, and James Maury.

Peter Jefferson had married Jane Randolph and come to the valley to build an image that is partly folk history and partly a mosaic of isolated facts. His son wrote of him, "My father's education had been quite neglected; but being of a strong mind, sound judgment, and eager after information, he read much and improved himself, insomuch that he was chosen, with Joshua Fry, Professor of Mathematics in William and Mary college, to continue the boundary line between Virginia and North Carolina . . . and was afterwards employed with the same Mr. Fry, to make the first map of Virginia which had ever been made."[4]

The tradition, as set down by Jefferson's earliest biographers, is that Peter was a big man, large in stature, strength, and presence, a portrayal that one historian calls "the Sampson legend."[5] He became a large landowner, a vestryman, justice of the peace, and sheriff. On his first western expedition in 1746, he and Thomas Lewis surveyed the Fairfax line, the boundary of a large grant from the crown to Lord Fairfax.[6] Other travels followed, and it is as a surveyor and mapmaker that Peter becomes important as a source of young Thomas Jefferson's attitudes toward land and its measurement, exploration, and husbandry.

In 1751, Joshua Fry and Peter Jefferson completed their *Map of the Most Inhabited Part of Virginia Containing the Whole Province of Maryland*. The two had been appointed to the task by the Virginia House of Burgesses, directed from London by the Royal Board of Trade. As the first mapping of Virginia done from actual surveys, it was quite accurate for the region east of the Alleghenies, which the two men knew best. Printed in four sheets in London about 1754, the map was followed by a corrected version—the emendations made chiefly by Fry, who had meantime done further exploring for the Ohio Company. It is impossible to say how much of the map is the result of actual observations by Fry or Jefferson, for, as cartographers frequently must, they may have used earlier surveys. In the same spirit, their own map was used with due acknowledgment by Lewis Evans when, in 1755, he published his famed *A General Map of the Middle British Colonies, in America.*[7]

The great mapmaking achievement of Fry and Jefferson was performed while Thomas was but a small child and could not have had an immediate effect upon him. Later he would become a collector and maker of maps, and a surveyor as well, using the Fry-Jefferson production as a basis for his only published cartographic work. He would learn to know the instruments of the surveyor and draftsman, and to think of land not just in terms of acres but of roods, poles, and perches. He would know mereing lines and meresmen, lead chainmen and hind chainmen.[8]

Among members of the group in Albemarle County who were beginning to think ambitiously of western lands was Dr. Thomas Walker, of Castle Hill, who was a neighbor, friend, and later an executor of Peter Jefferson's estate. He became a prime figure in a land operation that was to send him off in 1750 to make an important geographical visitation.

Land companies awarded charters by the crown were eager to establish patents in new regions between the East Coast and the Ohio Valley. The Loyal Company, often called the Loyal Land Company, was awarded 800,000 acres running west and north along the lower boundary of Virginia.[9] Members of the company included Peter Jefferson, Joshua Fry, Thomas Walker, James Maury, Peachy Gilmer, and other men of Albemarle. Dr. Walker was named field agent of the company in 1749 with the assignment of locating lands for its members. He left Castle Hill in March 1750, with a few men, heading for the region to become known as Kentucky; they traveled up the Shenandoah Valley southward until they reached a well-worn Indian trail leading west into the Appalachians. On 13 April Walker reached a gap in the range, on the divide between the Tennessee and Cumberland rivers. This cleft in the mountain, more than 1,600 feet above sea level and about 1,000 feet deep, was known to a few white men. Dr. Walker cannot be said to have discovered it, but he put it on the map, calling it Cave Gap in his journal, later renaming it Cumberland Gap, and assigning the same name to the mountain and the river. The gap soon appeared (though not by name) on Lewis Evans's map of 1755. It was a gateway through the Appalachian barrier that led to the bluegrass country of Kentucky. Through this gap Daniel Boone was to pass nineteen years later, followed in time by countless Americans pouring into the fertile valleys of the Midwest.[10]

During the years in which his father and Fry were making their map, and his future guardian Dr. Walker was reporting on the Cumberland Gap, young Jefferson lived not at Shadwell but at Tuckahoe. Peter's close friend William Randolph of Tuckahoe, in Goochland County, had died in 1745 and asked in his will that the Jeffersons move into his home and care for his three orphaned children. It was here that Thomas spent six of his first nine years, attending school in a small plantation schoolhouse. After the Jeffersons came home to Shadwell, the boy was sent to the classical school of a Scottish minister, the Reverend William Douglas, learning not only the rudiments of the classical languages but of French as well. For five years he stayed with the Douglases nine months of each year.

At fourteen, Thomas lost his father. He inherited about 5,000 acres of land with restrictions upon it until he became of age, a library of forty-two volumes, and a tremendous thirst for knowledge. The executors of Peter's estate, among themselves and doubtless in conference with his widow, decided to send Thomas to still another school. An autobiographical scrap has survived, upon which the lad wrote: "1758 Jan. 17. I went to Mr. Maury."[11]

James Maury, member of a Huguenot family that had fled France after the Edict of Nantes and settled in England, was pastor of the parish of Fredericksville, which included Albemarle County. Maury appears to have been an adequate but lackluster teacher. Between January 1758 and January 1760 he earned twenty pounds a year by giving Jefferson board, room, and instruction.[12]

Except for one quality, the Reverend Maury might have earned only a line or two in any study of Jefferson. That is about all that Jefferson himself gave the man in his brief autobiography, written late in life. But Maury was interested in geography and fascinated by tales of the West. Like all members of the Loyal Company, he hoped for riches in the forests and grasslands behind the Blue Ridge. He may have longed for adventure, too. He had seen in the home of Fry a book by Daniel Coxe, *A Description of the English Province of Carolana, by the Spaniards Call'd Florida, and by the French La Louisiane.* The book and its accompanying map caused James Maury to write a detailed description of the Mississippi drainage basin,[13] and some of Coxe's claims about the geography of the West led members of the Loyal Company into a more ambitious plan. No man westward bent could remain calm upon reading a passage such as this about "the Great Yellow River," actually called the Missouri: "so nam'd because it is Yellowish and so muddy, That tho' the Meschacebe [Mississippi] is very clear where they meet, and so many great Rivers of Christaline water below, mix with the Meschacebe, yet it discolours them all even unto the Sea. When you are up this River 60 or 70 Miles, you meet with two Branches. The lesser, tho' large, proceeds from the South, and most of the Rivers that compose it fall from the Mountains, which separate this Country from Mexico; notwithstanding which, there is a very easie Communication between them."[14]

Coxe's map shows the Missouri extending westward to an unnamed range of mountains. Encouraged by this report and perhaps by other descriptions of Louisiana appearing in *The Gentleman's Magazine* in 1753,[15] the Loyal Company devised a grand enterprise. We would know nothing of it today had not Maury written about it to Moses Fontaine in Janaury 1756: "Some persons were to be sent in search of that river Missouri, if that be the right name of it, in order to discover whether it had any communication with the Pacific Ocean; they were to follow the river if they found it, and exact reports of the country they passed through, the distances they traveled, what worth of navigation those river and lakes afforded, etc."[16]

These plans were laid in 1753, with Dr. Walker chosen to lead the expedition. The French and Indian War intervened and nothing came of the scheme. Young Jefferson was ten years old at the time, and must surely have heard the proposed expedition discussed at home. If not, then perhaps he learned of it in the Reverend Maury's classroom five or six years later.

It is conventional for historians to review these early influences

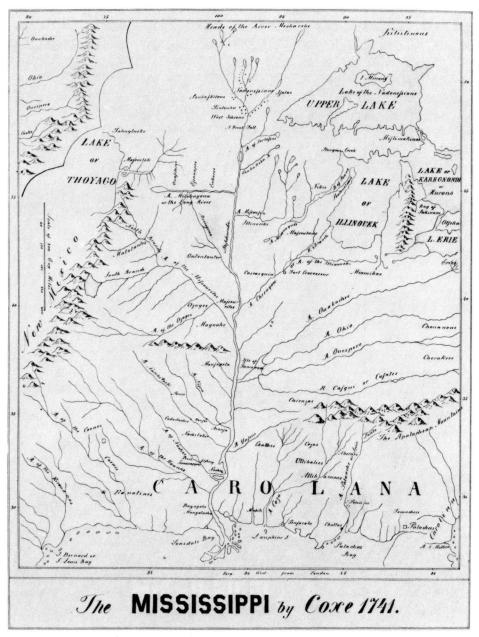

1. Tracing of Coxe's map of the Mississippi and "Carolana." LIBRARY OF CONGRESS

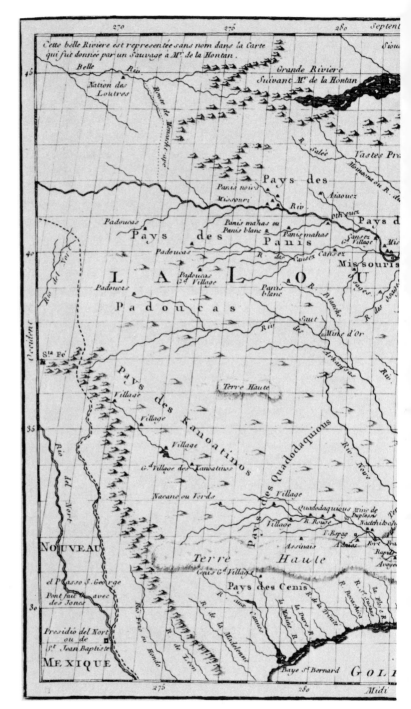

2. Louisiana, from Le Page du Pratz's *Histoire de la Louisiane*.

CARTE
DE LA LOUISIANE
Colonie Française
avec le Cours du Fleuve St. Louis,
les Rivieres Adjacentes,
les Nations des Naturels, les Etablissem.ᵗ Français
et les Mines.
Par l'Auteur de l'Histoire
de cette Province
1757.

on Jefferson and conclude that he was overpowered by the call of the wild.[17] They quote his famous line, penned years later, that he was "savage enough to prefer the woods, the wilds and independence of Monticello, to all the brilliant pleasures of this gay capital [Paris]."[18] In that passage he was merely indulging in word games: he loved to turn nice phrases. From his father he may have gained a love of maps and a disposition toward surveying; in Dr. Walker he gained an older friend, who would later serve with him in the House of Burgesses; James Maury had the interest and knowledge to imbue him with a romantic curiosity about the inner continent. The truth is, however, that none of these early associations with geographers, land speculators, and would–be discoverers played more than a small part in the early orientation of young Thomas Jefferson.

Other Virginians of his generation, such as George Washington and George Rogers Clark, joined land companies and became speculators. Jefferson, on the other hand, inherited a share of the Loyal Company and did nothing with it. We do not know if he ever read or bought books on the geography of the New World in those days, for his first library burned at Shadwell in 1770. He grew into a robust young farmer and a fine horseman, as able as any to endure the rigors of overland travel. But instead of adventure he craved learning. He seemed destined to learn of the West from the exploits of other men. Turning from the frontier of his childhood, he enrolled, in 1760, in the College of William and Mary at Williamsburg a few days before his seventeenth birthday.

• The Founding of Monticello •

Jefferson was at William and Mary for only two years, but he continued to read law and serve in the legislature, so that Williamsburg was his second home for nearly two decades. From this college and this provincial town he obtained as fine an education as he could have without traveling far to the north, or to Europe. He made friendships that would last a lifetime, and he gained stature—first in Virginia and then in the other colonies. That he was bookish, enchanted with learning, none could doubt. Frequently he claimed to have studied fifteen hours a day—especially in his second year—and when he tired of books he ran a mile out of the town and back at twilight. Yet he loved handsome horses, classical music, conviviality, and the company of comely women. Like Washington, he was fascinated by horse-racing, but only as an onlooker. Family tradition contains the names of his beloved horses Caractacus, Tarquin, Arcturus, and Eagle (his last horse, ridden when he was too feeble to mount by himself). He recalled practicing three hours a day on the violin in those years, and never gave up the instrument entirely until an injury to his wrist, long afterward, made playing impossible.[19]

In college, three men deeply affected Jefferson's life. He tells of their memorable influence himself:

It was my great good fortune, and what probably fixed the destinies of my life, that Dr. William Small of Scotland, was the Professor of Mathematics, a man profound in most of the useful branches of science, with a happy talent of communication, correct and gentlemanly manners, and an enlarged and liberal mind. He, most happily for me, became soon attached to me, and made me his daily companion when not engaged in the school; and from his conversation I got my first views of the expansion of science, and of the system of things in which we are placed. Fortunately, the philosophical chair became vacant soon after my arrival at college, and he was appointed to fill it *per interim:* and he was the first who ever gave, in that college, regular lectures in Ethics, Rhetoric and Belles Lettres. He returned to Europe in 1762, having previously filled up the measure of his goodness to me, by procuring for me, from his most intimate friend, George Wythe, a reception as a student of law, under his direction, and introduced me to the acquaintance and familiar table of Governor Fauquier, the ablest man who had ever filled that office. With him, and at his table, Dr. Small and Mr. Wythe, his *amici omnium horarum* [friends of all hours], and myself, formed a *partie quarée,* and to the habitual conversations on these occasions I owed much instruction. Mr. Wythe continued to be my faithful and beloved mentor in youth, and my most affectionate friend through life. In 1767, he led me into the practice of law at the bar of the General court, at which I continued until the Revolution shut up the courts of justice.[20]

Because Jefferson read so extensively and had an amazing diversity of interests, his career might have taken one of several turns. It is not easy to follow the influence of all the ideas to which he was exposed. Bacon, Newton, and Locke were his "trinity of three greatest men the world has produced." As he worshiped Newton, and was influenced by William Fauquier, whose father had worked with Newton, why did he not turn at once to science or mathematics? Perhaps he almost did. Years later he told Dr. Robert Patterson, "Before I entered on the business of this world I was much attached to astronomy & had laid a sufficient foundation at the College to have pursued it with satisfaction & advantage."[21]

There was less of the pure scientist in him, now and for a lifetime, than of the mechanic, the tinkerer, the gadgeteer, the amateur engineer. An early example is his work at the age of twenty to improve the Rivanna as a source of navigation. Learning that a canoe containing a family had passed several times along a section of the river that had been thought difficult, he explored the same area in a canoe "& found that section of the river could be made navigable for loaded boats by removing loose rocks only. I set on foot a subscription & obtained £200." With the aid of his friend, Dr. Walker, now in the House of Burgesses, he successfully encouraged an act to improve the nagivation of the Rivanna from its mouth upwards.[22]

These were days when he was reading law with George Wythe, managing his plantation, and looking hopefully to the hill overlooking his homestead where he would soon begin to build Monticello. It was clear that this spot was where he intended his life to center, but he yearned also to travel, especially in Europe. To his friend John Page he wrote that he planned to visit England, Holland, France, Spain, Italy, "where I would buy me a good fiddle," and Egypt, returning home by way of Canada.[23]

He was not to see Europe for another twenty-one years, but he made an early journey northward in 1766. He was in Annapolis when its citizens were celebrating the repeal of the Stamp Act. In Philadelphia, where he was no doubt sorely tempted by the array of books available in the shops, he was inoculated for smallpox by Dr. William Shippen, Jr. In New York he lodged in the same boardinghouse as Elbridge Gerry, of Massachusetts, a recent Harvard graduate who would later serve with him in the Continental Congress. Jefferson seems to have traveled overland mainly in a one-horse chair, a favorite kind of carriage.[24]

Back home again, he continued to prepare for a career in law and became an avid gardener. On a single day in April 1767, he planted nineteen kinds of flowers and fruiting plants, following with several vegetables during the next few days. On 28 May he wrote in his garden book—a diary of his plantings, harvestings, and related matters—"Strawberries come to table. Note this is the first year of their bearing having been planted in the spring of 1766 and on an average the plants bear 20 strawberries each." On 3 August he used the name Monticello for the first time, saying he had inoculated some common cherry buds into stocks of a larger kind at that place. He was then developing the grounds but the house was still to be built. He laid out specifications for the new home in 1768, contracting to have the top of the mountain leveled.[25]

Admitted to the Virginia bar, he began the practice of law in 1767. His account book lists sixty-eight cases during his first year, carrying him that fall to Staunton, Orange Court House, Culpeper Court House, Winchester, Fauquier Court House, and Richmond.[26] John W. Davis has speculated on what it was that turned his ambition toward the law. The mental exercise, perhaps, or the maternal tradition of his great-uncle, Sir John Randolph, who was attorney general under the crown. Two of his cousins, Peyton and John Randolph, were practicing in Williamsburg and would later become attorneys general.[27] There may have been a more persuasive attraction in the magnetic influence of George Wythe, under whom he had just finished five years of legal training.

Elected to the House of Burgesses in 1769, Jefferson soon became an effective and respected member. In the following year he lost Shadwell by fire. The loss could not have seemed a heavy one to Jefferson and his mother and sisters, for Monticello was well along toward completion and they would move into the house—when the southeast pavilion was partly done—in November. The larger loss was in the destruction of a major portion of his library. Except for those books he kept at Williamsburg, and perhaps some that he had already moved into the new house, he lost them all. Beginning immediately to replace the books with a new collection, he had gathered a library of more than a thousand books by 1773.[28]

If Jefferson showed little interest in western land speculation, he had of necessity to concern himself with Virginia properties, which—together with slaves—comprised the plantation system. In the 1770s his land totaled about 11,000 acres, located in Albemarle, Bedford, and Campbell counties. The land in the latter counties, eighty to ninety miles southwest of Monticello, he thought of collectively as Poplar Forest.[29] In later years he would comment on the reason he avoided the practice of western landholding. "I have never ventured in this way in my own country because being concerned in public business I was ever determined to keep my hands clear of every concern which might at any time produce an interference between private interests and public duties."[30]

His interest in mathematics, the tradition handed on by his father, and the sheer necessity for a large landholder to know what he has, made him a surveyor. He extended his craft beyond the boundaries of his own fields and, on 6 June 1773, accepted an appointment as surveyor of Albemarle County.[31]

His continuing interest in science seems to have been partly a product of his inquiring mind and partly another means of keeping up contact with his old Williamsburg circle. It is certain that he would have shown keen interest in the transit of Venus, an internationally observed event, in June 1769. His boyhood friend John Page wrote several articles for newspapers about the event, and Jefferson himself referred to it years later in a set of astronomical notes.[32]

Young Page, joining the respected botanist John Clayton and others, founded at Williamsburg in 1773 the Virginia Society for Promoting Useful Knowledge. Patterned after the Royal Society of London and the American Philosophical Society, it flourished for several years and at one time had a hundred members including Jefferson.[33] On 24 June 1778, at Monticello, Jefferson attempted to make observations on a total eclipse of the sun. He sent his notes for comment to the Reverend James Madison at Williamsburg, but was dissatisfied with his observations. It had been a cloudy day and he was hampered by the lack of a suitable timepiece. He wrote Philadelphia astronomer and instrument-maker David Rittenhouse, ordering an accurate clock for astronomical purposes.[34]

• Lawyer, Congressman, Governor •

In the context of this study, Jefferson's years from 1770 to 1781 can be covered briefly although they encompass some of the most momentous events in American history and in Jefferson's own career.[35]

On New Year's Day, 1772, he married Martha Wayles Skelton and brought her to the unfinished Monticello. His legal business was flourishing and he was still in the House of Burgesses. He owned fifty slaves in his own right and Martha had brought another 135 to the plantation. He was beginning to grow genuinely interested in agriculture along with his gardening. By the time the first of his children, Martha, was born in September 1772, Jefferson had become a rising member of the Virginia aristocracy.

Turmoil in the relationship with Britain had begun to occupy the minds of Virginians. Their royal governor, Lord Dunmore, dissolved one Assembly in Williamsburg and canceled the next before all the election returns were counted. But the freeholders of the colony called an unofficial convention of their own, in the summer of 1774, with Jefferson as a delegate from Albemarle. Although he became ill and could not attend, he sent the convention an extension of the ideas that had been brought forward by the Albemarle freeholders. Published without his consent, it became *A Summary View of the Rights of British America,* later reissued in Philadelphia and London. The pamphlet of twenty-three pages drew much attention and heightened Jefferson's reputation as a statesman.

In the following year he became a delegate to the first Continental Congress, in Philadelphia, and was chosen to return again in 1776. It was in June 1776 that he drafted that most desperate and inspired document, the Declaration of Independence. The War of the American Revolution had begun.

Believing that affairs in Virginia had first call upon his time and energy, Jefferson returned there in the fall of 1776 after first accepting, then declining, an appointment as commissioner to

France. Virginia was hardly touched by the war in its early stages; the captured army of mercenaries was sent to Charlottesville for confinement after the American victory at Saratoga, and the exploits of George Rogers Clark, at the head of Virginia forces, made news in victories over the British and Indians in the Ohio Valley. Later, Virginians were to know invasion and pillage, and during that time their governor was to be Jefferson—elected in June 1779.

After earlier invasions by Benedict Arnold and William Phillips, Virginia was ravaged by Cornwallis in 1781. She was ill-prepared, especially for inroads by sea. Governor Jefferson complained that when Arnold's fleet appeared in Hampton Roads on a Saturday, he was not even notified of it until Tuesday morning, and his call to the militia was all too late. Jefferson was a poor wartime governor, his decisions uneven and often timorous, his judgments not maturely developed.

Eventually the most decisive action of the war, the encounter at Yorktown, would be fought in Virginia. But Jefferson's closest personal encounter with the conflict, followed by his departure from the government, bore certain aspects of farce.

Dumas Malone calls it "retiring before the enemy under the inexorable pressure of events."[36] The government of the commonwealth had come unglued. Richmond had recently become the new capital, and the Assembly had been scheduled to meet there in early May 1781. But because of British activity that had threatened Richmond, a quorum of legislators failed to appear. Jefferson decided to move the seat of government temporarily to Charlottesville, and to convene the Assembly again ten days later. He rode to Tuckahoe, where his family had been relocated, then on to Monticello to await his colleagues. It was 28 May before a quorum was assembled.

Meanwhile a diversion arose—something that Jefferson was more able to cope with at the moment than the crumbling Virginia government. A delegation of Indians from the Mississippi Valley had crossed the mountains, come down the Shenandoah Valley on the old coach road, and journeyed in from Rockfish Gap to counsel with the governor. It was a routine that had been going on since the days of French and British rule—welcoming principal chiefs to the seat of government—and in earlier times such chiefs might find themselves sent all the way to Paris or London. The purpose of the white men in arranging these visitations was to pacify the tribes and remind them of the growing strength and power of the new order in America. To the Indians the trips were political junkets during which they haggled for concessions, begged for sustenance, or, in the case of the stronger tribes and confederations, threatened violent resistance. The trips were festive, for the Great Father was always generous with beads and other finery, as well as visits to the theaters and marketplaces of the eastern cities. But the hazards of travel were great, especially among a people who suffered diseases unknown to the Indians. It was usual for several members of each delegation from the distant tribes to die during the journey.

This deputation did not blunder innocently onto the fringes of war; the chiefs had been involved in it. The ranking member of the group was a bold and swart Kaskaskia Indian who had allied his kinsmen with George Rogers Clark in the recent western successes. He bore a Christian name, Jean Baptiste Ducoigne, for he had been converted to Catholicism by the Jesuits years earlier. His Indian name was Macouissa.

Jefferson had been a student of Indians and their history since boyhood, when the Cherokees sometimes stopped at Shadwell on their journeys to Williamsburg. Their language was the key, he supposed, to their common origin, and all his life he collected vocabularies of their varied tongues. Perhaps most of all he was fascinated by Indian oratory. He had heard it at Williamsburg, most memorably in a speech by Outasette or Outacity, a Cherokee chief who visited Williamsburg on his way to London in 1762. As a student, Jefferson had been near the Cherokee encampment when the chief had said farewell to the tribesmen who had come to see him sail for England. He had not understood a word of the Indian's prayer for the security of his people in his absence, or for his own safe return, but the man's stirring voice and the deep attention of his tribesmen had evoked in Jefferson an "awe and veneration" that never left him.[37]

Now Jefferson was Ducoigne's Great Father. Later, with the formation of the Union, that title would pass to George Washington and succeeding presidents.[38] It was Jefferson's duty, and no doubt a welcome digression from the sorry governmental business at hand, to write a speech to be read to the Indians. It surely was not his first Indian speech as Great Father, for other delegations must have appeared during his governorship, but it is the first one of which there is record. We do not know what Ducoigne said in his formal greeting to Jefferson, except to present some pictographs on animal skins and tell him that he had named his firstborn son Thomas Jefferson Ducoigne. Here is a part of Jefferson's reply:

I am very much pleased with the visit you have made us, and particularly that it has happened when the wise men from all parts of our country were assembled together in council, and had an opportunity of hearing the friendly discourse you held to me. We are all sensible of your friendship, and of the services you have rendered, and I now, for my countrymen, return you thanks, and, most particularly, for your assistance to the garrison [of George Rogers Clark] which was besieged by the hostile Indians. I hope it will please the Great Being above to continue you long in life, in health and in friendship to us; and that your son will afterwards succeed you in wisdom, in good disposition, and in power over your people. I consider the name you have given as particularly honorable to me, but I value it the more as it proves your attachment to my country. . . . I have carefully attended to the figures represented on the skins, and to their explanation, and shall always keep them hanging on the walls in remembrance of you and your nation. I have joined with you sincerely in smoking the pipe of peace; it is a good old custom handed down by your ancestors, and as such I respect and join in it with reverence. I hope we shall long continue to smoke in friendship together.[39]

The gaudily dressed Indians fade from the scene here, but another group of players in bright garb is about to appear. The red coats of Colonel Banastre Tarleton's force have been discerned, as British raiders advance on Charlottesville.

In a plan to disrupt the Assembly, Lord Cornwallis had sent a detachment of dragoons and mounted infantry, under Tarleton, marching toward Monticello. The news was brought to Jefferson from a breathless horseman named Jack Jouett, today thought of as a kind of southern Paul Revere, and the Assembly decided to adjourn to Staunton some forty miles to the west. Meanwhile, Jefferson had resigned as governor on 3 June and no successor had been elected.

Private citizen Jefferson sent off his house guests and, while the British were swarming in the streets of Charlottesville, left Monticello on horseback. His departure was either hastily or calmly planned, depending on how his friends and enemies later told the story. According to Dumas Malone, "The impression is inescapable that he remained at home too long for comfort, not that he left precipitately; and charges based on the circumstances of his flight would have been ridiculous when so many others were fleeing, and generally more hastily." Technically, Jefferson had retired from office because his term had expired, "but there must have been some people then, as there were more thereafter, who believed that he had abdicated in utter impotence."[40]

For a man destined to leave a long and richly detailed record in the chronicles of the American West, Jefferson was off to a slow start. He was thirty-eight and had been in public life since he first went to the state legislature a dozen years earlier. So far, his western horizon had been the war-ravaged middle Mississippi Valley, still part of Virginia. He knew Indians, knew natural history, loved geography, and soon would be developing his latent interest in the far West in rather indirect ways. But of the little boy who saw his father return bone-weary from journeys across the Blue Ridge, heard Dr. Walker's tales of the Cumberland Gap, and knew that his neighbors dreamed of an expedition to the great South Sea, there was in Jefferson the man no discernible trace.

NOTES

1. The date 2 April became 13 April when the Old Style calendar was changed in 1752. The narrative of the La Vérendrye brothers is most easily available, in both French and English, in BURPEE [2], 1:406–32. Throughout the notes to follow, three symbols are used repeatedly. TJ means Thomas Jefferson. LC means the Library of Congress, specifically the Papers of Thomas Jefferson unless otherwise noted. NARG denotes a record group in the National Archives and Records Service, Washington.

2. "He was the third or fourth settler, about the year 1737, of the part of the country in which I live." TJ, who wrote these lines about his father, appears to have been correct (AUTOBIOGRAPHY, 20).

3. ALVORD & BIDGOOD, 21.

4. AUTOBIOGRAPHY, 19–20. TJ tells us little of his father but even less of his mother, whose influence on his life is extensively discussed in BRODIE. No scrap of her handwriting is known to remain, although she lived for six years after a fire that consumed the family records.

5. BRODIE, 34. The image is drawn mainly from the biographical writings of RANDALL.

6. Peter reportedly kept a journal of this venture which was burned with the family papers. Lewis's journal has survived and is a tale of physical hardship, bad luck, treacherous watercourses, and dangerous wild animals (see LEWIS).

7. See CAPPON [1], 250–53, and Coolie Verner's introduction to FRY & JEFFERSON, a facsimile of the map presented in sections with colors overlaid as in the original.

8. A perch is 5½ yards, the same length as a pole, but also an area 5½ yards square. Forty square perches equal one rood, hence a quarter-acre. Mereing lines were boundaries; meresmen were those assigned to define the boundaries. Chainmen were surveyors' assistants who carried a chain of 100 links, totaling four poles or perches in length.

9. What apparently is a grant to this company appears in the *Executive Journals of the Council of Colonial Virginia* (Richmond: Virginia State Library, 1967), 2d ed., 5:296–97. The company itself is not named in the text of the grant, which is dated 12 July 1749.

10. NYLAND is a doctoral dissertation on Walker, whose journal of 1750 is reprinted in JOHNSTON [1], 8–75. See also HENDERSON.

11. Photostat, Alderman Library, University of Virginia, Charlottesville.

12. *Papers of the Albemarle Historical Society*, 2 (1942), 39n. TJ journeyed to Fredericksville to board with four or five other students, returning home on weekends (BRODIE, 54).

13. In MAURY, 389–90.

14. In COXE. The quotation is from p. 26 of a typed, mimeographed copy in the Alderman Library. The observation that the Yellow or Missouri River discolors the Mississippi all the way to the Gulf is based vaguely on fact. The Missouri brings so much silt into the Mississippi, with so powerful a current, that the brown coloration remains for at least a mile below the confluence of the two rivers.

15. The material was based on information from Antoine Simor Le Page du Pratz, who would later publish *Histoire de la Louisiane*. See *The Gentlemen's Magazine*, 23 (1753), 265–67, 358–59, 407–10, 459–60.

16. MAURY, 391. No original copy of this letter is present in the Maury papers at the Alderman Library, but other photostated letters

there check closely with Ann Fontaine Maury's published transcriptions.

17. For example, John Dos Passos: "Ever since he was a boy and heard James Maury holding forth on the subject at school on the Mountain, Jefferson had been preoccupied with the idea of exploration westward" (DOS PASSOS [1], 302). Also, Silvio A. Bedini: "From Boyhood his mind had been filled with the romance of the wilderness beyond the frontier that lay awaiting exploitation. . . . He was also influenced by one of his boyhood teachers, the Reverend James Maury, grandfather of the oceanographer Matthew Fontaine Maury, who was greatly preoccupied with the unknown northwest territory" (BEDINI, 311–13).

18. TJ to the Baron de Geismar, 6 Sept. 1785, BOYD, 8:499–500. Writing to Charles Bellini in the same month, he described himself as "a savage of the mountains of America" (30 Sept. 1785, BOYD, 8:568–70).

19. See RANDALL, 1:24 for his studiousness, 1:69 for the names of his horses, and 1:132 for his musicianship. If he engaged as extensively in fox-hunting as most Virginians, the fact is not as well documented as it is for Washington, whose diaries become at times a daily recital of his foxmanship.

20. AUTOBIOGRAPHY, 20–21.

21. CLARK, 323–24, remarks on the difficulty of tracing the early intellectual influences on TJ. The quotation on astronomy is from TJ to Robert Patterson, 29 March 1811, LC.

22. See his statement on the history of Virginia river navigation, 17 Aug. 1817, LC.

23. To Page, 20 Jan. 1763. TJ speaks of the voyage, particularly a trip to Britain, in other letters to Page, 15 July 1763 and 19 Jan. 1764, BOYD, 1:7–9, 9–11, 13–15.

24. He returned to Virginia by sea. MALONE, 1:98–101, recounts the journey. See also GARDEN BOOK, 1, 3.

25. This brief account of TJ's activities in 1767–68 is drawn from GARDEN BOOK, 1–12.

26. TJ's account book, an invaluable source, is at the Massachusetts Historical Society, Boston, with a typescript at the Alderman Library.

27. DAVIS [1], 119.

28. PEDEN discusses Jefferson as a book collector, including the loss of his first library, 99–100. For his new books, see his account book for 1773. TJ's books on American geography and history are discussed in Chapter 5.

29. PETERSON [1], 523–24.

30. To Francis Eppes, 15 Feb. 1783, BOYD, 6:244. TJ had been offered a partnership in a western land company and had declined.

31. BOYD, 1:99. The authority to issue such commissions rested with the president and masters of the College of William and Mary.

32. For TJ's notes, see BOYD, 2:210. Page carried on a lively correspondence with "X.Y." about the transit of Venus in the *Virginia Gazette*, 1769. See also HINDLE, 158n.

33. DAVIS [2], and HINDLE, 213–15 and his sources.

34. BOYD, 2:205, 206n, and TJ to Rittenhouse, 19 July 1778, Historical Society of Pennsylvania, Philadelphia. The eclipse was total in Williamsburg.

35. Among the many biographical works on TJ, the most reliable and extensive is MALONE. PETERSON [1] is a fine one-volume biography. BRODIE is a controversial but useful work. For others, see the bibliography at the end of this volume.

36. MALONE, 1:352. For a full account of the events of TJ's life in the summer of 1781, see MALONE, 1: chap. 25.

37. TJ to John Adams, 11 June 1812, CAPPON [2], 2:305–8. "He was always the guest of my father, on his journeys to and from Williamsburg."

38. Despite the ubiquitous use of the term "Great White Father" in contemporary fiction and films, the expression appears to have had no currency in the eighteenth and early nineteenth centuries.

39. BOYD, 6:60–64, using a previously printed text. The manuscript has not survived. Despite the turmoil and confusion, Jefferson wrote on 30 May to Richmond craftsman Robert Scot, ordering a medal for Ducoigne. He considered the matter important enough to send a messenger with instructions to wait until the medal was struck, saying he would attempt to detain Ducoigne—who was impatient to return home (BOYD, 6:43).

40. MALONE, 1:358. Although Tarleton did some damage in the area, and captured seven assemblymen, his raid was not a vicious one. Monticello was visited but left intact.

CHAPTER TWO

Some Notes on Virginia

Before resigning as governor, Jefferson already had assembled a large mass of data that would eventually become his only book, *Notes on the State of Virginia*. These papers went with him to Poplar Forest when he retired there with his family upon Tarleton's appearance at Monticello. A fall from a horse, probably Caractacus, injured him enough to render him sedentary for several weeks, with time to spend on the development of the manuscript. Not only is the work happily readable as a distinguished pioneer study in geography, and "may be properly regarded as the most important scientific work that had yet been compiled in America,"[1] it is of special concern to the student of Jefferson's role in the West. Within its remarkable passages on the geography, natural history, and political and social status of Virginia, we find Jefferson stretching his mind to encompass both his colony and the continent. Only those elements of the book bearing upon these proofs of Jefferson's expanding geographic horizon will be dealt with here.

In the summer or early fall of 1780, a questionnaire had reached Jefferson from François Marbois, first secretary of the French legation in the United States. The writer would later play a large role in negotiating the Louisiana Purchase and would become the Marquis de Barbé-Marbois. He wrote in 1780 strictly as a member of his legation, seeking information about the various colonies; his copy of the questionnaire, intended for some knowledgeable person in Virginia, reached Jefferson through Joseph Jones, a member of the Virginia delegation to the Continental Congress. Other recipients in other states either ignored the questions or sent perfunctory replies, but Jefferson, in his dogged way, used the opportunity to prepare a substantial treatise.

The book grew by accretion. He sent the main text of his response to Marbois in December 1781 but continued to circulate copies and to gather information from friends. Scrawling away at the additions and revisions during 1783–84 while at the Continental Congress, he then took the amended manuscript to France in 1784. Despite the urging of others, he had no thought of publishing it because he feared his remarks on slavery, and the Virginia constitution, would not be well received at home. Upon learning, however, that an unauthorized French edition was to be published (it appeared in an edition of 200 copies in 1785), he turned to the task of bringing out his own French version, bearing only his initials, and finally a definitive English edition carrying his full name. Even after publication he continued to add new material to his own copy, apparently with the thought of issuing a revision, and not until late 1814 did he concede that he no longer considered publishing a new edition.[2]

· The Refutation of Buffon ·

A theory abroad in Europe held that the climate of the New World was so hostile to animals and men, either indigenous or transferred from Europe, that they must inevitably degenerate physically and—in the case of men—mentally and morally. Much of Jefferson's commentary on the animal life and the Indian population of North America was directed at this theory, which he seemed to take as a canard and a personal affront.

Dutch scholar Cornelius de Pauw had opened the debate by declaring that colonial descendants of Europeans must decline in physical and mental vigor in America. There may have been some folk etymology at work in the formulation of this assumption, the term *nouveau monde* producing the notion of a newly created, thus raw and unevolved, world. De Pauw's book, *Recherches philosophiques sur les Américains* (Berlin, 1768), was given widespread credence by the more popular writings of the Abbé Raynal, whose *Histoire philosophique et politique des établissements et des commerces des Européens dans les deux Indes* (Amsterdam, 1770), was published in thirty-seven editions. The Abbé repeated De

Pauw's theory and asserted that colonialism was contrary to nature.

Although neither of these men enjoyed universal acclaim as scientists, a full measure of attention was accorded the man who gave the theory of American degeneracy a kind of scholarly respectability. Georges-Louis Leclerc, Comte de Buffon, was a French physician and botanist, superintendent of the famed Jardin du Roi in Paris, and author of the gigantic *Histoire naturelle*. In volume 9 (1761) he said that animal species in the New World were smaller, lacking in vigor, and produced fewer variations than those of Europe because the new continents had "remained longer than the rest of the globe under the waters of the sea." Considering the American Indian to be "a mere animal of the first rank," he applied the same strictures to the native population.

It is curious that Jefferson bothered to refute De Pauw, Raynal, and Buffon; a strong group in France already had done much to shout them down. By 1777 Buffon was divorcing himself from De Pauw's arguments and altering his earlier statements. Raynal had withdrawn his views on the degenerate American by 1781, saying, "Soon perhaps New England will be able to point to her Homer, her Theocritus, and her Sophocles." Jefferson lacked access to Raynal's retraction while writing his original version of the *Notes*, but did acknowledge it in a footnote to the 1787 edition. All in all, it seems quite probable that the few readers for whom Jefferson's work was intended had long been exposed to ample refutation.[3]

Jefferson's rebuttal, where animal life was concerned, was to concentrate mainly on the size of various species in North America as compared to their European counterparts. Lacking information of his own, he began to send out inquiries that would be bringing him responses for the next several years. A few examples: from Archibald Carey, of Tuckahoe, he received on 12 October 1783 reports on various animals he had encountered and their sizes, obviously in response to an inquiry from Jefferson. To Ezra Stiles, in Hartford, Conn., Jefferson wrote 10 June 1784 for information on the mammoth, because Buffon "has advanced a theory in general very degrading to America." Stiles replied a few days later. In a letter to the Marquis de

Chastellux, 7 June 1785, Jefferson wrote a discourse on the so-called degeneracy of animals in America. And Madison sent him a letter on 19 June 1786 about the weasel, giving detailed measurements. There are dozens of other exchanges, including Jefferson's request of 26 November 1782 to George Rogers Clark, asking for "Elk-horns of very extraordinary size."[4]

Jefferson devoted many pages of his *Notes* to the refutation of Buffon. Beginning with animals, he summarized Buffon's hypothesis, presented a table which he called "A comparative View of the Quadrupeds of Europe and of America," giving comparative weights, and—while carefully giving full credit to Buffon as a distinguished scientist—concluded that he was completely in error.

Extending the argument "to man in America, whether aboriginal or transplanted," Jefferson wrote vigorously in defense of the Indian. He called Buffon's protrayal of the Indian "an afflicting picture indeed, which, for the honor of human nature, I am glad to believe has no original."

Jefferson praised the physical development, mental prowess, bravery, and social mores of the Indian, saying in summary, "We shall probably find that they are formed in mind as well as in body, on the same module with the 'Homo sapiens Europaeus.'" He dwelt particularly on the Indian's eminence in oratory. "I may challenge the whole orations of Demosthenes and Cicero, and of any more eminent orator, if Europe has furnished more eminent, to produce a single passage, superior to the speech of Logan, a Mingo chief, to Lord Dunmore, when governor of this state." Jefferson referred here to a moving speech attributed to Logan after his family had been slain by whites in the spring of 1774.

Continuing his delicate destruction of Buffon's reasoning, he concluded, "It is one of those cases where judgment has been seduced by a glowing pen; and while I render every tribute of honor and esteem to the celebrated Zoologist, who has added, and is still adding, so many precious things to the treasures of science, I must doubt whether in this instance he has not cherished error also, by lending her for a moment his vivid imagination and bewitching language."[5]

Having written these passages, Jefferson had committed himself to years of searching for bigger animals and for taller, braver, and more eloquent Indians.

· The Great Chain of Being ·

In Jefferson's philosophy, all natural creations were thought to be links in an unbroken chain, from the mineral to the human being. This concept, says Daniel Boorstin, "was at once an expression of personal faith and a description of the material universe."[6] A part of this philosophy was the belief that no species ever became extinct. When Jefferson used the term "extinct" in referring to animals, he was alluding to individual specimens, not an entire species. This belief in nonextinction runs through all of Jefferson's writings on a favorite study of his, the then new science of paleontology.[7] His belief suggested the possibility that great creatures from the beginning of time might still exist in North America. "I cannot . . . help believing that this animal [the ground sloth], as well as the mammoth, are still existing. The annihilation of any species of existence, is so unexampled in any part of the economy of nature which we see, that we have a right to conclude, as to the parts we do not see, that the probabilities against such annihilation are stronger than those for it."[8]

In his *Notes*, Jefferson began his discussion of animals with the mammoth, a creature with which he and many other Americans had recently become fascinated. He said the Indians had a tradition that the mammoth still lived, and he related a tale: "A Mr. Stanley, taken prisoner by the Indians near the mouth of the Tanissee, relates, that, after being transferred through several tribes, from one to another, he was at length carried over the mountains west of the Missouri to a river which runs westwardly; that these bones abounded there; and that the natives described to him the animals to which they belonged as still existing in the northern parts of their country; from which description he judged it to be the elephant." The information apparently came to Jefferson from Arthur Campbell. Jefferson did not confuse the creature with the elephant, however. Because it appeared to be the largest of all living animals, and was—he assumed—unique to North America, it became one more bit of evidence with which to refute the errors of Buffon.[9]

Years later, when directing explorers who were going into the West, Jefferson would hope they might find recent remains or living specimens of these enormous creatures. He specifically mentioned the mammoth in his instructions to André Michaux in 1793, but had become more vague by the time he dispatched Lewis and Clark in 1803, directing them to look for rare or "extinct animals."[10]

• Botany and Agriculture •

Jefferson ranked botany with the most valuable of sciences, "whether we consider its subjects as furnishing the principal subsistence of life to man and beast, delicious varieties for our tables . . . the adornments of our flower-borders . . . or medi-caments for our bodies." He thought no country gentleman should be without "what amuses every step he takes into his fields."[11] He therefore turned with ease to the questions Marbois had put to him under the heading of "vegetables." Confining himself to native plants, and calling upon such sources as John Clayton and William Bartram, he listed those which would "principally attract notice," separating them into groups which he called medicinal, esculent, ornamental, and useful for fabrication. He followed the Linnaean system in affixing binomial Latin names, and in one instance, believing the pecan or "Illinois nut" unknown to Linnaeus and Clayton, he described it briefly in Latin. He had not only used the pecan himself, obtaining the nuts from the Mississippi Valley, but also had found it mentioned in Antonio de Ulloa's *Noticias Americas* (1772).[12] He passed over farm crops lightly, naming only the principal ones—knowing they would be familiar to European readers. The native crops he listed as tobacco, Indian corn, potatoes, pumpkins, and squash (cymlings).

Considering his lifelong engagement in agriculture, and the enthusiasm he felt for it in contrast to industry as the proper pursuit of his fellow Americans, it is surprising that Jefferson did not make his comments on farming the most extensive in his discourse. He produced, however, some notable quotes on the subject. "Those who labour in the earth are the chosen people of God, if ever he had a chosen people, whose breasts he has made his peculiar deposit for substantial and genuine virtue. . . . The mobs of great cities add just so much to the support of pure government, as sores do to the strength of the human body."[13]

Like so many of his fellow Virginians, Jefferson was a scientific farmer, although Washington seems to have excelled him in this pursuit. Washington was more experienced, having begun intensive farming and tobacco planting in the late 1750s, when Jefferson was still in his teens. Washington also was able to spend more years at Mount Vernon than Jefferson spent at Monticello; absentee direction did not lend itself to scientific agriculture.[14]

To Jefferson and Washington, diversification was the key to survival in the agricultural South. Washington raised or at least attempted nearly seventy different field crops; Jefferson's tally was not much less. This experimentation extended over a period of years, and many of the trials were failures; besides abandoning such minor crops as buckwheat and horsebeans, Virginia farmers eventually turned to the goal of giving up Indian corn and tobacco.

Diversification meant trying to cultivate many plants from other parts of the world, or to domesticate more of those native to North America. Jefferson's fields and gardens contained hop clover, hemp, bent grass, and winter vetch from England; alfalfa from the Mediterranean; Guinea corn and sesame from Africa; Nanking cotton from Asia; field peas, sainfoin, and turnips from Europe; sulla grass from Malta. His buffalo or Kentucky clover came from the inland grasslands of the Ohio Valley. All his prized orchard fruits—apples, pears, cherries, peaches—were introduced from abroad.

Thus it was not merely the botanist's eternal curiosity about nature's infinite diversity, but also the farmer's absolute need to find and develop new crops, that made plant collection a vital part of Jefferson's interest in the American West. Some day his fields and gardens would come alive with products from beyond the Missouri, some developed over centuries by the Indians of the Great Plains. Combined with Jefferson's almost naive faith in agriculture, which he envisioned as spreading gradually westward, this personal need to know the world of plants would one day be a further incentive to promote western exploration.

• The Earth Sciences •

Mineralogy appealed less to Jefferson than botany, but he devoted more space in his *Notes* to minerals than to plants. Although he personally viewed the study of minerals as useful but not very entertaining, he was careful to describe Virginia in terms of its deposits of gold, lead, copper, iron, black lead, coal, marble, salt, and precious stones.

While conceding that mineralogy was necessary to civilized man's survival, and that paleontology was fascinating because it spoke of the Chain of Being and told him something of past life, Jefferson cared not at all for the mother science, geology. "What difference does it make," he once asked, "whether the earth is six hundred or six thousand years old?" Nor does it matter much to know the composition of the various strata of the earth "if they contain no coal or iron or other useful metal." To Constantin Volney in 1805 he said that he had not indulged in geological enquiries "from a belief that the skin-deep scratches which we can make or find on the surface of the earth do not repay our time with as certain & useful deductions as our pursuits in some other branches." In his late years, when the newly forming American Geological Society sent him an invitation to join, he saluted the society and its officers but declined to become a member. In the last year of his life, he reaffirmed his belief in the practical study of minerals, but thought that theorizing on the origin of the earth "too idle to be worth a single hour of any man's life."[15]

His aversion to speculations about the formation of the earth did not prevent his remarking, in the *Notes*, on how one of his favorite landscapes might have been formed:

The passage of the Patowmac through the Blue ridge is perhaps one of the most stupendous scenes in nature. You stand on a very high point of land. On your right comes up the Shenandoah, having ranged along the foot of the mountain an hundred miles to seek a vent. On your left approaches the Patowmac, in quest of a passage also. In the moment of their junction they rush together against the mountain, rend it asunder, and pass off to the sea. The first glance of this scene hurries our senses into the opinion, that this earth has been created in time, that the mountains were formed first, that the rivers began to flow afterwards, that in this place particularly they have been dammed up by the Blue ridge of mountains, and have formed an ocean which filled the whole valley; that continuing to rise they have at length broken over at this spot, and have torn the mountain down from its summit to its base.[16]

Jefferson's respect, but not affection, for the science of mineralogy, and his disdain for the more basic geological studies, were to be precisely reflected in the instructions he would later give to exploring parties entering the West. The journals they kept would be attentive to deposits of coal, iron, lead, and salt, but would pay little attention to the vast eruptions, upheavals, and subsidences that formed the face of the West.

· Red Men, Black Men ·

There is no easy answer, perhaps no answer at all, to Jefferson's lifelong equivocation on the subject of slavery. That he abhorred it there is no doubt. That his solution, the removal of blacks from America, was nearly an impossible one is equally obvious. More complications arise when we see how carefully Jefferson distinguished the question of slavery from the question of race. In the *Notes*, as he discussed the differences between black and white men, and also between black and red men, Jefferson dared to place on the record a dangerously candid statement of his position. His reluctance to confide his views to public evaluation is part of the enigma. Not only did he decline at first to publish the *Notes*, but even tried to issue the first edition anonymously, "and to restrict its circulation to a few European savants, members of Congress and the students at the College of William and Mary."[17]

Jefferson cautiously presented the view that blacks might actually be a separate race, whereas the Indian was inherently different from the white man only in slightly different skin color.

Having propounded the view that slaves should be free, but that they were so inferior to whites that mixing the races was unthinkable, Jefferson had no alternative but to ponder the solution: deportation of the slaves. "Why not retain and incorporate the blacks into the state . . . ? Deep rooted prejudices entertained by the whites; ten thousand recollections, by the blacks, of the injuries they have sustained; new provocations; the real distinctions which nature has made; and many other circumstances, will divide us into parties, and produce convulsions which will probably never end but in the extermination of the one or the other race.—To these objections, which are political, may be added others, which are physical and moral."[18]

Because he had been born and reared in a society that proclaimed blacks to be inferior, and because, on the other hand, Indians were to him marvelously exotic people about whom he had devoted long hours of study, it is no surprise that he gave Indians a better score. Blacks were a part of the American scene through historic accident, while Indians were a part of the natural order. There were, he believed, insuperable biological differences between black man and white, but the differences between red and white were of a nature that could be overlooked. "Since the Indian was really a white man in moccasins and a breech-clout and the potential equal in every respect to his white relatives, Jefferson welcomed the mixture of Indian and Caucasian genes."[19]

A paradox was to come. When as president it became Jefferson's responsibility to "solve" the problem caused by the inexorable westward movement of the whites, it would be the Indian who seemed eligible for removal. A temporary removal, in Jefferson's plan, but still a separation because of irreconcilable life-styles. When the Indian had learned to live and behave like the whites, he would be free to return and intermarry. In the meantime, the first use that Jefferson would see for the new lands west of the Mississippi, after the Louisiana Purchase of 1803, would be as a vast camp where the Indians could be sent to rehearse the arts of civilization.

• A Lesson in Cartography •

When publication of the *Notes* seemed certain, the need for a map of Virginia became an essential part of the publication. The old Fry-Jefferson map made a splendid base upon which to build, but it was reliable only for the region east of the Alleghenies.

Jefferson turned to other works, especially a more recent map of the western parts of Virginia published by Thomas Hutchins in 1778. For the northern part of the map, which included all of Pennsylvania, Jefferson chose as his model a map prepared by William Scull and published in Philadelphia in 1770.

As he had done for the prose portions of the *Notes*, Jefferson then consulted not only his personal observations but the information possessed by his wide circle of acquaintances. He was eventually to call upon such men as David Rittenhouse, Thomas Hutchins, Bishop James Madison, and John Page.

Finally Jefferson had drawn all his data together and constructed a manuscript map. Considering it too crowded with topographic facts, and rather difficult to interpret, he sent it to his London engraver along with copies of Hutchins and Scull, and instructed him to use Fry-Jefferson and also Henry Mouzon's map of North Carolina as a check against his own.

The resulting map was drawn to a scale of one inch to twenty miles, with the zero degree of longitude assigned to Philadelphia. He gave this, his only published map, the title *A Map of the Country between Albemarle Sound, and Lake Erie, Comprehending the whole of Virginia, Maryland, Delaware and Pennsylvania, with Parts of Several Other of the United States of America. Engraved for the Notes on Virginia.*[20]

Jefferson was to be a collector and lover of maps all his life. But in this, his only experience at actually constructing one, he was unknowingly preparing himself to deal with and comprehend hundreds of maps when the West was opened to explorers, surveyors, and litigants in the inevitable boundary disputes following the acquisition of Louisiana.

• Oddments from Beyond the Mississippi •

What little Jefferson knew about the *terra incognita* in the west was still as much as any one man knew in those times. He had not assigned himself the task of discussing these regions in the *Notes*, but enough fact and lore crept into the pages to provide an indication of what he had gleaned from his growing library and from white and Indian informants.

He described the Missouri River because, although not a part of Virginia since the Treaty of Paris in 1763, it was a part of the Mississippi drainage system that did involve Virginia:

The *Missouri* is, in fact, the principal river, contributing more to the common stream than does the Missisipi, even after its junction with the Illinois. It is remarkably cold, muddy and rapid. Its overflowings are considerable. They happen during the months of June and July. Their commencement being so much later than those of the Missisipi, would induce a belief that the sources of the Missouri are northward of those of the Missisipi, unless we suppose that the cold increases again with the ascent of the land from the Missisipi westwardly. That this ascent is great, is proved by the rapidity of the river. . . . From the mouth of the Ohio to Santa Fe are forty days journey, or about 1000 miles. What is the shortest distance between the navigable waters of the Missouri, and those of the North [Rio Grande] River, or how far this is navigable above Santa Fe, I could never learn.[21]

The problem of learning the relationship between the headwaters of the Missouri and the Rio Grande would still be troubling Jefferson in 1802, when he was planning the Lewis and Clark expedition. Albert Gallatin, his secretary of the treasury and an eager student of the West, wrote him on 14 March 1803, "The most difficult point to ascertain is the latitude of the sources of the Rio Norte; and it is important. . . ." Gallatin was helping Jefferson gather information at the time, and to his comment Jefferson replied: "I do not find in my library any thing which can throw light on the geography of the Rio Norte. I do not believe that in modern times any thing has been added to the information given as to that river in early times."

The question eventually was left to Lewis and Clark. Jefferson instructed them to pay particular attention to the southern affluents of the Missouri, and to verify the assumption that the Rio Grande and the Colorado were the principal streams heading "opposite to the waters of the Missouri."[22]

Jefferson mentions a substance supposed to be volcanic lava, probably from the Missouri region. And yet, he reasons, since no volcano has been known at such a distance from the sea, the substance was probably not volcanic "pumice." Despite his skepticism, he later asked Lewis and Clark to report on "volcanic appearances."[23]

There is no specific reference in the *Notes* to mountains west of the Mississippi. Jefferson's information was scanty, his library yet to take on its special character as a storehouse of information on American geography, and he was especially lacking in access to Spanish sources. The extent of his ignorance is seen in his remark, "The mountains of the Blue Ridge, and of these the Peaks of Other, are thought to be of a greater height, measured from their base, than any others in our country [Virginia], and perhaps in North America."[24]

While he mentioned no western mountains by name, he did have something to say about the mountain systems east of the Mississippi. He wrote that they are "not solitary and scattered confusedly over the face of the country; but that they commence at about 150 miles from the sea-coast, are disposed in ridges one behind another, running nearly parallel with the sea-coast, though rather approaching it as they advance north-eastwardly." In a further observation, that "the courses of great rivers are at right angles with these," Jefferson is preparing himself for an extrapolation that he later will apply to the Rocky Mountains. As geographical historian John Logan Allen observes about Jefferson's reasoning, "And because the waters of the Potomac broke through the Blue Ridge transverse to their structure, it would seem possible [to Jefferson] that the Missouri broke through the Stony Mountains in the same fashion." Allen concludes that Jefferson's geographical ideas pertaining to the West did not change appreciably during the interval between his remarks in the *Notes* and his launching of the Lewis and Clark expedition in 1804.[25]

• A Field Wide Open •

In 1789 Jefferson was awarded a doctorate of laws from Harvard University. In sending an acceptance to Joseph Willard, the university president, he produced a burst of enthusiasm for American studies that might have served as a preface for his *Notes*:

What a feild [*sic*] have we at our doors to signalize ourselves in! The botany of America is far from being exhausted: it's Mineralogy is untouched, and it's Natural history or Zoology totally mistaken and misrepresented. As far as I have seen there is not one single species of terrestrial birds common to Europe and America, and I question if there be a single species of quadrupeds. (Domestic animals are to be excepted.) It is the work to which the young men, whom you are forming, should lay their hands. We have spent the prime of our lives in procuring them the precious blessing of liberty. Let them spend theirs in shewing that it is the great parent of science and virtue; and that a nation will be great in both always in proportion as it is free.[26]

Having written his only book—whetting his appetite for more ways in which to defeat Buffon and for further evidence that great creatures of the past might still live in unexplored areas, having felt the need for a greater knowledge of the useful plants and minerals now beyond his reach, and having organized his thoughts on the geography of his country and found them based on the scantiest of data—it was imperative for Jefferson to become one day the father of American exploration. The time was still far off.

NOTES

1. MALONE, 1:379. Every biography of TJ contains a mandatory treatment of his *Notes*. The most readily available scholarly edition of the work itself, edited by William Peden, is cited herein as NOTES. Merrill D. Peterson has said of TJ's work, "In a sense the book was a cultural accident. It was a by-product of revolutionary events and cannot be viewed in any other context. It had no prototype, belonged to no established genre, and answered to no speculative school. The very act of its creation expressed the amorphous and unpredictable character of American thought and imagination" (PETERSON [3], 50–51). The Peterson essay is an excellent introduction to the book.

2. This brief history of the work is from Peden's material in NOTES. TJ claimed to be appalled by the errors of translation in the French version made by André Morellet. But see MEDLIN for an analysis and the conclusion that the French edition was an acceptably accurate translation. Madison urged Jefferson to publish his own edition, 12 May 1786 (BOYD, 9:517). TJ comments on the quality of the French edition in a letter to William Carmichael, 15 Dec. 1787 (BOYD, 12:423). His own annotated copy is in the Alderman Library, University of Virginia, Charlottesville.

3. The discussion of the degeneracy theory and its proponents draws heavily upon ECHEVERRIA. Swedish naturalist Peter Kalm, who spent more than two years in the United States, wrote several pages on American settlers in his *Travels into North America* (London, 1770–71), claiming they died younger than Europeans, that their soldiers lacked endurance, and that cattle imported from Europe grew smaller with each generation.

4. Sources of this correspondence: for Carey, BOYD, 6:344; for Stiles, BOYD, 7:304, 312; for Chastellux, BOYD, 8:184; for Clark, BOYD, 6:204. The inquiry to Clark came at a time when Jefferson expected to be sent to France on a special mission. "You will perhaps hear of my being gone to Europe, but my trip will be short." Evidently he planned to take the antlers with him. For his actual experiences in France, see Chapter 3.

5. Quotations and summary of TJ's reaction to Buffon are drawn from NOTES, 48–64. For Buffon's life and work, including his role in the New World degeneracy controversy, see FELLOWS & MILLIKEN.

6. BOORSTIN, 35, in a discussion of the Chain of Being philosophy of TJ. The definitive work on this philosophy is LOVEJOY, especially the chapters covering the eighteenth and nineteenth centuries.

7. For an understanding of TJ's approach to the study of "extinct" creatures, SIMPSON is most useful. Simpson declares that TJ was not truly a paleontologist and that his contributions were slight, but that like most gifted amateurs, he brought together much material for study and preservation.

8. To John Stuart, 10 Nov. 1796, LC. TJ never gave up his doubts about the extinction of species, writing 9 Feb. 1818 to Francis Van der Kemp (LC), "It might be doubted whether any particular species of animals or vegetables which ever did exist, has ceased to exist."

9. For TJ's retelling of the story, see NOTES, 44. For Campbell to TJ, 29 Nov. 1782, see BOYD, 6:208. Allowing for some distortions in geography, the unidentified Stanley may have been describing the deposits of mammoth bones along the Osage River in present Missouri.

10. TJ's instructions to Michaux, 30 April 1793, and to Meriwether Lewis, 20 June 1803, are reprinted below, pp. 75–78 and 139–44.

11. To Dr. Thomas Cooper, 7 Oct. 1814, LC.

12. NOTES, 38–43.

13. NOTES, 164–65. TJ believed all his life that agricultural labor claimed a "moral and physical preference" over industrial labor. In 1816, having become more or less a protectionist, he was insisting that

agriculture produced a value greater than an equal expenditure of capital and labor on manufacturing, attributing the fact to the "spontaneous energies of the earth" (PETERSON [4], 140).

14. TJ's agricultural activities have been more extensively studied than Washington's, Edwin M. Betts having edited the TJ farm and garden books in two large volumes, cited herein as FARM BOOK and GARDEN BOOK. A start toward an understanding of Washington as a farmer has been made in Donald Jackson's horticultural and agricultural notes accompanying a recent edition of Washington's diaries (JACKSON & TWOHIG). Washington's correspondence, now being edited, will reveal much more on the subject.

15. See MARTIN [2], 46; TJ to Volney, 8 Feb. 1805, to the American Geological Society, 26 March 1820, and to John P. Emmet, 2 May 1826, all in LC. The founding officers of the American Geological Society, who approached TJ for membership, were William McClure, president, and Benjamin Silliman, vice-president. McClure is considered the father of American geological studies. When he sent a copy of his book on geology in the United States, TJ was complimentary of the work on minerals but could not resist remarking on the folly of man's scratching 100 feet below the surface of an earth 8,000 miles in diameter to conjecture about its internal structure (to McClure, 2 Nov. 1817, LC).

16. NOTES, 19. "This scene is worth a voyage across the Atlantic," TJ added.

17. MILLER, 38. John C. Miller's study of TJ and slavery is not only an instructive overview of TJ's position on race and slavery, but an analysis of the NOTES where these topics are concerned.

18. NOTES, 138.

19. MILLER, 65. The eventual extinction of racial differences through intermarriage was later to become an important part of TJ's long-range Indian policy.

20. The best source for TJ's preparation of the map is his own correspondence, all present in BOYD. A convenient summation is in VERNER. The final printed sheets were not only bound into copies of the *Notes*, but were issued for sale separately. See TJ to James Madison, 17 Sept. 1787 (BOYD, 12:136). He was sending Madison "100 copies of the map of Virginia, Pennsylvania, etc. which be so good as to put into the hands of any bookseller you please in New York and Philadelphia to be sold at such price as you think proper. Ready money only."

21. NOTES, 8–9.

22. For Gallatin to TJ, and for TJ's response of 20 March 1803, see

L & C LETTERS, 1:28, 32. TJ's instructions to Lewis concerning the Rio Grande are on pp. 141–42 below.

23. See L & C LETTERS, 1:275n, for a discussion of the substance as material derived from fields of burning lignite in the Badlands of the Dakota country. Clark later confirmed this in L & C LETTERS, 2:539.

24. NOTES, 20.

25. ALLEN [1], 376–79.

26. To Willard, 24 Mar. 1789, LC.

CHAPTER THREE

Assignment to France

When Jefferson resigned as wartime governor of Virginia in 1781, the world nearly lost him as a public servant. Grieving over the loss of his wife, who died the following year, and believing that his countrymen had disavowed his conduct of the Revolution in his colony, he went into seclusion. As John Dos Passos has said of him, "he had come to that period in his life, which seems to come to most men around their fortieth year, when all the blank checks of youth have been cashed and a man has to face himself as an adult, the way he's going to be until he dies."[1]

At the end of two years of self-doubt and indecision, when he accepted election as a delegate to the Continental Congress again, it was clear that Jefferson had not wasted those lonely times. He had discovered that with the death of Martha his dream of Monticello as a perpetual retreat was gone, and he decided to take his place once more in a life of public service. He had traveled some during an abortive assignment as peace commissioner, and he had accepted an honorary degree from his alma mater, the College of William and Mary. His most important work during his semiretirement had been preparation of the *Notes on the State of Virginia*. When he took his seat in Congress in November 1783, no man in America had taught himself more about his native land.

On 4 December 1783, he wrote to his longtime friend and compatriot George Rogers Clark, asking if Clark would consider leading an expedition into the West. "I find they have subscribed a large sum of money in England for exploring the country from the Missisipi to California. They pretend it is only to promote knolege. I am afraid they have thoughts of colonising into that quarter. Some of us have been talking here in a feeble way of making the attempt to search that country. But I doubt whether we have enough of that kind of spirit to raise the money. How would you like to lead such a party?"

At last Jefferson had put something on paper about the exploration of the American West. It is likely that he was speaking not as a congressman but as a member of the American Philosophical Society, based in Philadelphia, of which he had been a member for three years and a councilor since 1781. The society would later make other attempts to send teams westward.

Clark had to decline the opportunity. He wrote: "Your proposition respecting a tour to the west and North west of the Continent would be Extreamly agreable to me could I afford it but I have late discovered that I knew nothing of the lucrative policy of the world supposing my duty required every attention and sacrifice to the Publick Interest but must now look forward for future Support."[2] He was saying politely that the war had bankrupted him because of the private funds he had put into it, and that the commonwealth of Virginia showed little sign of repaying him with anything but honor and recognition.

How Jefferson had learned of British subscription of "a large sum of money" is unknown. He may have learned of a plan conceived by fur traders Peter Pond, Alexander Henry, or both, for making a giant step toward the Pacific. In October 1781, Henry drew up a memorandum for Sir Joseph Banks, president of the Royal Society, on "A Proper Rout, by Land, to Cross the Great Contenant of America."[3] By 1783 this information could easily have reached Jefferson through the American Philosophical Society, or through Benjamin Franklin—who worked with Pond on geographical matters in drawing up the Treaty of 1783 that ended the Revolution.

A notable service performed by Jefferson in Congress, in the spring of 1784, was chairmanship of a committee to determine how the new Northwest Territory should be governed. He and his fellow committee members proposed a plan under which settlers moving into the vast new area (beyond the Ohio and east of the Mississippi) could organize themselves first into territories, later into states, and do so on an equal basis with the original thirteen states. Although the proposal was somewhat altered by Congress, it became the foundation of the Northwest Ordinance of 1787.

Soon Jefferson was occupied with plans for moving to a country that he would come to love almost as much as his own. In May 1784, Congress named him minister plenipotentiary to the Court of France, with instructions to negotiate treaties that might improve commercial relations with the nations of Europe. He sailed from Boston in July, and after a month's voyage, during which he taught himself Spanish for amusement,[4] arrived in Paris. He was to spend five years abroad, replacing Franklin in 1785 as minister to France.

If the American people gained from Jefferson's time in France, it was not because of great diplomatic coups or outstanding day-to-day diplomacy, but because of his own personal development. Lacking Franklin's easy way with people, and coping with the fond memories of Franklin held by the French, Jefferson undertook—as he said—to succeed Franklin, not to replace him. "Whereas Franklin's effort had been mainly directed toward creating in the French mind a favorable picture of America, Jefferson's were directed toward creating an accurate one."[5]

During the Revolution, America had seen a strong delegation of French officers turning up on her doorstep to volunteer for service in the war. Now the tide seemed to surge in the other direction, and during Jefferson's tour the city of Paris was frequented by dozens of American tourists: artists, writers, schemers, and speculators. Men such as John Paul Jones, John Trumbull, Thomas Paine, and Gouveneur Morris were to become familiar figures on the streets of French cities.

Of these, none was more typically a tourist than Jefferson. His delight in French art, letters, and architecture is a familiar biographical theme. He did small things that one would expect of a tinkerer, inventor, inveterate shopper, and gifted amateur in countless pursuits. He hurried to send the latest new European books to his friends at home. He planted Indian corn in his garden at the Grille de Chaillot, while urging American gardeners to experiment with European varieties of field crops and ornamentals. While on an excursion to Germany he conceived the idea for an improved moldboard plow, which was to win him a French prize. To James Madison, who shared his delight in practical inventions, he sent some of the new "phosphoretic matches."[6] In a letter to George Rogers Clark, he introduced Dr. Antoine Saugrain, who was en route to Kentucky to establish himself and would later become a substantial resident of St. Louis.[7] He seemed impatient to devour all of French culture and export some of it, while paradoxically becoming more and more American.

If we are to investigate the ways in which Jefferson's stay in France affected his later attitudes toward America, but particularly toward the American West, we can profitably begin with John Ledyard.

• Ledyard and Lapérouse •

Before sailing for France, while he was sampling the bookstalls of Philadelphia, New York, and Boston, it is probable that Jefferson encountered two new books that dealt with a favorite topic, North American geography. Both were about the third voyage of Captain James Cook, who had touched upon the shores of the Pacific Northwest and who was, by any measurement, the most honored and talked-about voyager of his time. Neither of these new volumes was the official narrative of Cook's last voyage, which would not appear until the following year. They were written by members of Cook's crew, and the author of one was a young Connecticut soldier of fortune, John Ledyard, soon to become Jefferson's friend.

Ledyard had sold his manuscript to a Hartford publisher, who issued it in the summer of 1783 under the title *A Journal of Captain Cook's Last Voyage to the Pacific Ocean . . . in the Years 1776, 1777, 1778, and 1779.* The booksellers of Philadelphia soon had it in stock. William Prichard offered "Cook's Last Voyage," in two parts, in the *Pennsylvania Gazette* of 6 August. The other book, published anonymously but actually written by John Rickman, was offered by Philadelphia publisher Robert Bell in the *Gazette* of 8 October.[8]

John Ledyard had been the first American of record to set foot in the Pacific Northwest and the first American to meet the Russians in that region. Now he was the first American to write of it, and he did so in terms of the great potential for commerce. He remarked upon the "astonishing profits" with which the men of Cook's expedition sold sea-otter skins in Canton, China—nearly double what they had been paid at Kamchatka in Siberia—and he described copper jewelry and knives that he assumed the Indians had obtained from the Hudson's Bay Company. "Commerce is defusive," he said, "and nothing will impede its progress among the uninformed part of mankind . . . it seems intirely conclusive to suppose no part of America is without some sort of commercial intercourse, immediate or remote."[9]

It was in Paris that Jefferson first met John Ledyard and began to sense the young man's intensity, his excitement about the Pacific Northwest. Bernard DeVoto has said that Ledyard was "part genius and part moongazer."[10] Perhaps it is because the same can be said of Jefferson that the two men soon became friends.

Ledyard, who was born in Groton, Connecticut, in 1751, had been enrolled at Dartmouth for no more than a year, during which he spent at least three months living among the Indians of the Six Nations with the intention of becoming a missionary to the tribes.[11] But after a brief encounter with theological studies, his goals changed and he sailed off to Gibraltar, returned to the United States, then went to England and enlisted in the Royal Marines. In July 1776 he embarked on Cook's third expedition. The famous seafarer, voyaging in the *Resolution* and her consort the *Discovery*, traced the route so well known to history: Capetown, the Indian Ocean, Tasmania, and New Zealand, and by January 1778 had reached the Hawaiian Islands. From Hawaii Cook pressed on to look for a northwest passage. He sighted the coast of Oregon in March, then took anchorage in Nootka Sound. After that, the expedition headed northwest, investigated Cook Inlet, entered the Bering Sea in July, then proceeded northward into the Arctic Ocean, making a friendly call on the Russians of Unalaska. By February 1779 the expedition was back in Hawaii, where Cook was killed by the natives. Assuming command of the two vessels, a subordinate officer brought the expedition home in October 1780.[12]

For Ledyard the voyage had provided incentives for what might have been a rich and useful life, had his years been long. He was strongly interested in native peoples and wrote of them with empathy and a degree of scholarship. He lived among them when he could, got himself tattooed in their fashion, and in reflecting upon the welcome he had received from them he wrote: "Hospitality is a virtue peculiar to man, and the obligation is as great to receive as to confer."[13]

But for Ledyard as well as the other men of the Cook expedition, the big news was the creature called the sea otter. Ledyard was deeply impressed by the surprising profits that the skins from Nootka Sound brought the members of the expedition. Ledyard's most recent biographer has said, "In this visit lay the seed of two ambitions which dominated the rest of his life: the dream of setting up a fur-trading post and of crossing the North American continent."[14] We shall see, however, that the attempt to cross the continent was not a long-nourished dream but an act of desperation when all other schemes had failed and all other promises had been withdrawn.

With his newly published journal in hand and the sincerity of his purpose clear to all with whom he spoke, Ledyard set forth to interest others in his plans. He visited the scholar Ezra Stiles in February 1784 and said he did not believe there was a northwest passage.[15]

In New York the merchants all thought his ideas visionary, but Robert Morris, the famed financier of the American Revolution, was encouraging. Ledyard wrote of him: "What a noble hold he instantly took of the enterprise."[16] Morris worked with Ledyard in trying to find the right ship, and for a while they thought they had engaged the continental frigate *Trumbull*. Morris wrote John Jay in November 1783 that he was sending some ships to China to encourage the Pacific trade, but it is not possible to connect this venture with Ledyard's.[17] After many delays, Morris abandoned his role in the enterprise in the spring of 1784; the despairing Ledyard sailed off for Cadiz and from there to Brest. "The whole force of his mind," according to biographer Jared Sparks, "was now bent upon a voyage of trade and discovery to the Northwest Coast."[18]

In Lorient he thought at last he had a ship. But 1784 passed, and in February 1785 Ledyard wrote his brothers that after many delays he planned to sail from Lorient in August.[19] An expedition did sail from France in August, but it was not Ledyard's. It was instead the royal undertaking of Captain Jean François de Lapérouse, setting out with two vessels on what the French hoped would be a feat to rival that of Captain Cook. The expedition included the Pacific Northwest in its ports of call, and the merchants of Lorient caved in when confronted by such competition. Ledyard was again deeply disappointed.

Jean François de Lapérouse was probably the best man available to carry the French colors in the wake of Captain Cook. He had already been in the Far East as a naval officer and had fought in the American Revolution as commander of warships, successfully reducing the British establishment at Hudson Bay and capturing the company's governor, Samuel Hearne.

The purpose of the present expedition, organized by Louis XVI, was to search for the fabled Northwest Passage, explore the coasts of America, and penetrate the waters of Siberia, China, and the South Sea Islands. In a remarkably astute set of instructions prepared for him by Charles Claret, soon to become French minister of marine, Lapérouse was ordered to examine those areas not seen by Cook and to search "to see whether there be not some river or some narrow gulph, forming a communication, by means of the interior lakes, with some parts of Hudson's bay." He was to inquire whether the Hudson Bay people had managed to open trade with the Indians on the western shores of America. And also he was to try to find a suitable spot for a settlement in case a fur trade should be started by France.[20]

In Paris, Jefferson seems not to have heard of the Lapérouse expedition until it was almost ready to set sail. To John Paul Jones, who was in Lorient, Jefferson wrote on 3 August 1785, asking him to find out what he could of the nature of the forthcoming voyage.[21] His concern about the enterprise was voiced in a letter to John Jay on 14 August: "They [the French] give out that the object is merely for the improvement of our knowledge of the geography of that part of the globe. Their loading . . . and some other circumstances appear to me to indicate some other design; perhaps that of colonising on the Westn coast of America, or perhaps only to establish one or more factories there for the fur trade."[22] The real question, he told Jay, was whether the French were yet weaned from their desire to possess continental colonies in America.

By the time John Paul Jones could find out anything in the seaport of Brest, the Lapérouse expedition had sailed in two vessels, the *Boussole* and the *Astrolabe*. The voyage carried the good wishes of the international scientific community. In England, Sir Joseph Banks arranged for the loan of a dipping needle that had been used by Cook, "which I received," Lapérouse later wrote, "with feelings bordering almost upon religious veneration for the memory of that great and incomparable navigator."[23] Jones did not send Jefferson his report on the expedition until the autumn, and it was vague and confusing. The vessels carried, besides scientific equipment, some agricultural tools. There were mechanics and farmers on board, but no women. Jones thought the king might be planning to lay the groundwork for future fur trade on the Northwest Coast of America and then perhaps to establish colonies in the South Pacific.[24] Jefferson continued to view the expedition with suspicion and would of course have been even more disturbed if he had known that Lapérouse was specifically instructed to occupy a suitable spot upon which to establish a trading post.

During the summer of 1785, while he was fretting about the Lapérouse expedition, Jefferson met John Ledyard. The young adventurer had managed to dine once with Franklin in Paris before the aging minister returned home. And then Jefferson, as the new minister, somehow inherited Ledyard along with his appointment. By now, Ledyard was accustomed to seeking his goal among men in high places. During that same summer he met the Marquis de Lafayette and also John Paul Jones.

With Jones, Ledyard tried once again to mount an expedition to the Northwest and nearly succeeded. After meeting Ledyard, perhaps through Franklin or Jefferson, the famous naval captain set about finding two ships and the finances for a voyage to Nootka Sound and Alaska. They schemed to establish a post in the Northwest which Ledyard would manage while Jones sailed on to the Orient with the first shipment of sea-otter skins. As usual, the plan failed. The financing was difficult, and more important, the Spanish government raised an objection.[25]

After all his disappointments in what was actually a sound business idea, after so many men in high places had abandoned him, it is not surprising that Ledyard's dreams became more aggressively unrealistic. He decided to cross the American continent from west to east by first traversing the Russian Empire as far as the North Pacific. He was sardonic in describing his reverses in a letter to his brother Isaac in February 1786. "All the distresses that you can imagine . . . have most faithfully attached themselves to me . . . so curiously wretched have I been, that without any thing but a clean shirt was I invited from a Gloomy garret to the splendid Tables of the first characters of this Kingdom."[26] Curiously, it was the men at these splendid tables who now stood ready to help him realize his most impractical scheme. Jefferson, Lafayette, the Baron Friedrich von Grimm, and others bent to the task of convincing Catherine, the empress of Russia, that Ledyard should be given a passport and assistance in crossing the vast Russian continent, the snowy peninsula of Kamchatka, and the Bering Strait, where he would then begin the probably hopeless journey across the American continent alone.[27] During this period, Jefferson gave Ledyard money on several occasions.

It was not the methodical, logical kind of undertaking that Jefferson might have planned by himself, but he entered into the game with relish. According to one contemporary, Jefferson and Ledyard devised a method of keeping records by tattooing code symbols on Ledyard's already tattooed body and measuring the latitude by means of a twelve-inch distance marked off on his arm.[28]

Jefferson himself was to bring the news of one more disappointment. In August 1786 he wrote to Ledyard, who was then in London: "I saw Baron de Grimm yesterday at Versailles, and he told me he had received an answer from the Empress, who declines the proposition made on your account. She thinks it chimaerical. I am in hopes your execution of it from our side of the continent will prove the contrary."[29] It is apparent they had discussed a conventional overland expedition such as Jefferson already had proposed to George Rogers Clark a few years earlier.

When this bad news arrived, Ledyard was in London attempting to find passage on an English ship sailing for Nootka. The surviving correspondence does not indicate whether or not he ever got the message from Jefferson saying he was denied passage across Russia. He wrote Jefferson from London on 25 November 1786 that the English ship on which he planned to embark had been seized by the customhouse and that he was departing for St. Petersburg to begin his overland journey to the Bering Sea and the familiar sights of Nootka and the Pacific Northwest.[30]

By this time Jefferson had given up worrying about the Lapérouse expedition. During the summer he had given John Jay the news that Lapérouse had reached Brazil, was to touch at Tahiti, and would then proceed to California. "The presumption," he said, "is therefore that they will make an establishment of some sort on the North-west coast of America."[31] There is no further mention of Lapérouse in the remaining correspondence of Jefferson's lifetime.

The French expedition was doing very well. As Jefferson penned his letter to Jay, the *Boussole* and the *Astrolabe* were on a southern course down the Pacific Coast, and by mid-September had reached Monterey Bay, to become the first non-Spanish Europeans ever to visit the Indian tribes of that region.

Lapérouse had reached the Northwest Coast on 23 June 1786, and three days later had anchored at the entrance to Yakutat Bay. He had sighted Mount St. Elias in Alaska and measured its height by triangulation with a sextant. On 2 July, Lapérouse carried out one of his specific instructions. He took possession of a bay and named it "Port des Français," believing it sufficiently north of the region explored by the Spanish to be available under international custom. The place was Lituya Bay, showing on modern maps in Glacier Bay National Monument about a hundred airline miles north-northwest of Sitka. Lapérouse wrote in his journal that he had taken possession of the site, which a hundred men might easily defend against a considerable force, but he felt it was a useless gesture. The great distance of that port from Europe and the uncertainty of a ready sale in China convinced the captain that competition between the Spanish, Russians, English, and French would be undesirable. He did suggest, however, that the French might try three expeditions as an experiment. He was highly critical of Spain's policy of secrecy about its American holdings when he called at Spanish ports. He complained that he never would have learned about Monterey except for an English edition of the journal of Spanish explorer Francisco Mourelle, who had sailed the California coast a decade earlier.[32]

In carrying out the rest of his assignment, Lapérouse found himself short of time in charting the Northwest Coast; it would later require three successive seasons for George Vancouver to make such a chart. So Lapérouse amended his schedule in order to reach the Kamchatka Peninsula of Siberia during the following summer. As he sailed down the coast, adding now and then to the cumulative knowledge of the area, he guessed correctly that he was following a line of offshore islands and not the continent itself.[33] From Monterey, Lapérouse continued his investigations in the central Pacific and off the coast of Asia and arrived at Kamchatka in September 1787.

In the same month, John Ledyard came as close as he ever would to Kamchatka. He had departed from St. Petersburg in June 1787 in a hired carriage and by mid-July had crossed the Urals and reached Tobolsk in Siberia. Two weeks later he was in Barnaul, where he spent a few days, dined with the governor, and wrote a letter to Jefferson. He reported that he was about halfway from St. Petersburg to Okhotsk, which he must reach "before I see that Ocean which I hope will bear me on its boosom to the coast of America. How I have come thus far & how I am still to go farther is an enigma that I must disclose to you on some happier occasion."[34] His next town of consequence was Irkutsk, which he reached in mid-August, and from where he wrote to a benefactor, Colonel William S. Smith, a letter revealing something of his life-style. The travel by carriage, horseback, and boat was strenuous, but, he said, "at this place I am in a circle as gay, rich, polite, and as scientific, as if at Petersburg. I drink my French and Spanish wines: and have Majors, Colonels, and Brigadiers, by Brigades, to wait on me in the town, and disciples of Linnaeus to accompany me on my Philosophic walks. In Russia I am treated as an American with politeness & respect and on my account the healths of Dr Franklin and General Washington have been drunk at the tables of two Governors."[35] At this point, Ledyard might have reminded himself of the harsh lesson he had already learned: dining with governors and other persons of quality does not always clear away obstacles for a young man with an obsession.

Soon after providing this optimistic report, he traveled to Yakutsk and in September received the news that he would be unable to proceed during the winter to his destination, Okhotsk on the Pacific Coast. His journal does not make the reason clear, but the severity of the weather may have been the difficulty. The temperature often drops to 50° below zero there. Now he was to spend several months in western Siberia, observing native customs and chafing to be on the way again to the Pacific.[36]

Ledyard in Yakutsk and Lapérouse in Avacha Bay on the Kamchatka Peninsula both had an opportunity to form some conclusions about Russia's view of the Pacific region and how she planned to develop it, particularly that portion of the North American continent that lay so tantalizingly close across the Bering Sea.

Already Russia had a half-century head start on the rest of the world in the sea-otter trade. Until Cook's voyage and the publication of its results, those potential riches were unknown elsewhere. When Ledyard and Lapérouse appeared, there already was a three-year-old settlement on the southwest coast of Kodiak Harbor, established by the trader Shelikhov in 1785. Other settlements followed. Officially, at this time, permanent settlement in North America was not the Russian object. In 1788 Catherine had said, "Much expansion in the Pacific Ocean will not bring solid benefits. To conduct trade is one thing, to take possession is another."[37] But official viewpoints change, and this was long before the Russian-American Company had established Fort Ross in northern California and decided to challenge the Spanish, and later the Americans, for a foothold on the Pacific Coast. There was little time for Russia to lose, despite her running start in the fur trade. By August 1785 British seaman James Hanna had reached Nootka Sound, and the Americans were on the way.

What came particularly to the attention of Ledyard and Lapérouse was an expedition by the Russians, probably stimulated by advance reports of Lapérouse's voyage, to acquire more knowledge of the Pacific Northwest. In fact, the order by the empress establishing the project was issued in the very week of August 1785 when the French voyage sailed from Brest.[38] Commander of the Russian venture was Captain Joseph Billings, an Englishman who had served under Cook and who knew Ledyard. He was to explore the Kolyma River basin, the Chukotski Peninsula, and the islands of the North Pacific. Special attention was to be given to places visited by foreign fur traders.

Ledyard was in Yakutsk when Billings arrived there in November 1787, and they traveled together to Irkutsk the following January. A companion described Ledyard as a man whose haughty behavior made him several enemies. It was in Irkutsk that Ledyard, on the evening of 24 February, was arrested by order of the empress; his grand scheme was halted forever, and he was to be sent home the way he came. There seems to be nothing but coincidence in Ledyard's meeting with his old shipmate Billings. While Billings apparently did not intercede when Ledyard was arrested, he at least is not mentioned by Ledyard as the cause of the arrest.[39]

The vessels commanded by Lapérouse stayed about three weeks at Petropavlovsk on the Kamchatka Peninsula. Before he departed for the South Pacific to complete his assignment, Lapérouse sent a young officer overland toward St. Petersburg, and eventually Versailles, with dispatches and journal materials gathered by the scientists of the expedition. He had periodically sent such dispatches, and the courier he selected this time was his interpreter, Jean-Baptiste Barthélemy, Baron de Lesseps. The twenty-one-year-old Lesseps took leave of the expedition early in October 1787 and was still working his way up the peninsula of Kamchatka when Ledyard was arrested far inland at Irkutsk.[40]

Lapérouse and his ships never returned to France. He had completed his mission and anchored in January 1788 in Botany Bay, Australia. From there he sent home more letters and journals and wrote that he expected to sail in mid-February. After departing from Botany Bay he vanished. The wreckage of his vessels was found in 1826 on an island north of the New Hebrides.

Ledyard came back to London and Paris, chastened but still ebullient, convinced that he would one day cross the North American continent. He sent a note to his friend and mentor: "Mr. Ledyard presents his compliments to Mr. Jefferson— he has been imprisoned and banished by the Empriss of Russia from her dominions after having almost gained the pacific ocean. He is now on his way to Africa to see what he can do with that continent. . . ."[41] Ledyard had been hired by an English group—the Association for Promoting the Discovery of the Interior Parts of Africa—the goals of which included a study of the long and unknown Niger River. He went to Cairo, wrote two letters to Jefferson, and on 10 January 1789, he suddenly and mysteriously died.

How would Lapérouse and Ledyard have reacted to the suggestion that historians might one day be making a comparison of their travels? Lapérouse would have been content to let the facts speak. Ledyard, so brash and confident, so high in spirit, would have eagerly solicited our comparison and asked for a little financial help with his next adventure.

Lapérouse carried out his orders with fidelity and professional skill, and his personal courage was great. The scientific collections gathered by the naturalists disappeared in the wreckage of the ships, but Gilbert Chinard has declared the value of the observations retained in the journals to be of the first order— clearly superior to many of Lapérouse's predecessors and his immediate successors.[42] Geographically, the Lapérouse expedition added details to our knowledge of the Pacific, but little of great importance. As for the Pacific Northwest, the upper portion had already been explored by Captains Cook and Dixon and by the Spanish, and most of it below the Strait of Juan de Fuca had been covered by Spanish expeditions. Even more damaging to the usefulness of the journals, which were not published until 1797, was the fact that George Vancouver's account of his own voyage around the world appeared the very next year.[43]

But these French voyagers were not men of narrow vision. The chief engineer, M. Manneron, remarked that progress on the Pacific Coast would come only with the penetration of the Americans from the East, across the continent to California.

Jefferson, after his initial concern about the intentions of

Lapérouse, forgot about the expedition completely. Although his library contained the journals of Cook, Vancouver, Malespina, and others of his time and before, there is no evidence that Jefferson ever owned a set of the journals or read a line of what Lapérouse and his colleagues had given their lives to report.

Ledyard, on the other hand, affected Jefferson's thinking profoundly. If Jefferson could recognize a fellow moon-gazer, he could also see in Ledyard a man whose dreams made sense and were not unlike Jefferson's own dreams for American growth. There are several theories as to why Ledyard was expelled from Siberia. Perhaps it was simply because Catherine of Russia thought his plan was chimerical, as Jefferson reported; perhaps he was arrested because the Russians did not wish to have an American observer in the area at a time when their plans for exploration, trade, and colonization, which were sure to involve the Northwest Coast of America, were rapidly accelerating. In a sense, Ledyard's earlier voyage with Cook was almost as important as his abortive one into Siberia, for it was then that he caught the fever to engage in the sea–otter trade and to start American ships plying between Canton and the Northwest. The forces he set in motion then were not affected by his later flawed attempt to cross the American continent from west to east. But one man was affected, and that made all the difference.

Writing to a friend after Ledyard had returned from Russia and was on his way to Africa, Jefferson said, "He [Ledyard] promises me if he escapes through this journey, he will go to Kentucky and endeavour to penetrate Westwardly from thence to the South Sea."[44] It was a notion that would not die.

· Across the Alps ·

In September 1786, while walking along the Seine in the Cour la Reine, Jefferson attempted to leap over a fence. He fell, injuring his right wrist. His French surgeons called it a dislocation, but he may have broken a bone.[45] He began writing with his left hand, and complained constantly to recipients of his letters, but still he wrote on. Addressing Charles Thomson in December, he lamented the effect of the injury on his correspondence, although he had written a long letter to Madison the day before; in the

following week he wrote letters, some quite lengthy, to James
Monroe, John Trumbull, Nicholas Lewis, John Adams, and
Abigail Adams.[46]

When the discomfort did not abate, his friends nudged him
toward the standard treatment in such intractable cases: he was
urged to go to Aix-en-Provence and take the water. To make the
journey official and potentially useful to his country, Jefferson
decided to extend the tour into the ports of southern France and
northern Italy. Before leaving Paris he assembled all the maps he
could find of the towns through which he would pass, and on 28
February 1787 departed for Lyons, Nimes, Aix, Marseilles,
Nice, Milan, Rozzano, Genoa, Bordeaux, and Nantes. He was
back in Paris by 10 June.[47]

The meticulous note-taker was in his element. Even though he
was traveling in a populous and civilized part of the world, his
conduct of the trip made it something of a geographical exploration. Except for a botanizing tour into New England that he
would take with Madison in 1791 (see pp. 68–71 below), it was
his closest approach to an expedition of his own. He collected
seeds and plants, studied farms and vineyards, and of course kept
a journal.[48] He prepared a list of plants found in the mountains,
from the tenderest to the hardiest in order of their resistance to
cold, ranging from the delicate caper to the tough old almond
tree. In the process he spent four days on the back of a
mule.

Jefferson was excited about the prospect of introducing the
olive tree and a species of upland rice into America. Growing in
dry soil, the rice would replace the wetland variety of the
Carolinas and Georgia, then raised under such unhealthful conditions that he considered it "a plant which sows life and death
with almost equal hand." He believed the olive tree to be the
worthiest plant that he could introduce into America as a source
of oil, and sent 500 of them from Aix to be planted in the South.
While his rice experiment showed promise, his olive project
failed utterly. He blamed the "nonchalance of our Southern
fellow citizens" for the failure.[49]

A year after his return from Italy, he wrote this advice to two
acquaintances who were about to engage in some European
travel: "When you are doubting whether a thing is worth the

trouble of going to see, recollect that you will never again be so near it, that you may repent the not having seen it, but can never repent having seen it. But there is an opposite extreme, too, that is, the seeing too much. A judicious selection is to be aimed at, taking care that the indolence of the moment have no influence in the decision."[50]

The point is almost too fragile to belabor, but years later when Jefferson was surrounded by the journals, maps, and natural history specimens sent to him by explorers in the West, he might well have nodded with satisfaction as these things recalled the experience of riding across a mountain pass on muleback with notebook and collecting sack.

• Buffon in Person •

Four years before Jefferson was born, the Comte de Buffon had become the *intendant* of the Jardin du Roi. He was revered by the scholarly world. The vast collections in the royal garden, located east of the Latin Quarter, provided the working materials for Buffon's monumental series, *Histoire naturelle générale et particulière, avec la description du cabinet du Roi.* Because Jefferson had dealt with Buffon in veneration even as he had demolished his degeneracy hypothesis in the *Notes,* the two men felt no mutual enmity.

Jefferson had sent copies of his *Notes* to Buffon as soon as it was off the press, and had in turn received a hearty invitation to come and dine at the Jardin.[51] Escorted by the Marquis de Chastellux, a genial acquaintance who had traveled in America and visited Monticello, Jefferson dined several times with Buffon in 1786 and 1787. Our best account of the first encounter was related many years later, in a conversation between Jefferson and Daniel Webster:

"When I was in France, the Marquis de Chastellux carried me over to Buffon's residence in the country, and introduced me to him. It was Buffon's practice to remain in his study till dinner time, and receive no visitors under any pretense; but his house was open and his grounds, and a servant showed them very civilly, and invited all strangers and friends to remain to dine. We saw Buffon in the garden, but carefully avoided him; but we dined with him, and he proved himself then, as he always did, a man of extraordinary powers in conversation. He did not declaim; he was singularly agreeable."[52]

These affable conversations ought to have laid to rest Jefferson's uneasiness with the writings of Buffon on American degeneracy. Apparently they did not. Rather, they set him off on an armchair moose hunt that bordered on the ludicrous.

Having assured Buffon that the North American moose was so large that some species of European deer could walk under one without touching its belly, Jefferson set out to obtain the skin, skeleton, and antlers of such a creature. He was encouraged by the knowledge that there was, in one of the Indian towns of the north woods, a moose antler so large that it was used as a cradle for a child. He sought the aid of John Sullivan, governor of New Hampshire, an old revolutionary general whom he had met at the Continental Congress of 1774. Sullivan had corresponded with Jefferson about the North American moose during the writing of the *Notes*, and now turned with vigor to the assignment of obtaining the largest possible specimen.

It was nearly two years from the time of Jefferson's request to the delivery of the specimen to Buffon's office. Jefferson wrote Sullivan on 7 January 1786, accepting an offer that Sullivan had made earlier to obtain "the skin, the skeleton, and the horns of the Moose, the Caribou, and the Orignal or Elk." He was especially anxious to have the moose. Ideally, he would choose to receive the skin and skeleton so intact that a mounted specimen might be produced. "However I know they are too rare to be obtained so perfect; therefore I will pray you to send me the skin, skeleton and horns just as you can get them."

A year later, Sullivan wrote that he had at last obtained the moose specimen, and expected it to arrive in Portsmouth, N.H., as soon as the roads would permit the passage of a sleigh. In April he wrote again, saying a large box had been shipped with specimens of a moose and a few other zoological items. He enclosed an astonishing account of his expenses, totaling forty-six pounds sterling, which included payments to a hunter, tanner, and the "expence of 3 times sending to Effingham Connecticut River and the Province of Main to procure the skeleton."

By October 1787, Jefferson could write Buffon that the moose remains had arrived and that he was presenting them together with "the horns of the Caribou, the elk, the deer, the spiked horned buck, and the Roebuck of America. . . . I give you their popular names, as it rests with yourself to decide their real names." He said he suspected the animals were of a non-European species and that the moose might be of a new zoological class.

The specimens were acknowledged at once by associates of Buffon, and on 25 October Jefferson received an additional letter from the Comte de Lacépède, saying that Buffon was in poor health and could not write for himself. There was no further correspondence from Buffon. He died the following spring, succumbing to the infirmities of age. Perhaps he saw the enormous moose, perhaps not. Jefferson recalled years later that the specimen caused the savant to recant and brought a promise that his errors would be corrected in the next volume of his *Histoire naturelle*.[53] Jefferson's relationship with members of the Buffon circle remained close; throughout the years he sent many more specimens of North American fauna, recent and extinct, to the scientific friends he had made in France.

· The Expanding Dream ·

The man who drafted the Declaration of Independence was far from his homeland when the Constitution was formed in 1787. He watched, corresponded, and counseled. Despite the happy development, he felt the anguish of one who believes his country is drifting. He deplored the tendency of his countrymen to go into debt, and he hated what he considered their departure from the simple life. The repugnance of slavery dwelt stronger than ever in his mind, so strong that he played briefly with the notion that upon his return home he would free his slaves.[54] In the Mississippi Valley, where Spain had in 1784 closed the river to navigation, he saw the grave possibility that the people of that region—the Ohio Valley included—would go to war or even separate from the United States to gain the right of shipping their produce down the Mississippi. "They [the westerners] are able already to rescue the navigation of the Mississippi out of the hands of the Spanish, and to add New Orleans to their own territory.

They will be joined by the [French] inhabitants of Louisiana. This will bring on a war between them and Spain, in which the U.S. probably would be drawn on the side of the westerners."[55] Jefferson seemed ever convinced that his country was on the edge of a war with Spain, an event that was not to occur until 1898.

War of another kind, however, was at his doorstep. He had always sided with the rebels in the French Revolution, but the struggle took a turn that he did not anticipate. He had wanted the French to adopt a constitution patterned on the English rather than the American one, theorizing that a country cannot move too fast toward liberty without unnecessary disruption. He decided that France was able to sustain a limited constitutional monarchy. Then the Revolution overtook his thinking, in a sense, and leaped ahead to an intensity that he had not foreseen. It began, as he once said, "to wear a fearful appearance." There was some coldbloodedness in his detached observation of that struggle; he watched the killing of the upper classes, the storming of the Bastille, with a seemingly untroubled eye. "By August [1789] he had embraced not only the radical goals of the French Revolution but the idea, at first inculcated by Americanists like Lafayette . . . that it belonged to the same political universe as the American Revolution."[56]

The Revolution was only one of the factors that intensified Jefferson's Americanism. He never espoused theoretical systems, but after seeing the European system he felt in his soul the critical differences between his homeland and what he considered the tyrannical excesses of other nations. "My God! How little do my countrymen know what precious blessings they are in possession of, and of which no other people on earth enjoy," he wrote James Monroe. "I confess I had no idea of it myself. . . ."[57]

When he had spoken of "my country" in his early years, he had meant Virginia. Later the term meant to him the old republic, those original colonies and the states that followed them into the Union, reaching to the Mississippi. Then, during his stay in France, he had begun to envision still another enlargement in the dimensions of the American system. In an almost offhand comment to Archibald Stuart he had said, "Our confederacy must be viewed as the nest from which all America, North and South is to be peopled."[58] Spain was intractable and warlike, and the idea of extending the boundaries of an American republic beyond the Mississippi was still a formless kind of notion. It was stuck firmly, however, in the back of Jefferson's mind.

NOTES

1. DOS PASSOS [2], 68. Portions of the present chapter, including most of the section on Ledyard and Lapérouse, first appeared in JACKSON [5], and are used with permission of the *Western Historical Quarterly*.

2. For TJ's letter, BOYD, 6:371; for Clark's reply of 8 Feb. 1784, BOYD, 15:609. Clark may already have become unfit to endure the rigors of the adventure because of his use of alcohol. It was common knowledge seven years later that he was an alcoholic. TJ wrote: "I know the greatness of his mind, and am the more mortified at the cause which obscures it. Had not this unhappily taken place there was nothing he might not have hoped; could it be surmounted, his lost ground might yet be recovered" (to Harry Innes, 7 March 1791, LC).

3. The memorandum appears as an appendix in BURPEE [2]. Henry's activities are discussed in the same work, pp. 307–21.

4. On 31 May 1784, en route to his ship, TJ paid a New York bookseller four pounds for a Spanish dictionary (Account books, Massachusetts Historical Society, Boston).

5. ECHEVERRIA, 122–23. The paragraph following is suggested by ECHEVERRIA, 118.

6. Madison to TJ, 27 April 1785, BOYD, 8:110. Madison called the matches "a great treat to my curiosity."

7. To George Rogers Clark, 21 June 1787, BOYD, 11:487. He told Clark that Saugrain had been recommended to him "as a gentleman of skill in his profession, of general science and merit."

8. See RICKMAN. Ledyard's work is available in an edition edited by MUNFORD.

9. MUNFORD, 70, 77.

10. DE VOTO, 279.

11. Ledyard's first biographer was Jared Sparks, who went to Monticello to interview Jefferson (Sparks Manuscripts, 147b, Houghton Library, Cambridge, Mass.). SPARKS remains a reliable biography. The best modern source is WATROUS, containing Ledyard's manuscript journal, all pertinent letters, and a commentary by the editor. See also AUGUR.

12. The work which TJ listed in his library catalog as "Cooke's last

voiage" is COOK [1]. All three of the voyages are summarized in PALUKA.

13. MUNFORD, 94.

14. WATROUS, 8.

15. Reported in STILES, 3:106.

16. SPARKS, 172–73.

17. JAY, 3:97.

18. SPARKS, 192.

19. SPARKS, 199.

20. The official report of the expedition is LAPÉROUSE [1]. The citations which follow are from the later English edition, LAPÉROUSE [2].

21. BOYD, 8:339.

22. BOYD, 8:373.

23. LAPÉROUSE [2], 3:347.

24. BOYD, 8:587–88.

25. WATROUS, 15–16, summarizes this episode and lists sources.

26. WATROUS, 94–95.

27. Both SPARKS and WATROUS contain excellent accounts of the effort to get permission for Ledyard to enter Russia.

28. Diary of Nathaniel Cutting, Cutting Papers, Massachusetts Historical Society.

29. WATROUS, 108.

30. WATROUS, 114–15. Had the vessel sailed, Ledyard would have begun his overland journey from Nootka, not St. Petersburg. William S. Smith to Jay, 1 Sept. 1786, BOYD, 10:315n—16n.

31. BOYD, 10:221.

32. LAPÉROUSE [2], 3:299, 302, 310; 4:140–49.

33. DUNMORE, 266–76.

34. WATROUS, 127–28.

35. To William S. Smith, 20 Aug. 1787, WATROUS, 129–30.

36. WATROUS, 142–259, is an annotated transcript of Ledyard's manuscript journal from which this summary of his Siberian travels is drawn.

37. GIBSON, 6, 7.

38. SAUER, 1. Martin Sauer was secretary to the Russian expedition headed by Billings.

39. SAUER, 99–101.

40. LESSEPS, vii.

41. WATROUS, 252–53.

42. CHINARD [4], xl–xlv.

43. VANCOUVER, a work much relied upon by Jefferson in later years.

44. To the Rev. James Madison, 19 July 1788, BOYD, 13:382.

45. BUTTERFIELD & RICE. The date of TJ's fall, 18 Sept. 1786, and the place is confirmed in a letter of Louis-Guilliame de Veillard to William Temple Franklin, 20 Sept. 1786, American Philosophical Society, Philadelphia.

46. To Charles Thomson, 17 Dec. 1786, BOYD, 10:608.

47. See DUMBAULD, 83–109, or any standard biography.

48. His diary of the tour is in BOYD, 11:415–64. See also 11:515–18, in which he reports on the trip to John Adams, 1 July 1787.

49. See GARDEN BOOK, 380, 505. TJ called his upland or mountain rice *Oryza mutica*. Because American rice exports were down by half since the Revolution, he hoped to persuade Carolinians to raise this Mediterranean variety because the French liked it. He talked some French importers into buying the rice, and in 1789 more tons cleared the Charleston customhouse for France than ever before (PETERSON [1], 327–28).

50. To John Rutledge, Jr., 19 June 1788, BOYD, 13:268. The advice was intended for Rutledge and Thomas Lee Shippen.

51. RICE, 85, who conveniently summarizes Jefferson's personal relations with Buffon on pp. 83–86. The house in which Buffon lived still stands in the southwest corner of the Jardin du Roi.

52. Notes on TJ's conversations with Daniel Webster in 1824 are in WEBSTER, 1:371–78.

53. The TJ-Sullivan exchange is in BOYD, 9:160, 11:68, 11:320; TJ to Buffon, 12:194; Lacépède to TJ, 12:287. The affair of the moose is told at length in JONES. Writing years later, Lacépède told TJ that Buffon died "without being able to make use of the very valuable present you had given him. The American animals on which he had reported [i.e., described in print] were the species of reindeer, that of the roe and of the cougar" (Lacépède to TJ, 13 May 1803, LC). After Buffon's death in April 1788, Lacépède undertook to continue the *Histoire naturelle*.

54. On the simple virtues, see TJ to John Page, 4 May 1786, BOYD, 9:445–46. For his increasing sensitivity to slavery, see MILLER, 100–103.

55. To Madison, 30 Jan. 1787, BOYD, 11:92.

56. PETERSON [2], 50.

57. 17 June 1785, BOYD, 8:233.

58. To Stuart, 25 Jan. 1786, BOYD, 9:218. He added that he thought the South American countries could not be in better hands, for the time, "till our population can be sufficiently advanced to gain it from them peice by peice." Despite her hostility to American expansion, Spain would be an easier adversary than France or England.

CHAPTER FOUR

The Years with George Washington

Although he loved and understood America better than ever, Jefferson was not quite ready to leave France. He was planning a furlough, however, by late 1788 when he wrote John Trumbull that he hoped to be in Monticello by the next April, returning to France in the fall. He had to sail directly from Le Havre to Virginia "because I carry colonies of plants and birds for that country."[1]

Not only did his finances at home need attention, but Jefferson was anxious to see his two daughters safely back in Monticello. His authorization for leave came in August 1789 and he left Europe two months later. To James Madison, who had asked how he would feel about an appointment at home, he had written that he meant to take no other office. He wanted to finish out his service as minister to France and retire from public life. It was the old refrain, and perhaps he did not believe it himself. On the day that he sailed between the Virginia Capes and arrived on his native soil, he read in a newspaper that he had been appointed secretary of state by President Washington.[2]

All the steps had been taken. He had been nominated by Washington, with a title replacing the old title of "secretary for foreign affairs" held by John Jay, and the Senate had confirmed the appointment; everyone but Jefferson considered the matter settled. Only after he had been home for three weeks did he receive Washington's letter of appointment. He accepted in mid-February.[3]

Thus Jefferson began a decade in which he would serve for four years in the cabinet, return again to private life, then become vice-president under John Adams. It was a period in which matters pertaining to the West became increasingly important.

Although Washington is not looked upon as a man with a great western vision, he dealt authoritatively with western problems. Jefferson had much to learn from him.

· Dealing with Europe and the Indians ·

The first object of Jefferson's service as secretary of state was what Merrill D. Peterson has called "the redemption and pacification of the West," meaning western areas east of the Mississippi. Seven years after the end of the Revolution, Spain in the southwest and England in the northwest controlled great land areas claimed by the United States. The Spanish blockade of Mississippi navigation since 1784 and the British occupation of posts below the Great Lakes in violation of treaty provisions were vexing. Indian hostilities encouraged by the British took many American lives and hurt the fur trade.[4]

The Washington administration took hold of these problems with vigor. To reduce the threat of western separation, Washington gave appointments in civil and military affairs to influential westerners. Two important treaties were negotiated during his terms as president, although Jefferson—uneasy in office—had left the government before the treaties were put into effect. The first was Jay's treaty of 1794 with Great Britain, removing British forces from the Old Northwest and making the Indians an easier problem. The second was Thomas Pinckney's treaty a year later, the Treaty of San Lorenzo with Spain, restoring free access to the Mississippi for westerners and putting Spanish posts east of the Mississippi into American hands.

An early indication of Jefferson's views on American policy in world affairs came during his first summer in office. The British and Spanish clashed far away in the Pacific Northwest, in what became known as the Nootka Sound controversy. Spain had driven out British fur traders and captured two vessels at Nootka; Britain in turn sent an ultimatum to Spain, then unofficially inquired about the prospect of the United States permitting British troops to pass through American territory to attack Spanish Louisiana. To Jefferson's dismay, the inquiry was made through Alexander Hamilton, secretary of the treasury, and Hamilton took the matter directly to Washington. At a cabinet meeting, Washington set forth the question for discussion. Hamilton favored permitting British passage, Jefferson proposed making no official reply at all to the unofficial query. In the end, Spain backed down.[5] The incident marked the first of many differences with Hamilton which would spur Jefferson on to an early resignation.

Spain's intransigence about control of Mississippi navigation began while Jefferson was in France, and was not to be settled until he had left the secretariat, but he was nonetheless involved and active.

Determined to crush the hostile and British-dominated Indians of the Ohio Valley, the government sent out two unlucky expeditions. The first, under General Josiah Harmar, resulted in an ambush in which untrained militiamen were defeated. The second, in which General Arthur St. Clair led 3,000 men, ended in a debacle that resulted in more than 600 fatalities and nearly 300 men wounded in the fall of 1791. Negotiations with the British and Indians followed, with Jefferson participating. Under a new commander, General Anthony Wayne, a two-hour encounter called the Battle of Fallen Timbers crushed the Indians and persuaded them that Britain would be of no further help. At the Treaty of Greenville early in 1795, the tribes gave up most of the Ohio Valley and the way was cleared for new American settlements.

A problem arrived from France in the spring of 1793 with the debarkation of the minister from the French Republic, Edmond Charles Genêt. He was deprived of his protfolio within a few months, but not until he had started to organize expeditions on American soil to move against Spanish and British holdings, and had armed a captured British vessel, *The Little Sarah*. Breaking a pledge to Jefferson, he ordered the ship (now named *La Petite Democrate*) to sea. When it became obvious that Genêt's behavior was ill-advised and dangerous, and might involve the United States in war, Washington's cabinet decided to demand his recall. The recall presented little difficulty; the Jacobins newly come into power in France were quick to comply. Fearing that Genêt would be beheaded if he returned to France, Washington refused to extradite him. The affair touched Jefferson personally, in that his old friend George Rogers Clark had agreed to serve as a leader of armed incursions into Spanish Louisiana, and the André Michaux expedition to the Pacific arranged by Jefferson (see pp. 74–78 below) proved to be uncomfortably linked with Genêt's operation.

Already Jefferson had started discussions with Washington about leaving the cabinet, and he resigned at the end of 1793, removed, as he believed once more, from public life forever.

· Botanizing with Madison ·

Washington made two extensive tours of the States while in office, first into New England in the fall of 1789 and then into the southern states in the spring of 1791. During the second trip, time seemed to hang heavy on Jefferson's hands. He and his longtime Orange County friend, Madison, conceived a "botanizing excursion" into the north. The fact that these two Republicans were going plant-watching in Federalist strongholds brought charges that the trip was political.[6] While fence-mending may have been on their minds, Jefferson seemed to consider the jaunt primarily as a means of getting rid of a persistent migraine headache, a welcome withdrawal into the world of growing things, and a chance to study the advancing horde of Hessian flies that was destroying the wheat crops of northeastern farmers.

Leaving Philadelphia on 16 March, Jefferson joined Madison in New York and they spent a month traveling from there to Lake George and Lake Champlain, crossing into Vermont and coming down the Connecticut River Valley, returning by way of Long Island. An extract from the notes made by Jefferson has survived, of which the following is a portion (the brackets are Jefferson's):

May 22. Conklin's in the highlands. Found here the Thuja Occidentalis, called the white cedar & Silverfir, called hemlock. [The former with an imbricated leaf, the latter with single pinnated leaves.] Also the Candle berry myrtle.

23. Poughkeepsie. The white pine [5. leaved], Pitch-pine [3 leaved], Juniper [a shrub with decumbent stems about 8 f. long, with single leaves all round the stem, & the berries used for infusing gin.]

31. Lake Champlain is a much larger but less pleasant water than L. George. It is about 110 miles long & from one to 15 miles broad. It is narrow & turbid from Ticonderoga to beyond the Split rock about 30 miles, where it is said to widen & grow more clear. It yields catfish of 20 lb. weight, sturgeon, & salmon, also the fish found in L. George except the trout but in smaller quantities, & it is less infested with musketoes & insects. The eastern bank is of limestone laminated like slate, on the Western side is none, & it is remarkable that to the Westwd. of this & L. George, the people are obliged to come to them from great distances for their limestone. The Western end is closed by high mountains of very indifferent lands, on the East side the lands are champaign, the green mountains moving out of them at the distance of 20 or 23 miles & running parallel with the lake as far as the sight extends. These lands may be called good, & begin to be thickly seated. The growth on both sides the lake much the same as on Lake George, to which add the yellow or 2. leaved pine, & the thistle in such abundance as to embarrass agriculture in a high degree. This lake is conjectured to be about 100 f. lower than L. George, the difference of it's level in spring & fall is about 3 f. It closes with ice about the last of November & opens a few days before Lake George. It is to be noted that we have seen no poplar, dogwood nor redbud since we have passed the highlands, nor any fruit trees but apples, & here & there a cherry tree. We have seen no persimmons . . . in any place since crossing the Hudson.[7]

From Lake George, Jefferson wrote to daughter Maria: "I write to you on the bark of the Paper birch, supposed to be the same used by the antients to write on before the art of making paper was invented." Maria wrote back, politely avowing that the bark was "prettier than paper." In a letter to married daughter Martha Jefferson Randolph, he found an occasion to praise the Virginia climate. "Here they are locked up in ice and snow for 6. months. Spring and autumn which make a paradise of our country are rigorous winter with them, and a tropical summer breaks on them all at once. When we consider how much climate · contributes to the happiness of our cond[ition] . . . we have reason to value highly the accident of birth in such a one as that of Virginia."[8]

Although he loved plants for themselves, he was especially fond of those which promised new practical applications. In Italy it had been upland rice and olive trees, now it was the sugar maple. Here was a majestic tree not common in his part of

Virginia which, if properly cultivated, might free his region from dependence on sugar importation. He ordered sixty trees from nurseryman William Prince, of Flushing, N.Y., along with other plants, and a memorandum in his hand instructs that they were to be planted "below the lower Roundabout at the north east end. About 30 feet apart in a grove, not in rows."

From Bennington, Vt., Colonel Joseph Fay sent him some seeds to try. Acknowledging the gift, Jefferson said: "Many things seem to tend toward drawing the value of that tree into public notice. The rise in the price of West India sugars, short crops, new embarrassments which may arise in the way of getting them, will oblige us to try to do without them." The plants and seeds failed to grow. He later told his son-in-law that he would keep trying, as the maple tree was "too hopeful an object to be abandoned."[9]

What distinguished Jefferson the plant lover from a truly scientific botanist was shown in the chiding he must have received from members of the American Philosophical Society upon his return. He had not known how to collect systematically, and commented to Madison: "I am sorry that we did not bring with us some leaves of the different plants which struck our attention, as it is the leaf which principally decides *specific* difference." He urged Madison, who apparently was returning to New England from New York, to correct this oversight.[10]

In studying the Hessian fly, Jefferson was acting for the American Philosophical Society, which had appointed a committee of five to investigate means for eradicating this serious insect pest. Taking its name from the mistaken notion that Hessian soldiers had brought it to America, the insect was deadly to wheat crops and was moving south. Jefferson made detailed notes about the habits, life cycle, and depredations of the fly. He also solicited information from others, some of which was sent to him later. For example, Jonathan N. Havens and Sylvester Dering, whom he had met on his tour, sent him twenty-seven pages of such comments.[11] The fly moved slowly but inexorably down the coast, and Jefferson worried about it for years. In letters written nine years apart to Thomas Mann Randolph, he said in 1792 that the fly was now seen near Baltimore and that he was raising some for more information. "I have several of these now hatching." He said in 1801, after the seat of government had been moved to Washington: "The Hessian Fly is laying waste all the wheat in this quarter, the late as well as early sown." By this time, the fly had reached Monticello, having arrived in Albemarle County by 1798.[12]

Though Jefferson's botanizing had been too erratic to satisfy his scientific colleagues, and the news he brought of the Hessian fly was mostly bad, there was one singular outcome of the expedition that Jefferson felt worth recording. His migraines had abated. "I am in hopes the relaxation it [the trip] gave me from business has freed me from the almost constant headache with which I have been persecuted thro the whole winter and spring. Having been entirely clear of it while travelling proves it to have been occasioned by the drudgery of business."[13]

· Counseling with Indians ·

The arrival of new Indian delegations touched off Jefferson's appreciation of drama. Without discounting the terrible urgency of these visits, at a time when red and white men were slaughtering one another, he was able to admire the theatrical aspects of the occasion.

Some records of a particular visitation have been preserved, in the critical time between the defeat of St. Clair and the victory of Anthony Wayne. During that period many councils were held, and several treaties signed in an attempt to quell the belligerent tirbes and lure them away from British and Spanish influence.

In December 1792, a colorful group of Indian delegates, consisting of eight men and three women, with one French and two Indian interpreters, appeared in Philadelphia. They were referred to loosely by the government as "Wabash and Illinois Indians," but they represented seven tribes: Kaskaskias, Eel Rivers, Piankashaws, Weas, Mascoutins, Potawatomis, and Kickapoos.

Senior member of the group was Jean Baptiste Ducoigne, the Kaskaskia chief who had called on Jefferson in the final days of his Virginia governorship. Ducoigne inquired about Martha, and Jefferson was so pleased that he wrote her about it. "One of the Indian chiefs now here, whom you may remember to have seen at Monticello a day or two before Tarleton drove us off, remem-

bers you and enquired after you. . . . Perhaps you may recollect
that he gave our name to an infant son he then had with him and
who, he now tells me, is a fine lad."[14]

As traveling in winter back to their homes would be difficult,
the Indians were not rushed into negotiations. It was February
before they held the first of several meetings with Washington.
Besides the Indians, the dramatis personae at the first council was
impressive: George Washington, the president; Jefferson, secretary of state; Henry Knox, secretary of war; Arthur St. Clair,
governor of the Northwest Territory; General Rufus Putnam;
Captain Abner Prior, of the Third Sublegion; and Tobias Lear,
the presidential secretary.

There was also an English interpreter to translate the French
interpreter's version of the Indian statements, and to channel the
President's responses back through the linguistic relay to the
Indians. The ineptness of the English translator induced Jefferson
to keep his own transcript. Fluent in French, he followed the
words of the French interpreter and ignored the English one,
later making a copy of the resulting proceedings for Washington.
He gave it to Washington the same day with the remark, "He
[Jefferson] thinks he can assure the President that not a sentiment
delivered by the French interpreter is omitted, nor a single one
inserted which was not expressed. It differs often from what the
English Interpreter delivered because he varied much from the
other who alone was regarded [as proficient] by T. J."

It was not just a discussion to Jefferson, but fascinating pag-
eantry. His respect for the Indian, his delight in their oratory,
and his sense of theater is shown not only in his translation but
in the bracketed "stage directions" he inserts:

Feb. 1 1793. The President having addressed the Chiefs of the Wabash
& Illinois Indians, John Baptist de Coin, chief of Kaskaskias, spoke as
follows.

Father. I am about to open to you my heart. I salute first the Great
Spirit, the master of life, and then you.

I present you a black pipe on the death of the chiefs who have
come here and died in your bed. It is the calumet of the dead. Take it
and smoke it in remembrance of them. The dead pray you to listen to
the living and their friends. They are gone, we cannot recall them, let us
then be contented, for, as you have said, tomorrow perhaps it may be

our turn. Take then their pipe, and as I have spoken for the dead, let me now address you for the living. [He delivered the black pipe.]

[Here Three legs, a Piankishaw chief, came forward and carried around a white pipe from which every one smoked.]

John Baptist De Coin spoke again.

Father. The sky is now cleared, & I am about to open my heart to you again. I do it in the presence of the Great Spirit, and I pray you to attend.

You have heard the words of our father General Putnam. We opened our hearts to him, we made peace with him, and he has told you what we said. . . .

Gomo, a Potawatomi chief, then spoke on behalf of a dead tribesman, and delivered a strand of dark beads to Washington to honor the dead. He then spoke, as translated by Jefferson:

Father, I am happy to see you. The heavens have cleared away. The day is bright, and I rejoice to hear your voice. These beads [holding up a bundle of white beads] are the road between us. Take you hold at one end, I will at the other, and hold it fast. I will visit this road every day, and sweep it clean. If any blood be on it, I will cover it up; if stumps, I will cut them out. Should your children and mine meet in this road, they shall shake hands and be good friends. . . . Father, I take you by the hand with all my heart. I will never forget you; do not you forget me. [Here he delivered the bundle of white strands.]

The lengthy transcript contained several speeches, all with the usual Indian litany: resistance to aggression, resentment at the loss of lands and property. At one point Ducoigne exclaimed: "I am of Kaskaskia, and have always been a good American from my youth upwards. Yet the Kentuckians take my lands, eat my stock, steal my horses, kill my game, and abuse our persons. . . . Do not let the Kentuckians take my land nor injure me; but give me a line to them to let me alone."[15]

Succeeding councils had to be postponed because the sun did not shine—a bad omen to the Indians. When the clouds dispersed, the parties convened in mid-afternoon on 4 February, "whereafter making speeches & delivering a pipe & strings of wampum, they dined with the President."[16] On the 7th, Washington directed that a treaty with the Wabash and Illinois Indians be laid before the Senate; it had been negotiated earlier at Vincennes by General Putnam. After much delay the Senate failed to ratify the document on 9 Jan 1796.[17]

When the Indians decided to go home in the spring, they made a final call on the President. At the parting on 7 May, each received a letter of protection, a medal, and extracts from the current act to regulate Indian trade. Jefferson drafted a farewell speech to be intoned by Washington, and the delegates began the tedious journey by coach and keelboat back to their homeland.

· The Michaux Expedition ·

By the period 1792–93, several factors had directed the attention of the merchantile world to the waters of the Pacific Northwest. The narratives of James Cook and John Ledyard, awakening American interest, and the desire of British fur traders to push farther westward had resulted in several contacts and near-contacts by separately traveling explorers. The American sea captain Robert Gray had sailed his *Columbia* into the estuary of the Columbia on 11 May 1792. Later he met and traded information with Captain George Vancouver, who was making an official voyage of discovery for the British government. The next year, when Alexander Mackenzie of the North West Company pushed overland and bolstered British claims to priority in the general area, he was told by Indians that he had just missed Vancouver.

American claims in the region now rested solely on the enterprise of Captain Gray, a civilian; no action by the U.S. government was in sight.[18] The American Philosophical Society was pressing for an overland expedition, as member Caspar Wistar wrote to botanist Moses Marshall: "By a conversation with thy uncle [Humphrey Marshall], I find that thee is already acquainted with the wishes of some gentlemen here to have our continent explored in a western direction. . . . Mr. Jefferson and several other gentlemen are much interested, and think they can procure a subscription sufficient to insure one thousand guineas as a compensation to any one who undertakes the journey and can bring satisfactory proof of having crossed to the South Sea." Marshall was a Philadelphia physician and botanist who had traveled in Kentucky and Tennessee. There appears to be no correspondence between Marshall and Jefferson, and no evidence that the plan went any further.[19]

André Michaux was an important French botanist when he came to the United States in 1785, having collected and studied widely in Europe and England. Louis XVI sent him to the New World to accumulate seeds and plants for use in France, and to expedite his work, he established botanical gardens in New Jersey (nearly opposite what is now Fortieth Street in New York) and in Charleston. He visited George Washington in June 1786 at Mount Vernon, later writing, "I will accept of the Offer that you made me, in Sending to your Care, the Collections that I shall make in the Distant Counties, for the use of the King of France." He signed himself "Botanist to his Most Christian Majesty."[20]

Michaux seems to have tired of his assignment by 1791, advising the *intendant* of the Jardin du Roi on 15 April that he was preparing to return to France and that he felt an aversion to remaining in the United States.[21] Something during the next few months changed his mind. He approached the American Philosophical Society with a plan for an expedition to the Pacific. By December 1792 the idea was sufficiently advanced for Jefferson to suggest that Michaux might want to travel west with a delegation of Indians then in Philadelphia. He said that a Kaskaskia Indian then in Philadelphia (who else but Ducoigne?) would confer with Michaux about the projected journey to the South Sea.[22]

In the early months of 1793 Jefferson undertook to raise a subscription to finance the expedition. In an agreement to be signed by subscribers, Michaux was to receive the money in a prorated fashion, one-quarter in advance, the remainder on proof that he had reached the Pacific. If he failed he was to receive only a sum adjusted "to the extent of unknown country explored by him."[23]

The instructions given to Michaux in the spring were written by Jefferson, and are significant because the lines of inquiry set forth represent an outline of what Jefferson and the society knew, and wanted to know, about the West.

To Mr. Andrew Michaud.   [30 April 1793]
  Sundry persons having subscribed certain sums of money for your encouragement to explore the country along the Missouri, & thence Westwardly to the Pacific ocean, having submitted the plan of the enterprize to the direction of the American Philosophical society, & the

Society having accepted of the trust, they proceed to give you the following instructions.

They observe to you that the chief objects of your journey are to find the shortest & most convenient route of communication between the U.S. & the Pacific ocean, within the temperate latitudes, & to learn such particulars as can be obtained of the country through which it passes, it's productions, inhabitants & other interesting circumstances.

As a channel of communication between these states & the Pacific ocean, the Missouri, so far as it extends, presents itself under circumstances of unquestioned preference. It has therefore been declared as a fundamental object of the subscription, (not to be dispensed with) that this river shall be considered & explored as a part of the communication sought for. To the neighborhood of this river therefore, that is to say to the town of Kaskaskia, the society will procure you a conveyance in company with the Indians of that town now in Philadelphia.

From thence you will cross the Missisipi and pass by land to the nearest part of the Missouri above the Spanish settlements, that you may avoid the risk of being stopped.

You will then pursue such of the largest streams of that river, as shall lead by the shortest way, & the lowest latitudes to the Pacific ocean.

When pursuing these streams, you shall find yourself at the point from whence you may get by the shortest & most convenient route to some principal river of the Pacific ocean, you are to proceed to such river, & pursue it's course to the ocean. It would seem by the latest maps as if a river called Oregan interlocked with the Missouri for a considerable distance, & entered the Pacific ocean, not far Southward of Nootka sound. But the Society are aware that these maps are not to be trusted so far as to be the ground of any positive instruction to you. They therefore only mention the fact, leaving to yourself to verify it, or to follow such other as you shall find to be the real truth.

You will, in the course of your journey, take notice of the country you pass through, it's general face, soil, rivers, mountains, it's productions animal, vegetable, & mineral so far as they may be new to us & may also be useful or very curious; the latitude of places or materials for calculating it by such simple methods as your situation may admit you to practice, the names, numbers, & dwellings of the inhabitants, and such particularities as you can learn of their history, connection with each other, languages, manners, state of society & of the arts & commerce among them.

Under the head of Animal history, that of the Mammoth is particularly recommended to your enquiries, as it is also to learn whether the

Lama, or Paca of Peru is found in those parts of this continent, or how far North they come.[24]

The method of preserving your observations is left to yourself, according to the means which shall be in your power. It is only suggested that the noting them on the skin might be best for such as are most important, and that further details may be committed to the bark of the paper birch, a substance which may not excite suspicions among the Indians, & little liable to injury from wet or other common accidents. By the means of the same substance you may perhaps find opportunities, from time to time, of communicating to the society information of your progress, & of the particulars you shall have noted.

When you shall have reached the Pacific ocean, if you find yourself within convenient distance of any settlement of Europeans, go to them, commit to writing a narrative of your journey & observations & take the best measures you can for conveying it by duplicates or triplicates thence to the society by sea.

Return by the same, or such other route, as you shall think likely to fulfill with most satisfaction & certainty the objects of your mission, furnishing yourself with the best proofs the nature of the case will admit of the reality & extent of your progress. Whether this shall be by certificates from Europeans settled on the Western coast of America, or by what other means, must depend on circumstances.

Ignorance of the country thro' which you are to pass and confidence in your judgment, zeal, & discretion, prevent the society from attempting more minute instructions, and even from exacting rigorous observance of those already given, except indeed what is the first of all objects, that you seek for & pursue that route which shall form the shortest & most convenient communication between the higher parts of the Missouri & the Pacific ocean.

It is strongly recommended to you to expose yourself in no case to unnecessary dangers, whether such as might affect your health or your personal safety: and to consider this not merely as your personal concern, but as the injunction of Science in general which expects it's enlargement from your enquiries, & of the inhabitants of the U.S. in particular, to whom your Report will open new fields & subjects of Commerce, Intercourse, & Observation.

If you reach the Pacific ocean & return, the Society assign to you all the benefits of the subscription beforementioned. If you reach the waters only which run into that ocean, the society reserve to themselves the apportionment of the reward according to the conditions expressed in the subscription. [If you do not reach even those waters, they refuse all reward, and reclaim the money you may have received here under the subscription.]

They will expect you to return to the city of Philadelphia to give in to them a full narrative of your journey & observations, and to answer the enquiries they shall make of you, still reserving to yourself the benefits arising from the publication of them.[25]

When Genêt arrived as minister from France, Michaux's aims changed abruptly. Genêt decided to make the botanist an instrument of his own intrigues. Michaux finally set out on 15 July, apparently not with the Indian delegation, and traveled down the Ohio as planned—botanizing all the while. His principal aim, however, was no longer to reach the Pacific but to serve Genêt. Quite probably Jefferson knew before his departure that he no longer planned to act on his instructions from the American Philosophical Society. Carrying a letter of introduction from Jefferson, and credentials from Genêt, Michaux began to call upon Kentuckians. He visited General Benjamin Logan, Governor Isaac Shelby, and finally George Rogers Clark. From Clark, the proposed leader of a Genêt-sponsored filibustering expedition into Spanish territory, he learned that the scheme had gone sour. In November he started back, traveling overland through Virginia and arriving in Philadelphia in mid-December. During the next two days he called on Jefferson and society president David Rittenhouse, but the subject of their talks is not recorded.[26]

Michaux remained in the United States until 1796, apparently untainted by his venture into international intrigue. Later he published a distinguished work, *Flora Boreali-Americana* (Paris, 1802).

· Jefferson and the American Philosophical Society ·

When he left the government at the end of 1793, Jefferson was resolved to remain a farmer–planter at Monticello until the day he died. Although John Adams thought this was only a scheme to gain the presidency, it was actually another sincerely intended retirement to private life.[27] In the words of a favorite biblical passage of George Washington's, after his own retirement from the presidency, he was at last home "under his vine and his fig tree."[28] Also like Washington, he turned with new vigor to the profession of agriculture and the further development of Monticello. He wrote Edward Rutledge that a visitor "found me in a retirement I doat on, living like an Antediluvian patriarch among my children & grandchildren, and tilling my soil. . . ." And to David Rittenhouse he reported, "I am immersed in the concerns of a farmer, and . . . they in a great degree render me indifferent to my books, so that I read little and ride much."[29]

His correspondence dropped sharply during this period of his life. Among his papers in the Library of Congress, a single reel of microfilm holds all his correspondence from January 1794 to mid-June 1797.[30] In busier times, a reel might have stored only three months of correspondence.

An important connection with the world of scholarship during his retirement was his continued association with the American Philosophical Society. He had been elected to membership in 1780, ten years before the death of the society's founder, Benjamin Franklin. Since 1791 he had been vice-president. Philosophical Hall, which housed the society, had been a kind of club for him during his years in Philadelphia; through it he became a part of a distinguished circle. "The association stimulated him and enlarged his powers; while his constant correspondence with members such as David Rittenhouse, Charles Thomson, Benjamin Rush, Caspar Wistar . . . and other intellectual worthies clarified his concepts and crystallized them on paper."[31]

After an absence of three years, during which he did not visit Philadelphia, Jefferson was coaxed back into politics. Although he did not seek nomination to the vice-presidency under Adams, he did not refuse it, and was elected in the autumn of 1796. It was welcome news to his friends in Philosophical Hall, who were seeking a successor to the late David Rittenhouse as president of the society. Benjamin Rush wrote, even before Jefferson had accepted his election, and said the society proposed to elect him its president. The action had been taken on the assumption that Jefferson would accept the vice-presidency of the United States and would thus be living again in Philadelphia. It may be that Jefferson valued this offer more than the offer of the people to make him the second officer of the land. In responding, after the society actually elected him, he wrote: "The suffrage of a body which comprehends whatever the American world has of distinction in philosophy and science in general is the most flattering incident of my life, and that to which I am the most sensible."[32]

Jefferson attended a meeting of the society on the evening of 10 March 1797, his first as president, and read a paper entitled "Memoir on the Discovery of Certain Bones of a Quadruped of the Clawed Kind in the Western Parts of Virginia." Believing it a new species, and one which offered another chance to repudiate Buffon about the size of animals in the New World, Jefferson named it the megalonyx. Before his paper was published, however, he was reminded that the creature had been described a few years earlier, and that he had been sent a drawing of the bones by William Carmichael in Madrid. He revised the paper and restored to the prehistoric giant the name it already had been given, the megatherium.[33]

Fulfilling his duties with distinction, Jefferson was to serve the society as president for eighteen years. It had expanded all his horizons including the geographical horizon in the west; in all his future contributions to western exploration and study, this organization founded "to promote useful knowledge" would play a significant part.

· Jefferson, Washington, and the West ·

It is easy to place Jefferson in a favorable light when comparing his and Washington's interest in the American West, but it must be done cautiously.[34] We can ascribe the differences to personality, to divergent life-styles, to a wide disparity in their interests and education, and of course to their differences in philosophy. It is important, however, not to overlook the eleven-year difference in their ages and the changes wrought in the world during those important years. Washington grew up under the influence of men to whom great landholdings were the source of power and status—and these lands lay in the West. He sought to build his fortune in that way. When young Jefferson was writing a friend in 1763 of his dreams of going to Europe, Washington was helping to form the Mississippi Company, designed to obtain a grant of land east of the Mississippi which the French had surrendered in 1763. The nineteen members of the company included Washington's brother John Augustine and four members of the famous Lee family. Washington lost in that enterprise but more than regained his losses by means of the military bounty lands he obtained in the Ohio Valley.[35]

Washington served the West in his own way. He belived, as did Jefferson and others, that the western settlers might eventually break away from the United States if they could not maintain adequate ties with the East and could not have access to channels of trade. He not only worked to maintain open navigation of the Mississippi but also proposed a system of waterways, carrying the trade of the Ohio Valley along the Potomac to the sea. Engineering skills of the day were inadequate to implement his vision; his hopes were never realized.

So cautiously did Washington express himself that comments revealing his deep feeling for the West are rare. It was he, not Jefferson, who went three times to the Ohio Valley, once as a young man on a military mission, twice later on matters pertaining to land. He had seen these regions before settlement; he had hunted bison along the Kanawha; he had dragged a surveyor's chain, like Jefferson's father, Peter, where only Indians had trod before.

At the end of the Revolution, Washington wrote several letters in which he expressed a desire to travel, if not to explore, the western corners of his world. He told his former comrade-in-arms, Lafayette, that he would like to make a tour into Canada, up the St. Lawrence, through the lakes to Detroit, then "thro' the Western Country by the river Illinois, to the river Mississippi, and down the same to New Orleans. . . ." He wanted Lafayette to go along. "A great tour this, you will say, probably it may take place no where but in imagination, tho' it is my *wish* to begin it in the latter end of April of next year."[36]

It is almost impossible to nail down a poetic impulse in Washington's writings; he could not help associating everything about the land with a practical application. But he was almost off guard when he wrote to Chastellux, describing a trip he had made into some of the areas of New York in which he had lately fought. "I could not help taking a more contemplative and extensive view of the vast inland navigation of these United States, from maps and the information of others; and could not but be struck with the immense diffusion and importance of it; and with the goodness of that Providence which has dealt her favours to us with so profuse a hand. Would to God we may have wisdom enough to improve them. I shall not rest contented 'till I have explored the Western Country, and traversed those lines (or great part of them) which have given bounds to a New Empire."[37]

It was a dream not to be realized, and it had tighter boundaries than the dreams of Jefferson. In the vast collection of letters and documents that Washington produced in his lifetime, one will encounter few of the western place names that are so common in the letters of Jefferson. Look for Oregon; it is not to be found. Look for the Columbia River or the Rio Grande, for the Missouri or the Colorado River, for Mexico and the Sandwich Islands. Look for mention of the towering mountains that captured the fancy of countless men. They are nowhere mentioned in the papers of Washington.

It is not that Washington was behind his times in his view of the West, but rather that Jefferson was so far advanced. When Washington died in 1799, an era of rapid change lay just ahead. If the Father of his Country could have lived as many years as Jefferson, he would have witnessed not only the Louisiana Purchase but also the Lewis and Clark expedition, the Zebulon Pike expedition, the penetration of the Trans-Mississippi region by American fur traders, and the establishment of Astoria on the Pacific Coast. He would have experienced the War of 1812 and known the great movements for independence in Mexico and South America that furthered Jefferson's goal of a totally non-European hemisphere.

Washington had to deal with the West as a succession of problems, and he did what he could to solve them. Jefferson saw the West as an opportunity and, more than any other man in American history, seized that opportunity.

NOTES

1. To Trumbull, 1 Nov. 1788, BOYD, 14:44.
2. To Madame de Corny, 2 April 1790, BOYD, 16:289. "I made light

of it, supposing I had only to say 'no' and there would be an end of it. It turned out however otherwise."

3. For his nomination of 25 Sept. 1789 and confirmation the following day, see *Journal of the Executive Proceedings of the Senate,* 1 (1828), 32–33. Washington wrote him 21 Jan. 1790, "I know of no person, who, in my judgement, could better execute the Duties of it than yourself," and TJ replied 14 Feb., "Your desire that I should come on as quickly as possible is a sufficient reason for me to postpone every matter of business, however pressing, which admits postponement" (BOYD, 16:117, 184).

4. PETERSON [1], 397–98.

5. For the Nootka Sound controversy, see MANNING and PETERSON [1], 415–18. Jefferson's recommendations are in TJ to Washington, 12 July 1790, BOYD, 17:108–11.

6. "In the view of some New York Federalists the secret purpose of the Virginians' tour was to cement an alliance between the Madisonians of the South and the Clintonians of the North. . . . If any alliances or bargains were struck . . . they were very secret indeed, for they left no trace" (PETERSON [1], 439–40).

7. The notes are in Jefferson's papers for 1791, LC, beginning with fol. 11190.

8. To Maria, 30 May 1791, and Maria to TJ, 10 July 1791, BETTS & BEAR, 83, 87; to Martha Randolph, 31 May 1791, BETTS & BEAR, 84–85.

9. To Fay, 30 Aug. 1791, and to Thomas Mann Randolph, 14 April 1792, LC.

10. To Madison, 21 June 1791, LC. TJ also asked Madison to continue inquiries about the Hessian fly.

11. Havens and Dering to TJ, 1 Nov. 1791, LC. See his own six pages of notes made while traveling in the fly country, beginning with fol. 11907, LC.

12. The two letters to Randolph are 15 June 1792 and 16 Nov. 1801, LC. The arrival of the fly in Albemarle is reported in the *American Farmer,* 1 (1819), 301. Scientific farmers thought that plant selection and breeding were the best weapons against the fly. Washington, among the best of farmers, wrote: "What an error it is, and how much to be regretted, that the Farmers do not confine themselves to the Yellow-bearded Wheat, if, from experience, it is found capable of resisting the ravages of this, otherwise, all conquering foe" (to Samuel Powell, 15 Dec. 1789, JACKSON & TWOHIG, 5:13–14).

13. To Martha Jefferson Randolph, 23 June 1791, BETTS & BEAR, 85.

14. To Martha Jefferson Randolph, 31 Dec. 1792, BETTS & BEAR, 108.

15. TJ's transcript and covering letter to Washington, 1 Feb. 1793,

LC. The transcript is a blurred letterpress copy; the original is not among Washington's papers.

16. "Journal of the Proceedings of the President," Papers of George Washington, LC. This manuscript, edited by Dorothy Twohig, is scheduled for publication by the University Press of Virginia.

17. TERR. PAPERS, 2:414n.

18. In December 1789, the War Department had instigated a plan to send Lieutenant John Armstrong, stationed at a post on the Ohio, to ascend the Missouri in an attempt to reach the Pacific. Armstrong went as far as St. Louis but was persuaded that going farther would be hazardous. See L & C LETTERS, 2:661–67, 685. Although a flurry of correspondence resulted, the attempt was not pressed, and there is no evidence that TJ knew of it at the time.

19. Wistar to Marshall, 20 June 1792, in L & C LETTERS, 2:675. Marshall had studied medicine in Wilmington, Del., early in the Revolution, and had attended wounded soldiers at the Battle of Brandywine in 1777. After a brief career in medicine he became involved in shipping plants and seeds to Europe, and helped his more famous uncle in the preparation of *Arbustrum Americanum* (Philadelphia, 1785). See DAR-LINGTON, 545–47n.

20. JACKSON & TWOHIG, 4:350; Michaux to Washington, 20 June 1786, Papers of George Washington, LC. See ROBBINS & HOWSON for general background on Michaux in the United States.

21. ROBBINS & HOWSON, 363–64.

22. To Benjamin Smith Barton, 2 Dec. 1792, LC. TJ reported that the Indian was then in the process of being inoculated against smallpox.

23. L & C LETTERS, 2:668–69. Some minor letters dealing with fundraising are also present. In August 1979, while going through some papers in a vault in Philosophical Hall, staff members of the American Philosophical Society found a bundle labeled "Treasurers Accounts, 1790–1899." In it was a copy of the subscription agreement, in Jefferson's hand, followed by the names of the subscribers in their own hands. George Washington led the group with a subscription of one hundred dollars, followed by John Adams with twenty. Among the list of thirty signers were James Madison, Alexander Hamilton, Henry Knox, and other notable members of the society.

24. In the margin beside the preceding two paragraphs, Jefferson wrote: "Here it is proposed to insert the contents of the annexed paper." The paper is not present.

25. Reprinted, L & C LETTERS, 2:669–73, from the copy in the library of the American Philosophical Society, Philadelphia. The bracketed passage in the next to last paragraph was stricken by TJ.

26. MALONE, 3:104–8, discusses the political aspects of the 1793 trip, and TJ's ambiguous attitude toward it in the light of what he knew of Genêt's plans.

27. PETERSON [2], 64. Yet it was Adams who was to become president in 1797, with Jefferson his vice-president. Their famous estrangement was still years away.

28. The allusion occurs at least eleven times in Washington's letters of 1796 and 1797. The passage reads this way in 1 Kings 4:25: "And Judah and Israel dwelt safely, every man under his vine and under his fig tree." For similar passages, see 2 Kings 18:31 and Micah 4:4.

29. To Rutledge, 30 Nov. 1795, BETTS & BEAR, 239; to Rittenhouse, 24 Feb. 1795, LC.

30. There are, of course, other papers for the period in the holdings of the Massachusetts Historical Society, American Philosophical Society, Historical Society of Pennsylvania, Huntington Library, etc.

31. SCHACHNER, 225.

32. Rush to TJ, 4 Jan. 1797, and TJ to the Secretaries of the Society, 28 Jan. 1797, both in the American Philosophical Society library.

33. For the story of TJ and the megalonyx-megatherium, see Julian P. Boyd's article, listed in the bibliography under MEGATHERIUM. For carbon-dating evidence regarding the disappearance of the ground sloth, see LONG & MARTIN, who state that *Nothrotheriops shastense* existed as recently as 11,000 years ago, disappearing with the arrival of human hunters. Organic remains such as dung and hair, preserved in caves of the arid Southwest, led paleontologists of the nineteenth century to believe the sloths were not extinct.

34. Portions of this section are drawn from a lecture entitled "Washington, Jefferson, and the American West," delivered by the writer 9 Nov. 1976 at Mary Baldwin College, Staunton, Va.

35. At his death, Washington owned four tracts on the east side of the Ohio between Wheeling and the mouth of the Kanawha, and five on the Kanawha above and below Charleston. The total of more than 33,000 acres occupied almost fifty-two square miles (PRUSSING, 322–23; KNOLLENBERG, 89, 181n).

36. Washington to Lafayette, 12 Oct. 1783, Papers of George Washington, LC.

37. Washington to the Marquis de Chastellux, 12 Oct. 1783, Papers of George Washington, LC. Note that this letter and the one immediately preceding were written on the same day, from Princeton.

CHAPTER FIVE

A Geographer's Bookshelf

Jefferson did not turn to the extensive buying and reading of geographical works—especially books on American geography—until he went to France. Before then he had been an eclectic reader with interests ranging from classical literature to works on horseshoeing and gardening. During his lifetime he assembled four libraries. The first had as a core the forty-two books left him by his father and those he had bought mainly in Williamsburg before 1770. After the Shadwell fire and his move to Monticello, he started to amass a second library, and by 1773 he could record that he owned 1,250 volumes.[1] This, his largest library, grew until 1815, when he sold it to the government as the start of the Library of Congress. But Monticello was not the same to him after those 6,000 books had gone off in wagons to the Capitol. As he told John Adams, "I cannot live without books."[2] So he began to build his third library, the one he owned at his death in 1826. The fourth, which he assembled but did not own, was acquired for the newly established University of Virginia in the years just before his death.

Until he visited Philadelphia in 1766, Jefferson's principal source of books had been the printing office of the *Virginia Gazette* in Williamsburg. The proprietors of that newspaper, William Hunter, Jr., and John Dixon, were able at one time to publish a list of more than 300 titles in stock. The daybooks of the firm show two early purchases by Jefferson. In the spring of 1764 he bought William Stith's *The History of the First Discovery and Settlement of Virginia* (Williamsburg, 1747), and the *Dictionary of Arts and Sciences* (2d ed., London, 1764).[3]

An early indication of what Jefferson thought were useful books is an exchange of letters with young Robert Skipwith, who married the half-sister of Jefferson's future bride. Skipwith asked him in July 1771 for a list of books "suited to the capacity of a common reader who understands but little of the classicks." Jefferson responded with a splendid list covering the fine arts, politics, religion, law, ancient and modern history, and natural history. Although the list ranged wide, it contained only two titles relating to America; both were histories of Virginia. One was Stith and the other Sir William Keith's *History of the British Plantations in America* (London, 1738).[4]

"While I was in Europe," Jefferson told a correspondent, "I purchased everything I could lay my hands on which related to any part of America, and particularly had a pretty full collection of the English and Spanish authors on the subject of Louisiana." To another he wrote of his library, "That which respects America, is the result of my own personal searches in Paris for 6 or 7 years, & of persons employed by me in England, Holland, Germany, and Spain to make similar searches. Such a collection on that subject can never be made again."[5]

Except for Spanish works, which he got through such contacts as William Carmichael, the U.S. chargé d'affaires in Madrid, Jefferson bought mainly from three bookmen. He placed orders with John Stockdale, in London, who also was publisher of his *Notes on the State of Virginia,* and with London bookseller James Lackington, who issued an extensive catalog. Lackington, who had risen from bootmaker's apprentice to wealthy bookman, offered 12,000 volumes in his catalog of 1778. By 1795 the publication contained 683 pages and offered half a million books.[6] Although Jefferson used Lackington's catalog as a want list, he often placed the orders with Stockdale and others. He preferred to shop in Paris, because "all books except English, Latin and Greek are bought here for about two thirds of what they cost in England."[7] Jefferson dealt with several Parisian booksellers, mainly on the Left Bank, but his primary source was J.-F. Froullé, on the Quai des Augustins. He called this old *libraire* one of the most conscientiously honest men he had ever dealt with.[8]

In the summer of 1787 Jefferson made especially heavy purchases. In August he sent James Madison three boxes of books, one for Madison, one for Franklin, and one for William Hay of

Richmond. In the letter announcing the shipment, he told Madison he had been most anxious to collect the original Spanish writers on American history, and had commissioned Carmichael to make the purchases. "They came very dear, & moreover he was obliged to take duplicates in two instances. I have packed one copy of these in Mr. Madison's box, & will beg the favor of him to sell them for me if he can."[9]

There are several reasons for the heightened interest Jefferson was showing in Spanish works. He had been studying the language, was realizing the future importance of Spanish America to the course of events at home, and had better access in Europe to Spanish books.[10] Truly informative studies and maps reflecting current Spanish explorations were scarce, perhaps purposely so, and the nature of the books Jefferson bought—some of which had been published two centuries earlier—suggests that he was buying some as history, and for the pleasures of a bibliophile, rather than as a source of immediately usable knowledge.

On a single day, 17 April 1789, Jefferson bought these Spanish and Portuguese works from Froullé:

Acosta, José de. *Historia natural y moral de las Indias*. Seville, 1590.

Casas, Bartolomé de las. *Tratado cõprobatorio del Imperio soberano universal que los Reyes de Castilla y Leon tienen sobre las Indias*. Seville, 1553.

Diaz del Castillo, Bernal. *Historia verdadera de la conquista de la Nueva-España*. Madrid, 1632.

Fernandez, Diego. *Primera, y segunda parte, de la historia del Peru*. Seville, 1571.

João, José de Santa Thereza. *Istoria delle guerre del Regno del Brasile accadute tra la Corona di Portogallo*. Rome, 1698.

López de Gómara, Francisco. *Historia de Mexico*. Anvers, 1554.

Pizarro y Orellana, Fernando. *Varones illustres del Nuevo Mundo*. Madrid, 1639.

Tamayo de Vargas, Tomas. *Restauracion de la Ciudad del Salvador, i Baia de Todos-Sanctos, en la Provincia del Brasil*. Madrid, 1628.

Vargas, Machuca Bernardo de. *Milicia y descripcion de las Indias*. Madrid, 1599.

Veitia Linage, José de. *Norte de la contratacion de las Indias Occidentales*. Seville, 1672.

Zarate, Augustin de. *Histoire de la decouverte et de la conquete de Perou*. Amsterdam, 1700.[11]

His collection of works on American geography and exploration occupies 197 pages in Millicent Sowerby's annotated catalog. Only a sampling can be discussed here, limited to writers who seem to have influenced him more than others. The editions named are those owned or used by Jefferson, although earlier editions may be mentioned. They are discussed in chronological order, although this may not represent the sequence in which they came to his attention.

Louis Hennepin was a Franciscan missionary and explorer, born in Belgium, who went to Canada in 1675. He was assigned as chaplain to La Salle on the Illinois River in 1679–80. Jefferson owned three Hennepin works of great importance, the first entitled *Description de la Louisiane, nouvellement decouverte au sud'ouest de la Nouvelle France* (Paris, 1683). Hennepin's travels on the Mississippi and its tributaries bore the authenticity of firsthand accounts, augmented (and occasionally embroidered) by secondhand data. Jefferson used two later Hennepin works in preparing his 1804 memorandum on Louisiana after the Purchase: *Nouvelle decouverte d'un tres grand pays situé dans l'Amerique* (Utrecht, 1697), and *Nouveau voyage d'un pais plus grande que l'Europe avec les reflections des enterprises du Sieur de la Salle, sur les mines de St. Barbe, &c.* (Utrecht, 1698).

A travel writer who fascinated Jefferson was the Baron Louis Armand de Lom d'Arce de Lahontan, a French soldier who served in Newfoundland for a year and then deserted. His *Voyages du Baron de La Hontan dans l'Amerique Septentrionale* (Amsterdam, 1705) contained a few geographical truths, distorted but close to reality, but in the main the book was lyrically inventive. The French in America quickly discredited it, but it retained a certain vogue in Europe and England. Lahontan wrote journals and letters supposedly based upon his own travels, and developed the idea of a "Rivière Longue" or Long River, rising in a range of mountains and flowing eastward into the Mississippi. Not far from its headwaters another river was said to flow westward into the South Sea.

Jefferson included Lahontan's work in a list of books he recommended in 1785, along with Hennepin and Charlevoix.[12]

Perhaps the earliest work on American geography that came to

Jefferson's attention was Daniel Coxe's *A Description of the English Province of Carolana, by the Spaniards Call'd Florida, and by the French La Louisiane* (London, 1741). The author was the eldest son of Dr. Daniel Coxe, of London, who claimed a large part of the lower Mississippi Valley—which he called Carolana. The younger Coxe visited the American colonies in 1702–16, then returned to prepare his *Description,* first issued in 1722. He returned to New Jersey in 1725, and at the time of his death in 1739 was a judge of the colonial supreme court. The influence of this book on members of the Loyal Company has been noted in Chapter 1. Jefferson still considered it of value in later life, retaining a copy until the sale of his library to Congress. From Coxe and other British writers came the concept of "symmetrical geography," by means of which Jefferson and his contemporaries tried to visualize the American West. In theory, for example, the rivers of the unknown West ought to lie and behave like the known ones in the East. Jefferson's old mentor, James Maury, was using the concept when he pointed out how far the eastern branches of the Mississippi extend eastward, and how near they come to the Potomac and other rivers which enter the Atlantic. It could be expected, then, that the western branches of the Mississippi would approach other rivers that empty into the Pacific. [13]

The French Jesuit explorer and historian Pierre François Xavier de Charlevoix taught in Quebec in 1705 and later traveled along the Great Lakes and down the Mississippi. His special assignment was to gather information about routes to the Pacific; thus he questioned traders who had returned from the West and was able to suggest several routes to the South Sea. As an indication of his influence, his *Histoire et description generale de la Nouvelle France, avec le journal historique d'un voyage fait par ordre du Roi dans l'Amérique Septentrionnale* (Paris, 1744) prompted Pierre La Vérendrye to travel in the upper Missouri watershed and to suppose that the Missouri was indeed the route to the South Sea. Charlevoix reported what he and other French travelers had come to believe: that the Missouri originated in a range of mountains, and that another river probably flowed westward from the same range. Like Coxe, he discussed the possibility of wagon roads across the mountains. His contribution to conceptual geography was the promotion of the pyramidal "height-of-land" theory in which the Mississippi, Missouri, and Minnesota rivers all rose near the same elevated location.[14]

Also important to Jefferson was a work by Antoine Simor Le Page du Pratz, *The History of Louisiana, or of the Western Parts of Virginia and Carolina* (London, 1763). Surely Jefferson was familiar with the original French version, *Histoire de la Louisiane* (Paris, 1758), but it was the English translation that he bought, used, and commended to Lewis and Clark. The fact that Lewis borrowed a copy from Benjamin Smith Barton, returning it after his expedition, and that citations to it appear in the Lewis and Clark journals, is documented elsewhere (p. 133 below). We have already seen that material from the work may have been known to members of the Loyal Company in Jefferson's boyhood community. It also was one of the works he cited in his 1804 memorandum on Louisiana, giving it a usefulness that spanned more than half a century. Le Page du Pratz was a French architect and naturalist who published his work about twenty-five years after he had lived and traveled in America.

Probably the first writer to speak of the river "Ouragan," and one who early promoted the concept of the height-of-land from which rivers flowed in several directions, was Robert Rogers. The leader of "Rogers' Rangers," who gained fame as an adventurer in the French and Indian War, returned to England after that conflict and published *A Concise Account of North America: Containing a Description of the Several British Colonies on That Continent, Including the Islands of Newfoundland, Cape Breton, &c.* (London, 1765). Jefferson knew of this work as early as 1783, when it appeared on a list of books recommended to Congress and based on his own reading and collecting.[15]

In his *Notes*, Jefferson presented a list of ninety-three birds compiled from a monumental work by Mark Catesby, *The Natural History of Carolina, Florida, and the Bahama Islands* (London, 1771). Jefferson's set of this work was a late one, the first edition having been issued in 1731–43. Perhaps because he was using an edition less well produced than the original, he thought the coloring in the drawings of flora and fauna was too brilliant.[16] Catesby has been described as "the colonial Audubon." Like the Bartrams (pp. 92–93 below), he was not content merely to describe and protray wildlife; his narrative was wide-ranging. He lived in Virginia from the spring of 1712 until the autumn of 1719, before accepting a commission to study in the Carolinas, and his work thus became an important tool for Jefferson's own studies of the natural history of Virginia.

Thomas Hutchins, an engineer and mapmaker who served as geographer to the United States during Washington's administration, was the author of *A Topographical Description of Virginia, Pennsylvania, Maryland, and North Carolina* (London, 1778). Because Jefferson had become so familiar with his father's own map (the Fry-Jefferson collaboration), and was soon to produce one of his own for the *Notes,* he detected a number of errors committed by Hutchins. Jefferson's two-page list of corrections brought an anguished response from the cartographer: "How to account for so egregious a blunder in calculation, I am really at a loss, as a moment's reflection on the subject would have set me right."[17] Jefferson was not demeaning an inferior work; he was improving a superbly useful one.

That epic of sea travel and Pacific exploration, Captain James Cook's *A Voyage to the Pacific Ocean* (London, 1784), was among Jefferson's books. This account of Cook's third and last voyage was the official one, but there were several others—attesting to the importance of Cook's achievement. John Ledyard's association with Cook, before his friendship with Jefferson, is covered in Chapter 3. Lewis and Clark were thoroughly familiar with Cook's third voyage, which carried him along the coast of the Pacific Northwest.

In the field of natural history, William Bartram's work was more current and more important to Jefferson in his later years than Catesby's. *Travels through North & South Carolina, Georgia, East & West Florida* was published in Philadelphia in 1791, but Jefferson did not obtain his own copy until 1805. Bartram's fame led Jefferson to invite him, unsuccessfully, to accompany an expedition up the Red River. Bartram and his father, John, were widely read for the geographical observations they made as well as for the plants they collected (Jefferson also owned a copy of John Bartram's *A Description of East-Florida,* London, 1769). William spent almost four years, from 1773 to 1776, traveling by horseback, canoe, and on foot, studying natural history and learning about the Creeks, Cherokees, and Seminoles. The literary excellence of his observations made his work a popular one. Undoubtedly the investigations and writings of Bartram were a model for the kind of journals that Jefferson hoped would come from the western expeditions he was to sponsor.

A less knowledgeable but perhaps more notable traveler was Jonathan Carver. He was born in Connecticut, served in the French and Indian War, and then became an explorer determined to find a passage by land across the continent. His published account was *Three Years Travels throughout the Interior Parts of North-America, for More Than Five Thousand Miles* (London, 1778). Jefferson's edition was a much later one—Boston, 1797. Carver's firsthand observations were cheapened by his borrowings without credit from Hennepin, Lahontan, and Charlevoix, and for many years his work has been discounted as an authentic eyewitness account. Lawrence J. Burpee suggests that the narrative may be that of Dr. John Coakley Lettsom, a writer and editor who worked from Carver's notes and the published work of others. Burpee quotes a 1792 letter from Oliver Wolcott to Jedediah Morse: "He doubtless resided a number of years in the western country, but was an ignorant man, utterly incapable of writing such a book."

The value of his work to Jefferson might have lain in his borrowing, for he adapted the French height-of-land idea and, on a map accompanying his work, depicted four large rivers rising very near each other at the center of the continent and flowing in four directions.[18] He perpetuated the name "Oregan" for the great river that flowed westward from the mountains, following the example of Robert Rogers.

With the publication of George Vancouver's *A Voyage of Discovery to the North Pacific Ocean* (London, 1798), Jefferson had access to a work with direct application to the coming expedition of Lewis and Clark. Published posthumously, the work reported on a voyage by the sloop-of-war *Discovery* and the auxiliary tender *Chatham,* commanded by Vancouver, who was seeking data about the fur trade of the Pacific Northwest and the possible existence of a northwest passage. The expedition arrived off California in April 1792 and sailed northward. In a fateful miscalculation, Vancouver saw the mouth of the Columbia but failed to recognize it as the entrance to a mighty river. However, he did enter the Juan de Fuca Strait and explored Puget Sound. After meeting American sea captain Robert Gray, who told him of his own venture into the Columbia, Vancouver explored the lower reaches of that river. His charts were excellent, more detailed than Cook's, and would be studied—and even traced—by Lewis and Clark. There is no record that Jefferson ever owned a copy of Vancouver's work, but ample indication that he knew it well.

From these and other works, especially those of the French, Jefferson had received geographical concepts which were largely to be borne out later by actual exploration. From Alexander Mackenzie, however, he received a kind of personal challenge, making Mackenzie's *Voyages from Montreal . . . through the Continent of North America, to the Frozen and Pacific Oceans* (London, 1802) the most important geographical work in Jefferson's possession. How the work figures in Jefferson's response, the Lewis and Clark expedition, is discussed in Chapter 7.

Mackenzie, a partner of the North West Company operating in Canada, descended the Mackenzie River to the Arctic Ocean in 1789, under the illusion that it might lead him to the Pacific. He may have traveled primarily on his own behalf rather than as a member of the fur company, but in any case his first journey was a disappointment; even his geographical reports were discounted because he was not trained to make celestial observations. After determinedly studying the methods of finding latitude and longitude, he set out toward the Pacific in the fall of 1792, wintered at a company fort, and continued on in the spring of 1793. In June he reached the Fraser River, mistaking it for the fabled River of the West—the Columbia—and a month later had become the first man to cross the continent north of Mexico, reaching the Pacific at the mouth of the Bella Coola.

Voyages was published late in 1801 in London, probably ghostwritten for Mackenzie by a professional writer named William Combe.[19] The explorer was hardly learned enough to have written the book in its published form. His letters and journals have not survived in original form.

When the American Philosophical Society met on 10 March

1797, Jefferson was present and probably presiding, as he had been elected president of the society in January. On the agenda was the recording of gifts from Judge George Turner, including a sea-otter skin brought from the Pacific Coast by Mackenzie in 1794.[20] This incident may have marked the first time that Mackenzie's travels had come to Jefferson's attention. In the early months of 1798, Mackenzie was in New York for several months trying to solve some problems connected with the fur market in China and Europe. He made a trip to Philadelphia during that time, but there was little reason for him to meet Jefferson or members of his circle. Still, he was becoming so well known that the Polish diarist Julian Niemcewicz called him "the celebrated traveler Mackenzie," and recorded a conversation with him. "He has made a journey which is the most astonishing that has ever been undertaken, having crossed the whole breadth of the immense continent of North America."[21]

Jefferson may not have known much about Mackenzie's work until fellow society member Caspar Wistar called his attention in January 1802 to the recently published book.[22] For him, the most important part of the work would be the final "geographical review," in which Mackenzie urged Great Britain to develop a land passage to the Pacific for trade with Asia.

But whatever course may be taken from the Atlantic, the Columbia is the line of communication from the Pacific Ocean, pointed out by nature, as it is the only navigable river in the whole extent of Vancouver's minute survey of that coast: its banks also form the first level country in all the Southern extent of continental coast from Cook's entry, and, consequently, the most Northern situation fit for colonization, and suitable to the residence of a civilized people. By opening this intercourse between the Atlantic and Pacific Oceans, and forming regular establishments through the interior, and at both extremes, as well as along the coasts and islands, the entire command of the fur trade of North America might be obtained, from latitude 48. North to the pole, except that portion of it which the Russians have in the Pacific. To this may be added the fishing in both seas, and the markets of the four quarters of the globe [p. 411].

Mackenzie's account of his journey, and his remarkable proposal, marked the beginning of true rivalry among nations for domination of the Columbia River basin and the Pacific North-west. Jefferson would soon accept the challenge and put America into the race to claim that river and that land.

NOTES

1. An account book entry for 4 Aug. 1773, Massachusetts Historical Society, Boston. He did not list the books by title, and we have little knowledge of that first library. The most complete catalog of his later acquisitions is SOWERBY.

2. To Adams, 10 June 1815, CAPPON [2], 2:441–43.

3. The daybooks of the *Gazette* for 1750–52 and 1764–66, edited by James Southall Wilson, are at the Alderman Library, University of Virginia, Charlottesville.

4. Skipwith to TJ, 17 July 1771, and TJ to Skipwith, 3 Aug. 1771, BOYD, 1:74–75, 76–81.

5. To William Dunbar, 13 March 1804, LC, and to L. W. Tazewell, 5 Jan. 1805, Alderman Library. On the same theme: "While residing in Paris, I devoted every afternoon I was disengaged, for a summer or two, in examining all the principal bookstores, turning over every book with my own hand, and putting by everything which related to America" (to Samuel H. Smith, 21 Sept. 1814, LC).

6. For Lackington see PASTON. A copy of his 1795 catalog is in the Alderman Library.

7. To James Currie, 27 Sept. 1785, BOYD, 8:560. He told Currie he had attempted to send live partridges, pheasants, hares, and rabbits to Virginia, but the destination of the vessel was changed "and the poor colonists all died" while another ship was being sought.

8. RICE, 77–78, deals with Jefferson's Parisian booksellers—including Froullé.

9. To Madison, 2 Aug. 1787, BOYD, 11:662–68. He paid thirty-five dollars for the duplicates, which were works by Garcilaso de la Vega and Andrés de Garcia Carballido y Zuñiga.

10. To young John Quincy Adams, whom Jefferson befriended while they both lived in Europe, he teasingly said that Spanish was so easy he had learned it in nineteen days at sea. Adams noted the remark in his diary for 23 Nov. 1804, ADAMS, 1:317. When Jefferson sent Peter Carr a list of books worth reading, 10 Aug. 1787, he recommended the study of Spanish because "our future connection with Spain and Spanish America will render that language a valuable acquisition." He

also reminded Carr that the ancient history of much of America was written in Spanish (BOYD, 12:14).

11. Works and dates of purchase are compiled from SOWERBY, *passim*.

12. To Walker Maury, 19 Aug. 1785, BOYD, 8:409–12. "I have inserted several books of American travels th[inking] they will be a useful species of reading for an American youth."

13. Symmetrical geography is one of the concepts discussed in ALLEN [1] and [2]. Other aspects of conceptual geography, such as the height-of-land theory, are also set forth in these two studies.

14. ALLEN [2], 14, 358n; DE VOTO, 199.

15. ALLEN [2], 62. See also BOYD, 6:316, for a note on the list. Although it is in Madison's hand, Boyd suggests it is based largely on a much longer list compiled by Jefferson about 1782, including books he owned or intended to buy.

16. NOTES, 65–70. FRICK & STEARNS is a biography of Catesby.

17. Hutchins to TJ, 11 Feb. 1784, SOWERBY, no. 525.

18. BURPEE [1], 293–94.

19. MONTGOMERY presents a brief account of Combe's role in the preparation of Mackenzie's work. Combe had written travel narratives for other voyagers. At the time Mackenzie's book was published he was in debtor's prison, where he was to spend the rest of his life.

20. Early proceedings of the American Philosophical Society, 10 Mar. 1797, American Philosophical Society library, Philadelphia. Turner, a native of England, was a judge in the Northwest Territory.

21. NIEMCEWICZ, 39.

22. Wistar to TJ, 8 Jan. 1802, LC.

CHAPTER SIX

Researching the New Territory

From the time he entered public life, Jefferson had a problem with Christmas: he was almost never able to spend it at home. For example, when he returned happily to Monticello after his long assignment in France, in December 1789, it was his first Christmas at home since 1774.[1]

At times after 1800, when the federal government moved to Washington and thus closer to Monticello, he invited members of his family to spend the holidays with him. Because Congress did not recess at Christmas in those days, he felt that as president he must remain on hand, even if the House and Senate were not accomplishing much. At one holiday season he wrote to daughter Maria, "When Congress will rise, no mortal can tell: not from the quantity but from the dilatoriness of business."[2]

Of special concern here is Jefferson's Christmas holiday in 1803. A grateful mood was abroad in the land because, after many months of negotiation with France, much Federalist-Republican wrangling in Congress, and Jefferson's own anguish about the constitutionality of the move, the Louisiana Purchase was complete. Two transfer ceremonies were scheduled, the first in New Orleans and the second—set for the following spring—in St. Louis. New Orleans was now the destination of two American representatives who would watch the French flag come down. One was William C. C. Claiborne, the new governor of the lower part of the territory, the other General James Wilkinson, commanding general of the army.

Jefferson waited in Washington for word of the transfer. He knew the time it took to travel the roads in winter, and he had estimated the exact time when he might receive mail from the south and know that the ceremony had been accomplished.

Writing to his son-in-law, Thomas Mann Randolph, about a week before Christmas, he said that if all went well with the transfer, "we shall hear of it Christmas night."[3] There was a disappointing delay, however, and on the day after Christmas Jefferson had moved his expectation ahead to still another holiday, writing to Maria, "On New Year's day . . . we shall hear of the delivery of New Orleans to us."[4] The actual transfer had been made on 20 December. The President learned of the transfer in the middle of January and reported it immediately to Congress, precipitating another round of festivities. Whether the transaction was a gift from Jefferson to the American people or a magnificent gift from them that was to bring him endless fascination, the Purchase was surely one of the most significant events of his presidency, if not of his lifetime.

The mechanics of the Louisiana Purchase are not under discussion here; they are too readily available for study. What follows is not an analysis of how the territory was bought by Robert Livingston, minister to France, and James Monroe, a special commissioner, but of what Jefferson did to learn all he could, as early as possible, about the new acquisition. Typically, he took hold of this project with doggedness, using every means he could devise to gather data about the extent, the boundaries, the terrain, the people and their ways, the potential of the country for development by the United States.

· The Informants ·

For the moment Jefferson's great library failed him. He needed more than the outdated conjectures of a fifty-year-old *Histoire de la Louisiane,* for the new territory was not only unchanging rivers and mountains, but a country of new U.S. citizens waiting to be governed. During the first few years, Jefferson supplemented his printed literature with letters, narratives, and maps provided by men who knew the frontier. The material came in slowly at first, then in a flood, and always it was uneven in veracity and usefulness. The suppliers of these facts and nonfacts are discussed here, more or less in the order of their appearance as correspondents.

James Wilkinson. This knavish general, unique in American history, has a leading and heavy role in Chapter 12. Here, however, he is an ingratiating figure, doing what he can to advise his commander-in-chief of all that is "marvellous" in the West. As early as 1797 he was sending information and artifacts in from the field.[5] By 1800, stationed on the lower Mississippi, he was submitting meteorological records, "some petrefactions, an Indian knife, and a map of the parts of Mississippi Territory."[6] In 1802 he sent bottles of water from the Mississippi and the Arkansas, for comparison, describing the samples as "remarkable for their difference to each other & to the Waters of all other Rivers within my knowledge."[7]

Among the data sent in 1804 was a long memorial on Louisiana, enclosing a collection of manuscript maps relating to Texas, New Mexico, and the Interior Provinces of New Spain. He correctly reported that the left branch of the Red River headed on the east side of an elevated plain, and that west of this plain were waters which ran south, "probably those of the Rio Bravo." Beyond these, he said, was a high ridge of mountains.[8]

In 1805, after he had been sent to St. Louis as military and civil commander, he continued to send Jefferson natural productions of the territory "to amuse a leisure Moment," and geographical and population data obtained from the Indians. The latter included "An Enumeration of Some of the Indian Nations South West of the Missouri River" given him by a principal Arikara chief.[9]

Wilkinson sent these materials partly to curry favor with officials at the head of government, as he declared a few years later. "From the period of Genl. Washington's administration, down through the times of his successors, I have been taught to believe that it was my duty, to acquire every information topographical, and political, which might . . . become interesting to our Country. My labours have not been totally unproductive, and for my little services in this way, I have received the acknowledgments of Washington, Adams, and Jefferson."[10]

Philip Nolan. This Kentuckian, who made a living by venturing into Spanish Texas to capture wild mustangs, is a man of some mystery. After several illegal ventures (there was no trade between Texas and Louisiana at the time), he was killed with his party in March 1801, about 150 miles west of Nacogdoches. His relationship with Wilkinson suggests intrigue that went beyond wild horses. "I look forward to the conquest of Mexico by the United States; and I expect my patron and friend, the General, will, in such an event, give me a conspicuous command."[11]

After learning of Nolan from Wilkinson, Jefferson wrote the horse trader in 1798, asking for information about wild horses west of the Mississippi. He explained that the environment did not permit these animals to exist in the Old World and they were fast becoming extinct in the New. On behalf of the American Philosophical Society, he asked for all the data that Nolan could provide. Nolan had planned to visit Monticello after receiving the letter, but instead he set out again on his last foray into alien territory in search of mustangs. He could have taught Jefferson much that went beyond horse lore. As Wilkinson said in his letter of introduction, "I am persuaded you will find pleasure, in his details of a Country, the Soil, clime, population, improvements & productions of which are so little known to us."[12]

Daniel Clark, Jr. When Jefferson wrote Nolan, who was away in Texas, a reply arrived from Daniel Clark, Jr., who said the letter had come into his hands. Clark then introduced himself and offered his own expertise in providing Jefferson with knowledge of the area. Clark had gone to New Orleans to enter business with his uncle, Daniel Clark, Sr., in 1786. He was obviously well informed, knew much about the people of New Orleans and their ways. Jefferson wrote him in June 1799, Clark replied, and the brief exchange had two significant results. Jefferson appointed Clark consul in New Orleans in 1801, and through him made the acquaintance of a much more significant frontiersman, William Dunbar.[13]

William Dunbar. When Clark first wrote Jefferson, he not only extended his own good offices but spoke highly of his friend William Dunbar, of near Natchez, a man of learning and accomplishment. Jefferson began a lively correspondence with Dunbar in 1800 and soon brought him into his learned circle. A distinguished Scottish botanist, surveyor, astronomer, and physician, Dunbar had established "The Forest," a plantation southeast of Natchez, in 1792. He had served as one of the Spanish commissioners in the survey of the thirty-first parallel (southern boundary of Mississippi) in 1798.

Apparently his first letter to Jefferson had dealt in part with

Indian sign language, Jefferson replying that it was the first information he had ever had on the subject. Soon Dunbar sent some notes about his work on the Spanish surveying commission and a promise to send information later about the Mississippi River. In 1801 he gave Jefferson some details about fossil bones west of the Mississippi and a curious aquatic animal reported by the Indians of New Mexico. He also reported at that time on the killing of Nolan by the Spanish. Although, as he said, politics was not a favorite subject with him, by 1803 he felt sufficiently at ease with Jefferson to abandon his stance as a scientific and philosophic country gentleman, and to write seven pages on the political aspects of the region. He was particularly concerned about the possible occupation of Louisiana by France, and had heard that 30,000 Frenchmen had obtained passports to migrate to the Mississippi River region.[14]

Dunbar's exchanges with Jefferson were literate and useful. The part he played in exploring the new territory is detailed in Chapter 11.

William C. C. Claiborne. When Claiborne was offered the governorship of the Territory of Orleans—the lower portion of the new purchase—in 1804, he may have been mystified by a passage in Jefferson's letter proffering the assignment: "This office was originally destined for a person whose great services and established fame would have rendered him peculiarly acceptable to the nation at large."[15] He was speaking of the Marquis de Lafayette, still a hero more than twenty years after the Battle of Yorktown and the end of the Revolution he had helped to win.

Perhaps the idea of appointing Lafayette governor of Orleans had come to Jefferson when he received a congratulatory letter from him: "In the joy of my Heart I Congratulate You on the Happy Arrangement which Has lately taken place." Lafayette was speaking for the entire pro-American group in France, the Idealogues, who thought of the Purchase as an enlargement of republicanism. Their official publication, the *Decade,* was currently speaking of the new advantages the French people of Louisiana would enjoy.[16]

The prospective appointment of Lafayette got into the newspapers, and into the pages of at least one senator's diary, but it never materialized. Congress did vote the marquis a large grant of land north of the Ohio for his services in the war, and Jefferson got the location switched to Louisiana. The two discussed several times the possibility of Lafayette's settling in Louisiana and holding an appointment. Jefferson referred to it during the Burr conspiracy fever when he told Lafayette: "Certainly, had you been, as I wished, at the head of the government of Orleans, Burr would never have given me one moment's uneasiness."[17]

As the only representative from Tennessee, Claiborne had cast his vote for Jefferson in the election of 1800. His patronage prize was first the governorship of Mississippi Territory in 1801, then the governorship of Orleans. Although he was something of a garrulous complainer, and not a statesman of high stature, he served in a place of turmoil for many years as an adequate public servant. Soon after taking the post at New Orleans, he joined the little band of correspondents upon whom Jefferson was relying for intelligence.[18]

John Sibley. Describing himself as a physician who had lived for the past ten months at Natchitoches, on the Red River, Dr. Sibley first wrote to Jefferson in March 1804. It was the beginning of an active period for the doctor; he lived in a region vital to the United States and was interested in two of Jefferson's avocations, botany and Indian ethnology. In his first letter he discussed the wood called by the French "Bois d'Arc, or Bow Wood," sending some samples of dyes he had extracted. It was the Osage orange (*Maclura pomifera*), famed more for the durability of its wood than for its coloring qualities, and Jefferson was soon to receive cuttings from St. Louis also.

Later, but perhaps still in 1804, Sibley sent enough information for Jefferson to produce, in a small and compact hand that he often adopted when much material was to be digested, four pages of data headed "Sibley's Acct. of the Indians." Sibley was then appointed Indian agent for Orleans, with headquarters at Natchitoches, and Secretary of War Henry Dearborn urged him to cultivate the friendship of the tribes in the event of a conflict with Spain.[19]

Alexander von Humboldt. When Baron Friedrich Heinrich Alexander von Humboldt visited Washington in the spring of 1804, he was a world-famous traveler who merited every attention from Jefferson. Not only was the Prussian savant one of the great explorers of his time, just arrived from South America and Mexico, but he came at a time when the personal knowledge he had amassed through travel was vital to Jefferson's plans. The conversations at dinner must have reminded Jefferson of his visits with old Buffon in Paris. The President was especially interested in the disputed area between the western boundary of the Purchase as claimed by Spain and that claimed by the United States. Wilkinson, too, pressed for information. Writing Jefferson he said, "I lament the sudden departure of Baron Humboldt as I feel a strong interest in haveing his answers to the queries which I take the liberty to enclose you." A map which Humboldt lent to Gallatin was surreptitiously copied by Wilkinson, and later appeared with minor alterations in Pike's own map of the West (see pp. 273–74 below). In later years Jefferson unfailingly obtained Humboldt's published works, issued in parts and often sent directly by the baron himself.[20]

· The Big Questionnaire ·

Perhaps he remembered that a list of questions from Marbois was what had started him writing his *Notes on the State of Virginia*. He had often used the device himself in the learning process. So now Jefferson set about drawing up a questionnaire to send his frontier acquaintances. Originally he made a list of seventeen questions and had several clerk's copies made for distribution. Then he began to edit and rearrange the list, and to consult Albert Gallatin, secretary of the treasury. Gallatin's prolific curiosity more than doubled the list, and by the time it was ready to mail it contained forty-five queries.[21]

Apparently the list went out first with letters written 17 and 18 July 1803 to Claiborne, Clark, Dunbar, and Ephraim Kirby, a land commissioner for the district east of the Pearl River. There may have been other submissions at about this time. The recipients each responded in his own way, choosing the questions he felt qualified to answer and turning to other informants for help—Claiborne applying to Clark, for example, and Dunbar to Dr. Sibley. Claiborne's response was the earliest and most complete, but he was unable to answer most of the questions fully. He was asked about the best available maps; the boundaries of

Louisiana; the political divisions of Lower Louisiana; and information about the population, the militia, the clergy, commerce, mining, military capabilities, the Indian tribes, and other matters important to the U.S. government. Although he did his best, his reply is filled with such statements as "I have not been able to obtain any satisfactory information" and "The information I have as yet been able to collect . . . is not sufficiently authentic, to justify my hazarding an answer in detail to this question."

Claiborne decided to stop after responding to thirty-six questions. They were getting harder and more detailed. For example, one question of Gallatin's read in part: "What is the annual amount of imports under the following heads: 1. Articles of the growth of the United States coming down the Mississippi. 2. Articles of the growth of the United States arriving by sea. 3. Articles of the growth of other countries distinguished as follows: what quantity of spirits, brandies, coffee, teas, pepper & spices, cocoa and chocolate, salt, sugars, Spanish tobacco. . . ."

· Determining the Boundaries ·

At no time did Jefferson wish more earnestly to get home to his library than in the summer of 1803. In negotiations with France, the essence of the transactions was the "limits," as he called them, of the territory. No man knew what they were. The terms of the transfer were vague—deliberately so, according to the French, who may have hoped to see Spain and the United States go to war over the question. France ceded "the colony or province of Louisiana, with the same extent that it now has in the hands of Spain, and that it had when France possessed it; and such as it should be after the treaties subsequently entered into between Spain and other states."[22]

Eventually Jefferson would come to realize that the real boundaries were only a short-term problem; they would take shape according to the best interests of the United States. In day-to-day transactions, however, with Spain watching angrily from the sidelines for the least infraction of her rights, the negotiating parties needed a body of historical documentation as precedent.

Upon reaching Monticello for his usual summer recess from the heat and the cares of Washington, he began at once to sort through the books he had been collecting since the 1780s. Before his research began, he had a general mental picture of the territory which he conveyed to John Dickinson. He said the "unquestioned" bounds of Louisiana were the Mississippi and the Iberville on the east, the Mexicana (Sabine) or the highlands east of it, on the west; then from the head of the Sabine to the highlands, which included the waters of the Mississippi, "and following those highlands round the head spring of the western waters of the Mississippi to its lower where we join the English or perhaps the Lake of the Woods."

In other words, he said, the territory was a kind of triangle with the Missouri as one leg, the Mississippi another, and the hypotenuse extending from the mouth of the Mississippi to the source of the Missouri.[23]

Using the library of English, French, and Spanish authors he had collected in Europe, he prepared a memorandum on the boundaries.[24] His old favorites came down from the shelves: Hennepin, Le Page du Pratz, Coxe; Henry Tonti's *Derniers Decouvertes,* Thomas Jeffrey's *Natural and Civil History of the French Dominions in North and South America,* and the *Memoires historiques sur la Louisiane,* by Louis Dumont de Montigny. He had completed a draft of the memorandum by September, with revisions in January 1804, and was sending copies to his friends. The document was not to be published until a century later.[25]

While researching in his books, Jefferson also was listening to Madison, Livingston, and Monroe, who were less concerned at the moment with reading history than with making policy plausibly and advantageously. A troublesome matter which took priority over all other boundary matters at the time was the question of the two Floridas, especially West Florida. In 1803, after centuries of give and take, East and West Florida lay below the southern boundary of the United States (the thirty-first parallel) and included not only present Florida but parts of what are now Alabama and Mississippi. West Florida, bordering the Mississippi on the east, remained a threat to New Orleans if it were in Spanish hands. What Jefferson sought in his books, and his negotiators sought in their dealings with France and Spain, was a way to define West Florida—or a part of it—as part of the Purchase. By the time he had finished his memorandum in

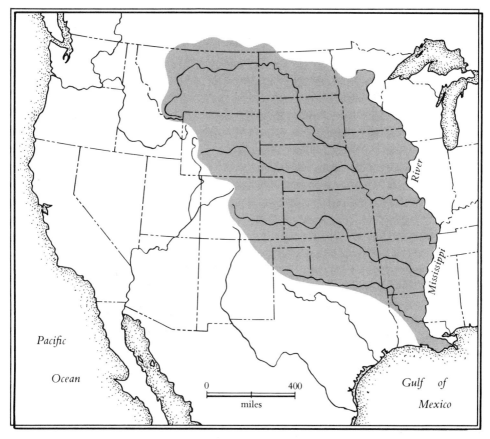

3. Jefferson's conception of the Louisiana Purchase boundaries (after MARSHALL).

THE EXPANDING BOUNDARIES OF THE LOUISIANA PURCHASE

	Jefferson's Early View	Jefferson's Final View	Boundaries as of 1819
Eastern boundary	Mississippi River[a]	Mississippi River	Mississippi River
Northeastern	Mississippi headwaters or Lake of the Woods; indefinite[b]	Discrepancy to be corrected[c]	From Lake of the Woods along 49th parallel to Rocky Mountains[d]
Northwestern	Missouri River headlands	Missouri River headlands and Oregon Country[e]	Joint occupancy with Britain for ten years in Oregon Country, by Convention of 1818; no defined boundary
Western	Rocky Mountains	Rocky Mountains[f]	Adams–Onís Treaty line of 1819[g]
Southwestern	Red River, headlands of Sabine, to Rocky Mountain headlands	Rio Grande River and Texas[h]	Adams–Onís line
Southeastern	Undecided about West Florida	Convinced that West Florida east to the Perdido River was in the Purchase[i]	West Florida seized during War of 1812; East Florida ceded in Adams–Onís Treaty

ᵃ Established by the Anglo–American Peace Treaty of 1783. See CAPPON [3], 14, 87, with discussion of some disputes about the upper end of the boundary.

ᵇ TJ to Dickinson, 9 Aug. 1803, LC. At the same time, he wrote Madison that he was using his library on the limits of Louisiana and was satisfied that U.S. right to the Perdido was substantial and that the land westward to the Bay of St. Bernard "may be strongly maintained" (MARSHALL, 11).

ᶜ The Treaty of 1783, based on incomplete information and an error in John Mitchell's map used in the negotiations, ran the northeastern boundary from the upper tip of the Lake of the Woods due west along the forty-ninth parallel to intersect the headwaters of the Mississippi. By the time he had finished his Sept. 1803 memorandum, Jefferson had concluded that such a line could not intersect the Mississippi headwaters. Hence the line would not "close," an untenable situation for a man trained as a surveyor.

ᵈ The Convention of 1818 between Britain and the United States ran the line from the Lake of the Woods west along the forty-ninth parallel, considerably above the sources of the Mississippi, to the Rockies.

ᵉ By 1808 it was apparent that Jefferson considered the Oregon Country to be a part of Louisiana. During the discussion of a boundary treaty with Britain, when he agreed to the forty-ninth parallel from Lake of the Woods to the Rockies, he specified "that nothing in the present article shall be considered to extend to the north-west coast of America or to the territories belonging to or claimed by either party on the continent of America to the westward of the Stony Mountains" (MARSHALL, 14).

ᶠ Jefferson maintained his view of the Rockies as the western limit despite efforts of Republican enthusiasts on the House Committee of Commerce and Manufactures, who urged that the claim should include the lands beyond the Rockies "between the territories claimed by Great Britain on the one side, and Spain on the other, quite to the South Sea." Samuel Latham Mitchill, chairman of this committee and influential with Jefferson, was a strong proponent of this position. See ABERBACH, chap. 4.

ᵍ A treaty of 12 Feb. 1819, negotiated by John Quincy Adams, secretary of state, and Luis de Onís, Spanish minister to the United States. Besides giving up the two Floridas to the United States, the treaty established the western and southwestern boundaries between Spain and the United States. Following in zigzag fashion certain river courses and parallels of latitude, the new line reached the Pacific at the forty-second parallel, thus separating Spanish California from the Oregon Country.

ʰ In writing the 1803 memorandum, Jefferson came to hold the Rio Grande as the southwestern boundary. He immediately asked Livingston to obtain supporting documents. "The statement that the Rio Grande was the boundary did not even have the backing of administrative precedent, since the western limit of the Spanish province of Texas was at the Nueces, farther east" (BROOKS [1], 54n).

ⁱ Memorandum of 3 Sept. 1803. Thomas Maitland Marshall, an excellent source, sums up Jefferson's changing view of the boundaries. "Starting with the idea that the purchase was confined to the western waters of the Mississippi Valley, Jefferson's conception had gradually expanded until it included West Florida, Texas, and the Oregon Country, a view which was to be the basis of a large part of American diplomacy for nearly half a century" (MARSHALL, 14).

September, Jefferson had convinced himself that West Florida, as far east as the Perdido River, was a part of the Louisiana Territory. This interpretation allowed the Mississippi to flow peacefully along to New Orleans without the menacing presence of Spanish soldiers along its eastern shore.[26]

The evolution of Jefferson's thinking about all boundaries is shown in the accompanying table.

· The Northern District ·

The southern end of the Purchase was socially complex, and there were touchy matters of jurisdiction, but at least the area was better known to Americans than the northern region. That part, with St. Louis as its de facto capital, was all but unfathomable. Jefferson knew so little of its government (legally French, actually Spanish) that he addressed a letter to Henry Peyroux, thinking he was in command at Ste. Genevieve and St. Louis. He learned long months later that Peyroux had never been in command at St. Louis, and had not been commandant of the Ste. Genevieve district for the past ten years.[27]

Most of the tall tales, and the weird but true tales, came from the upper region. There was the mountain of salt. "Tomorrow I set out for Saint Louis," wrote Thomas T. Davis, "to see a French man named Shoto [Chouteau] who it is said has just returned from Santa Fee & reports that he has found a Salt Rock of immense size on the dividing ridge that separates the Head Waters of the Arkansaw River from the head waters of the Missouri."[28] And there were the volcanoes. Based on pieces of burned-out lignite from the Badlands, which floated down the Missouri, the rumors of volcanoes were so persistent that Lewis and Clark would later investigate them. No coincidence, perhaps, that during this information-gathering period Jefferson bought a copy of Claude Nicholas Ordinare's *Histoire naturelle des volcans* (Paris, 1802).

If the volcanoes and the salt mountain were myths, the lead mines were real and exciting to think about. Not everyone took them seriously, especially grouchy Senator Plumer, who reminded his diary that in 1802 Jefferson was talking of salt mountains and now in 1804 was boasting of the many rich lead mines in Upper Louisiana. "Baits like these are well calculated to keep alive the expectation of the credulous, & draw their attention from the immense debt we own for that country."[29]

John Heckewelder, longtime friend of the eastern tribes, sent a notice to a journal claiming that a Mohawk Indian named Daniel Green had spent two years in the northwestern parts of Louisiana. He mentioned a white bear (obviously the grizzly), the moose, "goats which climb up the rocks"—an early reference to the mountain goat—and a sheep with large horns which could only be the Rocky Mountain sheep or bighorn. It is obvious that Daniel Green had indeed been to the Northwest.[30]

To render the Louisiana Purchase governable, Congress decided to divide it into the District of Orleans, lying south of the thirty-third parallel, and the District of Louisiana, comprising the rest. For administrative purposes, the upper district was made a part of Indiana Territory under the governorship of William Henry Harrison. Dissatisfaction with this system caused Congress a year later to form a separate territorial government, establishing the Territory of Louisiana in the north. Various combinations of districts were discussed for the new upper territory, and Jefferson finally divided the region exactly as it had existed under the Spanish. The districts were St. Charles, St. Louis, Ste. Genevieve, Cape Girardeau, and New Madrid.[31]

While he governed the upper territory as a district of Indiana, Harrison did what he could to provide information for Jefferson. He sent descriptions, proposals for districts, and an estimate of the population at 9,373 persons including 1,497 blacks. The leading citizens of St. Louis were soon volunteering data. Pierre Chouteau provided an estimate of the Indian tribes, thought to be 34,680 persons, the largest tribes being the Sioux with 12,000 and the Ietans (Comanches) with 15,000. Charles Gratiot sent additional information, and enclosed five pages in French from B. Cousin, of Cape Girardeau, describing that district.[32]

· What It All Meant ·

Jefferson reported the gist of what he had learned about Louisiana to Congress on 14 November 1803. His "An Account of Louisiana" contained a digest of his questionnaire returns, his reading, and some common knowledge already at hand. Two weeks later he submitted a digest of the laws of Louisiana as an appendix to his Account.

Considering the time he had spent in deliberating the boundaries, his comment was sparse—purposely so. He told William Dunbar that he had deliberately said little about boundaries "because we thought it best first to have explanations with Spain."[33] He omitted Texas from his comments, but could not forbear getting in an early word on the matter of West Florida:

> The precise boundaries of Louisiana, westward of the Mississippi, though very extensive, are at present involved in some obscurity. Data are equally wanting to assign with precision its northern extent. From the source of the Mississippi, it is bounded eastwardly, by the middle of the channel of that river, to the thirty-first degree of latitude; thence, it is asserted upon very strong grounds, that, according to its limits when formerly possessed by France, it stretches to the east as far, at least, as the river Perdido, which runs into the bay of Mexico, eastward of the river Mobile.

He was now doing some hard thinking about how the Purchase had affected the future of his country. As usual, his pondering ranged from the most immediate of practical applications to the grandest of visions. He had begun to fit the territory into his Indian policy, thinking of those still unmapped lands as a temporary home for the tribes east of the Mississippi (while they were learning to become white men). He told Dupont de Nemours that "our policy will be to form New Orleans, and the country on both sides of it on the Gulf of Mexico, into a state, and as to all above that, to transplant our Indians into it, constituting them a Marechaussee [mounted constabulary] to prevent emigrants crossing the river, until we shall have filled up the vacant country on this side."

By mid-June 1804, government officials were talking of exchanging Indian lands for equivalent tracts west of the Mississippi. But, as Jefferson wrote to his secretary of war, "Before we can offer lands on the other side of the Missisipi to any tribe, we should be well informed of the title to lands there." An even more ambitious notion was to induce the French citizens of the upper regions to exchange their holdings for lands east of the Mississippi and immigrate there, leaving all the west side to the Indians.[34] The plan was humanitarian in intent, but there were ominous suggestions of what would later become the notorious Indian-removal policy of his successors.

On the larger scale, Louisiana was not fitting itself into Jefferson's pan-American daydreams. He had said in 1786 that the United States was the nest from which all America, north and South, was to be feathered. Here were the first whisperings of Manifest Destiny, though Jefferson had a way of making it sound not only logical and inevitable, but something devoutly to be wished by all men. To John Breckinridge, in the context of the possibility that western settlements might break away from the United States and form their own governments, he wrote:

> Besides, if it should become the great interest of those nations [formed from Louisiana] to separate from this, if their happiness should depend on it so strongly as to induce them to go through that convulsion, why should the Atlantic States dread it. But especially, why should we, their present inhabitants, take sides in such a question. . . . The future inhabitants of the Atlantic and Mississippi states will be our sons. We leave them in distinct but bordering establishments. We think we see their happiness in their union, and we wish it. Events may prove it otherwise; and if they see their interest in separation, why should we take sides with our Atlantic rather than our Mississippi descendants? God bless them both, and keep them in union, if it be for their good, but separate them, if it be better.[35]

Alexander von Humboldt reported many years after his 1804 visit with Jefferson that they had discussed the political future of America and "the project of a future division of the American continent into three great republics which were to include Mexico and the South American states which at that time belonged to the Spanish crown."[36]

There were matters of greater priority before Jefferson now. Where did the Missouri River really come from? Was there a backbone of mountains down the length of the continent, and on the other side a great river that ran to the sea? The maps and books said so, and Jefferson had studied them all. He was as familiar as anyone could be with the geography of the American West, yet it was all theory. Someone had to go there, and to this enterprise Jefferson had already turned his attention.

NOTES

1. Julian P. Boyd describes the holiday season in TJ's neighborhood in CHRISTMAS, an Oxford University Press keepsake edition.

2. Maria to TJ, 22 Jan. 1791, BETTS & BEAR, 70.

3. To Thomas Mann Randolph, 19 Dec. 1803, LC.

4. To Maria, 26 Dec. 1803, BETTS & BEAR, 250. No word had come as of 13 Jan., according to a letter from TJ to Meriwether Lewis, LC.

5. Mentioned in Wilkinson to TJ, 22 May 1800, LC.

6. Wilkinson to TJ, 29 Nov. 1800, LC. John Logan Allen suggests that some "modern manuscripts" sent by Wilkinson this year may have been provided by Antoine Truteau, a trader on the upper Missouri. Wilkinson described them as coming from an employee of the Missouri Fur Company who had made a trip to the Mandans (ALLEN [2], 68).

7. Wilkinson to TJ, 18 Jan. 1802, LC.

8. Wilkinson to Dearborn, 13 July 1804, NARG 107, W-349. Wilkinson describes the maps as being based on the observations of Philip Nolan.

9. Wilkinson to TJ, 22 Oct. and 23 Dec. 1805, LC. The Arikara enumeration is separated from the December letter and cataloged as vol. 146, fol. 25409.

10. Wilkinson to Eustis, 3 Sept. 1809, NARG 107, W-687. By this time William Eustis was secretary of war and Madison was president, neither much interested in collecting the kind of western miscellany that amused TJ.

11. LOOMIS, 131, 132.

12. TJ to Nolan, 24 June 1798, LC. See also PETERSON [1], 588–89, and Wilkinson to TJ, 22 May 1800, LC, in which the general introduces Nolan. Daniel Clark, Jr., had planned to send with Nolan a special horse as a gift to TJ. "In your Country where fine horses are so common he will be only remarkable for Colour" (Clark to TJ, 29 May 1800, LC).

13. Clark to TJ, 12 Feb. and 12 Nov. 1799, LC. Clark later became a delegate to Congress from the Territory of Orleans.

14. See TJ to Dunbar, 16 Jan. 1800, acknowledging Dunbar's first letter of 6 Oct. 1799 (not found), and Dunbar to TJ, 14 July 1800, 22 Aug. 1801, and 10 June 1803, all in LC.

15. To Claiborne, 30 Aug. 1804, LC. TJ did not reveal Lafayette's name (Claiborne probably knew), but did assure Claiborne of fullest confidence and support.

16. Lafayette to TJ, 17 May 1803, CHINARD [2], 220. For the attitude of the Idealogues, see ECHEVERRIA, 276.

17. See PLUMER, 219; MALONE, 4:357 and his sources; TJ to Philip Mazzei, 18 July 1804, Dearborn to TJ, 25 March 1805, and TJ to Lafayette, 14 July 1807, all in LC. Plumer, an irascible Federalist, judged Claiborne to be a man of little talent or ability.

18. Much of Claiborne's public career is covered by his correspondence in TERR. PAPERS and CLAIBORNE. HATFIELD is a biography and BRADLEY an article on his dealings with Spain under Jefferson and Madison.

19. See biographical material by GARRETT and WHITTINGTON. Sibley's first letter to TJ is 20 March 1804, LC. On his agency, see Dearborn to Sibley, 25 May 1805, NARG 75, letters sent, 2:80. Sibley's report on the Indians was included in Jefferson's 1805 message to Congress (see MESSAGE).

20. Humboldt's visit to Washington is related in FRIIS. For his correspondence with TJ, see DE TERRA. Humboldt's nineteen-page "tableau satistique" reporting population and other data from Mexico, responding to TJ's inquiry of 9 June 1804, is filed at fol. 25355. See also Wilkinson to TJ, 11 June 1804, LC, and his list of queries beginning at fol. 25405. Wilkinson included some questions to which he already knew the answers, "because by such answers [we] shall be able to determine the accuracy of his information."

21. The rough drafts, as drawn by TJ and augmented by Gallatin, are filed as fols. 23030–36 in the undated 1803 material, LC. Claiborne's lengthy response of 24 Aug. 1803 is in its proper chronological location, LC.

22. MALONE, 4:303, quoting the language of the treaty. No one knew what the Purchase meant in terms of square miles, or what the terrain was like. A dispatch from the Spanish court in 1804 speaks of the Missouri River as passing through a part of Texas. General Nemesio Salcedo, commanding the Internal Provinces of New Spain, considered the Missouri to be the northern boundary of his command *after* the Purchase, and especially believed that he controlled the Missouri "west of its confluence with the Platte" (Salcedo to Alencaster, 9 Sept. 1805, Cunningham Transcripts, Illinois Historical Survey, Urbana). Of course the Missouri does not run west at that point, but north.

23. To John Dickinson, 9 Aug. 1803, LC.

24. See TJ to Dunbar, 13 Mar. 1804, LC, in which he says he did the research at Monticello at the first opportunity after the Purchase. He sent Dunbar a copy of his report.

25. His original draft of 7 Sept. 1803 is in LC. A later memorandum, "A Chronological Series of Facts Relative to Louisiana," which includes a separate section on the limits and is dated 15 Jan. 1804, is in the

American Philosophical Society library, Philadelphia. The published version is PURCHASE DOCS.

26. With West Florida under Spanish control, not only did Mississippi River traffic have to pass under Spanish guns at Baton Rouge, eighty miles to the northwest, but the two principal roadways to New Orleans from the northeast crossed Spanish lands (DARGO, 23–24).

27. To Peyroux, 3 July 1803, LC, and Peyroux to TJ, 20 March 1804, Colonial Williamsburg Library, Williamsburg, Va.

28. Davis to TJ, 5 Oct. 1803, LC. Senator Plumer discussed the salt mountain in his diary, based on information from TJ, and said the Indians considered it a sacred place (PLUMER, 221).

29. PLUMER, 192. Lead mines were an invaluable part of the mineral resources of the territory; some Indian tribes, such as the Sauks and Foxes on the upper Mississippi, had devised crude smelters for extracting the lead.

30. *Philadelphia Medical and Physical Journal,* 1 (1804), pt. 1, 75–76. The journal was published by Jefferson's old scientific friend, Benjamin Smith Barton, of the Medical College of the University of Pennsylvania.

31. L & C LETTERS, 1:183n.

32. Harrison to TJ, 24 June 1804, Chouteau to TJ, 19 Nov. 1804, and Gratiot to Meriwether Lewis, 13 Nov. 1804, all in LC.

33. To Dunbar, 13 March 1804, LC. The account is reprinted in AM. ST. PAPERS, Misc., 1:344–56, 362–84.

34. To Dupont de Nemours, 1 Nov. 1802, CHINARD [3], 80, and TJ to Dearborn, 6 June 1804, LC. For his plan to transplant French settlers, see pp. 147–48.

35. To Breckinridge, 12 Aug. 1803, LC.

36. Quoted in KELLNER, 62.

CHAPTER SEVEN

The Response to Mackenzie

Nothing in the Lewis and Clark story is more firmly believed than the tradition that Jefferson hired Meriwether Lewis in 1801 not merely as a secretary and aide but as a trainee for a transcontinental expedition. The tradition is highly suspect.

Lewis was a local youth whom Jefferson had known for many years. Born in 1774 on a plantation called Locust Hill, a few miles west of Charlottesville, he had made the Blue Ridge his playground. His father, William, was killed in the Revolution and his mother, Lucy, had married again to John Marks. When the Marks family moved for a time to the Broad River in Georgia, Meriwether went along—but returned to Charlottesville before the rest of the family came back from the Georgia adventure. Mrs. Marks, widowed once more, reestablished her home at Locust Hill.

The boy received some conventional grammar school education with classical overtones and absorbed a greater than average interest in natural history. Much of his knowledge was self-acquired. He seemed born to rise, in the agricultural-mercantile circles of Virginia, and he chose one of the most routinely traveled routes, a career in the army.[1]

Joining the militia during the Whiskey Rebellion in 1794, Lewis moved north and languished in various cantonments in western Maryland and Pennsylvania, deciding the following year to try life in the regular army. He was appointed ensign in the Second Sublegion in 1795, transferring the next year to the First Regiment of Infantry. This was to be his outfit during the rest of his military career.[2]

After the Whiskey Rebellion, his remaining duty was spent

either on furlough, in the recruiting service, or as regimental paymaster. He fought neither Indian nor white man, but he traveled much. General Anthony Wayne gave him a leave late in 1796, during which he went to Washington with dispatches from the general, and apparently the leave was extended well into 1797. During this furlough he spent some time on the Locust Hill plantation, went to Kentucky on family business, and to Georgia. His assignment to recruiting duty in Virginia, headquartering in Charlottesville with occasional visits across the Blue Ridge to Staunton, lasted from January 1798 to April 1799. While he was paymaster to the First Regiment, beginning in September 1800, he traveled from fort to fort in the Ohio Valley, visiting Fort Wayne, Detroit, Pittsburgh, and Cincinnati.[3]

What happened next turned a humdrum frontier army career into something like a miracle. It is told best by Lewis himself, writing excitedly to his company commander and tent mate, Captain Ferdinand L. Claiborne, 7 March 1801, from Pittsburgh:

> I cannot withhold from you my friend the agreeable intelligence I received on my arrival at this place by way of a very polite note from Thomas Jefferson, the newly elected President of the United States, signifying his wish that I should except the office of his private Secretary; this unbounded, as well as unexpected confidence, confered on me by a man whose virtue and talents I have ever adored, and always conceived second to none, I must confess did not fail to raise me somewhat in my own estimation, insomuch that I have almost prevailed on myself to believe that my abilities are equal to the task; however be that as it may I am resolved to except it, and shal therefore set forward to the City of Washington in a few days; I deem the prospect two flattering to be neglected by a man of my standing and prospects in life. By excepting this appointment I do not sacrifice my rank in the Army, but only suspend my pay and rations in lue of which my Salary will be $:500 annually & by becoming one of the President's family shal be at no expence of boarding lodging &c. &c.[4]

The position of secretary to the president was an honorable one, as taxing as the president wished to make it. Tobias Lear, secretary to Washington, had been a family friend, tutor to children, and a witness if not a participant in Washington's struggle to set strong precedents for heads of state to come. Jefferson described his own requirements for the position in a letter to another potential secretary: "The office itself is more in the nature of that of an Aid de camp. . . . The writing is not considerable. . . . The care of our company, execution of some commissions in the town occasionally, messages to Congress, occasional conferences & explanations with particular members, with the offices, & inhabitants of the place where it cannot so well be done in writing, constitute the chief business."[5]

Observing military courtesy, Jefferson sent his request to Lewis under cover to General Wilkinson with the request that it be forwarded. He told Wilkinson he thought it would be advantageous "to take one who possessing a knolege of the Western country, of the army & it's situation, might sometimes aid us with informations of interest, which we may not otherwise possess." He used similar words in his letter to Lewis: "Your knolege of the Western country, of the army and of all it's interests & relations has rendered it desireable for public as well as private purposes that you should be engaged in that office."[6]

At this point, historians go astray by piling one misconstruction upon another. They reason that Jefferson had long wished for an expedition to the Pacific; that he was at last in a position to authorize such a plan; that he placed Lewis on his staff so that he could personally guide the study and preparation needed for such an expedition.

While it is true that Jefferson had since 1783 shown sporadic signs that he wanted a transcontinental exploration, he had done so as a private citizen or as a member of the American Philosophical Society. During the three years he served as secretary of state, and four as vice-president, he had done exactly nothing to press for a government expedition. His purchases of geographical books were minimal. There is other evidence to consider before we can conclude that in early 1801, as the new president, he realized that he would use the power of office to send an exploring team across the Mississippi.

The two key phrases in Jefferson's message to Lewis are: (a) *Your knolege of the Western country,* and (b) *of the army and of all it's interests and relations.* Perhaps the wrong phrase has attracted our attention. By "Western country" Jefferson of course meant the Ohio Valley. It is true that Lewis had traveled there, both on furlough and on trips to pay the troops of the First Infantry. He knew the reaches of the Ohio, the main roads of Kentucky, the burgeoning towns of Cincinnati, Wheeling, and Louisville along the river. He certainly knew what the western people were thinking—a matter of deep concern to Jefferson, who had to be alert to the separatist elements on the outer edges of his constituency. An intelligent young officer who had recently traveled among those people could be useful, especially if he were someone long known and trusted by Jefferson.

The second phrase, about "the army and . . . all it's interests and relations," must be examined more fully in the light of a document among Jefferson's papers. Opposing the Federalists, Jefferson had run on a platform that included a reduction of the standing army. He held firm to the Republican belief that a strong militia could handle the country's lesser military problems, and thus it became necessary for him to remodel and reduce the U.S. army—a strong and influential element in American life of which he had very little personal knowledge. Although he commanded the forces of Virginia as governor, and dealt with army matters later as a federal official, he did not know the officer corps on a personal basis. How was he to retain the good officers (especially Republican ones, for party patronage was solidly established in the military), and how would he decide who must be among those "reduced" to Republican specifications?

A roster of officers, listed by outfit, was given to Jefferson in the early months of his presidency. It has long been of interest to students of Jefferson and his times, because there is a code symbol beside the name of each man which evaluates him as a party member and an officer. Accompanying the roster is a sheet explaining the symbols, so that Jefferson could tell at a glance whether an officer was a strong or weak Republican, avid or lukewarm Federalist, or perhaps nonpolitical. He could also consult the symbols for an estimate of each man's military proficiency, including a few "unworthy of the commissions they bear."

What has gone unnoticed until recently is the handwriting on the sheet which explains the symbols. It is the hand of Meriwether Lewis.[7]

It seems probable that uppermost in Jefferson's mind, when he asked Lewis to join his staff, was the young officer's thorough knowledge of the army and "of all it's interests and relations." There is no indication that Lewis began at once to plan and study for his expedition. Instead, his job involved long hours at the writing desk, performing menial tasks. For example, he drew up a list of all U.S. postmasters, with their locations and compensation, totaling twenty pages.[8] He went to Capitol Hill with mail from Jefferson's office, including official messages to Congress. He may have sat in on cabinet meetings and Indian councils as Tobias Lear had done with Washington. It was by all indications a monotonous routine.

Lewis stayed on the job for nearly two years before he found himself preparing for a western expedition. During that time he spent many days in Charlottesville, and paid a visit to a new Philadelphia friend, Mahlon Dickerson—a young lawyer and ardent Republican. Apparently he was enjoying his proximity to the heads of state, despite the modest nature of his own role in government. There had been a hint of his instinct for politics, as well as an air of self-importance, in that first euphoric letter he had written his army tent mate Claiborne when he accepted the new position: "I . . . shal take the liberty of informing you of the most important political occurrences of our government or such of them as I may feel myself at liberty to give."[9]

Late in 1801 a publishing event stirred the western world, jolted Jefferson back into thinking in terms of hemispheric geography, and changed the course of Lewis's life. Alexander Mackenzie's *Voyages* was published in London, and copies were circulating in New York and Philadelphia within a short time. Mackenzie had been knighted for his travels. Jefferson's first knowledge of the book probably came in a letter from Dr. Caspar Wistar, who frequently sent down from Philadelphia bits of new information for the President. "Have you seen McKenzie's account of his journeys across the Continent & to the Northern Ocean?" Wistar asked. "He had very peculiar advantages for such an enterprize, & happily availed himself of them. It is reported here that he is at New York, on his way to the North West Country, & that he has provided himself with the vaccine virus for the benefit of the unfortunate natives. His melancholy acount of the effects of the Small Pox in that country must add

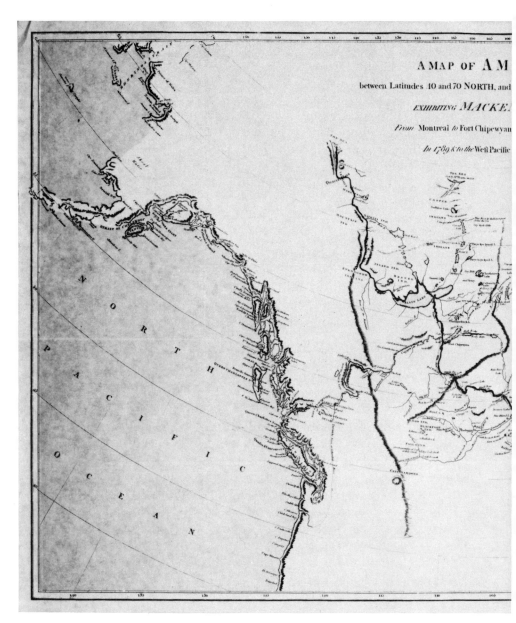

4. The Mackenzie map of 1801, carried by Lewis and Clark. LIBRARY OF CONGRESS

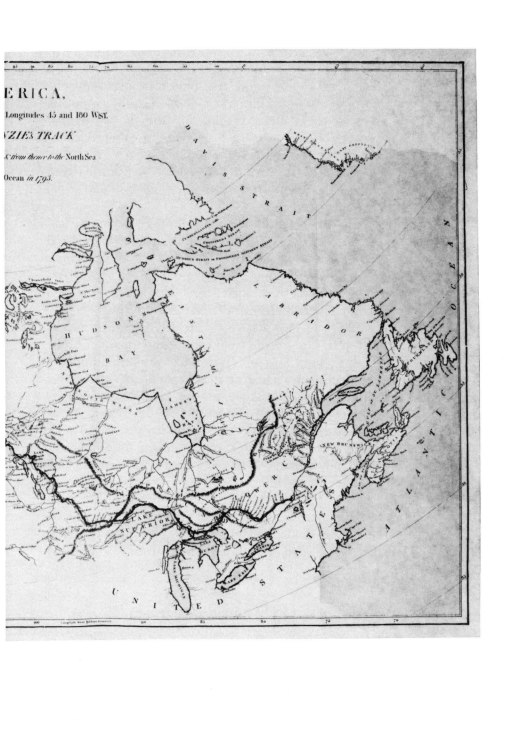

greatly to your satisfaction on account of your exertions to diffuse the benefits of that very happy discovery."[10]

Wistar had missed the big point. As a physician and scientist he had reported what interested him most, and Jefferson was indeed a strong advocate of smallpox vaccination. But the words that would have caught Jefferson's attention were those that Mackenzie said he had inscribed, with vermilion and melted grease, on the face of a rock near the Pacific: "Alexander Mackenzie, from Canada, by land, the twenty-second of July, one thousand seven hundred and ninety-three."[11]

At Monticello for the summer, going through papers he had saved for the easier days on his little mountain, Jefferson ordered a copy of Mackenzie's book from New York dealer James Cheetham. At the same time he ordered a copy of Aaron Arrowsmith's latest map of the United States, just off the press with new observations gleaned from other British voyagers.[12]

For two weeks in August that year, Jefferson's house guest was Benjamin Smith Barton, an old friend and fellow member of the American Philosophical Society. Barton had been on a botanizing tour into Virginia, traveling up the Shenandoah Valley, over to Warm Springs, back through Lexington, Staunton, and Charlottesville. He stayed at Monticello from 10 to 25 August, keeping a daily journal which—for the Monticello period—is now missing. Had Jefferson begun to formulate plans for an expedition, he would almost surely have conferred with Barton, who had been involved in the plan of 1793 to sponsor the travels of André Michaux. Apparently nothing was said about a new expedition, for six months later, when Jefferson would write Barton of his decision to send Lewis west, the tone of his letter would make it clear that he was advising Barton for the first time.[13]

· Addressing Diplomatic Questions ·

Early in December 1802, the Spanish *encargado de negocios* in Washington wrote his home office for instructions. He was Carlos Martínez de Irujo, minister to the United States from the court of his Most Catholic Majesty, Carlos IV. Addressing the minister of foreign affairs in Madrid, he told of a curious conversation with Jefferson.

The President asked me the other day in a frank and confident tone, if our Court would take it badly, that the Congress decree the formation of a group of travelers, who would form a small caravan and go and explore the course of the Missouri River in which they would nominally have the objective of investigating everything which might contribute to the progress of commerce; but that in reality it would have no other view than the advancement of the geography . . . its object would not be other than to observe the territories which are found between 40° and 60° [north latitude] from the mouth of the Missouri to the Pacific Ocean, and unite the discoveries that these men would make with those which the celebrated Makensi made in 1793. . . .[14]

Irujo had tried to talk Jefferson out of his scheme by giving him a superfluous lesson in Pacific exploration. He dropped the names of Cook, Vancouver, Malaspina, and others, and said that Jefferson's hope of finding a water passage, or a passage with very little water travel, had already been settled by Mackenzie. There was no such passage. Still, Irujo told his superior, Jefferson might try the expedition anyway. "The President has been all his life a man of letters, very speculative and a lover of glory, and it would be possible he might attempt to perpetuate the fame of his administration . . . by discovering or attempting at least to discover the way by which the Americans may some day extend their population and their influence up to the coasts of the South Sea." If this should happen, what were the instructions from home?[15]

Late in January Irujo again wrote to the foreign minister, saying that Jefferson was pressing him for a passport, had confided his plan to the Senate, and seemed ready to go ahead. Again, what should he do?[16]

There is no record of the minister's responses but there is much to document the stir that Jefferson's plan was creating in Spain and in the provinces of New Spain. Apparently no Spanish passport was issued,[17] and the Spaniards—so confused and truculent about the recent Louisiana Purchase—prepared to obstruct and even intercept the proposed expedition.

The British and French officials were not so difficult, easily accepting Jefferson's assertion that the expedition would be a "literary" one in the interest of science. Edward Thornton, the minister from London, wrote the home office that he had issued a passport for Lewis and hoped the secretary of state for foreign affairs "will not think that in paying this mark of personal attention to the President's wishes, I have materially exceeded the limits of my duty." Thornton described the expedition as the only one left for the United States in the Northwest region, "the Northern Communication having been so ably explored and ascertained by Sir Alexander Mackenzie's journeys."[18] Had Thornton actually read Mackenzie's *Voyages,* especially the author's plea for British control of the mouth of the Columbia, he might have been less willing to issue a passport to Britain's strongest potential competitor in that region.

The secretary of the French legation, Louis André Pichon, was even easier to deal with, borrowing the British passport to serve as a model for the one he prepared. Pichon then wrote to Talleyrand, the French minister of foreign affairs, explaining his action and saying that the only occasion on which the passport might be useful would be if "Capt. Merryweather" and his men had to return from the West Coast by sea. Pichon was impressed by Jefferson's enthusiasm. "He explained his purpose to me, on the big map by Arrow Smith."[19]

All these negotiations with foreign representatives were executed before anyone in Washington realized that Napoleon and Talleyrand were about to put the Louisiana Territory up for sale.

· Relations with Congress and the Cabinet ·

Jefferson inserted a request for a small appropriation, to get the expedition plans going, in his annual message to Congress in December 1802. When he circulated the draft among his cabinet members, however, he was persuaded by Secretary of the Treasury Albert Gallatin that the proposal ought to be confined to a separate, confidential message, "as it contemplates an expedition out of our own territory." So Jefferson left the matter out of the regular message and sent up a special, confidential one, on 18 January 1803. Even then he buried his request in a discourse that spoke primarily of renewing the provision for Indian trading houses and his desire to purchase more Indian lands in the months and years ahead. Then he got to the matter of the expedition, couching it in terms of commerce. If the Indians were to be persuaded to abandon the hunt and take up farming, U.S. citizens would be deprived of the profits from the fur trade. It might be well to look into the practicality of establishing relations with Indians west of the Mississippi for purposes of trade.

The river Missouri, & the Indians inhabiting it, are not as well known as is rendered desireable by their connection with the Missisipi, & consequently with us. It is however understood that the country on that river is inhabited by numerous tribes, who furnish great supplies of furs & peltry to the trade of another nation carried on in a high latitude, through an infinite number of portages and lakes, shut up by ice through a long season.

He said that the Missouri, traversing an area with a more moderate climate, might offer a better source of transportation, "possibly with a single portage, from the Western ocean," and then he came to his real purpose:

An intelligent officer with ten or twelve chosen men, fit for the enter-prize and willing to undertake it, taken from our posts, where they may be spared without inconvenience, might explore the whole line, even to the Western ocean, have conferences with the natives on the subject of commercial intercourse, get admission among them for our traders as others are admitted, agree on convenient deposits for an interchange of articles, and return with the information acquired in the course of two summers. . . . The interests of commerce place the principal object within the constitutional powers and care of Congress, and that it should incidentally advance the geographical knowledge of our own continent can not but be an additional gratification.

He asked for an appropriation of $2,500 "for the purpose of extending the external commerce of the U.S." Congress bought the whole package, perhaps little realizing that $2,500 was only the beginning of the cost, and the proposal became law as of 28 February 1802.[20]

If the Spanish, French, and British knew of the plan, and if Congress had provided the money, and if the expedition were truly constitutional as described by Jefferson, then why all the secrecy? Jefferson seemed to fear intervention and criticism by his political foes. Attorney General Levi Lincoln mentioned "the perverse, hostile, and malignant state of the opposition" in commenting on the expedition. The rumor was purposely spread that Lewis and his men were bound up the Mississippi. Even as late as 13 July 1803, with Lewis already on his way, Jefferson could write to Caesar A. Rodney, "Capt. Lewis left this on the 5th on his journey up the Missisipi."[21] It was a foolish and near-paranoid attempt at secrecy that could never work. Word had already spread to Louisville. When the secret could no longer be kept, Jefferson winced at the criticism in the opposition press, writing to Lewis, "The Feds. alone still treat it as philosophism, and would rejoice in its failure. Their bitterness increases with the diminution of their numbers and despair of a resurrection."[22]

Most members of Jefferson's cabinet played but small roles in the planning of the expedition. Henry Dearborn, secretary of war, was compliant though sometimes dilatory. Levi Lincoln looked over a draft of Lewis's instructions, suggested information to be sought from the Indians, proposed that cowpox vaccine be carried to the tribes, and said he hoped Lewis would not be inclined to push too far in case of difficulty. Madison, secretary of state, might have been expected to make a substantive contribution. He was content to return the draft instructions with four minor suggestions.[23] The secretary of the treasury was the big surprise, exhibiting knowledge and enthusiasm in an area of learning far removed from his fiscal assignments.

· Albert Gallatin, Unexpected Expert ·

Gallatin was a Swiss emigrant who had established himself in western Pennsylvania, serving as a member of Congress while Jefferson was vice-president. As Jefferson's secretary of the treasury, he had the touchy job of changing the nation's fiscal policies from Federalist to Republican. He managed to lower the national debt, despite some unexpected expenses such as the Louisiana Purchase. Finance, it developed, was only one of his interests. He was an earnest student of Indian life, and when plans were growing for Lewis's trip, Gallatin suddenly was discovered to know more about western geography than anyone in government except Jefferson.

He had observed that in the United States the source of every river north of 42° latitude originated in a lake, and that those rising south of 41° issued from a mountain range. He postulated an east-west chain of mountains dividing the northerly headwaters of the Rio Grande from the southerly affluents of the Missouri, and thought the width of that chain would determine the extent of country watered by the Missouri. He stressed the importance of observing how far to the north the affluents of the Missouri rose, "as their position would generally determine the extent of territory watered by the Missouri." He stressed the importance of discovering what part of the country was fertile enough to support a large population.[24]

Gallatin's greatest contribution to the expedition was probably the blank map that he ordered for Lewis. Drawn by cartographer Nicholas King, it was to contain all known information that might be useful: the Ohio as charted by Andrew Ellicott, the Pacific Coast from Cook and Vancouver, the upper reaches of the Missouri from Mackenzie and Arrowsmith, and the Rio Grande from the older charts of Jean Baptiste d'Anville and Guillaume Delisle. That such a blank map was made and carried on the expedition has now been verified. Historical geographer John Logan Allen has within recent years published and described it for the first time.[25]

It was Gallatin who knew that only one set of Vancouver's charts existed in the United States, and was for sale at fifty-five dollars by a Philadelphia bookseller. Later, when Lewis went to Philadelphia to prepare for the journey, he would talk bookseller F. Nichols into letting him make tracings of the charts pertinent to his needs.[26]

Gallatin's interest in geography and Indian ethnology and linguistics was to continue throughout a long career. It is incredible to find him helping to plan the Lewis and Clark expedition, and a whole generation later writing to John Charles Frémont for information about Indian languages and certain geographical features of the West.[27]

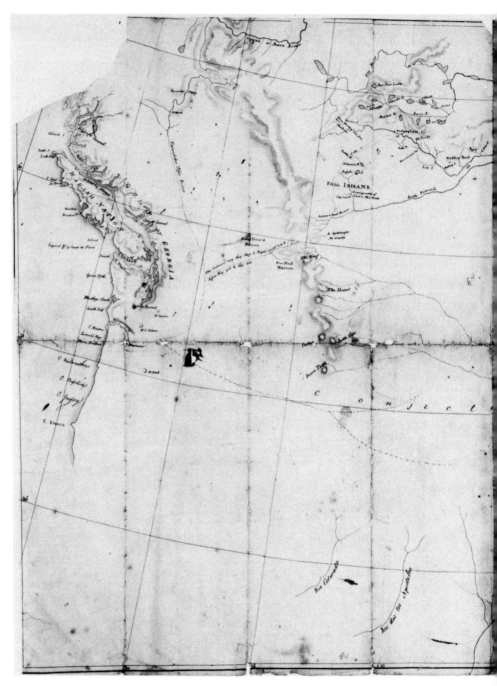

5. Nicholas King's 1803 map, carried by Lewis and Clark. LIBRARY OF CONGRESS

• Maps, Books, and Ciphers •

From his own library Jefferson could have produced a respectable collection of maps for Lewis to use. Besides old favorites of varying reliability, such as Mitchell, Jeffreys, and Hutchins, and those maps included in books by Le Page du Pratz, Carver, Mackenzie, and others, there was one in particular to which Jefferson and Lewis paid special attention.

Aaron Arrowsmith was a prominent British mapmaker whose peculiar advantage was his access to the records of the Hudson's Bay Company. He could thus add to his own long experience in collecting data of the recent findings of Mackenzie, David Thompson, Peter Fidler. Perhaps the most important map available to Lewis, and definitely carried on the expedition, was Arrowsmith's *A Map Exhibiting All the New Discoveries in the Interior Parts of North America . . . with Additions to 1802* (London, 1802). This map was sufficiently up-to-date to show Mackenzie's route to the Pacific, including the Tacoutche-Tesse River, the name Mackenzie applied to the Fraser, which he erroneously thought was the Columbia. Much of the detail in the watershed of the upper Missouri was from the observations of another Hudson's Bay man, Peter Fidler. It was the soundest and most recent map available, and it bore comforting confirmation of what Jefferson believed from his study of French writers since the days of Hennepin: the Missouri rose in a range of mountains, and flowing westward from that range was a great river running to the sea. Here was the water communication to the Pacific and then the Orient that Lewis was being sent to find, and his success would depend on whether those two rivers intertwined, or lay near one another, at their sources.

We cannot know for sure the complete list of maps taken by Lewis. Certainly Arrowsmith, Mackenzie, tracings from Vancouver, and a copy of David Thompson's 1798 map made after a visit to the Mandans. A tracing of the Thompson map is still among the Lewis and Clark documents at the Library of Congress, and the latitude and longitude given for the Mandan villages were to be a pivotal point in the mapping done by Lewis and Clark themselves.

The large blank map made under Gallatin's direction, and the ancillary maps that formed it, contained known latitudes and longitudes of such reliability that they were vital guideposts for Lewis and Clark. These known locations were St. Louis, from astronomical observations of French observers there; the Mandan villages, from Thompson, an astute astronomer; and the readings of George Vancouver on the Northwest Coast. Without making it sound easy, we can observe that Lewis and Clark had only to connect those three known locations with an accurately drawn line. It was to be a heartrending job.[28]

The books to be taken were judged both for content and weight. Lewis had seen at once that the Vancouver set was too bulky to consider for his traveling library. Jefferson felt the same about the original quarto edition of Mackenzie. Writing to bookseller Cheetham again, he said, "I have understood there is to be had in New York an 8vo edition of McKenzie's travels with the same maps which are in the 4to edition: I will thank you to procure it for me." He also asked for another copy of Arrowsmith.[29]

A fairly accurate list of books taken on the expedition can be compiled, partly from remarks in the journals and partly from Lewis's record of purchases. The works are listed here with only brief comment; the serious student may consult an entire article on the subject.[30]

Barton, Benjamin Smith. *Elements of Botany; or, Outlines of the Natural History of Vegetables* (Philadelphia, 1803). The first American work in elementary botany.

Kelly, Patrick. *A Practical Introduction to Spherics and Nautical Astronomy; being an attempt to simplify those . . . sciences. Containing . . . the discovery of a projection for clearing the lunar distances in order to find the longitude at sea . . .* (London, 1796). Important because Lewis was planning to use lunar distances, rather than the moons of Jupiter, to determine longitudes (see pp. 173–76 below).

Kirwan, Richard. *Elements of Mineralogy* (London, 1784; 2d ed., 1794). There is evidence in the journals that this work was consulted en route.

Le Page du Pratz, Antoine. *The History of Louisiana, or the Western Parts of Virginia and Carolina* (London, 1763; 2d ed., 1774). A favorite book of Jefferson's. For proof that Lewis borrowed Benjamin Barton's copy, and returned it after the expedition, see CUTRIGHT [2].

Mackenzie, Alexander. *Voyages* (London, 1801; American ed., 1802). Previously discussed.

Miller, John. *An Illustration of the Sexual System of Linnaeus,* vol. 1 (London, 1779); *An Illustration of the Termini Botanici of Linnaeus,* vol. 2 (London, 1789). Lewis's descriptions and terminology are definitely Linnaean.

The Nautical Almanac and Astronomical Ephemeris . . . published by order of the Commissioners of Longitude (London, 1781–1804). Contains daily locations of the sun, moon, and planets in respect to the earth. A necessary complement was *Nevil Maskelyn's Tables Requisite to be Used with the Nautical Ephemeris for Finding the Latitude and Longitude at Sea* (London, 1781).

A New and Complete Dictionary of Arts and Science; comprehending all the branches of useful knowledge, with accurate descriptions as well of the various machines, instruments, tools, figures, and schemes necessary for illustrating them, as of the classes, kinds, preparations, and uses of natural productions, whether animals, vegetables, minerals, fossils, or fluids. By a Society of Gentlemen (London, 1753; 2d ed., 1764). Owned and recommended to others by Jefferson. The journals bear evidence of its use, and Clark refers to it in a letter to Jefferson.

No doubt the expedition also carried at least one medical treatise and the current edition of the rules and articles of war.

As a gadget lover, Jefferson was naturally fascinated by codes and ciphers. They were an essential part of governmental communications then, as today, and in the papers of Washington, Jefferson, and Madison are many examples of their routine use in foreign affairs. Mathematician Robert Patterson devised a special cipher for the expedition. With Jefferson retaining one copy and Lewis the other, encrypted messages could easily be exchanged. A key word was required; the cipher made for Lewis was based on the word "artichokes." In playing with the system during their preparations for the expedition, Jefferson and/or Lewis enclosed one brief sample message full of hope and optimism: "I am at the head of the Missouri. All well, and the Indians so far friendly."[31]

· Shopping and Learning in Philadelphia ·

About a week after Congress approved the expedition, Jefferson was writing to his scientific acquaintances in Philadelphia, all fellow members of his beloved American Philosophical Society. He wrote first to Barton, but almost at the same time to Wistar, Patterson, and Dr. Benjamin Rush. Another letter went to Andrew Ellicott in Lancaster. The thrust of all letters was the same: an expedition was authorized but was still confidential; Lewis, the chosen leader, needed advice and instruction; he was sending Lewis to Philadelphia (and Lancaster) to be guided by the best minds he knew.

Of Lewis, he said to Patterson: "If we could have got a person perfectly skilled in botany, natural history, mineralogy, astronomy, with at the same time the necessary firmness of body & mind, habits of living in the woods & familiarity with the Indian character, it would have been better. But I know of no such character who would under take an enterprise so perilous." He said Lewis had been practicing with the sextant for some time to perfect his celestial observations, and needed more training.[32]

Lewis's schedule called for him to go first to the arsenal at Harpers Ferry, Va., and arrange for the acquisition of rifles, pistols, tomahawks, knives, and a folding iron-framed boat which he planned to cover with bark or skins, caulk with tar or pitch, and use on the upper Missouri (another gadget, and Jefferson must surely have had a hand in designing it). Lewis was to go then to Lancaster for lessons in the use of the sextant, chronometer, and printed tables for finding the longitude and latitude. He would then proceed to Philadelphia with a long shopping list of equipage and supplies, and letters of introduction to the savants who were to sharpen up his skills as an amateur scientist and navigator.

After a month at Harpers Ferry, where the construction of the boat frame had presented many problems, Lewis reported his arrival in Lancaster on 19 April 1803, saying he had commenced at once to practice the use of navigational instruments under Ellicott's tutelage.[33] In the meantime, Jefferson had set about finding a new secretary, eventually hiring Lewis Harvie, who set aside his plans to study law in Georgetown. He said he hoped he would have some time free for study.[34]

After two weeks in Lancaster, Lewis moved on to Philadelphia. Because the time was short, and it is clear that he spent some of it in socializing, he cannot have learned more than a smattering of what his teachers had to offer. He was occupied also with the procurement of many items from private and public vendors.

He hastened to renew his association with Mahlon Dickerson, with whom he had visited the year before. The two dined together on 12 and 14 May, and on Sunday, the 15th, they dined with Dr. George Logan and spent the evening with Pennsylvania governor John McKean. On the 19th they dined with Henry Sheaff, a prominent merchant who had formerly provided wine for the table of George Washington. On the 24th, Dickerson reports a "conference" with Lewis. They dined together in Dickerson's quarters on the 29th and were at the governor's home again on the 31st.[35]

Philadelphia was the headquarters of Israel Whelan, purveyor of public supplies and Lewis's official outfitter. There was a list which Lewis and perhaps Jefferson had prepared in advance, detailing mathematical instruments, arms and accoutrements, ammunition, clothing, camp equipage, food items, medicine, Indian presents, and "Means of Transportation." It was at best only a guide to his purchases, for he changed his requirements as he conferred with his suppliers and saw what was available. He bought a surprising lot of material from the merchants of Philadelphia: fishing tackle from George Lawton; lead canisters from George Ludlam; medicines from Gillaspy & Strong; dry goods from William Chancellor & Co.; tobacco from Thomas Leiper. He had shirts made by Matilda Chapman, and Francis Bellet concocted 193 pounds of "portable soup" which cost $289.50.

Through purveyor Whelan he purchased of Thomas Whitney this array of navigational and surveying equipment:

A Spirit level
Case of plotting Instruments [for drafting]
two pole Chain [for measuring distances]
Silver plated pocket Compass
Brass Boat Compass
3 Brass pocket Compasses
a Magnet
Tangent screw Quadrant [similar to sextant]
Metal Sextant

Making a Microscope and fixing Ditto on the Index of the Sextant
Sett of Slates in a Case
log line, reel & log ship
parallel glass for a horison
4 ounces of Talc [for artificial horizon]

Lewis had already spent most of the $2,500 appropriated by Congress. He had bought from private vendors materials totaling $2,324. Even when he deducted from the amount the $462.67 chargeable to other government funds, the total spent was $1,861.33. He had spent as much for dried soup as he had originally estimated for mathematical instruments, arms, and ammunition.[36]

After arranging wagon transportation to Pittsburgh for all his purchases, Lewis left Philadelphia during the first week in June, his head crammed with instructions and new learning. He had received navigational training from both Ellicott and Patterson, botanical and zoological advice from Barton, and tips on health and hygiene from Rush. Now he was going back to Washington for a most important task, the selection of a co-commander and partner.

· Clark Makes It "Lewis and Clark" ·

As a captain under Anthony Wayne, William Clark had once commanded the company in which Lewis served. He was four years older than Lewis, had been born in Albemarle County but moved early, and the two were friends who respected each other—not intimate buddies since childhood as is often believed. Clark had been down the Mississippi as far as Natchez on army business, was a tough woodsman and good practical surveyor, and was the younger brother of that fading national hero, George Rogers Clark.

Before Jefferson decided that prudence dictated a pair of commanders for the expedition, the enterprise had been to him "Mr. Lewis's Tour." Even later, when Clark had proved himself Lewis's equal in performing the divided duties of the exploring party, Jefferson rather thought of it as a Meriwether Lewis success. Lewis himself first used the term "Lewis and Clark's Tour" in a prospectus for the published journals, at about the time

Sergeant Patrick Gass, a member of the expedition, was also offering the public a journal of his travels "under the command of Captain Lewis and Captain Clarke."

In one of the most famous invitations to greatness the nation's archives can provide, Lewis wrote to Clark in June 1803 and offered him joint command (and a captaincy in the army): "From the long and uninterrupted friendship and confidence which has subsisted between us I feel no hesitation in making to you the following communication under the fulest impression that it will be held by you inviolably secret untill I see you, or you shall hear again from me."

After this awesome admonition, Lewis described the forthcoming expedition. Then he said: "If therefore there is anything under those circumstances, in this enterprise, which would induce you to participate with me in it's fatiegues, it's dangers and it's honors, believe me there is no man on earth with whom I should feel equal pleasure in sharing them as with yourself." Lewis declared that Jefferson had authorized him to offer a captain's commission, adding, "your situation if joined with me in this mission will in all respects be precisely such as my own."[37]

The mails were always slow and time was pressing. In case Clark should decline, or his reply should not return from Louisville until too late, Lewis was authorized to choose a stand-in. Lieutenant Moses Hooke, of the First Infantry, was approached and had consented to go, but Clark's acceptance came through.

"The enterprise &c. is Such as I have long anticipated and am much pleased with," he wrote Lewis, "and as my situation in life will admit of my absence the length of time necessary to accomplish such an undertaking I will chearfully join you . . . and partake of the dangers, difficulties, and fatigues, and I anticipate the honors & rewards of the result of such an enterprise, should we be successful in accomplishing it. . . . My friend I do assure you that no man lives whith whome I would perfur to undertake Such a Trip."[38]

The letter reached Lewis in Pittsburgh, where he had gone to await his wagons from Philadelphia and Harpers Ferry, and to arrange for the building of a large keelboat in a Pittsburgh boatyard. Responding, Lewis said, "I feel myself much gratifyed with your decision; for I could neither hope, wish, or expect from a union with any man on earth, more perfect support or further aid in the discharge of the several duties of my mission, than that, which I am confident I shall derive from being associated with yourself." He added some news that Clark may already have heard. "The session of Louisiana is now no secret; on the 14th of July the President recieved the treaty from Paris."[39]

· Instructions from the President ·

His directions to Lewis, like those to Michaux a decade earlier, are essential to an understanding of Jefferson's developing attitude toward the West. They embrace years of study and wonder, the collected wisdom of his government colleagues and his Philadelphia friends; they barely conceal his excitement at realizing that at last he would have facts, not vague guesses, about the Stony Mountains, the river courses, the wild Indian tribes, the flora and fauna of untrodden places—perhaps even some evidence of the late, great creatures whose bones he loved to collect.

[20 June 1803]

To Captain Meriwether Lewis esq. Capt. of the 1st regimt. of Infantry of the U.S. of A.

Your situation as Secretary of the President of the U.S. has made you acquainted with the objects of my confidential message of Jan. 18, 1803 to the legislature; you have seen the act they passed, which, tho' expressed in general terms, was meant to sanction those objects, and you are appointed to carry them into execution.

Instruments for ascertaining, by celestial observations, the geography of the country through which you will pass, have been already provided. Light articles for barter and presents among the Indians, arms for your attendants, say for from 10. to 12. men, boats, tents, & other travelling apparatus, with ammunition, medecine, surgical instruments and provisions you will have prepared with such aids as the Secretary at War can yield in his department; & from him also you will recieve authority to engage among our troops, by voluntary agreement, the number of attendants above mentioned, over whom you, as their commanding officer, are invested with all the powers the laws give in such a case.

As your movements while within the limits of the U.S. will be better directed by occasional communications, adapted to circumstances as they arise, they will not be noticed here. What follows will respect your proceedings after your departure from the United states.

Your mission has been communicated to the ministers here from France, Spain & Great Britain, and through them to their governments; & such assurances given them as to it's objects, as we trust will satisfy them. The country having been ceded by Spain to France, the passport you have from the minister of France, the representative of the present sovereign of the country, will be a protection with all it's subjects; & that from the minister of England will entitle you to the friendly aid of any traders of that allegiance with whom you may happen to meet.

The object of your mission is to explore the Missouri river, & such principal stream of it, as, by it's course and communication with the waters of the Pacific ocean, whether the Columbia, Oregan, Colorado or any other river may offer the most direct & practicable water communication across this continent for the purposes of commerce.

Beginning at the mouth of the Missouri, you will take observations of latitude & longitude, at all remarkeable points on the river, & especially at the mouths of rivers, at rapids, at islands, & other places & objects distinguished by such natural marks & characters of a durable kind, as that they may with certainty be recognised hereafter. The courses of the river between these points of observation may be supplied by the compass the log-line & by time, corrected by the observations themselves. The variations of the compass too, in different places, should be noticed.

The interesting points of the portage between the heads of the Missouri, & of the water offering the best communication with the Pacific ocean, should also be fixed by observation, & the course of that water to the ocean, in the same manner as that of the Missouri.

Your observations are to be taken with great pains & accuracy, to be entered distinctly & intelligibly for others as well as yourself, to comprehend all the elements necessary, with the aid of the usual tables, to fix the latitude and longitude of the places at which they were taken, and are to be rendered to the war-office, for the purpose of having the calculations made concurrently by proper persons within the U.S. Several copies of these as well as of your other notes should be made at leisure times, & put into the care of the most trust-worthy of your attendants, to guard, by multiplying them, against the accidental losses to which they will be exposed. A further guard would be that one of these copies be on the paper of the birch, as less liable to injury from damp than common paper.[40]

The commerce which may be carried on with the people inhabiting the line you will pursue, renders a knolege of those people important. You will therefore endeavor to make yourself acquainted, as far as a diligent pursuit of your journey shall admit, with the names of the nations & their numbers;

the extent & limits of their possessions;

their relations with other tribes of nations;

their language, traditions, monuments;

their ordinary occupations in agriculture, fishing, hunting, war, arts,
& the implements for these;

their food, clothing, & domestic accomodations;

the diseases prevalent among them, & the remedies they use;

moral & physical circumstances which distinguish them from the
tribes we know;

peculiarities in their laws, customs & dispositions;

and articles of commerce they may need or furnish, & to what extent.

And, considering the interest which every nation has in extending &
strengthening the authority of reason & justice among the people
around them, it will be useful to acquire what knolege you can of the
state of morality, religion, & information among them; as it may better
enable those who may endeavor to civilize & instruct them, to adapt
their measures to the existing notions & practices of those on whom
they are to operate.

Other objects worthy of notice will be

the soil & face of the country, it's growth & vegetable productions,
especially those not of the U.S.

the animals of the country generally, & especially those not known in
the U.S.

the remains or accounts of any which may be deemed rare or extinct;

the mineral productions of every kind; but more particularly metals,
limestone, pit coal, & saltpetre; salines & mineral waters, noting
the temperature of the last, & such circumstances as may indicate
their character;

volcanic appearances;

climate, as characterised by the thermometer, by the proportion of
rainy, cloudy, & clear days, by lightning, hail, snow, ice, by the
access & recess of frost, by the winds prevailing at different seasons, the dates at which particular plants put forth or lose their
flower, or leaf, times of appearance of particular birds, reptiles or
insects.

Altho' your route will be along the channel of the Missouri, yet you
will endeavor to inform yourself, by enquiry, of the character & extent
of the country watered by it's branches, & especially on it's Southern
side. The North river or Rio Bravo which runs into the gulph of
Mexico, and the North river, or Rio colorado which runs into the
gulph of California, are understood to be the principal streams heading
opposite to the waters of the Missouri, and running Southwardly.
Whether the dividing grounds between the Missouri & them are moun-

tains or flat lands, what are their distance from the Missouri, the character of the intermediate country, & the people inhabiting it, are worthy of particular enquiry. The Northern waters of the Missouri are less to be enquired after, because they have been ascertained to a considerable degree, & are still in a course of ascertainment by English traders, and travellers. But if you can learn any thing certain of the most Northern source of the Missisipi, & of it's position relatively to the lake of the woods, it will be interesting to us.

[*Two copies of your notes at least & as many more as leisure will admit, should be made & confided to the care of the most trusty individuals of your attendants.*] Some account too of the path of the Canadian traders from the Missisipi, at the mouth of the Ouisconsing to where it strikes the Missouri, & of the soil and rivers in it's course, is desireable.

In all your intercourse with the natives, treat them in the most friendly & conciliatory manner which their own conduct will admit; allay all jealousies as to the object of your journey, satisfy them of it's innocence, make them acquainted with the position, extent, character, peaceable & commercial dispositions of the U.S.[,] of our wish to be neighborly, friendly & useful to them, & of our dispositions to a commercial intercourse with them; confer with them on the points most convenient as mutual emporiums, and the articles of most desireable interchange for them & us. If a few of their influential chiefs, within practicable distance, wish to visit us, arrange such a visit with them, and furnish them with authority to call on our officers, on their entering the U.S. to have them conveyed to this place at the public expence. If any of them should wish to have some of their young people brought up with us, & taught such arts as may be useful to them, we will receive, instruct & take care of them. Such a mission, whether of influential chiefs or of young people, would give some security to your own party.[41] Carry with you some matter of the kinepox; inform those of them with whom you may be, of it's efficacy as a preservative from the smallpox; & instruct & encourage them in the use of it. This may be especially done wherever you winter.

As it is impossible for us to foresee in what manner you will be recieved by those poeple, whether with hospitality or hostility, so is it impossible to prescribe the exact degree of perseverance with which you are to pursue your journey. We value too much the lives of citizens to offer them to probable destruction. Your numbers will be sufficient to secure you against the unauthorised opposition of individuals or of small parties: but if a superior force, authorised, or not authorised, by a nation, should be arrayed against your further passage, and inflexibly determined to arrest it, you must decline it's farther pursuit, and return. In the loss of yourselves, we should lose also the information you will have acquired. By returning safely with that, you may enable us to renew the essay with better calculated means. To your own discretion therefore must be left the degree of danger you may risk, and the point at which you should decline, only saying we wish you to err on the side of your safety, and to bring back your party safe even if it be with less information.

As far up the Missouri as the white settlements extend, an intercourse will probably be found to exist between them & the Spanish posts of St. Louis opposite Cahokia, or Ste. Genevieve opposite Kaskaskia. From still further up the river, the traders may furnish a conveyance for letters. Beyond that, you may perhaps be able to engage Indians to bring letters for the government to Cahokia or Kaskaskia, on promising that they shall there recieve such special compensation as you shall have stipulated with them. Avail yourself of these means to communicate to us, at seasonable intervals, a copy of your journal, notes & observations, of every kind, putting into cypher whatever might do injury if betrayed.

Should you reach the Pacific ocean inform yourself of the circumstances which may decide whether the furs of those parts may not be collected as advantageously at the head of the Missouri (convenient as is supposed to the waters of the Colorado & Oregan or Columbia) as at Nootka sound, or any other point of that coast; and that trade be consequently conducted through the Missouri & U.S. more beneficially than by the circumnavigation now practised.[42]

On your arrival on that coast endeavor to learn if there be any port within your reach frequented by the sea-vessels of any nation, & to send two of your trusty people back by sea, in such way as shall appear practicable, with a copy of your notes: and should you be of opinion that the return of your party by the way they went will be eminently dangerous, then ship the whole, & return by sea, by the way either of cape Horn, or the cape of good Hope, as you shall be able. As you will be without money, clothes or provisions, you must endeavor to use the credit of the U.S. to obtain them, for which purpose open letters of credit shall be furnished you, authorising you to draw upon the Executive of the U.S. or any of it's officers, in any part of the world, on which draughts can be disposed of, & to apply with our recommendations to the Consuls, agents, merchants, or citizens of any nation with which we have intercourse, assuring them, in our name, that any aids they may furnish you, shall be honorably repaid, and on demand. Our consuls Thomas Hewes at Batavia in Java, Wm. Buchanan in the Isles of France & Bourbon & John Elmslie at the Cape of good Hope will be able to supply your necessities by draughts on us.

Should you find it safe to return by the way you go, after sending two of your party round by sea, or with your whole party, if no conveyance by sea can be found, do so; making such observations on your return, as may serve to supply, correct or confirm those made on your outward journey.

On re-entering the U.S. and reaching a place of safety, discharge any of your attendants who may desire & deserve it, procuring for them immediate paiment of all arrears of pay & cloathing which may have incurred since their departure, and assure them that they shall be recommended to the liberality of the legislature for the grant of a souldier's portion of land each, as proposed in my message to Congress: & repair yourself with your papers to the seat of government [*to which I have only to add my sincere prayer for your safe return*].

To provide, on the accident of your death, against anarchy, dispersion, & the consequent danger to your party, and total failure of the enterprize, you are hereby authorised, by any instrument signed & written in your own hand, to name the person among them who shall succeed to the command on your decease, and by like instruments to change the nomination from time to time as further experience of the characters accompanying you shall point out superior fitness: and all the powers and authorities given to yourself are, in the event of your death, transferred to, & vested in the successor so named, with further power to him, and his successors in like manner to name each his successor, who, on the death of his predecessor, shall be invested with all the powers & authorities given to yourself.

Given under my hand at the city of Washington this 20th day of June 1803.[43]

TH: J. PR. U.S. OF A.

· Descending the Ohio ·

Lewis and Clark buffs in certain states derive some chauvinistic pleasure from convincing themselves that the expedition "started" in their area. The most fortunate claimants include the Virginians, who point out that some of the planning had to be done at Monticello and that Jefferson, Lewis, Clark, and some of their men were Virginians; residents of Illinois, who can cite the Wood River encampment where the first winter was spent; Missourians, who have the whole St. Louis and St. Charles area to consider as the basic departure point. Pennsylvanians seldom speak up for Pittsburgh in this friendly competition, but it was to Pittsburgh that Lewis hauled his gear, hired the construction of a fifty-five-foot keelboat, and headed down the Ohio in August

1803. That river was no trackless waste and did not need mapping or exploring, but the trip provided an arduous journey—a breaking-in period for the boat and the man. Lewis wrote often to Jefferson, as if reluctant to break away from the person so singlehandedly responsible for what was about to happen to him.

From Wheeling he wrote of the struggle to get a negligent and heavy-drinking boat-builder to complete his work on the craft. By departure time, the last day of August, water in the Ohio was so low that Lewis had to send part of his cargo ahead by wagon. "On many bars the water in the deepest part does not exceed six inches." He said he was averaging about twelve miles a day, but on some days could not travel more than four or five.[44]

At Cincinnati he received letters from Clark describing the actions he was taking in the Louisville area and discussing the recruitment of soldiers. He sent a long report to Jefferson on his visit to the Big Bone Lick, a deposit of prehistoric animal bones in Boone County, Ky., southwest of present Covington. He asked for more smallpox vaccine, believing that his supply might have lost its potency.[45]

Jefferson answered Lewis's Ohio River letters in one long response, enclosing copies of the treaties dealing with Louisiana and extracts from the journal of Jean Baptiste Truteau, who had lived among the Indians of the Missouri. He also enclosed a copy of his *Account of Louisiana,* just off the press.[46]

Clark met Lewis joyfully at Louisville and presented for his approval nine young recruits he had selected for intelligence, daring, and willingness to tackle the unknown. Lewis may already have recruited one or more men on his way down the Ohio, and others would be chosen from soldiers serving at frontier posts. By December the growing band had visited Fort Massac, turned northward into the Mississippi, stopped at Fort Kaskaskia, and finally reached the St. Louis area. For Lewis, who had come so laboriously from Pittsburgh, and for Clark, who had done an incredible amount of work to prepare for the journey, the expedition had already begun.

• At the Staging Ground •

To understand the situation in St. Louis, and the decision of Lewis and Clark to spend the first winter on the American side of the Mississippi, two facts are essential. First, although Spain had retroceded the Louisiana Territory to France in 1800, French officials had never taken over the government—so the governor of Upper Louisiana, soon to meet with Lewis, was Spanish. Second, no word of the Louisiana Purchase agreement with France had as yet reached St. Louis; copies of the treaty sent by Jefferson had not arrived, and Lewis was determined not to speak of the matter until he had an official document to back him up.

On 8 December, Lewis crossed the river and called on Governor Carlos Dehault Delassus. He presented his credentials, including British and French passports, explained the object of his expedition, and asked permission to winter a little way up the Missouri—which joins the Mississippi a few miles above St. Louis. The governor was cordial but correct: Lewis could not ascend the Missouri until some word could be received from higher up. So, on the advice of settlers who lived on the east bank in a small village called Cahokia, Lewis and Clark decided to push on to the mouth of a stream a few miles higher and make winter camp there. Knowing that Delassus would soon have news of the Louisiana Purchase, Lewis agreed with him "that by the ensuing spring all obstructions would be removed to my asscending the Missouri."[47]

At the campsite, Clark made the last entry in the journal that Lewis had started at the beginning of the Ohio trip: "I came to the mouth of a little River Called Wood River. . . . The hunters which I had sent out to examine the Country in Deferent directions, returned with Turkeys and Opossoms and informed me the country was butifull and had great appearance of Gaim."[48]

In a division of labor that was quite sensible, considering the background and temperament of the two men, Lewis decided to headquarter for the winter at Cahokia (possibly boarding with postmaster John Hay), and Clark was to command the Wood River camp and see to the training of the men, the stockpiling of supplies, and the making of their first map. The big keelboat was pulled ashore and the building of huts was started. With recruitment still going on, a detachment from South West Point in Tennessee arrived on 23 December.

When the Christmas revels were over, Lewis sent off his

second report to Jefferson from Cahokia. His early weeks had been spent usefully, and it must have satisfied Jefferson to receive at last a trustworthy account of the situation in St. Louis.

Along the waterfront of the town, the river bluff broke into a plunging scarp of yellowed rock that sharply divided land from water. On the elevation above this horizontal ribbon of limestone, extending for a mile and a half along the shore, ran the three principal streets of St. Louis. First the Grand Rue, then the Rue de l'Eglise, and then the Rue des Granges. Somewhat less than 200 houses sat there, and when first approached by a river traveler they seemed to rest in orderly rows, compact and gleaming white. On closer inspection their orderliness vanished; they were scattered, varied, and often crude. It was the coat of lime that had set them glittering from afar.

Most of the houses were built *poteaux en terre* with upright posts set in the ground and chinked with clay. Some, however, were of stone, of which the most imposing was the galleried, two-story home of Auguste Chouteau in the center of town. Beyond the town were low hills and prairies where cattle and horses foraged. Barely visible on the western horizon was the edge of the hardwood forests. Within this settled area between forest and shore there lived perhaps a thousand persons, more than half of whom were white. The rest were mulattoes, free blacks, and slaves.

St. Louis was not a mean and lowly village. The French residents not born there had come up from New Orleans or down from Canada, and had been building their town on the basis of fur trade since its founding in 1764. Viewing this thriving place, Lewis must surely have realized that his first assignment there was bound to fail. For Jefferson had asked him to inquire into the prospect that these prosperous and busy Frenchmen might trade their town and their homes for land on the east side of the Mississippi, leaving the west side to the Indians. "The advantages of such a policy has ever struck me as being of primary importance to the future prosperity of the Union," Lewis wrote dutifully. No such thing; it was a chimerical idea. "I gave it my earlyest and best attention," he continued, preparing the President for the bad news. And he never really said it could not be done.

I am fully persuaded, that your wishes to withdraw the inhabitants of Louisiana, may in every necessary degree be affected in the course of a few years, provided the gouvernment of the U. States is justly liberal in it's donations. The American emigrants will be much more readily prevailed on to come into this measure than the French, the French may be said almost exclusively to be the slave holder, they own at least five sixths of that property. I fear that the slaves will form a source of some unwillingness in the French to yeald to the wishes of the government. They appear to feel very sensibly a report which has been circulated among them on this subject, that *the Americans would emancipate their slaves immediately on taking possession of the country,* this however false, is sufficient to show the Opinions and disposition of the people on that subject; there appears to be a general objection not only among the French, but even among the Americans not slave holders, to relinquish the right which they claim relative to slavery in it's present unqualifyed shape.[49]

Within a short time, Lewis had met the leading figures of the region: René Auguste Chouteau (a founder of the town) and his half-brother Jean Pierre, heads of a mercantile dynasty; Charles Gratiot, Swiss-born trader and landowner, brother-in-law of the Chouteaus; Manuel Lisa, a Spaniard, soon to become a powerful figure in the Missouri River trade; Antoine Soulard, surveyor-general of Upper Louisiana for the Spanish government, who would later be held over in that post by Jefferson.

Lewis marveled at the ways in which these men and their families had devised a pattern of civilized living under hard circumstances. Once he had witnessed and enjoyed their kind of life, he said no more about their selling out and moving to the wilderness east of the Mississippi. Jefferson never mentioned it again to Lewis, but kept trying for a while, concentrating not on St. Louis but on the less densely settled areas of Upper Louisiana.[50]

Antoine Soulard proved to be cautiously helpful in obtaining census data for Jefferson and geographic information for the expedition. To obtain more facts, Lewis borrowed Jefferson's technique and prepared a questionnaire to circulate among the citizens. What is the present population? How many emigrants from the United States per year? What is the condition of agriculture? What is exported and at what charge? What are your mines and minerals? What are the animals, birds, and fish of Louisiana?[51]

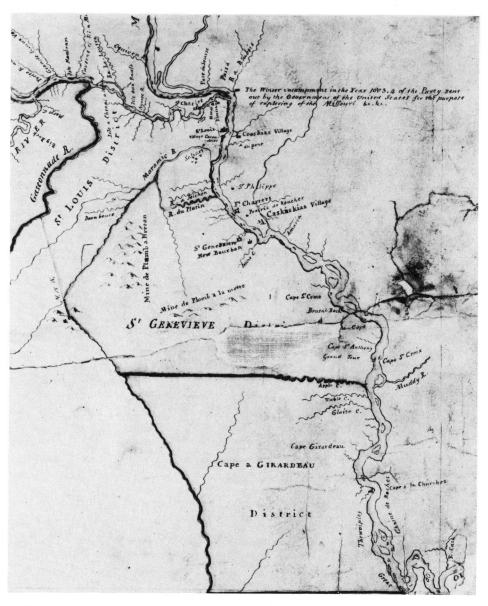

6. Redrawn excerpt from the first map sent home by Lewis and Clark, 1804.

NATIONAL ARCHIVES AND RECORDS SERVICE

Early in the spring, Lewis sent some cuttings of the wild plum and the Osage orange, which Jefferson and his fellow gardeners on the East Coast considered little more than a curiosity. They had missed its greatest potential: it could be made into impenetrable hedges, substituting for rail or stone fences, and Virginians were needing this kind of material. Both Jefferson and Washington imported large quantities of various hedge plants, including many species of hawthorn, when the supply of trees for rails began to dwindle. A generation later, the Osage orange would become the standard fencing plant of the grasslands of the Midwest, where stones and rails were also hard to obtain.[52]

Lewis also sent Jefferson his first zoological specimen. Commonplace today, even a pest in some areas, like many of the creatures that were to amaze Lewis and Clark when first encountered, "this large hare of America . . . is said to be remarkably fleet, and hard to be overtaken on horseback even in their open plains." It was, of course, a jackrabbit.[53]

For his own use in the months ahead, Lewis had obtained a general map of Upper Louisiana done by Soulard; a chart of the Missouri from its mouth to the Mandan Indian country, by James Mackay; and a journal kept by Mackay and John Evans, both of whom had traveled on the Missouri. This material went up to Clark at the Wood River camp, to be added to the expedition's records and to be used in drawing the first map to be sent back to Jefferson.[54]

· Disappointment for Clark ·

In the huts and on the parade ground at Camp Dubois, as Clark sometimes called the Wood River encampment, the men were being tested. While some were rejected, some showed signs of leadership: George Drouillard, hunter and interpreter; John Colter, all-round woodsman; the Field brothers, John Ordway, Patrick Gass, Charles Floyd—all are names revered today by devotees of the expedition's history. Because the camp was not wholly isolated, there were frequent visitors. Settlers from surrounding farms provided food and the women hired out to do laundry. Dr. Warren Cottle, who lived upstream on the Cuivre River, stopped by frequently, and rations were brought up from

St. Louis by an army contractor. Lewis and Clark kept up a steady flow of correspondence. Clark, for example, sent down a "Memorandon of Artecles which may be wanting" that included red lead and oil paint, nails, rawhide, and swivels with which to hang two muskets on the stern of the keelboat.[55]

An unsettled matter was the rank that Clark was to bear. No commission had arrived as the time for departure drew near. Both men expected that Clark would have a captain's commission as Jefferson had promised. Then came the news that might have destroyed the entire operation, had Clark been a man of lesser character. Word came in a letter from Secretary of War Dearborn to Lewis. "The peculiar situation, circumstances and organisation of the Corps of Engineers is such as would render the appointment of Mr. Clark a Captain in that Corps improper—and consequently no appointment above that of a Lieutenant in the Corps of Artillerists could with propriety be given him, which appointment he has recd. and his Commission is herewith enclosed."[56]

Furious, Lewis sent the commission up to Clark along with Dearborn's letter. "I think it will be best to let none of our party or any other persons know any thing about the grade, you will observe that the grade has no effect upon your compensation, which by G——d, shall be equal to my own."[57]

The men have gone down in history as "the two captains." Neither left any record of Clark's immediate reaction. In certain official communications that he prepared during the expedition, he signed himself as "Wm. Clark Capt., &c." There was more than pride involved; if he was to command—especially in case something happened to Lewis—he had to have authority, not only in the eyes of his men but in his dealings with fur traders and Indian chiefs along the way. After the expedition he would turn in his commission with no hostile comment; but when questioned about his feelings, upon receipt of the lesser rank, he would reply to Nicholas Biddle: "I did not think myself very well treated as I did not get the appointment which was promised me. As I was not disposed to make any noise about the business have never mentioned the particulars to any one, and must request you not to mention my disapointment & the Cause to any one."[58]

Jefferson's behavior in the matter is subject to criticism. Obviously, he could not appoint army officers without the advice and consent of the Senate, and there were army regulations and seniority to be considered. But when Dearborn sent a list of nominations to Jefferson on 24 March, including Clark as second lieutenant, Jefferson sent the list off to the Senate without protest. He offered no explanation to Lewis or Clark. To interpret the matter generously, he may have sent the nomination to the Hill with never a thought of his promise, or without studying the names.

• The Transfer Ceremony •

The residents of St. Louis received word in January that their country had been bought by the United States. Clark gave his version of the situation in a letter to his brother-in-law:

I have postponed writing to you untill this time with a view of haveing something worth informing you relitive to this Country, but have been disaptd. and this hasty scraul will do little more than inform you that I am in tolerable health. I have not been from Camp to any house since my arrival here. It is hourly expected that the American's will take possession of the other side of the Mississippi. All the Inhabitents appear anxious except the people of St. Louis, who are ingaged in the Indian trade which they are doubtfull will be divided, amongst those whome will trade on the best terms. Capt. Amos Stoddard of the Corps of Artillerists, who is now stationed at Kaskaskia is appointed the Commandant of the Upper Louisiana, and to take possession of St. Louis with his Compy. as soon as orders arrive from New Orleans to the Spanish Lt. Govr. to give up possession which is hourly exptd. . . .

The Missouri which mouths imedeately opposet me is the river we intend assending as soon as the weather will permit. This Great River which seems to dispute the preeminence with the Mississippi, coms in at right angles from the West, and forces its great sheets of muddy Ice (which is now running) against the Eastern bank. We are collecting what information we can of this river and its rises so as we may make just Calculations, before we set out.[59]

The transfer which was "hourly exptd." did not occur until 10 March. Lewis signed the cession document, along with Governor Delassus, Captain Stoddard, Soulard, and Gratiot. To provide a new government for the District of Louisiana, it was attached for the time to Indiana Territory. But the only American official in charge, while Lewis and Clark were preparing to embark, was Amos Stoddard, now elevated from commander of a single company at Kaskaskia to temporary governor of a vast and almost empty land.

· Spanish Countermeasures ·

Nemesio Salcedo was commandant-general of the Internal Provinces of New Spain, with headquarters in Chihuahua. To command so huge a region with communications so poor was manifestly impossible, but he tried. For the next several years he was to be constantly preoccupied with the ambitious Americans. Not only were they insisting that the boundaries of the Purchase were much more extensive than Salcedo and other Spaniards believed, but they were attempting to push their explorations even beyond the limits of their own claims.

Now Salcedo had received a suggestion from New Orleans that seemed incredibly difficult to execute. He was advised that "Mr. Merry Weather Lewis," often to be called just "Captain Merry" by the Spanish, intended to "penetrate the Missouri River in order to fulfill the commission which he has of making discoveries and observations." "The only means," the letter continued, "which presents itself is to arrest Captain Merry Weather and his party, which cannot help but pass through the nations neighboring New Mexico, its presidios or rancherias."[60]

The Spanish decision to intercept Lewis and Clark came precisely at a time when General James Wilkinson, now stationed in New Orleans, was conniving with those officials for profit. In March he prepared a dossier on recent American actions, for the guidance of Spanish officials, which contained this sentence: "An express ought immediately to be sent to the governor of Santa Fe, and another to the captain-general of Chihuaga, in order that they may detach a sufficient body of chasseurs to intercept Captain Lewis and his party, who are on the Missouri River, and force them to retire or take them prisoners."[61]

When Salcedo received news of the expedition, in Chihuahua, five months had passed since Lewis's arrival in St. Louis, and two months since Casa Calvo had dispatched his warning. Still, it was necessary to attempt a countermove. Salcedo ordered the governor of New Mexico, Fernando de Chacón, to enlist the aid of the Comanches or other tribes in reconnoitering the Missouri. "Nothing would be more useful than the apprehension of Merry," Salcedo said, "and even though I realize it is not an easy undertaking, chance might proportion things in such a way that it might be successful. . . ."[62]

Chacón responded by sending Pedro Vial, a French explorer and trader who knew the Missouri and Red rivers thoroughly, had forged overland routes from San Antonio and Natchitoches to Santa Fe, and then had established a trail from Santa Fe to St. Louis. Vial left Santa Fe with a detachment of soldiers, in search of news about Lewis and Clark, on 1 August 1804, and spent a month traveling to the Pawnee villages in central Nebraska. By this time Lewis and Clark were near the Nebraska–South Dakota border and well out of danger.

The second attempt to intercept the party was made by Chacón's successor, Governor Joaquín del Real Alencaster, who dispatched Vial to the Pawnees and other tribes near the Missouri in the fall of 1805. The mission failed when the party was attacked by unidentified Indians near the junction of the Purgatoire and Arkansas rivers in present Colorado. A third attempt was made by Vial, in the spring of 1806, but was terminated within a month for unknown reasons.[63] The Spanish response to Lewis and Clark was inadequate and ill-timed, but their forays were to become better organized and more precisely scheduled when later American expeditions took the field.

• "Under a Jentle Brease" •

By mid-May, Lewis and Clark were fully ready to head their flotilla up the Missouri. They had channeled as much information as they could to Jefferson, done what was possible to ease the transition of governments, and now knew as much as any American about the upper reaches of the Missouri and the tribes that roamed there.

Continuing an old tradition, Lewis had sent a delegation of Osages to Jefferson with gifts, complaints, questions, and the intention of signing a treaty of amity and alliance. He had given Amos Stoddard signed authority to act as his agent, a task that changes of personnel in St. Louis would later pass to Charles Gratiot and then to Pierre Couteau.

The record gives us little by which to sense the excitement of the party as the day of departure approached. Lewis's last letter to Jefferson was a routine description of specimens being carried by the Osage delegation. Clark wrote to brother-in-law William Croghan to introduce Pierre Chouteau, who was chaperoning the Indians. Of the enlisted men who could write, only Sergeant Ordway has left an expression of the eagerness and anxiety that gripped the camp. "Honored Parence. I now embrace this opportunity of writing to you once more to let you know where I am and where I am going. . . . I am now on an expedition to the westward, with Capt. Lewis and Capt. Clark, who are appointed by the President of the united States to go on an expedition through the interior parts of North America . . . and I am So happy as to be one of them pick'd Men from the armey, and I and all the party are if we live to Return, to Receive our Discharge when ever we return again to the united States if we chuse it. . . . We are to Receive a great Reward for this expidition, when we Return."[64]

Not all the men who filled the Wood River camp in the final days were scheduled to complete the expedition. A corporal and six privates had been detached to accompany the party only as far as the Mandan villages, then bring the keelboat back to St. Louis the following spring. Also hired for the same period were several French *voyageurs* or watermen, who would assist in getting the boats up the fast-flowing Missouri. Ordway said the party—meaning the permanent party—consisted of twenty-five men. By departure time the number of permanent members had grown to twenty-seven plus Lewis and Clark, and the whole party probably numbered forty-seven. One of these was York, a slave whom Clark had inherited in 1799 from his father. (Two other colorful figures, Toussaint Charbonneau and his wife, Sacagawea, would not be joining the expedition until they were encountered at the Mandan villages during the winter.) Completing the roster was a black Newfoundland dog named Scannon, perhaps brought by Lewis all the way from Washington.

On 14 May 1804, the heavily laden keelboat and two smaller pirogues, accompanied by men on horseback following the shoreline, set out from the Wood River camp. Lewis was to come from St. Louis to join the group at St. Charles, a short way up the Missouri, a week later. As the expedition crossed the Mississippi and traversed those first exciting miles up the Missouri, Clark began a journal of adventure and discovery that has become an American classic.

"I Set out at 4 oClock P.M., in the presence of many of the neighbouring inhabitents, and proceeded on under a jentle brease up the Missouri."

NOTES

1. DILLON is the conventionally cited biography of Lewis; it contains no annotation. BAKELESS, an excellent work, appeared too early (1947) to benefit from recent scholarly studies. L & C LETTERS is of little help for Lewis's early years, as it deals primarily with correspondence generated by the Lewis and Clark expedition.

2. A few letters from Lewis to his mother, written from army camps, are in the Missouri Historical Society, St. Louis. His regular army career is cataloged briefly in HEITMAN and shows him serving in the First Regiment continuously from 1796 to March 1807; but a roster drawn by Alexander Hamilton, adjutant and inspector, lists him as a second lieutenant in the Fourth Infantry as of Oct. 1799.

3. An unsigned note in Wayne's hand, 2 Nov. 1796, granting Lewis's furlough, is in the Historical Society of Pennsylvania, Philadelphia. For his mission to Washington: "I certify that there is due to Ensign Meriwether Lewis the sum of Twenty Dollars & 50/100 being the balance of his account of Expenses of himself, a dragoon & servant from Headquarters of the Army [Greenville, Ohio] with despatches from the Commander in Chief [i.e. the commanding general, Wayne] to this City," signed by William Simmons and addressed to the Secretary of War, 5 Dec. 1796, copy in Missouri Historical Society. Lewis wrote Nicholas Lewis 2 May 1797 from Charlottesville, saying he was going to Kentucky and then to Georgia. From Shelbyville, Ky., he wrote Mrs. Marks 24 July 1797, reporting that he was setting out for Georgia at once. For his Fort Pickering assignment, see BAKELESS, 70, and DILLON, 24. In a memoir written for inclusion in BIDDLE, the 1814 narrative of the Lewis and Clark expedition, TJ recalled that Lewis

had applied in 1792 to carry out the expedition that was assigned to Michaux. Lewis was only eighteen at the time, and there are enough discrepancies in Jefferson's account to cast some doubt on his recollection. TJ relates that the idea for the 1793 expedition was his, when actually it appears to have been Michaux's; and he says that Lewis was "stationed at Charlottesville on the recruiting service" at the time, when actually he had not yet joined the army. There are no corroborating documents. See the memoir in L & C LETTERS, 2:589.

4. Misc. Collections, LC. When the letter was written, Claiborne was stationed at Fort Massac on the lower Ohio. In a postscript, Lewis casually remarks that he has been promoted to captain.

5. TJ to Burwell, 26 March 1804, LC. This letter, and the one from Lewis to Claiborne previously cited, are reprinted in L & C LETTERS. Original sources are usually cited in the present volume, except where editor Jackson himself has added useful material in annotating the L & C LETTERS.

6. TJ to Wilkinson, 23 Feb. 1801, and to Lewis, 23 Feb. 1801, LC. Lewis was in Pittsburgh when he received TJ's letter. He acknowledged it and accepted the offer 10 March, making immediate arrangements to leave for Washington. On the road, a lame horse and difficult traveling after spring rains delayed him, and he did not reach Washington until 1 April. He turned his paymaster records over to his successor, Lieutenant Ninian Pinkney, of Maryland.

7. The roster, dated 24 July 1801, begins with fol. 19697 in Jefferson's papers, LC. For a discussion of the document and Lewis's relation to it, see JACKSON [7]. For a briefer discussion, in which the handwriting is also identified as Lewis's, see CUNNINGHAM, 127.

8. The list is dated 5 Jan. 1802. An eye trained to recognize Lewis's hand can find many other routine documents of his in Jefferson's papers for 1801–3. Examples: a list of prisoners in the Washington jail as of 29 March 1802; an extract of a letter from W. C. C. Claiborne to Thomas J. David, 6 March 1802; four pages of Benjamin Latrobe's report on the cost of a naval arsenal, 4 Dec. 1802—all in LC.

9. See L & C LETTERS, 2:677–84, for excerpts from Dickerson's diary, published there for the first time (and not in the first edition). Lewis visited Dickerson again in 1803 and 1807, apparently after they had met at TJ's dinner table on 19 April 1802. Congress adjourned in May, TJ went off to Monticello, and Lewis took advantage of the slack time to make his first visit to Philadelphia. The comment to Ferdinand Claiborne is from Lewis's 7 March 1801 letter, excerpted earlier.

10. Wistar to TJ, 8 Jan. 1802, LC.

11. MACKENZIE, 349.

12. Cheetham's bill for Mackenzie and the Arrowsmith map, dated 22 Feb. 1802, LC, shows 21 June 1802 as the date of the order. Cheetham was also a journalist, publishing a biweekly New York newspaper, *The Republican Watch-Tower.*

13. For Barton's trip, see MC ATEE. See also TJ to Barton, 27 Feb. 1803, LC: "What follows in this letter is strictly confidential," etc. Barton seems to have been the first member of TJ's circle of Philadelphia friends to be advised of the forthcoming expedition.

14. Irujo to Pedro Cevallos, 2 Dec. 1802, NASATIR, 2:712–14. The translation is Nasatir's. Although Irujo was later to fall out with the Jefferson administration, he was on friendly terms at this time, was married to the daughter of Governor Thomas McKean of Pennsylvania, and had even helped Jefferson to find a cook (MALONE, 4:97n). Irujo's name was often spelled Yrujo, and after he became a marqués a few years later, it was Casa Irujo or Casa Yrujo.

15. NASATIR, 2:712–14.

16. NASATIR, 2:715–16. The originals of this and the preceding letter are in the Archivo Histórico Nacional, Madrid.

17. Although no Spanish passport has been found, and TJ believed eventually that none was required, a French trader who met Lewis and Clark claimed he saw passports and letters of recommendation "from the French, Spanish, and British ministers" (MASSON, 1:303).

18. Thornton to Lord Hawkesbury, 9 March 1803, Public Record office, London, FO5/38, pp. 56–59. The LC has a transcript in the Foreign Office Records. The passport itself exists only as a French transcript in the Archivo General de Indias, Seville. It is reprinted in L & C LETTERS, 1:19.

19. Pichon to TJ, 4 March 1803, and transcript of Pichon to Talleyrand, 4 March 1803, LC. The passport is presented in transcript, the original being in Correspondance Politique, Affaires Étrangères, E.-U., 55:320. For an English translation, see L & C LETTERS, 1:20.

20. Gallatin's suggestion, undated, was received by TJ on 21 Nov. 1802. Source of the figure $2,500 is an undated memorandum in Lewis's hand, probably written while TJ was preparing his message; it itemizes such needs as mathematical instruments, camp equipage, Indian presents, and the hire of guides and interpreters. All these documents are in LC, including the confidential message.

21. Lincoln to TJ, 17 April 1803, and TJ to Rodney, 13 July 1803, LC.

22. TJ to Lewis, 13 Jan. 1804, LC. Lewis was in St. Louis by this time, spending the first winter of the expedition there. TJ's concern with criticism from the Federalist press often led him to contemplate

excesses. When such journalists were offending him early in 1803, he suggested to Thomas McKean a selective prosecution of the "most prominent offenders," taking care not to make it look like a persecution. TJ to McKean, 19 Feb. 1803, LC.

23. Lincoln to TJ, 17 April 1803, and Madison to TJ, 14 April 1803, LC.

24. Gallatin to TJ, 13 April 1803, LC. In the same letter he suggested that Lewis might spend the first winter somewhere on the lower reaches of the Missouri rather than in the St. Louis area—an idea that TJ later overruled.

25. See ALLEN [2], 97–102. At least one of Lewis's annotations on the map could not have been made until he had reached the Mandans on the upper Missouri.

26. TJ to Gallatin, rec'd 21 Nov. 1802, and Lewis to TJ, 29 May 1803, LC. Of the tracings Lewis wrote, "They were taken in a haisty manner, but I believe they will be found sufficiently accurate to be of service in composing the map . . . the maps attached to Vancouver's voyage cannot be procured separately from that work, which is both too costly, and too weighty, for me either to purchase or carry."

27. See Gallatin to Frémont, 15 Sept. 1847, and Frémont to Gallatin, 10 Oct. 1847, Gallatin Papers, New-York Historical Society, New York City. Frémont promised to prepare a map (not found) of his routes in the Great Basin country for Gallatin's use.

28. References to Lewis and *Clark* are necessary, even though Clark has not yet entered the story. In fact, we cannot be sure exactly when Jefferson and Lewis conceived the idea of adding a co-commander to the expedition.

29. TJ to Cheetham, 17 June 1803, LC.

30. JACKSON [1].

31. The cipher, in LC, is reproduced in L & C LETTERS, 2:10. For notes on its operation, see "Method of using Mr. Patterson's cypher," fol. 22130 in Jefferson's papers, LC.

32. TJ to Patterson, 3 March 1803, to Rush, 28 Feb. 1803, to Wistar, 28 Feb. 1803, and to Barton, 27 Feb. 1803, all in LC. His letter to Ellicott of 26 Feb. has not survived; an acknowledgment from Ellicott is dated 6 March 1803, LC.

33. TJ had complained that he had heard nothing from Lewis since leaving for Monticello on 7 March (TJ to Lewis, 23 April 1803, LC). Adding a few assignments to those he already had given Lewis, TJ asked for "a Leopard or tyger skin, such as the covers of our saddles were cut out of," and the robe of the Peruvian sheep or llama. By this time, Lewis's letter of 20 April (LC) was on the way to reassure TJ.

34. TJ to Lewis Harvie, 22 April 1803, LC. Within less than a year, Harvie had an assignment to France and was succeeded as secretary by William Burwell.

35. Dickerson's diary in L & C LETTERS, 2:677–84.

36. Much of the information about Lewis's Philadelphia purchases is in L & C JOURNALS, 7:231–46, but not the vouchers from private vendors. All surviving documents are in a single consolidated file, NARG 92, Box 560A. L & C LETTERS, 1:69–99, contains them all, with annotation and identifications not found elsewhere.

37. Lewis to Clark, 19 June 1803, Missouri Historical Society. Clark had been living for many years in Louisville, Ky., and at Clarksville, across the Ohio in Indiana Territory.

38. Clark to Lewis, 18 July 1803, LC. His first draft, with several changes in wording, is in the Missouri Historical Society.

39. Lewis to Clark, 3 Aug. 1803, Missouri Historical Society. "Write & direct to me at Cincinnatti," he added in a marginal note.

40. The last sentence in this paragraph appears in smaller letters, as if added later.

41. This sentence is inserted in smaller letters as if added later. TJ's reference to the security of the party may have given rise to the common belief that the Osages who left St. Louis for Washington in the spring of 1804 were "hostages" for the safety of the expedition.

42. This paragraph and the preceding one were written vertically in the righthand margin, as insertions.

43. The document presented here is a draft. TJ also retained a duplicate of his fair copy, which is in LC. Passages in brackets were deleted by TJ.

44. Lewis to TJ, 8 Sept. 1803, LC. Lewis left Wheeling on 9 Sept., leaving behind Dr. William Ewing Patterson, son of the Philadelphia professor, who had expressed a desire to go along. Lewis agreed to take him as far as the Mississippi and await TJ's permission if he could be ready by 3 P.M. the following day. "He thought he could and instantly set about it," Lewis wrote, but Patterson failed to meet the deadline (LEWIS & ORDWAY, 39–40). In addition to his correspondence, Lewis was keeping a daily journal, cited here together with Sergeant John Ordway's because the two were published together in 1916.

45. Lewis to TJ, 13 Sept. 1803, LC; Lewis to Clark, 28 Sept. 1803, Missouri Historical Society; Lewis to TJ, 3 Oct. 1803, LC. TJ would acquire many fossil bones from the Big Bone Lick as a result of Clark's work there in 1807, the greater part of the collection being destined for the Museum of Natural History in Paris. "The collection was probably the most extensive that was ever seen together at one display. As they

lay on the floor of one of the great saloons in the President's [in Washington], the present narrator surveyed them in company with the owner . . ." (MITCHILL, 30).

46. TJ to Lewis, 16 Nov. 1803, LC. "Your friends & acquaintances here & in Albemarle are well as far as I have heard . . . present my friendly salutations to Mr. Clarke, & accept them affectionately yourself." All his life TJ spelled Clark's name Clarke.

47. Lewis to TJ, 19 Dec. 1803, Historical Society of Pennsylvania, was Lewis's first report upon arriving at Cahokia. The governor's version of the meeting is Delassus to the Marqués de Casa Calvo and Juan Manuel de Salcedo, 9 Dec. 1803, NASATIR, 2:719–20. Casa Calvo was military governor of all Louisiana, stationed in New Orleans, and Salcedo was a Spanish military official there.

48. LEWIS & ORDWAY, 75–76. Clark began his own journal 13 Dec. 1803, hereafter designated as FIELD NOTES. While the origin of the name Wood River is obscure, it appears that Clark or someone who did not understand the meaning of the French *à* in the Mississippi Valley mistranslated *Rivière à Dubois*. Actually the little stream was named for a Frenchman named Dubois (MC DERMOTT [1], 144). At that time the mouth of the stream was directly opposite the mouth of the Missouri. Today the Missouri joins the Mississippi farther to the south.

49. Extract from Lewis to TJ, 28 Dec. 1803, Historical Society of Pennsylvania.

50. See FOLEY and his sources. Moses Austin, developer of lead mines in Missouri, warned Gallatin against pressing for removal, saying that "the United States will have cause to regret the moment they became possessed of Louisiana, such a project can never be effected but with immense expence and trouble and after all the exertions of the Government would prove abortive (Austin to Gallatin, [Aug. 1806?], FOLEY, 15).

51. A copy of the questionnaire in French, addressed to Auguste Chouteau, survives in BILLON, 384–85.

52. Lewis to TJ, 26 March 1804, LC. The Osage orange thrives in TJ's old neighborhood as an ornamental tree. Several large specimens grow on the grounds of Morea, a guest house at the University of Virginia. The slips sent by Lewis were forwarded to Philadelphia nurseryman Bernard McMahon, who planted some in front of his store on Fourth Street. Today, a row of the trees beside the adjacent St. Peter's Episcopal Church, at Fourth and Spruce streets, almost certainly dates from that time (EWAN, 170, and personal confirmation by Harold B. Billian, of Villanova, Pa.).

53. Lewis to TJ, 26 March 1804, LC. Lewis said the hare was found

on the upper part of the Arkansas and in the country south and west of that river, to "the mountains which seperate us from New Mexico."

54. The maps and journals obtained by Lewis in the final weeks before the departure up the Missouri were vital, but their nature and provenance are too complicated to be dealt with here. See ALLEN [2], 140–77 *passim,* and L & C LETTERS, 1:135–36, 193–94, and *passim.*

55. Clark to Lewis, [April 1804], Missouri Historical Society.

56. Dearborn to Lewis, 26 March 1803, NARG 107, letters sent, 2:202. Dearborn sent the letter to the commanding officer at Kaskaskia, asking him to forward it by special messenger. Clark's date of rank was 26 March, and thus he was not allowed the seniority that would have accrued had the commission been backdated to the time of his agreement to join the expedition.

57. Lewis to Clark, 6 May 1804, Missouri Historical Society. Clark thus received the news about a week before the expedition was scheduled to depart.

58. Clark to Biddle, 15 Aug. 1811, L & C LETTERS, 2:571–72. At that time, Biddle was preparing an account of the expedition for publication (see BIDDLE), and had written Clark for additional information.

59. Clark to William Croghan, 15 Jan. 1804, Missouri Historical Society. Croghan was married to Clark's sister Lucy, and had built an estate in Louisville known as Locust Grove.

60. Salcedo to Cevallos, 8 May 1804, enclosing Casa Calvo and Salcedo to Cevallos, 5 March 1804, in NASATIR, 2:729–35.

61. Wilkinson's "Reflections on Louisiana," originally attributed to Vicente Folch, governor of West Florida, is in ROBERTSON, 2:323–47.

62. COOK [2], 457. Warren Cook's account of Spanish attempts to intercept Lewis and Clark is the latest and fullest. See his pp. 460–90.

63. COOK [2], 477–83, believes that a later attempt allegedly directed at Zebulon Pike's expedition was actually a fourth try at intercepting Lewis and Clark.

64. Ordway to his parents, photostat, Oregon Historical Society, Portland. As published in the *Oregon Historical Quarterly,* 23 (1922), 268–69, the letter was addressed to Stephen Ordway, Hebron, N. H.

CHAPTER EIGHT

An Odyssey in Bitter Snows

Akeelboat was a useful but ungainly craft. Load it with ten or twenty tons of cargo and it was a faithful, wallowing drudge. Arm it with a swivel gun, set a guard with firearms at the gunwales, and it became a little warship. Navigating it downstream was easy if you kept an eye out for submerged logs, but going upstream there was no ideal way to keep it moving. If the wind was fair you ran up a sail. When the wind failed you broke out the iron-pointed setting poles and started pushing. If the bottom was deep enough, you could row. If the current was too swift for rowing you could bend a forty-fathom length of cordelling cable to the mast and put the crew ashore to haul on the line. Failing all this, you could tie up to the bank and wait for the wind to rise and blow fair.

The Lewis and Clark keelboat rode with a small artillery piece at the bow, a cabin aft, and lockers along each side that could serve as breastworks when the heavy lids were raised. Her escort consisted of the two pirogues—one red, one white—flat-bottomed craft of smaller size, one of which required six oars and the other seven. A writer partial to John Ledyard's plan of traveling unencumbered complains that Lewis and Clark were hampered and "encysted" in their equipage and supplies. She is quite mistaken; those tons of food, tools, and Indian gifts carefully baled and stowed were to save the expedition, not endanger it.[1]

The lower reaches of the Missouri were much traveled. The names of the creeks, islands, and prominent landforms were mainly French, easily obtained from maps or information provided by the *voyageurs* who accompanied the entourage. The confluence with the Osage River, a stream that led traders off to the lands of the Osage and Kansas tribes, was for those times a bustling intersection. The same was nearly true for the mouth of the Kansas, farther upstream, and to a lesser extent the mouth of the Platte in what is now southeastern Nebraska. To have navigated past the mouth of the Platte was the riverman's equivalent of crossing the equator or slipping over the international dateline.

· The Expedition as a Military Detachment ·

If there is an antidote to the infectious habit of considering the Lewis and Clark expedition a kind of high-risk romp, a bunch of guys out camping and collecting, it is the realization that Lewis and Clark were army men going by the book. And the book was the collection of dicta and proscriptions commonly called the "Rules and Articles of War." Clark wrote in his orderly book at Wood River: "No Man is to absent himself from Camp on any pretence what ever without permission from the Comdgn. officer present."[2] Although there were French civilian boatmen in the group, and some new recruits from Kentucky who might not know the army routines, the core of the detachment was a group of men who knew the army from the vantage point of a private earning five dollars a month. Such soldiers knew that military discipline was not suspended when a detachment marched out of a garrison and took to the trail.

Lewis and Clark built three forts sufficient in size and durability to house and protect their men during three winter encampments. Once established, those forts became military posts with routines laid down by regulation and tradition. Some adaptation of the rules was of course necessary when the expedition was traveling, but the men were soldiers still in the terminology of their daily assignments and in the performance expected by their captains. If the typical army unit of 1804 was a one-company fort on the western borders of the United States, the expedition can be considered near the norm. In numbers the men with Lewis and Clark fell not far short of the usual strength of some one-company posts, especially posts decimated by desertions, disease, and scanty reenlistment.[3]

At the garrisons to which most of the Lewis and Clark men had become accustomed, life was a series of responses to drumbeats. Taps for reveille were beaten at daylight (when a sentinel could see clearly for a thousand yards), and reveille was beaten twenty minutes later. After reveille the guards ceased challenging, the wicket gate was opened, the morning gun was fired to alert any drowsy men who had slept through reveille, and no man fit for duty was allowed to remain in his bunk. The whiskey drum (the first of two) sounded just before breakfast and the men fell into line for a half gill of liquor. The breakfast call, "Peas upon a Trencher," sounded at 7 A.M. in summer and 8 A.M. in winter. After a day dominated by the drum calls, the most demanding of which was "Fatigue," which sent everyone off to work, retreat was beaten at sunset. Colors and flags were struck and the evening gun fired. The men paraded at arms and usually witnessed at least one flogging. They answered to roll call, heard instructions for the next day's fatigue parties and any daily orders then in effect. Often they listened to the reading of a section from the rules and articles of war. Then the gate of the fort slammed shut and the day was all but ended: tattoo, then taps, and the officer of the day made sure that all men were in their bunks. The sentinels began calling "all's well" to one another throughout the night.[4]

A regimen very close to this had governed the lives of the Lewis and Clark men; they expected no more or less upon the river. They knew exactly what they would be fed when there was food, exactly how much whiskey they would receive while it lasted, and almost exactly what would happen to them if they provoked the thumbs-down verdict of a court-martial.

Although they were superior soldiers for their time, nine of the twenty-four privates considered to belong to the permanent party had been court-martialed before the expedition reached its wintering ground in the fall. Privates John Shields, John Colter, and Robert Frazer had been tried for misconduct and acquitted while the expedition was still at Wood River. Three days after departure, as a result of a ball given by the citizens of St. Charles on the lower Missouri, Werner, Hall, and Collins were tried for being absent without leave, and Collins faced additional charges of unbecoming behavior and disrespectful language. All were found guilty by a court-martial consisting of enlisted men, Werner and Hall receiving sentences of twenty-five lashes and

7. Route of the Lewis and Clark expedition, 1804–6.

Collins fifty. "The Commanding Officer approves of the proceedings & Decision of the Court martial and orders that the punishment of John Collins take place this evening at Sun Set in the Presence of the Party. The punishment ordered to be inflicted on William Warner & Hugh Hall, is remitted under the assurance arriseing from a confidence which the Commanding officer has of the Sincereity of the recommendation [for leniency] of the Court."[5]

The importance of whiskey to the morale of the men is seen in the next court-martial episode. On 29 June, Collins was charged with dispensing whiskey while it was in his care as a sentinel, and Hall was charged with drinking it. The court of enlisted men, obviously aware that the kegs of good Monongahela whiskey could not last throughout the expedition, handed down a severe sentence. Collins received one hundred lashes, Hall fifty.[6]

The next offense was much more serious. On 12 July Alexander Willard was charged with falling asleep at his post, and because this was a capital crime punishable by death, both Lewis and Clark sat on the court. Willard pled guilty to lying down but not to sleeping. He was found guilty of the whole charge and sentenced to receive one hundred lashes in four installments, the punishment to be administered at sunset by members of the guard then on duty.

Two other courts-martial were to cause the defendants to be physically punished and dismissed from the permanent party, destined to be sent home. Moses B. Read was convicted of desertion in August and John Newman of mutinous expression in October.[7]

Trial and punishment were the most spectacular aspects of army discipline, but every hour of the day contained lesser indications. The detachment was divided into squads, the squads into messes. Lewis kept an orderly book and other required records, for submission to the War Department later. When the boats got under way at daybreak, flankers were posted and hunters sent out. A system of signaling was devised for communication between shore parties and the boats, probably involving the tin trumpets listed in the invoices (there is no mention of drum signals). Upon coming to in late afternoon, near a bank or sandbar, the first precaution was to post out the guard. Food was prepared in the evening by the cooks (who were exempt from most other duties except rowing), to be served while under way on the following day. Besides items from the standard army ration,[8] the cooks were issued three basic menus in rotation: hominy and lard one day; salt pork and flour the next; cornmeal and pork the next. No salt pork was issued when the hunters had provided fresh meat.

The keelboat was a small military base in itself. Precise handling was required to get more than fourteen miles of sailing out of the lumbering craft, as on 9 August when the expedition was traversing the Iowa shoreline.[9] The messes of the three sergeants formed the crew of the vessel. When the boat was under way, one sergeant was stationed at the helm, one in the center at the rear of the starboard locker, and one at the bow.

The Sergt. at the helm, shall steer the boat, and see that the baggage on the quarterdeck is properly arranged and stowed away . . . The Sergt. at the center will command the guard, manage the sails, see that the men at the oars do their duty . . . he will keep a good lookout for the mouths of all rivers, creeks, Islands and other remarkable places . . . he will attend to the issues of sperituous liquors . . . it shall be his duty also to post a centinel on the bank, near the boat whenever we come too and halt in the course of the day. . . . It shall be the duty of the sergt. at the bow, to keep a good look out for all danger which may approach, either of the enimy, or obstructions which may present themselves to the passage of the boat; of the first he will notify the Sergt. at the center, who will communicate the information to the commanding officers, and of the second or obstructions to the boat he will notify the Sergt. at the helm. . . .[10]

A somber manifestation of military tradition occurred 20 August upon the death of Sergeant Charles Floyd. He had been ill for several days and died near present Sioux City, Iowa, probably of a ruptured appendix. He was buried with military honors, which meant that his comrades paraded without arms while a select guard fired salvos over the new grave. "This Man," Clark wrote in his journal, "at all times gave us proofs of his firmness and Determined resolution to doe Service to this Countrey and honor to himself."[11]

· To the Mandans for the Winter ·

Lewis and Clark ran the military side of the expedition with aplomb, secure in the growing confidence they felt in ranking sergeant John Ordway and in the general shaping-up of the men. The captains were free to turn more fully to Jeffersonian pursuits. As they approached the domain of the Teton Sioux, they already had counseled with the Oto, Missouri, Omaha, and Yankton Sioux, all Siouan tribes. They had gathered Indian vocabularies and given out medals, flags, and gifts. Certain chiefs had been dispatched downriver to join delegations bound for Washington. The captains had collected a few plants new to science, such as rabbit brush, pink cleome, and buffaloberry, but their greatest contributions to botany were still ahead. They had encountered some animals scarcely heard of in those days but common today, such as the pronghorn, coyote, prairie dog, and mule deer. They had collected the badger in the belief that it was new among American mammals, unaware that it had been described from Canada in 1778.[12]

Besides naming many new topographical features, they had made useful geographic notes, astronomical observations, and mineralogical findings. Lewis gathered and described specimens with apparent confidence; Clark sensed the limitations they both must have felt. "What a field for a Botents [botanist] and a natirless [naturalist]."[13]

The weeks of river travel had been made less arduous by days spent ashore making rope, mending oars, jerking meat, dressing skins, drying out wet cargo and sails, repairing arms, and inspecting ammunition. They had killed their first bison and would encounter them again and again in unthinkably large herds. Lewis and Clark were hardened plainsmen now and ready for their first unsettling experience with a new kind of Indian.

By far the largest tribe along the upper Missouri was the assemblage of bands known as the Teton Sioux. Traders estimated their numbers at about 11,000. They were aggressive, loved intertribal warfare, and were a constant threat to French traders from St. Louis. Weaker tribes in the region feared them—the Omahas downstream, the Arikaras and Mandans farther north. Sergeant Gass counted eighty lodges of about ten persons each at the village visited by the expedition.

Beginning on 24 September, Lewis and Clark bluffed their way through a four-day encounter. Although warned in St. Louis about the Tetons, the captains were only expecting their usual routine: distribute gifts and certificates to the chiefs, spread the gospel of the new Great Father in Washington, and proceed upstream. But the Tetons, who promptly stole the last hunting horse, had their own set of procedures. During several exchanges of visits they threatened to terminate the expedition, then turned nice and carried Lewis and Clark separately to a council site on painted buffalo robes. There was a translation difficulty. All in all, the experience was a critical one, with Clark at one point drawing his sword, and later threatening to light the fuse of the bow gun, which was charged with sixteen musket balls. "These are the vilest miscreants of the savage race," Lewis wrote later, declaring that the upper Missouri would be of little use to the United States until the Teton Sioux were "reduced to order."[14]

Although the affair was something of a standoff, it was an American victory in the eyes of the neighboring tribes, putting a new face on the forthcoming visits of the expedition to the upstream Indians.

The Arikaras greeted the expedition amiably—although they were to become the harassing force on the upper Missouri in the years immediately following—and the captains made valuable observations during their visit. The chief whom they persuaded to go to Washington the following spring was an astute and intelligent man. His death from disease while on the journey was to become a factor in the later truculence of the Arikaras. Like other tribes along the route, they were captivated by the black skin and kinky hair of York, Clark's servant; he played out the role of Strange Being for his own amusement and, as Clark said, "did not lose the opportunity of [displaying] his powers Strength &c."[15]

In late October the expedition reached the country of the Mandans. These relatively fair-skinned people, agricultural and sedentary, with a long record of hospitality to Europeans, lived in two villages below the confluence of the Knife River with the

Missouri. As planned, the explorers reconnoitered the area for a few days, getting acquainted not only with the Mandans but with three villages of Minitaris and Amahamis a little way up the Knife; then they chose a site for their winter encampment. On the east side of the river, below the first Mandan town and near the future site of Bismarck, N.D., they began to build the rude but serviceable structure they would call Fort Mandan.

They had spent their first winter in the formidable cold and snow of western Illinois and St. Louis. Now they were to reside in the truly wretched weather of a North Dakota winter. Sleds were to be a common means of hauling meat, frostbite would be a common ailment, and Clark would record in disbelief the temperature readings he obtained. During the months of December, January, and February, he noted almost forty days when the thermometer registered below zero. The fluctuating river level and accumulating ice encased the keelboat and the pirogues while snow drifted across their decks. Clearing the ice away from the boats was to become a major operation. At one time the pirogues were icebound to the tops of their gunwales.

· Reporting to Jefferson ·

There had been no direct word of Lewis since he had written Jefferson just before departure, reporting—in a letter which has not survived—that the expedition was leaving St. Louis about the middle of May. Since then Jefferson had relied on the few scraps of rumor and fact that came his way. He had greeted the first delegation of Osages in July, referring to the "beloved man, Capt. Lewis" whom he had sent into the West.[16] Amos Stoddard sent Jefferson some vocabularies of the Iowa and Sioux languages that Lewis had left with him. Someone, perhaps a trader, had seen and talked with the explorers at about the time they were visiting the Oto in early August near the mouth of the Platte. "Two of his men had deserted from him," Jefferson wrote Lewis's brother Reuben. "He had with him 2. boats and about 48 men. He was then setting out up the river. One of his boats & half the men would return from his winter quarters." In January, Jefferson wrote again to Reuben that as of 19 August all was well with the expedition, which would winter with the Mandans.[17]

At Fort Mandan, the captains were trying to think like Jefferson. As soon as the ice broke up, they were sending the weary keelboat downstream with letters, journals, maps, and specimens. To this burden of paperwork was added the need to gather all the intelligence they could about the route ahead. Much of this would be Indian data rendered less reliable by translation; more useful information would come from British traders who came in from the North West Company posts in Canada.[18]

Their relationship with the Mandans was close. Lewis went hunting with a principal chief, Sheheke or Big White, who would join the expedition on its return trip and visit Jefferson in Washington. When a hostile party of Sioux was expected, the expedition turned out to aid the Mandans and fell into a military posture described by Private Joseph Whitehouse: "The Captn. [Clark] formed his men on the S.W. Side of the river Missourie and told them off in Sections, from the right, and Sent out a Noncommissioned Officer and a file of men on Each flank to Reconitere the woods at the distance of neerly One Hundred Yds. from the head of Company."[19]

One of Clark's preoccupations was with the large map he was making for Jefferson and the War Department. Using the base map provided by Gallatin as a guide, he was creating "a connection of the countrey" that was to become a landmark in American cartography (see illus., pp. 174–75 below). Besides information from informants, he was working with two kinds of data: the tried and true collection of headings and distances, so faithfully kept by himself or the sergeant in command of the keelboat, and time-honored by mariners as the system called dead reckoning; and the highly suspect astronomical observations that he and Lewis had been making with the quadrant since the establishment of the Wood River camp a year earlier. Clark had practiced constantly there, and probably was more proficient than Lewis in using the Hadley's quadrant (forerunner of the sextant) brought from Philadelphia. He had a background in surveying that gave him an edge over Lewis. Neither man, however, was to distinguish himself as an astronomical observer.

Latitude was no problem, being determined by a noon observation of the sun—or observations in midmorning and midafternoon—and a few simple calculations. The tough part

8. Clark's 1805 map, sent from the Mandan country. LIBRARY OF CONGRESS

A MAP
of part of the Continent of
North America

Between the 35 and 51 degrees of North
Latitude, and extending from 89 Degrees of
West Longitude to the Pacific Ocean

Compiled from the Authorities of the best
informed travellers by M. Lewis

Note The Missouri River from Fort Mandan
in Lat 47 21 47 N. and in Long. 101 west from
the Meridian of Greenwich, is erected by
Celestial Observation. The Country
West of Fort Mandan is laid down
principally from Indian information.

Copied by Nicholas King
Scale 50 miles to an Inch

was the longitude. Here the captains were handicapped not only by their lack of experience but by the fact that their advisors had taught them to use a difficult method. They employed lunar distances involving the movement of the moon in relation to the sun or another celestial body. The advantage over the other common method, the immersion and emersion of Jupiter's satellites, was that no powerful telescope was required; the small telescope on the quadrant was sufficient to observe the moon, the apparent movement of which is the fastest of the solar bodies. The disadvantages were the need for absolutely precise timing and some difficult calculations in spherical trigonometry.

Calculations for longitude were left to be done months later, and they were no better than the timed measurements made on the spot. In the use of lunar distances, an error of one minute of arc produces an error of about thirty minutes of longitude. Here the ineptness of Lewis and Clark was compounded by the fickleness of their chronometer. It had been carefully regulated in Philadelphia, and its "rate of going" ascertained so that its daily error could be fed into the calculations. It ran down several times, however. The popular assumption that this threw off their entire body of calculations is erroneous; local time could easily be regained by observing equal altitudes of the sun to establish the moment of noon.[20] The observations for longitude were later turned over to Ferdinand Rudolph Hassler, instructor of mathematics at West Point and future organizer of the U.S. Coast and Geodetic Survey. After a good deal of trial and error, Hassler declared he could make nothing of the observations. Although errors by Lewis and Clark may be primarily to blame, it is also possible that Hassler did not understand their procedures. He had no way of knowing that although the chronometer was regulated on mean solar time, the observations were entered according to local time.[21]

Lewis and Clark would have been well advised to forget about longitude, except for the key readings they had been given in advance for St. Louis, Fort Mandan, and the mouth of the Columbia. Their most useful data proved to be their dead-reckoning records, particularly those showing their westering, combined with their observations for latitude.

Early in April 1805, the keelboat was eased into the channel for its descent to St. Louis. It would be of little use in the busy and narrow waters that faced the expedition above Fort Mandan. Commanded by Corporal Richard Warfington, it bore a precious cargo for transshipment to Jefferson and mail for others. Among the materials were Clark's rough journals kept at Wood River, the only record of that period of the expedition; his all-important map of the country traversed thus far; and a long letter from Lewis to Jefferson describing their progress.

Dear Sir.   Fort Mandan, April 7th 1805[22]

Herewith inclosed you will receive an invoice of certain articles, which I have forwarded to you from this place. Among other articles, you will observe by reference to the invoice, 67. specimens of earths, salts and minerals; and 60 specimens of plants; these are accompanyed by their rispective labels expressing the days on which obtained, places where found, and also their virtues and properties when known. By means of these labels, reference may be made to the Chart of the Missouri forwarded to the Secretary at War, on which, the encampment of each day has been carefully marked; thus the places at which these specimens have been obtained may be easily pointed out, or again found, should any of them prove valuable to the community on further investegation. These have been forwarded with a view of their being presented to the Philosophical society of Philadelphia, in order that they may under their direction be examined or analyzed. After examining these specimens yourself, I would thank you to have a copy of their labels made out, and retained untill my return. The other articles are intended particularly for yourself, to be retained, or disposed off as you may think proper.

You will also receive herewith inclosed a part of Capt. Clark's private journal, the other part you will find inclosed in a seperate tin box. This journal is in it's original state, and of course incorrect, but it will serve to give you the daily detales of our progress, and transactions. Capt. Clark dose not wish this journal exposed in it's present state, but has no objection, that one or more copies of it be made by some confidential person under your direction, correcting it's grammatical errors &c. Indeed it is the wish of both of us, that two of those copies should be made, if convenient, and retained untill our return; in this state there is no objection to your submitting them to the perusal of the heads of the departments, or such others as you may think proper. A copy of this journal will assist me in compiling my own for publication after my return. I shall dispatch a canoe with three, perhaps four persons, from the extreem navigable point of the Missouri, or the portage betwen this river, and the Columbia river, as either may first happen; by the return of this canoe, I shal send you my journal, and some one or two of the best of those kept by my men. I have sent a journal kept by one of the Sergeants,[23] to Capt. Stoddard, my agent at St. Louis, in order as much as possible to multiply the chances of saving something. We have encouraged our men to keep journals, and seven of them do so, to whom in this respect we give every assistance in our power.

I have transmitted to the Secretary at War, every information relative to the geography of the country which we possess, together with a view of the Indian nations,[24] containing information relative to them, on those points with which, I conceived it important that the government should be informed. If it could be done with propriety and convenience, I should feel myself much obliged by your having a copy taken of my dispatches to the Secretary at War, on those subjects, retaining them for me untill my return. By reference to the Muster-rolls[25] forwarded to the War Department, you will see the state of the party; in addition to which, we have two Interpreters, one negroe man, servant to Capt. Clark, one Indian woman, wife to one of the interpreters, and a Mandan man, whom we take with a view to restore peace between the Snake Indians, and those in this neighbourhood amounting in total with ourselves to 33 persons. By means of the Interpreters and Indians, we shall be enabled to converse with all the Indians that we shall probably meet with on the Missouri.

I have forwarded to the Secretary at War, my public Accounts[26] rendered up to the present day. They have been much longer delayed than I had any idea that they would have been, when we departed from the Illinois, but this delay, under the circumstances which I was compelled to act, has been unavoidable. The provision perogue and her crew, could not have been dismissed in time to have returned to St. Louis last fall without evedently in my opinion, hazarding the fate of the enterprise in which I am engaged, and I therefore did not hesitate to prefer the sensure that I may have incurred by the detention of these papers, to that of risking in any degree the success of the expedition. To me, the detention of those papers have formed a serious source of disquiet and anxiety; and the recollection of your particular charge to me on this subject, has made it still more poignant. I am fully aware of the inconvenience which must have arisen to the War Department, from the want of these vouchers, previous to the last session of Congress, but how to divert[27] it was out of my power to devise.

From this plase we shall send the barge and crew early tomorrow morning with orders to proceed as expeditiauly as possible to St. Louis, by her we send our dispatches, which I trust will get safe to hand. Her crew consists of ten ablebodied men well armed and provided with a sufficient stock of provision to last them to St. Louis. I have but little doubt but they will be fired on by the Siouxs; but they have pledged themselves to us that they will not yeald while there is a man of them living.

Our baggage is all embarked on board six small canoes and two perogues; we shall set out at the same moment that we dispatch the barge. One or perhaps both of these perogues we shall leave at the falls of the Missouri, from whence we intend continuing our voyage in the canoes and a perogue of skins, the frame of which was prepared at Harper's ferry. This perogue is now in a situation which will enable us to prepare it in the course of a few hours. As our vessels are now small and the current of the river much more moderate, we calculate on traveling at the rate of 20 or 25 miles pr. day as far as the falls of the Missouri. Beyond this point, or the first range of rocky Mountains situated about 100 miles further, any calculation with rispect to our daily progress, can be little more than bare conjecture. The circumstance of the Snake Indians possessing large quantities of horses, is much in our favour, as by means of horses, the transportation of our baggage will be rendered easy and expeditious over land, from the Missouri, to the Columbia river. Should this river not prove navigable where we first meet with it, our present intention is, to continue our march by land down the river untill it becomes so, or to the Pacific Ocean. The map,[28] which has been forwarded to the Secretary at War, will give you the idea we entertain of the connection of these rivers, which has been formed from the corresponding testimony of a number of Indians who have visited the country, and who have been seperately and carefully examined on that subject, and we therefore think it entitled to some degree of confidence.

Since our arrival at this place we have subsisted principally on meat, with which our guns have supplyed us amply, and have thus been enabled to reserve the parched meal, portable soup, and a considerable proportion of pork and flour, which we had intended for the more difficult parts of our voyage. If Indian information can be credited, the vast quantity of game with which the country abounds through which we are to pass leaves us but little to apprehend from the want of food.

We do not calculate on completeing our voyage within the present year, but expect to reach the Pacific Ocean, and return, as far as the head of the Missouri, or perhaps to this place before winter. You may therefore expect me to meet you at Montachello in September 1806.

On our return we shal probably pass down the yellow stone river, which from Indian informations, waters one of the fairest portions of this continent.

I can foresee no material or probable obstruction to our progress, and entertain therefore the most sanguine hopes of complete success. As to myself individually I never enjoyed a more perfect state of good health, than I have since we commenced our voyage. My inestimable friend and companion Capt. Clark has also enjoyed good health generally. At this moment, every individual of the party are in good health, and excellent sperits; zealously attached to the enterprise, and anxious to proceed; not a whisper of discontent or murmur is to be heard among them; but all in unison, act with the most perfect harmoney. With such men I have every thing to hope, and but little to fear.

Be so good as to present my most affectionate regard to all my friends, and be assured of the sincere and unalterable attachment of Your most Obt. Servt.

MERIWETHER LEWIS CAPT.
1st U.S. Regt. Infty.

[Enclosure]

Invoice of articles[29] forwarded from Fort Mandan to the President of the United States through Captn. Stoddard at St. Louis and Mr. H. B. Trist the Collector of the Port of New Orleans.

No.	Package	Contents
1	Box	Skins of the Male and female Antelope,[30] with their skeletons. [came. P.]
"	do	2 Horns and ears, of the Black tail, or Mule Deer.[31] [came]
"	"	A Martin[32] skin [came] containing the skin of a weasel[33] [came. P.] and three small squirels[34] of the Rocky Mountains & the tail of a Mule deer fully grown. [came.]
"	"	Skeletons of the small, or burrowing wolf[35] of the Praries, the skin haveing been lost by accedent. [some skeletons came, not distinguishable. sent to P.]
"	"	2 skeletons of the White Hare.[36] [as above. P.]
"	"	A Mandan bow with a quiver of arrows [came] the quiver containing some seed of the Mandan tobacco.[37] [came]
"	"	A carrot[38] of Ricara tobacco. [came.]

2	Box	4 Buffalow robes, [came] and an *ear* of Mandan corn.[39]
3	Box	Skins of the Male and female Antelope, with their skeletons [undistinguishable. P.] and the skin of a brown, or yellow Bear.[40]
4	Box	Specimens of earths, salts, and minerals, numbered from 1. to 67. [came]
,,	,,	Specimens of plants numbered from 1 to 60. [came.] [A. Ph. Society.]
,,	,,	1 earthen pot, such as the Mandans manufacture, and use for culinary purposes. [came]
,,	,,	1 tin box containing insects, mice &c.
,,	,,	a specimen of the fur of the Antilope.
,,	,,	a specimen of a plant, and a parsel of its roots, highly prized by the natives as an efficatious remidy in the cure of the bite of the rattle snake, or mad dog.
	in a Large Trunk	Skin of a Male and female Braro, or burrowing Dog of the Praries,[41] with the skeleton of the female. [came. P.]
,,	in a large Trunk	1 skin of a red fox[42] containing a Magpie.[43] [came.]
,,	,,	2 cased skins of the white hare. [came. P.]
,,	,,	1 Minetarre Buffalow robe, [came] containing some articles of Indian dress. [came]
,,	,,	1 Mandan Buffalow robe, [came] containing a dressed skin of the Lousivire[44] [came] and two cased skins of the burrowing squirels of the praries. [came P.]
,,	,,	13 red fox skins [came.]
,,	,,	4 horns of the mountain ram, or *big horn*.[45] [came.]
,,	,,	1 Buffalow robe[46] painted by a Mandan man representing a battle which was faught 8 years since, by the Sioux & Ricaras, against the Mandans, Minitarras & Ahwahharways. [came.]
6	Cage	Containing four liveing Magpies. [1. came P.]
7	do.	Containing a liveing burrowing squirel of the praries. [came. P.]
9	do.	Containing one liveing hen of the Prarie.[47]
10	—	1 large par of Elk's horns connected by the frontal bone.

NOTES

1. AUGUR, 187–88.
2. Undated order, FIELD NOTES, 31.
3. Example: at one time during the War of 1812, the commander of the one-company post of Fort Madison submitted a report listing forty-six soldiers present including three unfit for duty. Horatio Stark to Daniel Bissell, 7 Feb. 1812, TERR. PAPERS, 14:521. Normal complement for a company would have been one captain, one first and one second lieutenant, one ensign, four sergeants, four corporals, four musicians, and sixty-four privates (CALLAN, 142).
4. The daily routine presented here has been compiled from many sources, including CALLAN; GRISWOLD; Cantonment Orderly Book, Belle Fontaine, 1808–10, Missouri Historical Society, St. Louis; Fort Adams Garrison Orders, 8 Nov. 1807–17 June 1808, NARG 95, vol. 149.
5. L & C JOURNALS, 1:19–20. While at Wood River, Clark had drawn plans for courts-martial, with a sergeant as president and at least one noncom and five privates as members. In capital cases, one of the captains was to preside (FIELD NOTES, 21). Unless the offense was serious, a court-martial was considered routine; nearly everyone faced military courts during an army career. Lewis himself had been court-martialed in 1795, charged with provocative speech and conduct unbecoming an officer. He was acquitted (DILLON, 20–21).
6. L & C JOURNALS, 1:62. Perhaps by now Clark was recalling his earlier appraisal of Collins and Hall. At Wood River, on some rough notes, he had written "blackguard" after Collins's name. After Hall's he had noted "Drink" (FIELD NOTES, 12). These men were to commit no further infractions deserving court-martial. Neither was Thomas P. Howard, after whose name Clark had written "never drinks water."
7. L & C JOURNALS, 1:112, 192. Although flogging was cruel, and the practice had begun to abate by the War of 1812, there was a certain unhappy logic in the administration of beatings. If you put a man in the guardhouse you lost his services—perhaps to the peril of his comrades. If you flogged him, he might spend a bad night or two but would soon be back on the duty roster and responding to the whiskey drum. It was not practical to confine a man in the course of an expedition moving daily upriver; he was needed at the oars.
8. Edible portion of the daily ration was 1¼ pounds of beef or ¾ pound of salt port; 18 ounces of bread, flour, or cornmeal; 1 gill of rum, whiskey, or brandy. For every 100 rations there were 2 quarts of salt, 4 quarts of vinegar, 4 pounds of soap, and 1½ pounds of candles. The

two captains were entitled to three rations a day or the equivalent in money, on the theory that they owned servants or were expected to entertain. A day's ration for a horse was typically 14 pounds of hay and 12 quarts of oats or 8 of corn (CALLAN, 144).

9. "The Wind blew south had Good sailing for better than 14 Miles" (Whitehouse journal entry, L & C JOURNALS, 7:49).

10. Lewis's orderly book entry for 26 May 1804, L & C JOURNALS, 1:31–32. It is noteworthy that the French *voyageurs,* experienced boatmen, were not used in the navigation of the keelboat. They were assigned to the red pirogue. Corporal Richard Warfington and his army crew in the white pirogue were scheduled to return to St. Louis in the spring.

11. L & C JOURNALS, 1:114–15. After an election by the men, Private Patrick Gass was picked from the ranks and promoted to sergeant.

12. CUTRIGHT [1], 70. Paul R. Cutright's work on the natural history of the expedition is definitive.

13. A note of 1 Aug. 1804 in FIELD NOTES, 95.

14. In Lewis's tabulation of data, "Estimate of the Eastern Indians," L & C JOURNALS, 6:98. Clark's account of the episode, L & C JOURNALS, 1:161–74, becomes clearer if read along with that of Sergeant Ordway in LEWIS & ORDWAY. Clark's stern bearing and his obvious anger may have influenced the Indians to back down. "I felt My Self warm & Spoke in verry positive terms (L & C JOURNALS, 1:165).

15. For the chief, see L & C LETTERS, 1:242, 257, 261–62, 272–73. James Wilkinson called him a great traveler, warrior, and geographer, and "certainly a *learned* Savage." After his death, TJ sent a special messenger to the Arikara nation with the chief's possessions, presents for the tribe, and a speech of condolence. "We buried him among our own deceased friends & relatives, we shed many tears over his grave, and we now mingle our afflictions with yours on the loss of this beloved chief. But death must happen to all men; and his time was come" (to the Arikaras, 11 April 1806, LC). Clark's remark about York is in L & C JOURNALS, 1:185.

16. To the Osages, 16 July 1804, LC. The term "beloved man" was English for what the Indians understood to be a trusted official representative of the President. At times the term "nephew" was used in the same way.

17. Stoddard to TJ, 29 Oct. 1804, and TJ to Reuben Lewis, 6 Nov. 1804 and 4 Jan. 1805, all in LC. John Hay wrote TJ 12 Feb. 1805 with no new information but with the prediction that Lewis and Clark would reach the Pacific in July (Missouri Historical Society).

18. They found Hugh McCracken and another British trader at the

villages when they arrived. Clark immediately wrote their superior, Charles Chaboillez, enclosing a copy of the British passport and asking for information about the geography of the land and other facts "which might be serviceable to us in the prosecution of our voyage" (L & C JOURNALS, 7:307–8). Chaboillez, in charge of the Department of the Assiniboine for the North West Company, sent Hugh Heney with a reply to the letter in December; another party under François-Antoine Larocque had arrived earlier. One member of that party, Charles McKenzie, detected a bit of anglophobia in Lewis's manner: "It is true, Captain Lewis could not make himself agreeable to us. He could speak fluently and learnedly on all subjects, but his inveterate disposition against the British stained, at least in our eyes, all his eloquence" (MASSON, 1:336).

19. Whitehouse in L & C JOURNALS, 7:70. While Whitehouse's journal is clearly supplementary to those of the captains and Sergeant Ordway, he frequently contributes small details overlooked by other journal keepers.

20. In fact, trained surveyors later carried printed forms for exactly this purpose. Colonel William Ludlow, engineering officer with General George Custer's 1874 expedition to the Black Hills, used a form headed: "Determination of the Time by Observed Equal Altitudes of the Sun's Limb to Correct the Chronometer at Noon" (NARG 77, Papers of the Black Hills expedition). Even the highly accurate marine chronometers of later generations required careful handling, and precise adjustment at the beginning and end of a voyage (BEDINI, 362).

21. The Hassler correspondence with Clark, Nicholas Biddle, and Robert Patterson is in L & C LETTERS. Lewis's note on mean time *vs.* local time is in L & C JOURNALS, 6:232.

22. LC, received by TJ 13 July 1805. The enclosure is in Clark's hand. In the enclosure the words in brackets, in Jefferson's hand, show whether the materials were sent to Charles Willson Peale or to the American Philosophical Society. Those marked only "came" were probably retained by TJ. A penciled notation at the head of the letter, in the hand of Elliott Coues, reads: "This letter was originally printed, *revised,* with Jeff's. Message to Congr. of Feb. 19, 1806, and afterwards in many other places, always misdated 'April 17th.' " Another annotation by Coues, at the end of the enclosure, reads: "Above is original of the invoice of presents etc. to Mr. Jefferson, shipped by the Barge from Fort Mandan April 7th. Coues." The editor of several travel narratives at the end of the nineteenth century, Coues marked up rare manuscripts with a soft pencil, almost as if they were printer's copy. The annotation

presented here is adapted from L & C LETTERS, 1:236–42, with many deletions and some additions.

23. Probably the journal of the late Sergeant Floyd.

24. A large table in Clark's hand, now at the American Philosophical Society, Philadelphia. From it Jefferson prepared as part of his *Message from the President* a section entitled "A statistical view of the Indian nations inhabiting the Territory of Louisiana and the countries adjacent to its northern and western boundaries."

25. None found. The muster rolls of the regular army for this period are not numerous; those which have survived are in the National Archives, NARG 94.

26. Not found as such, but represented in a statement of Lewis's accounts, L & C LETTERS, 2:419–31. Total cost of the expedition as shown there is $38,722.25.

27. The word "divert," altered in pencil to "avert" in the hand of Coues.

28. Original not found, but the War Department copy is in the Cartographic Records branch of the National Archives, entitled: "A Map of part of the Continent of North America, Between the 35th. and 51st. degrees of North Latitude, and extending from 89 Degrees of West Longitude to the Pacific Ocean. Compiled from the Authorities of the best informed travellers, by M. Lewis. . . . Copied by Nicholas King, 1806." Other copies in King's hand are in the library of the Boston Athenaeum and the Geography and Map Division of the Library of Congress. For an illustration, see pp. 174–75 above. For the best discussion, see ALLEN [2], 226–52. Samuel L. Mitchill saw the map when it reached Washington but declined to publish it in his *Medical Repository,* declaring that that privilege should be reserved for Lewis.

29. "I think I sent you Capt. Lewis's original catalogue of the articles he had forwarded to me. I retained no copy of it, & having occasion to turn to it, would thank you for it" (Jefferson to Peale, 1 Jan. 1806, LC). For a duplicate that Clark inserted in his journal, see L & C JOURNALS, 1:280–82.

30. The pronghorn. Lewis and Clark were the first to put specimens and a detailed, firsthand description into the hands of scientists, although the existence of the animal had long been known. Benjamin Smith Barton, in the *Philadelphia Medical and Physical Journal,* supp. 2 (1807), 194, reports that the animal had been known for more than 150 years. Jefferson had heard of the pronghorn through the Osages and discusses it in a letter to naturalist William Bartram, 7 April 1805 (LC): "I dare say you know that Westward of the Misipi there is an animal of

the Capra kind; & tho by some it is called a deer, & by some a goat that
would not authorise us to call it the Cervicapra of the East. . . . The
Osage Indians shewed me a specimen of it's leather, superior to any
thing of the kind I ever saw. . . . I count on special information as to
this animal from Capt. Lewis, and that he will enrich us with other
articles of Zoology, in which he is more skilled than in botany."

31. *Dama hemionus hemionus* (Rafinesque). The specimens were collected in what is now South Dakota, in September 1804. "Colter killed
. . . a curious kind of Deer of a Dark gray colr. more so than common,
hair long & fine, the ears large & long . . . the Taile about the length of
Common Deer, round (like a Cow) a tuft of black hair about the end"
(L & C JOURNALS, 1:152).

32. *Martes americana americana* (Turton).

33. The long-tailed weasel, *Mustela frenata longicauda* Bonaparte.

34. The red squirrel, perhaps either *Tamiasciurus hudsonicus fremonti*
(Audubon and Bachman) or *Tamiasciurus hudsonicus richardsoni*
(Bachman). Such common names as "Fremont's squirrel" and
"Richardson's red squirrel" have been discarded by mammalogists,
who now designate all such subspecies by one name, "red squirrel."

35. The coyote, *Canis latrans latrans* Say.

36. The white-tailed jackrabbit, *Lepus townsendii campanius* Hollister,
first mentioned by Lewis in a letter to TJ, 26 Mar. 1804, LC, while the
expedition was still in St. Louis.

37. *Nicotiana quadrivolvus* Pursh. Lewis and Clark observed a difference between Arikara and Mandan tobacco, and sent back specimens of
what they thought were two species of Arikara tobacco, differing
mainly in size of leaf and flower. For Lewis's description of both species
and the manner of cultivation, see L & C JOURNALS, 6:150–51. A sample
of tobacco that Jefferson sent to Philadelphia tobacconist Thomas
Leiper may have been brought back by the explorers, or even grown by
Jefferson from the seed mentioned here. Leiper reported to Jefferson 20
Aug. 1807 (LC): "I returned you by Major Lewis Two Bundles of
segars manufactured from the Tobacco you sent me by him. From the
manner the Tobacco was packed it was not possible it could retain
much of its original flavour. From the smalness of the sample I had it
not in my power to manufacture it into any thing else but segars and I
believe it to be the kind of tobacco that the very fine segars are made of
for it has as little substance as the Kitefoot owing no doubt to its being
top't high . . . ."

38. A length of tobacco leaves twisted together, roughly resembling
a carrot.

39. Maize or Indian corn, *Zea mays* L. Seed collected by Lewis and

Clark was said by PURSH, 1:46, to produce "as excellent ears as any sort I know." Jefferson experimented with two varieties sent back by the explorers, the Mandan and the Pawnee [Arikara], and took special pains to compare them with some European corn sent him by his old friend André Thouin (b. 1747), chief of the Jardin des Plantes in Paris. Hence this entry in Jefferson's weather memorandum, GARDEN BOOK, 336: "Aug. 11 [1807]. my Quarentine corn planted May 1 gave rosten ears in the last week of June. Being about 8. weeks. It is now dry enough to grind, to wit 3½ months. My Pani corn planted the same day was a week or fortnight later. But Shoemaker [a tenant] planted Pani corn about the 2d. week of May, & had rosten ears the last week of June. . . ." By quarantine corn, Jefferson seems to mean corn that matures in about forty days—from the original meaning of the word. He was still raising the Pawnee or Arikara variety some years later. An entry of 9 April 1811 in his garden book reads: "Planted Pani corn in the middle part of grounds below Bailey's alley. Come to table July 18" (GARDEN BOOK, 446). English botanist John Bradbury wrote William Roscoe, of the Liverpool Botanic Garden, 12 Aug. 1809, that Jefferson planned to send to England "a New Variety of Zea Maize which was brought by Capn. Lewis from . . . a Tribe of Cultivating Indians in Latitude 49° and a Country so much elevated as to render it almost a Greenland climate." On 10 May 1809, Bradbury wrote Roscoe that he had planted the corn in his own St. Louis garden. "I have no doubt of its doing very well in England & it will be an immense National benefit. . . ." In the fall he sent some seed to Roscoe. "I send you herewith some varieties of Maize amongst which are two kinds which will I think succeed in England as they will frequently come to maturity here in 10 or 11 weeks whereas the common variety requires the whole summer . . ." (RICKETT, 59–89).

40. The grizzly bear, *Ursus horribilis horribilis* Ord. This subspecies is now probably extinct, but three others are listed by MILLER & KELLOGG. The story of the grizzly demonstrates the fact that a species may be known to many men, including scientists, and still be "unknown to science." The species was not named and described until 1815, when Ord presented it on the basis of the Lewis and Clark specimens and descriptions. On the evidence which follows here, it is difficult to understand why it remained unknown for so long.

Perhaps the first white man to report the grizzly was Henry Kelsey, while exploring for the Hudson's Bay Company on the Canadian prairies in the summer of 1691. He wrote in his journal, "This plain affords Nothing but short Round sticky grass & Buffillo & a great s[ort] of a Bear w[hi]ch is Bigger then any white Bear & is Neither White nor

Black But silver hair'd like our English Rabbitt . . ." (DOUGHTY & MARTIN, 12–13). It is not clear whether he was reporting from hearsay or actual sightings.

Sir Alexander Mackenzie saw the grizzly in 1793. "We this day saw two grisly and hideous bears" (MACKENZIE, 1:164). And on 8 June 1805, Charles Willson Peale wrote in his museum memoranda (Historical Society of Pennsylvania, Philadelphia), "a Claw of the Grisly Bear brought from the interior of American by Alexr. McKenzie. . . ." William Henry Harrison reported to Jefferson that he was sending him what may have been a grizzly in 1803. "The Lieut. Governor [of Upper Louisiana] was so obliging as to give me one of two bears that were brought from a great distance up the Missouri & is of a kind not hitherto described that I know of. This shall be sent with the other articles as soon as I get some one to take them" (29 Oct. 1803, LC). There is no further record of this specimen.

The first opportunity for eastern scientists to see the bear may have come in the summer of 1803, when Peale had one on display. As Peale told the story to Jefferson: "A french-man; an Indian trader from New Orleans, brought here in the sickly season last summer a Grisley-bear to exhibit. Enclosed is one of his Bills—he expected to make a fortune by the Animal, but he was disappointed, altho' it differed considerably from the common, yet nevertheless it was a Bear, & as such did not excite much curiosity." Peale said he bought the bear and kept it until early March 1804, when it broke loose and had to be shot. "Please to accept a hind quarter which I have sent by the Mail stage, directed for you." And he added: "I much suspect that this species of Bear has not been described and therefore I shall shortly write some observations & give a drawing of it, which I mean to send to you" (Peale to Jefferson, 18 March 1804, LC).

A handbill which Peale enclosed with the letter reads in part: "THE FAMOUS GRISLY BEAR, hitherto unseen in the inhabited countries, and entirely unknown untill the celebrated A. Mackenzie gave some account of that extraordinary animal, having met him in the neighbourhood of the Rocky Mountains. . . . This animal was born in the spring of the year 1802 not far from the sources of the river Missory, about 4500 miles from Philadelphia, in a country inhabited by an indian nation called the Cattanahowes. He is the first of his specie that ever was seen, and seems to be a separate class of White Bear, which differs from those known to and described by the naturalists, as well in point of colour, as in point of inclinations. His hair is a kind of straw colour or light sorrel, neither hard nor stiff, but somewhat like wool. . . . By the size of this one, who has hardly attained the third part of his bigness, by the length of his claws, when yet so young, one may form an idea of the powerful strength of that dangerous animal. . . ."

41. The American badger, *Taxidea taxus taxus* (Schreber). "Braro" is Clark's version of the French *blaireau*.

42. *Vulpes fulva regalis* Merriam.

43. The black-billed magpie, *Pica pica hudsonia* (Sabine).

44. *Lynx canadensis canadensis* Kerr. For Clark's "Lousivire" read the French *loup-cervier*.

45. The Audubon mountain sheep, *Ovis canadensis auduboni* Merriam. This is the species which Lewis and Clark called the ibex or argali, as well as the bighorn, and which early naturalists thought of in connection with the *Ovis ammon* or Siberian argali of Cuvier. Its existence came as no surprise to Lewis and Clark; the animal was known in St. Louis, and word of it had passed to American settlers east of the Mississippi, as shown in a letter written by George Turner, territorial judge in Kaskaskia in 1794–95: "[Mr. Chouteau] tells me that at a great distance up that River [the Missouri], you will meet with some new—animals—animals unknown in our Natural History: particularly one, of the size and nearly the colour of the elk, but with much longer hair. Under this hair, he is clothed with a fine and very long fur. He has two large horns—which, issuing from behind the ears and turning backwards in a circle, terminate in two points projecting before the head, in a horizontal direction" (to John Evans, 10 March 1795, Archivo General de Indias (Seville), Papeles de Cuba, legajo 213, printed by NASATIR and DILLER). Diller believes that Turner also wrote an account of the Missouri, mentioning the mountain sheep, which Samuel L. Mitchill published in his *Medical Repository,* 2nd hexade, 1 (April 1804), 412–14. It is possible that Lewis and Clark already knew of the mountain sheep before coming to the West. In a note on the animal, Barton said that its existence had been known to Spanish historians before 1633 (*Philadelphia Medical and Physical Journal,* suppl 2. (1807), 193–94). Mitchill, in an introduction to an article by Duncan McGillivray (d. 1808) in the *Repository* ((MC GILLIVRAY, 237), asserted that Father Picolo, a Spanish missionary in California, had reported in 1697 having seen such animals and eaten their flesh. Mitchill probably was referring to an account by Francis Maria Picolo, published in 1708. Miguel VENEGAS described and illustrated the mountain sheep in 1:36 of his *Natural and Civil History of California* . . . (London, 1759), which was the English edition of his *Noticia de la California* . . . (Madrid, [1757]). Thomas PENNANT followed Picolo's account in his *Arctic zoology* (London, 1784–87). McGillivray collected a specimen while traveling in the fall of 1800 with explorer David Thompson in the Rockies, between the Saskatchewan

and Missouri rivers; he included a woodcut with his published description. The drawing of the animal in DOUGHTY, 1:193, was done partly from the male and female specimens, presented by Lewis and Clark, in Peale's museum. Lewis left a slip of paper among his effects, upon his death, reading "History of quadrupeds published by A. Anderson N. York Page 526—the american Argali discribed—copy of this work in the possession of the A.P. Socyety—Philadelphia" (MoSHi). He was referring to the first American edition of Thomas Bewick's *A General History of Quadrupeds* (New York, 1804), issued by engraver Alexander Anderson with an appendix containing descriptions of some American animals. After the expedition, Lewis asked Manuel Lisa to try raising some of the young sheep, but lack of milk was a handicap. Lisa told Thomas Nuttall in 1810 that he was still trying to raise some, using domestic goat's milk (Nuttall to Barton, 22 April 1810, transcript in the Philadelphia Academy of Natural Sciences).

46. This robe may be the one now at the Peabody Museum, Harvard University. For a note on recent doubts about the identification of the Peabody robe, see L & C LETTERS, 2:734.

47. The black-billed magpie, *Pica pica hudsonia* (Sabine), the black-tailed prairie dog, *Cynomys ludovicianus ludovicianus* (Ord), and the sharp-tailed grouse, *Pedioecetes phasianellus jamesi* Lincoln. The five birds and one prairie dog were sent live to St. Louis to the attention of Lewis's agent, for transshipment via New Orleans and Baltimore to Washington. One magpie and the prairie dog survived, resided for a time in the presidential mansion, then were sent on to Peale in Philadelphia. The prairie dog was unknown to science when the specimens and the living animal arrived on the East Coast. Jefferson was spending the summer at Monticello when his maitre d'hotel, Etienne Lemaire, wrote him that he had received "a kind of cage in which there is a little animal very much resembling the squirrel, and in the other a bird resembling the magpie of Europe." Jefferson instructed Lemaire "to have particular care taken of the squirrel & pie which came with the things from Baltimore that I may see them alive at my return. Should any accident happen to the squirrel his skin & skeleton must be preserved" (Lemaire to TJ, 12 Aug. 1805, Massachusetts Historical Society, Boston, and TJ to Lemaire, 17 Aug. 1805, LC).

CHAPTER NINE

"With Unspeakable Joy"

Leaving Fort Mandan 7 April 1805 in six recently built canoes and the two pirogues, the Lewis and Clark expedition set out upon new waters. A few personnel changes had been made: the French boatmen were gone, as were the temporary men under Corporal Warfington and the two soldiers discharged for cause. Private Robert Frazer had transferred from Warfington's detachment and a new private—Jean Baptiste Labiche —had been recruited at Fort Mandan. History has taken greater notice of a half-blood interpreter named Toussaint Charbonneau, and more particularly his young wife, Sacagawea, a captured Shoshoni girl who was traveling with a baby slung on her back.

Lewis was pleased with his trained detachment and the carefully packed vessels. The party now totaled thirty-three persons and the black Newfoundland. "This little fleet altho' not quite so rispectable as those of Columbus or Capt. Cook, were still viewed by us with as much pleasure as those deservedly famed adventurers ever beheld theirs; and I dare say with quite as much anxiety for their safety and preservation."[1]

Game became more plentiful and scientifically interesting. The monstrous grizzly bear would soon appear to challenge and even terrorize them. New plants appeared at every bend in the river, some to be collected and pressed, others to be only described. On the second day out, Clark reported seeing great numbers of brant in the air, and said the maple, elm, and cottonwood were budding. "I saw flowers in the praries to day, juniper grows on the Sides of the hills, & runs on the ground." And the first foreboding of coming summer wretchedness: "I saw a Musquetor to day."[2]

Two weeks later, the expedition paused at the point of land formed by the junction of the Missouri and the Yellowstone. It was a notable river, so interesting that Clark would descend it on the homeward journey. He had found, on a low plain apparently not subject to overflow, "a butifull commanding situation for a fort near the commencement of the Prarie."[3]

· The Mystery of the White Pirogue ·

Students of the expedition have noted that, except for a few fragments, there are no surviving journal entries in Lewis's hand for the trip as far as the Mandans. After the departure from Fort Mandan, Lewis records his entries regularly. Some scholars have concluded that he kept no journal on a routine basis during the early months of the expedition.[4]

The red morocco notebooks at the American Philosophical Society, which contain most of the journal material, are not original drafts. They are copied in the hands of the explorers from rough-draft material now mostly lost. In copying their notes, Lewis and Clark were usually careful to date an observation in keeping with their original drafts; but sometimes they worked their data in wherever they could. Now and then we read a few lines about the day's happenings, then we get some data on the Indians, or on natural history, set down as if it had been observed on that day, when in fact it has been put there only for convenience.

For example, Lewis includes a description of the California condor in his entry for 17 February 1806, and is thus the author of a very early description of that remarkable bird. But in copying him, Clark got the description a day early, in his entry for 16 February.[5] He could hardly have examined the bird on that day, because the two enlisted men who brought in the carcass did not arrive from a hunting trip until the following day. But here it is, preceding Lewis's description by a full day. Scholars have been led by this inadvertence to attribute to Clark the first full description of the bird.

Another example, one of the clearest indications that Lewis and Clark often worked their descriptions of plants and animals into their journals wherever they could: Lewis describes a species of cherry in his entry for 12 August 1806: "I must notice a singular Cherry which is found on the Missouri in the bottom lands about the beaver bends and some little distance below the white earth river. . . . The stem is compound erect and subdivided or branching without any regular order. It rises to the hight of 8 or 10 feet," etc. Now here is Clark's entry for 10 August, two days earlier than Lewis's: "I found a Species of Chery in the bottom, the shrub of which are different from any which I have ever Seen. . . . The Stem is compound, erect and subdivided or branching without any regular order. It rises to the hight of 8 to 10 feet," etc.[6]

Not only did Clark fail to alter the passage from the first person, as drafted by Lewis, but he gave it an impossible date: Lewis and Clark were separated on that day and Clark could not possibly have copied Lewis's description at the time. But these are exceptional cases, telling us something about how the journals were made. In the long run the journals seem to reflect a day's happenings and observations quite accurately, and are usually made on the day such occurrences were observed.

Perhaps we can learn something from this rather helter-skelter organization of the journals, and from Clark's method of copying Lewis. While they were wintering at Fort Mandan, the two prepared the material they were to send downriver. When they dispatched the keelboat, Lewis wrote to Jefferson (p. 177 above) that he was sending along a record that Clark had kept until that time, but that he (Lewis) had not had a chance to put his own notes into acceptable form. He said he would send a canoe back later with a copy of his own journal—but this proved impractical.

The party thus set out from Fort Mandan apparently carrying Lewis's unrevised notes of the journey so far, continuing the daily habit of setting down their observations. Although Lewis and Clark were keeping a double record at this time, that simply means that both men were keeping journals. Until now there had been little attempt by Clark to enter Lewis's observations on ethnology and natural history into his own record. They move on toward the Rockies, and by 1 May Clark is still not copying these scientific entries. On that day, Lewis describes a "bird of the plover kind" in great detail, while Clark's description is much shorter. The same situation appears a few days later, when Lewis describes a bear in detail but Clark does not. Three days later, Clark makes no attempt to duplicate Lewis's long description of the *pomme blanche* or whiteapple (*Psoralea esculanta*), and on 12 May he lets Lewis's description of the wild cherry alone.

But on 25 May, something noteworthy appears in the journals. Lewis describes in rather full detail their encounter with the mountain goat, and Clark copies the entry in what amounts to substantial duplication. From that time on, virtually all of Lewis's scientific observations are duplicated in Clark's journal. Had something happened to make these men reconsider their procedures? Were they suddenly reminded that they should not only keep separate journals, but that the information in them—especially that of a scientific nature which only Lewis could satisfactorily produce—should be duplicated?

Something *had* happened, on 14 May, which could have influenced this decision. One of the boats had turned on its side and filled with water.

Sergeant Ordway's description of the accident is succinct: "About 5 oClock the white perogue of the Captains was Sailing a long, there came a violent gust of wind from the N.W. which was to the contrary to the course they were Sailing. It took the Sail and before they had time to douse it it turned the perogue down on one Side So that she filled with water, and would have turned over had it not been for the oarning [awning] which prevented it."

On the following day they spread all their gear and supplies out to dry. Private Whitehouse wrote: "Some of the papers and nearly all the books got wet, but not altogether spoiled."[7]

Suppose that the damage proved to be greater than at first assumed, and that Lewis's notes for the entire first leg of the expedition were either badly water-soaked or entirely lost (his recent notes, still extant, would have been with him—and he was not aboard). These were honest men, and Lewis might have been expected to tell Jefferson, upon returning, that he had lost most of his journal for the period of May 1804 through March 1805, but there would have been little point in announcing it to the world.

If Lewis's journal was lost or damaged in the accident, a

number of questions are resolved. The accident would explain, of course, why there is no Lewis journal—except for fragments—covering the early period. It would explain why Clark copied into his journal the very next scientific observation made by Lewis after the boat incident, and kept on doing so for the remainder of the journey. It would explain why, perhaps in an effort to salvage the information in some of the water-soaked documents, both copied into their journals after the accident a few entries which had been made much earlier. For example, they did not deal with the chokecherry until a long time after they had seen it, nor did they promptly describe the horned toad.

Finally, the loss or damage of Lewis's journal during the capsizing would account for one of the most puzzling aspects of all. It is not precise to say that we have *no* Lewis journals for the first part of the expedition. We have a few loose sheets on paper apparently torn from the regular notebooks. One section of four leaves was found fastened inside a notebook with sealing wax. The paper is worn and discolored. On it, in Lewis's hand, are journal entries for 15 to 20 May 1804, at the very start of the journey, making it clear that Lewis was setting out in earnest to keep a daily record. Another section of four leaves covers the period of 16 and 17 September 1804. These sheets, too, are badly worn and the edges appear to have been repaired at a later date. They are with the other journals at the American Philosophical Society library.

By stacking one conjecture upon another, we may venture the strong probability that Lewis did keep a journal in 1804, at least a possibility that it was damaged during the voyage, and that some parts of it were salvaged and now appear in the revised manuscripts—combined with entries for a later period.

• To the Great Falls •

At the mouth of the Marias, entering the Missouri from the north, there was some confusion as to which stream was the main branch of the Missouri. The Marias, an unexpected river which Lewis named for a cousin, appeared to be the main branch; but to take the wrong fork might bring disaster to the enterprise. Of the Marias Lewis wrote, "In short the air and character of this

river is so precisely that of the Missouri below that the party with
very few exceptions have already pronounced the N. fork to be
the Missouri." Holding a minority opinion, the two captains
believed that the southern river was the one that would lead them
to Columbia waters. While it seemed unlike the Missouri they
had been ascending, its depth and clarity, and its bottom of
round and smooth stones, seemed most like a stream issuing
from the mountains. Because of the strong difference of opinion,
it was decided that each officer would take a detachment "and
ascend these rivers until we could perfectly satisfy ourselves of
the one, which it would be most expedient for us to take on
our main journey to the Pacific."[8] Their observations sustained
their first conclusion and they continued to follow the true
Missouri—the southern fork.

Reaching the Great Falls in western Montana, the men faced
a portage of eighteen miles that tested their endurance and
ingenuity. They made crude wheels cut from sections of cottonwood logs to move the pirogues along, and even tried a sail on
one of these improvised wagons. The episode was a cruel experience. "The prickly pears were extreemly troublesome to us,"
wrote Lewis, "sticking our feet through our mockersons." The
next day he added: "During the late rains the buffaloe have
troden up the praire very much which having now become dry
the sharp points of earth as hard as frozen ground stand up in
such abundance that there is no avoiding them . . . at every halt
these poor fellows tumble down and are so much fortiegued that
many of them are asleep in an instant . . . yet no one complains,
all go with cheerfullness."[9]

· To the Pacific by Land ·

Having cleared the Falls, Lewis was able to test his "leather
boat," the iron frame of which had been hauled from Pittsburgh.
Bitterly disappointed when the craft, covered with skins and
caulked, would not stay afloat, he abandoned the vessel.

At the Three Forks of the Missouri another geographical analysis had to be made. One of these forks—they named them the
Jefferson, Madison, and Gallatin—was a branch of the Missouri
that would lead them into the mountains. As they had done at the

confluence with the Marias, they decided correctly, following the Jefferson branch until it dwindled away in the Rockies. The task then was to cross the mountains and find Pacific-bound waters that would take them to the coast.

A fortunate meeting with the Shoshonis provided horses that were essential to travel now that they had cached their river craft. Dealings with the Shoshonis were made simpler by a surprising coincidence. One of the first chiefs they met, Cameahwait, was Sacagawea's brother.

Life on the river had been strenuous and risky but without prolonged suffering. Now came hunger, cold, and sickness. The crossing of Lolo Pass in the Bitterroots was an awful one. Deterred by snow and hail, and half starved, the men killed horses and drank melted snow. Sergeant Gass thought the Rockies were "the most terrible mountains I ever beheld," a fair conclusion, as he had known only the Appalachians until now.

And what of Mackenzie's "short portage" across the mountains? The Englishman had written that he crossed the Rockies near the fifty-fifth parallel over a very low pass—perhaps 3,000 feet above sea level. South of this point, he reasoned, the passes would be even lower. He had misled himself—and Lewis and Clark—by a piece of conceptual geography that had proved false.

In these hard surroundings, references to geographical phenomena seldom crept into the journals. The forbidding mountains, what forces made them, how the great canyons were cut, what ingredients were fused to make the craggy skyline—of these things Lewis and Clark had little to say. At the beginning of the expedition their journals had contained random observations on potentially useful mineral deposits, and a collection of rocks and minerals had been sent back with the keelboat. In all the journals, their descriptions of the terrain necessarily dealt with landforms and certain geological processes. But even here in the Rockies, where observations about the earth might have crowded the pages of the journals, they concentrated on plants and animals. It was a blank spot in Lewis's thinking that he almost surely had acquired from Jefferson. The Rockies were too far away for mining, for any commerce but the fur trade, and so were not an object of study and speculation but only a wretchedly cold obstacle between men and the sea.

Clark, writing on 16 September: "Began to Snow about 3 hours before Day and continued all day. The Snow in the morning 4 inches deep on the old Snow . . . I walked in front to keep the road and found great difficuelty in keeping it as in maney places the Snow had entirely filled up the track. . . . I have been wet and as cold in every part as I ever was in my life."[10]

West of the Lolo Trail the expedition met the Nez Perce Indians, found the going easier (once they had rejected the impossible Salmon River), and continued by land and water to the Columbia.

When they reached what they thought was the Pacific, though they were still in the estuary of the Columbia, Clark penned a phrase that has come to epitomize the exaltation and relief felt by the entire party. On 7 November he wrote: "Ocian in view! O! the joy."[11] Another quotation of Clark's is equally meaningful, evoking as it does the international rivalry that had given rise to the expedition. In Mackenzie's *Voyages,* documenting the travels of the first white man to cross the continent north of Mexico, was the taunting phrase the explorer had scrawled on a rock at the end of his trip: "Alexander Mackenzie, from Canada, by land, the twenty-second of July, one thousand seven hundred and ninety-three." Now it had been done again. Americans had come across the land to link up with the river that another American, Captain Gray, had been first to enter from the sea. It was a triumph for the United States, and Clark could afford to mimic Mackenzie in the inscription he put on a tree on 23 November 1805: "I marked my name the Day of the Month & year on a Beech tree & 'By Land.' "[12]

After wintering on the coast in the third fort of their own construction, and enduring more cold and privation, the expedition started home in the spring of 1806. Lewis made a side trip north to scout along the Marias, believing it to be the northernmost arm of the Missouri watershed and thus important in boundary negotiations; Clark examined the Yellowstone.

During his scouting of the Marias, Lewis and his detachment had an encounter with a small band of renegade Piegan Indians, a division of the Blackfoot nation. He had been encamped for several days northwest of present Cut Bank, Mont., to rest his men and horses and try to establish the longitude. He then began a southeasterly journey toward the Missouri, making botanical observations in his journal—noting the buffaloberry and three species of cottonwood all growing together. On 26 July 1806, he camped on the Two Medicine River in company with eight Piegans who, traveling with thirty horses, had fallen in with his party that afternoon. Fearful that the Indians might attempt to steal their horses, Lewis and his men spent a restless and wakeful night, and at daylight their apprehensions became a fact. While crowding around the fire at daybreak, the Piegans seized several guns. In the resulting fray, with the Indians trying to drive off Lewis's horses, two of the marauders were killed.[13]

In the meantime, Clark with twenty men and Sacagawea were on the Yellowstone, traveling in canoes that had been removed from the cache and repaired. Dugouts were built later. Clark's party, too, lost horses—probably stolen by Indians—but the descent of the river was mainly uneventful. They reached the Missouri on 3 August, and camped downstream to wait for Lewis.

When the reunited party reached the Mandan villages, two arrangements were made that were to extend the history of the expedition long beyond its termination in late September. First, the Mandan chief Sheheke agreed to join the party, with his wife and an interpreter, and to accompany Lewis on to Washington at the end of the river voyage. This agreement was to have fateful consequences for Lewis in the years immediately following the expedition. Second, Clark demonstrated the solicitude he had come to feel for Sacagawea and her baby, Jean Baptiste. In a letter to her husband, Charbonneau, he made a generous offer. "Your woman who accompanied you that long dangerous and fatigue-ing rout to the Pacific Ocian and back diserved a greater reward for her attention and services on that rout than we had in our power to give her. . . . As to your little Son (my boy *Pomp*) you well know my fondness for him and my anxiety to take and raise him as my own child. I once more tell you if you will bring your son Baptiest to me I will educate him and treat him as my own child."[14]

As they descended the Missouri and approached St. Louis, Lewis and Clark engaged in a kind of ruse that demonstrates what made their relationship distinctively selfless. Aware that publication of their letters home was inevitable, and that Clark's mail would reach his relations in Louisville before Lewis's arrived in Virginia, the two men addressed the fact that Clark was not an astute grammarian or skillful speller. As usual, they did the sensible thing: Lewis wrote Clark's letter for him. In St. Louis, Clark copied it and sent it off to one of his brothers, either Jonathan or George Rogers Clark. The draft in Lewis's hand is in the Clark papers at the Missouri Historical Society.

Upon reaching St. Louis on 23 September, Lewis immediately wrote to Jefferson. "It is with pleasure that I announce to you the safe arrival of myself and party at 12 OClk. today at this place with our papers and baggage. . . . With rispect to the exertions and services rendered by that esteemable man Capt. William Clark in the course of [the] late voyage I cannot say too much; if sir any credit be due for the success of that arduous enterprize in which we have been mutually engaged, he is equally with myself entitled to your consideration and that of our common country."

Lewis said he felt he had discovered the most practicable route across the continent, a belief to which he was certainly entitled, although other men were to find better routes. He added, however, that 140 miles of the route lay over "tremendous mountains which for 60 mls. are covered with eternal snows." He discussed the future of the fur trade in the light of their findings, and said, "If the government will only aid, even in a very limited manner, the enterprize of her Citizens I am fully convinced that we shal shortly derive the benifits of a most lucrative trade from this source, and that in the course of ten or twelve years a tour across the Continent by the rout mentioned will be undertaken by individuals with as little concern as a voyage across the Atlantic is at present."[15]

Jefferson had heard nothing authoritative about the expedition since the documents and specimens had reached him in the summer of 1805. Although he knew nothing of Spanish attempts to cut off Lewis and Clark, there had been rumors of catastrophe. While amusing himself with the journals and specimens he had received, he contemplated the sorry prospect that the party had been lost. When a delegation of chiefs from several plains tribes appeared, Jefferson thanked them for their treatment of the expedition. "I therefore sent our beloved man Capt. Lewis one of my own family, to go up the Missouri river. . . . Some of you who are here have seen him & heard his words. . . . My children I thank you for the services you rendered him, and for your attention to his words. When he returns he will tell us where we should establish factories to be convenient to you all, and what we must send to them."[16]

A month later he wrote his French friend, C. F. C. Volney: "Our last news of Captn. Lewis was that he had reached the upper part of the Missouri and had taken horses to cross the highlands to the Columbia River."[17] It was true, even though the word had passed from tribe to tribe and reached him through the Osage delegation. It took a month for Lewis's letter to arrive from St. Louis. The ecstatic Jefferson immediately consulted Albert Gallatin about how Lewis should be rewarded for his accomplishment. Apparently the governorship of Louisiana Territory had already been discussed. Now Gallatin sent a note: "If you select him for Governor, ought not provision to be made for the contingency of his leaving that place for Washington before the arrival of a commission?"[18]

Jefferson then wrote to Lewis. "I received, my dear Sir, with unspeakable joy your letter of Sep. 23 announcing the return of yourself, Capt. Clarke & your party in good health to St. Louis. The unknown scenes in which you were engaged, & the length of time without hearing of you had begun to be felt awfully."[19]

It was as close as Jefferson ever would come to putting tears of relief and gratitude on paper.

NOTES

1. L & C JOURNALS, 1:284.

2. L & C JOURNALS, 1:292. Clark had also resumed keeping course and distance records, logging more than twenty-three miles on 9 April.

3. L & C JOURNALS, 1:342. The confluence of the two rivers was to become the site of Fort Union and other posts as the West developed.

4. The discussion in this section was first presented by the author at the Centennial Conference of the Missouri Historical Society, St. Louis, 31 March 1967. The thesis it presents was not challenged at the

meeting and has not been questioned since, but it does rest on conjecture. The material appears in JACKSON [4].

5. L & C JOURNALS, 4:79–83. "I believe this to be the largest Bird of North America. It was not in good order and yet it wayed 25 lbs. Had it have been so it might very well have weighed 10 lb. more or 35 lbs."

6. Lewis's entry is in L & C JOURNALS, 4:243–44; Clark's, 4:328.

7. LEWIS & ORDWAY, 212, and Whitehouse in L & C JOURNALS, 7:83. The white pirogue was a vessel of eight tons burden, an open craft more than thirty feet long, equipped with sail. Clark blamed the accident on the carelessness of Charbonneau and credited Sacagawea with saving much of the cargo.

8. L & C JOURNALS, 2:116. ALLEN [2], 272–77, contains a useful discussion of the decision made at the Marias.

9. L & C JOURNALS, 2:180–83.

10. L & C JOURNALS, 3:69.

11. L & C JOURNALS, 3:207n. Elsewhere in his notes for the same day, and in a more restrained passage, Clark wrote, "We are in view of the opening of the Ocian, which creates great joy."

12. L & C JOURNALS, 3:244.

13. L & C JOURNALS, 5:223–25. Lewis wrote, "I called to them as I had done several times before that I would shoot them if they did not give me my horse and raised my gun, one of them jumped behind a rock and spoke to the other who turned arround . . . and I shot him through the belly, he fell to his knees and on his wright elbow from which position he partly raised himself up and fired at me."

14. Clark to Charbonneau, 20 Aug. 1806, Missouri Historical Society, St. Louis. Historians now believe that Sacagawea died while still in her teens (see L & C LETTERS, 2:639, 749). Young Jean Baptiste did receive an education in St. Louis under Clark's direction, and later traveled to Wurttemberg, Germany, as the ward of Prince Paul, who met the lad while on a trip up the Missouri and took him abroad in 1824. "Pomp" and "Pompey" were nicknames Clark had given the child.

15. Lewis to TJ, 23 Sept. 1806, LC. A draft of the letter at the American Philosophical Society library is written in a shaky and uneven hand, as if it were penned on the boat traversing the final miles to St. Louis.

16. L & C LETTERS, 1:280–81.

17. TJ to Volney, 11 Feb. 1806, LC. Volney had written TJ on 7 May 1804: "Nous sommes aux grandes scenes de d'histoire. Quoique ma part ne soit pas mauvaise, j'aimerais autant etre le l'expedition des voyageurs a l'Ouest" (CHINARD [1], 166–67).

18. Gallatin to TJ, 25 Oct. 1806, LC.

19. TJ to Lewis, 26 Oct. 1806, LC.

CHAPTER TEN

Jefferson's Indian Policy:
A Case Study

The Sauks and Foxes were the first Indians to feel new pressures created by the Louisiana Purchase. The treaty they signed in 1804 contained something impossible before: a provision for their eventual removal to the west side of the Mississippi. They also were the first among the tribes to surrender claim to lands actually lying west of that river. Their experience with Jefferson's Indian policy, and later with the policies of Madison, Monroe, Adams, and Jackson, provides an excellent picture of white-Indian relations as they were affected by Jefferson's determination that the Purchase was to be used for resettlement of the tribes.

· The Cuivre River Murders ·

Upstream a few miles from where William Clark had trained his men at the Wood River camp, the Cuivre River comes east from the high prairies of Missouri and loses itself in the willowed flats of the Mississippi. In the late summer of 1804, the Cuivre was the scene of a common and ugly occurrence: three white men were killed by Indians.

The raiding party consisted of five warriors from the loosely allied Sauk and Fox nations, whose summer villages were strung along both banks of the Mississippi, beginning just below the mouth of the Des Moines. They had wandered more than a hundred miles downstream, to the very northern edge of the settlements, risking peace with the white men without apparent provocation. Perhaps they were restless at the start of the new hunting season; perhaps they were thoughtless because their old chiefs were far away and could not counsel them. They killed in

[203]

the Indian way: musket fire, followed by ritualistic scalping, mutilation, and dismemberment.

On the following day a volunteer searching party led by Dr. Warren Cottle came upon the three bodies. He sent word at once to St. Louis, but by the time his message reached the commandant the five Sauk braves were nearing their village among the so-called lower towns of the Sauks and Foxes at the mouth of the Des Moines.

At first the Indians in the village were jubilant, for they profoundly disliked what they had seen of the Americans. Earlier in the year, soon after Louisiana had changed hands and Captain Stoddard had taken control in St. Louis, some cocky young Sauks had reportedly tied the U.S. flag to a horse's tail and dragged it across the ground.

The jubilation in the Sauk village lasted but a short time—perhaps no longer than it takes to mount a scalp dance—and then alarm spread. The four towns below the mouth of the Des Moines began to break up and move north. Into the dugout pirogues, and onto the backs of their horses, went everything the distraught villagers had brought with them for the summer. Leaving only their loaf-shaped lodges of elm bark, and the ashes of their kicked-out campfires, they pushed across the Des Moines to join forces with three villages on the north side, for added safety.

Two chiefs then volunteered to go to St. Louis, taking as their interpreter and spokesman a swart Creole trader named Louis Honoré, who had lived near the lower towns for several years. When confronted by Major James Bruff (who had just taken over as commandant from Captain Stoddard), the chiefs admitted that the killings on the Cuivre had been committed by three of their young men; the fourth had neither fired nor scalped, and the fifth had actually hung back, opposing the deed. The chiefs told Bruff they had put their lives into his power by coming down to inquire what satisfaction was demanded of them. They said they hoped the Americans would be merciful and not punish the innocent with the guilty. It was possible that they would not be able to persuade their nation to give up the slayers.

The whole trouble, they said, was the way the Americans had been treating those favored Indians to the west, the Osages. An

Osage delegation was even now on the way to see the Great Father in Washington. When Osages came to St. Louis they always went home with gifts, but when a Sauk or Fox war party ventured out to wreak vengeance on the Osages, the Americans stepped in and turned back the party. The Osages were a powerful tribe. Was it any wonder that the young Sauks began to think that Americans gave the most gifts to the tribe they feared the most? All right, thought the young men, we will show the Americans how to fear us also.

Bruff gave the chiefs a stern lecture and sent them home with orders to bring back the three men who had done the killing. Apparently he sent a paper along, to be read at the council fires by Honoré, but it has disappeared. Writing a few days later to General Wilkinson, Bruff said: "Enclosed is my Message to the Saukies [a variant of Sauk]—there is but one opinion here—that is—unless those Murderers are Demanded: given up and examples made of them; our Frontier will be continually harrassed by Murders and Robberies—I hope suffering their chiefs to return will at least induce a large proportion of them to attend the Treaty they are invited to by Governor Harrison—when measures may be taken that will produce those warriors."[1]

• A Call to Council •

Late in October their trader appeared with another message from St. Louis. This time it was from Pierre Chouteau, who had been named agent for the government during the summer. In translation, this is the message he sent up the river:

My brothers. The great chief of the seventeen great cities of America, having chosen me to maintain peace and union between all the Red skins and the government of the United States, I have in consequence just received the order from the great Chief of our country, who has just arrived from the post of Vincennes, to send for the chiefs of your villages with some important men, and to bring with them those of you who recently killed his children; I enjoin you to come at once, and if some great reasons prevent you from bringing the murderers with you, this is not to prevent you from obeying the orders which I transmit to you. When you carry them out, you will be treated as chiefs and you will go home after having listened to the word of your Father, and then you can make it understood by your elders and your young people; so open your ears and come at once. You will be treated as friends and allies of the United States.

Chouteau had given Honoré the message on 18 October, instructing him to "go immediately and get the chiefs and some important men *considerés* of the Sauk and Fox nations. . . ." He was also to pry slightly into the present relationship of the Indians to the British in Canada, "employing only methods of gentleness and persuasion." He was soon on his way back to St. Louis with most of what he had been sent for.[2]

In response to this summons, seven men went down the river in the last week of October. Honoré was one, gliding down to civilization in his cottonwood pirogue as he had done countless times. With him were six men from the Sauk-Fox confederation—two Fox chiefs, three Sauk chiefs, and a forlorn hostage from the unwise little party that had slaughtered the men on the Cuivre.

The hostage was not chained nor was he in arrest; he was simply going to surrender. When the council of chiefs and *considerés* had decided to give him up, there had been no force to use upon him but persuasion and moral pressure. Senior members of the tribes often complained that they had no control over their young men. But when they needed a hostage they managed somehow.

Except for one, the chiefs who accompanied the hapless warrior have left little record but their names. Only Quashquame has prevailed, somewhat more tangible than a shadow, a man reconstructible from bits and tatters of history. His name means Jumping Fish. Quashquame was a civil chief and hence a hereditary one, not a war chief, whose post was appointive. He was not a tall man; his body was stocky, shining with grease and the soot of many cooking fires. From his head he had plucked all the hair except a short tuft on top, and when he reached St. Louis he would unroll a gaudy headdress of roached deer hair and fasten it to the tuft with thongs and wooden pegs. An eagle plume would dangle from a bone tube at the back of the roach. His face was painted with vermilion and Prussian blue; his nose and ears were pierced for rings and pendants. About his neck he may have worn a necklace of bear claws, and perhaps a medal bearing the image of George III, for the Americans had not yet got around to issuing presidential medals to all the Sauk and Fox chiefs.

The white men who knew Quashquame said that he was not a profound thinker or a respected statesman, although he had the knack of commanding respect through oratory. He was a great beggar, they said, and of little influence in the long run. One thing more: he was a drunkard. No pirogue could ever carry him fast enough to the French taverns in St. Louis.[3]

The 27th of October, the day the chiefs arrived in town, was Saturday. They surrendered their hostage to Major Bruff and he was taken off to the garrison guardhouse because there was no jail. Most army posts in the West maintained log huts for visiting Indians; Quashquame and his colleagues probably spent the weekend in one of these, drinking whiskey that protocol required Bruff to dispense to chiefs on official business. (Officially, the army prohibited all issuance of liquor to Indians, but every post commander kept a barrel of common spirits for the use of visiting chiefs and *considerés*.) Certainly no business would have been conducted with them over the usually riotous Sabbath in St. Louis, but on Monday morning there probably was a meeting of the Indian delegation with William Henry Harrison.

Harrison was the "great Chief of our country" mentioned by Chouteau in his message to the Sauks and Foxes. He had arrived in town on 12 October from Vincennes, on the Wabash, had been met on the prairies east of the river by an escort of citizens, and since then had been the guest of Auguste Chouteau. As governor of Indiana Territory, his primary mission was to organize the District of Upper Louisiana as part of the territory. But now he had at hand the matter of the Sauks and Foxes, and he was by far the most important American figure to confront representatives of these tribes since the Purchase. He was a small, long-nosed gentleman of thirty-one years with a forelock slanting down toward his right eye. With his black suit and big black ascot tie, and his sallow plainness, he must have confirmed what the Indians already believed about Americans—that they were stiff-necked and unyielding—but he was not quite as dour as he looked, and at home had a reputation for occasional vivacity. Though he seemed rather young to be a governor, it was but one of the titles he had won in the few years since he had set out as an ensign in the First Infantry, with a volume of rhetoric and an edition of Cicero, to fight Indians under General Anthony Wayne.

First at the council, the general cry of *bon jour!*—a phrase understood by every Indian in the valley. Then the matter of the murders and the hostage.

Our account of this deliberation comes from James Bruff, who wrote Secretary of War Dearborn after the series of councils had ended. He said that Harrison offered to pardon the other murderers if they would come down and appear as witnesses against the prisoner. Indeed, Harrison and some of the other officials would have let the hostage go free, but Bruff had opposed this. He wanted the prisoner *and* the fugitives, as a matter of law and order. A legal tangle arose when Amos Stoddard and Judge John Griffin (of the Harrison party) argued that none of the Indians could be brought to trial. First, the crime had been committed under Spanish rule. Second, how could you swear in an Indian witness, with his red heathen hand on the Bible, when he was not a Christian?

At this sophistry, Bruff snorted and wrote, "With *due* difference to the *legal* knowledge of those gentlemen: I must doubt the law, as it is not founded on reason. If christian testimony to identify Indians . . . is insisted on—none will ever be condemnd: and what wou'd be the consequences I leave those who know our frontier people to judge!"[4]

To dispose of the problem Harrison kept the hostage in the guardhouse, applied to President Jefferson for his pardon, and brought up a new matter that Quashquame and the other chiefs were ill-prepared to discuss. The real subject on Harrison's mind was this: he wanted to buy land from the Sauks and Foxes.

• Harrison as Land Buyer •

As the power behind Jefferson's land policy in the West, Harrison had been obtaining cessions from the Indian nations in tremendous amounts. Judging from the clamor that arose among the Indians after some of his treaty-making, he did not always reach a meeting of the minds with the sellers. Historians would later berate him for his unseemly haste and say that he was

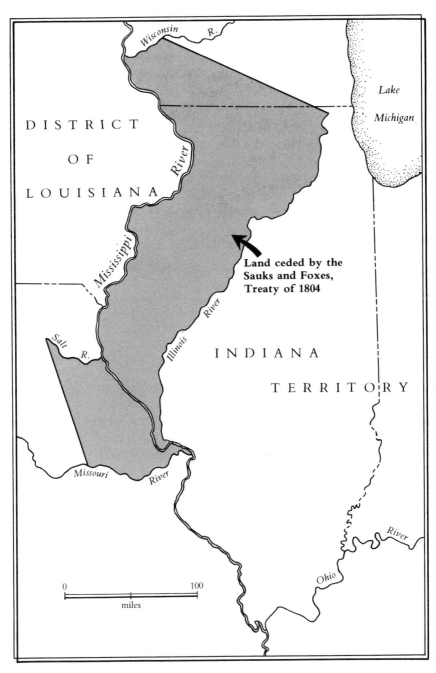

9. Lands ceded by the Sauks and Foxes in 1804.

courting the approval of land-hungry westerners, hoping to draw attention from his unpopular civil administration. If his methods were his own, and not too savory, certainly his basic instructions came straight from the pen of Jefferson. The President had written him in the winter of 1803:

. . . to be prepared against the occupation of Louisiana by a powerful and enterprising people, it is important that setting less value on interior extension of purchases from the Indians, we bend our whole views to the purchase and settlement of the country on the Missisipi from its mouth to it's Northern regions, that we may be able to present as strong a front on our Western as on our Eastern boarder, and plant on the Missisipi itself the means of its own defence. . . . For this purpose we have given you a general commission for treating. The crisis is pressing. Whatever can now be obtained, must be obtained quickly. The occupation of New Orleans, hourly expected, by the French, is already felt like a light breeze by the Indians. You know the sentiments they entertain of that nation. Under the hope of their protection, they will immediately stiffen against cessions of land to us. We had better therefore do at once what can now be done.[5]

Of course the French threat was now gone, but there were always the British up in Canada, sending traders down the river with better goods for the Indians than they could get from American traders. The woodland nations still made annual treks to Fort Malden across the Detroit River to receive gifts and friendly un-American counsel from the British commandant. This bolstered the natural inclination of the Sauks, Foxes, and Winnebagoes to be surly toward the United States. A solid boundary along the Mississippi would be an advantage if real trouble ever developed with Great Britain and her potential Indian allies.

The Sauks and Foxes had never really been parties to a treaty with the United States, even though two Sauks had signed the Fort Harmar treaty negotiated by Arthur St. Clair in January 1789. That treaty, mainly involving the Wyandot, Delaware, Ottawa, Chippewa, and Potawatomi nations, had never been taken very seriously by anyone concerned, and had been superseded in 1795 by the important Treaty of Greenville. The Sauks had been invited to Greenville but mistook the date and missed the council. This left them utterly free of commitments to the

United States in regard to such matters as mutual exchange of prisoners, and so on. It also left them in possession of a big segment of the Mississippi that Harrison had long eyed with interest.

He had written Secretary Dearborn in July 1801 that the Sauks were "very willing to treat if they are put upon the same footing that the rest of the Indian Nations are." And seven months later, on the same topic, "They are now extremely desirous to be put on a footing with the other tribes, and receive an annual present, and it appears reasonable that they should."[6]

The Sauks were not anxious enough to put in an appearance, however, when Harrison arranged a treaty date for them. He had suggested to Dearborn that they be dealt with in the summer of 1802. Dearborn had given him permission to grant them an annuity of $500 if their conduct merited it. But when Harrison scheduled a council for August, no Sauk chiefs appeared.

A year later Harrison was still determined to bring them to terms. He wrote Jefferson in October 1803, saying that no part of the President's plan for land cessions remained unaccomplished except the settlement of boundaries in the Illinois country with the Sauks, Potawatomis, and Kickapoos.[7]

All this correspondence fails to mention the Foxes (the French called them Renards and they called themselves Mesquakies), who were affiliated with the Sauks. The government apparently did not know of this alliance, although the Americans in St. Louis did.

By 1804 the Sauks and Foxes had begun to see the advantages of a treaty. They had told Amos Stoddard in June that they would like a government factory or trading house to supply them with goods. And Harrison had received instructions from Secretary of War Dearborn: "It may not be improper to procure from the Sauks such cessions on both sides of the Illinois as may entitle them to an annual compensation of Five or Six hundred dollars; they ought to relinquish all pretensions to any land on the southern side of [the] Illinois and a considerable tract on the other side."[8]

On his arrival in St. Louis, Harrison instructed agent Pierre Chouteau to invite the Indians down to a council. Bruff mentions the word "treaty" in a letter to Washington. But there was no mention of a treaty in the message Chouteau sent up the river. Was the omission Harrison's or his? The missing Bruff message to the Indians may have mentioned a treaty, but even so, "treaty" did not necessarily mean "land cession" to an Indian. It may have meant merely a pact of friendship and the receipt of gifts such as those the British gave them yearly.

Had the two Indian nations expected to sell land they would have sent a large delegation to St. Louis. In it would have been some of their shrewdest chiefs and most persuasive orators. Chief White Skin of the Sauks, for example, or Black Thunder of the Foxes. Instead, they sent five chiefs of middling caliber, expecting only to placate the Americans by handing over a hostage. They had clearly sent their second team.

A treaty was drawn on 3 November 1804 that transferred fifteen million acres of land lying in what is now Illinois, Wisconsin, and Missouri. The land was to remain in Indian hands until the government had sold it off in parcels to white men, and the Indians were to get $1,000 a year in annuities, plus the services of a trader, a blacksmith, and a man to teach them farming. And most important: eventually they were to vacate the east side of the Mississippi.[9]

The names of the five chiefs were written at the end of the document and they solemnly touched the quill while the clerk made a cross after each name. For the Sauks: Layouvois, Pashepaho, and Quashquame. For the Foxes: Outchequaha and Hahshequaxhiqua. For the United States: Harrison and two officials from Indiana Territory—his secretary William Prince, and Judge John Griffin. Also Bruff and Stoddard, Pierre Chouteau and his brother Auguste, Charles Gratiot, Stephen Worrell, and Daniel Delaunay. Finally the two sworn interpreters, Joseph Barron and Hypolite Bolon.

A sworn interpreter was one who swore he had made every word of a treaty clear to the Indians who signed it. What the two Frenchmen could never have made clear to the Sauks and Foxes was the abuse, disgrace, and heartache they had contracted for in signing away fifteen million acres of land. The furor broke the moment the men had returned home and reported to their tribal councils. It would terminate, after years of struggle and ill will, with the Black Hawk War of 1832.

James Bruff claimed that the delegation wanted the treaty and eagerly signed away the land to get protection from the Osages. But a Sauk and Fox group that came to St. Louis the following summer complained bitterly. "We were desirous to oblige the United States," they said, "but we had never before Sold Land, and we did not know the value of it, we trusted our beloved white men traders and interpreters to Speak for us, and we have given away a great Country to Governor Harrison for a little thing, we do not say we were cheated, but we made a bad bargain and the Chiefs who made it are all dead, deposed, yet the bargain Stands, for we never take back what we have given, but we hope our Great Father will . . . allow us Something in addition, to what Governor Harrison has promised us."[10]

The claim that the chiefs who made the treaty were deposed is exaggerated, though they obviously lost much prestige. Quashquame remained head of a village for many years, and traveled to Washington at least once with a delegation of Sauks. He continued to sign treaties during his lifetime (he died in 1830). The name of Pashepaho, a principal Sauk chief, appears on later treaties but there were two men of that name. Hahshequaxhiqua probably was the same as Chahecahaqua, a Fox who signed the 1805 treaty with the Osages.

Yet they lived in shame. "This old man is the one who has made us all unhappy!" cried Keokuk at a council with white men in 1829, pointing to the aging Quashquame.

In self-defense the signers sought alibis. Quashquame insisted that Pierre Chouteau had offered to free the hostage in exchange for all the land claimed by the Sauks and Foxes east of the Mississippi. In opposition is the comment by Major Bruff, previously cited, that Harrison wanted to set the prisoner free. Quashquame also said he had only agreed to sell the land as far north as the Rock River but that one of the Foxes had agreed to the larger tract. At no time, insisted Quashquame, did he ever realize he was selling out completely on the east side of the Mississippi.[11]

The most spectacular excuse set forth by the signers was their repeated cry: "We were drunk! We did not know what we were doing!"

Commenting on this claim a few years later, Dr. Isaac

Galland, who knew Quashquame and the other signers, said:
"The writer had no doubt, from his own personal knowledge of
Quas-Quaw-ma, that he would have sold to Gov. Harrison, at
that time, all the country east of the Rocky Mountains, if it had
been required."[12]

Harrison, like most western officials, held equivocal views
toward prohibition for Indians. As a matter of long-range policy
he wanted liquor kept away from them, and he sounds sincerely
appalled when he is describing the effects of alcohol: "I can at
once tell by looking at an Indian whom I chance to meet whether
he belong to a Neighbouring or a more distant Tribe. The latter
is generally well Clothed healthy and vigorous the former half
naked, filthy and enfeebled with Intoxication. . . ."[13]

But given a particular delegation of chiefs and a particular
transaction to accomplish—well, a man had to be practical about
these things.

What he really thought about the treaty is hard to say. The
letter he wrote Secretary of War Dearborn on 21 November,
forwarding the agreement and commenting on it, was received
and registered by clerks in the secretary's office but cannot now
be found. Pierre Chouteau wrote somewhat smugly to Jefferson,
"I see with satisfaction that my credit and influence with these
two nations have finally brought these chiefs to conclude a treaty
which I dare believe you will find advantageous."

Jefferson's own comment was forthright. To Secretary Dearborn he wrote: "The late purchase is important as it fortifies our
right to keep the British off from the Missisippi." In his message
to Congress on the subject he said, "This cession giving us a
perfect title to such a breadth of country on the eastern side of the
Mississippi, with a command of the Ouisconsin, strengthens our
means of retaining exclusive commerce with the Indians, on the
western side of the Mississippi: a right indispensable to the policy
of governing those Indians by commerce rather than by arms."[14]

One dubious advantage accrued to the Indians; it brought to
them, in theory at least, the protection afforded by the act of
Congress of 30 March 1802 to regulate trade and intercourse with
the Indian tribes. The act described boundary lines between the
United States and various tribes, and it laid down certain stipula-
tions against trespassing on tribal lands, committing offenses

against the Indians, etc. Until the Sauks and Foxes had been welcomed into the Great Father's official arms they could not receive the benefits of this legislation, which accomplished little.

That the five signers did not "sell" the land in the absolute sense is obvious; they merely surrendered their particular claim to it, and the government would have to buy most of it again from other Indian nations. In 1816 the United States would buy from the Ottawa, Chippewa, and Potawatomi nations a large share of the Sauk and Fox cession east of the Mississippi, and by 1833 would have re-purchased, through various stages of cession and retrocession, all of the original area.

The Sauk prisoner who had triggered this interaction between Indians and whites lay in a guardhouse cell all winter and into the spring, glanced at now and then by a sergeant of the guard but apparently forgotten by those who were to say what should be done with him. No one in St. Louis knew that Jefferson had pardoned him in February 1805.

By early May the pardon had reached Harrison in Vincennes and had been forwarded. In the letter accompanying the pardon, Secretary of War Dearborn said that Jefferson believed "we ought to commence our intercourse with the Indians in Louisiana in such a manner as to show not only our regard for justice, but our benevolent and tender feelings for the unhappy. . . ."[15] But the forlorn young man could wait no longer. Before the pardon reached St. Louis, he broke away and was fired upon, as he fled, by a sentinel whose musket was charged with buckshot. His body, or at least the body of an Indian felled by buckshot, was found outside St. Louis later in May.

· Implementing the Treaty ·

At last the hand of the Great Father was raised to bless his Sauk and Fox children. In 1805 the government moved frequently but ponderously on behalf of the tribes; always the moves were inept, unfruitful, or too late. By April a site was being discussed for the factory or trading house called for in the treaty. But when it finally was built at Fort Belle Fontaine, on the south bank of the Missouri four miles above its mouth, the location was too far away for the convenience of the tribes. Failing to understand the economy of the Indians, the government hesitated to extend credit even though Jefferson himself advocated it. It would take a while to weaken the Poor-Richard caution of the men who ran the Office of Indian Trade.

While being transported in a keelboat on the Ohio, the first year's shipment of annuity goods sank in a gale. The boat crew spent eight days drying the blankets and bolts of yard goods on the river bank, but they were ruined. Too bad, said General Wilkinson, reporting the loss to Washington, but the goods were of poor quality anyway and the selection was not suitable for the Sauks and Foxes.

Land remained the biggest problem even after the treaty had transferred ownership of fifteen million acres. The Indians were still there and would be allowed to remain until the land passed into private hands. And who knew how gracefully they would leave when the time came? Only three weeks after the treaty, Surveyor-General Jared Mansfield had been ready to move crews into a portion of the new area. In March an act of Congress had provided that the land office at Kaskaskia could open the territory to settlers.[16]

To most white men the Indian's notions about land were damned foolishness. A band of Sauks, say, rode twice a year through a tract as big as a couple of eastern states, and claimed it as their own. The settlers were willing to give the Indian two choices: he could pack up his cooking pots and beaver traps and disappear over the horizon, or he could die. As Jefferson and the men about him knew, sensible planning required a third alternative. Give the Indian a workable substitute for his wide-ranging winter hunts and eventually he might be able to live beside the white man. Better still, he might quietly leave the settled areas without resistance. As Jefferson explained:

When they withdraw themselves to the culture of a small piece of land, they will perceive how useless to them are their extensive forests, and will be willing to pare them off from time to time in exchange for necessaries for their farms & families. To promote this disposition to exchange lands which they have to spare and we want for necessaries, which we have to spare and they want, we shall push our trading houses, and be glad to see the good and influential individuals among them run into debt, because we observe that when these debts get beyond what the individuals can pay, they become willing to lop them off by a cession of lands. . . . In this way, our settlements will gradually circumscribe and approach the Indians, and they will in time either incorporate with us as citizens of the United States or remove beyond the Missisipi. The former is certainly the termination of this history most happy for themselves. But in the whole course of this, it is essential to cultivate their love. As to their fear, we presume that our strength and their weakness is now so visible that they must see we have only to shut our hand to crush them. . . .[17]

· The Policy in General ·

On paper, the Indian policy of the United States had always been pretty much the same: keep the peace, civilize the tribes, trade with them, and get title to their lands. These ends could be accomplished by fair or foul means, and fair was better, especially if it cost less. "The Indians can be kept in order only by commerce or war," Jefferson said. "The former is the cheapest. Unless we can induce individuals to employ their capital in that trade, it will require an enormous sum of capital [for war] from the public treasury."[18]

That is Jefferson at his most pragmatic. He could put it much more delicately: The Indian could be controlled

by introducing among them a knowledge of agriculture & some of the mechanic arts, by encouraging them to resort to these as more certain & less laborious resources for subsistence, than the chace; & by withholding from them pernicious supplies of ardent spirits. They are our brethren, our neighbors; they may be valuable friends, & troublesome enemies. Both duty & interest then enjoin, that we should extend to them the blessings of civilized life, & prepare their minds for becoming useful members of the American family.[19]

To understand Jefferson's Indian policy, we must remember first that he was a benevolent man facing an insoluble situation. We need also to see his attitude toward the Indian as multifaceted, for he must deal with them as a problem in his role as their Great Father, yet could view them as a delightful source of study in his other role as an amateur ethnologist and collector of Osage headdresses.

One way of looking at his policy is to separate out its component parts:

1. Indians are almost as capable as Europeans, but they are not ready for assimilation. (In contrast, the blacks will never be ready for it.)

2. They must sell their lands and learn to support themselves by other means. Otherwise, there is no room for them.

3. For a generation or so, the eastern Indians must move to the western side of the Mississippi while they learn the white man's ways.

4. Eventually, the blood of the two races will flow together and complete assimilation will occur.[20]

Could Jefferson have chosen his own timetable, the policy might have worked, especially if he also could have controlled the temperament and unabating land hunger of the American people. As always, events ran ahead of Jefferson's schedule.

· A Spark in the Willows ·

For a while the government tried to honor the treaty terms. A young Pennsylvania farmer, William Ewing, was sent to the Des Moines Rapids to teach the Indians agriculture. The irony was that the Sauk and Fox women, with their corn, bean, and squash fields, knew more about farming than Ewing did. The Indians also got a blacksmith to repair the shoddy traps and cheap firearms that came to them through the U.S. factory system. Finally they were given a factory of their own, above the Rapids where Fort Madison, Iowa, now stands. The factory needed protecting, especially when a "British band" of Indians came under the influence of English traders in the uneasy years before the War of 1812. So Fort Bellevue, later named Fort Madison, was established in 1808. For a while it thrived, along with its sister post on the Missouri, Fort Osage, built at the same time. But in 1813, under constant siege by the warring faction and deserted by the army contractor who was supposed to supply it, Fort Madison was abandoned. It burned, probably set afire by the withdrawing soldiers of the First Infantry.

After the War of 1812, new factories and new forts would appear in Sauk and Fox country, but encroachment by the whites created constant incidents. The lead mines of the Indians were one focus of trouble.

In the region where Wisconsin, Iowa, and Illinois come together, rich lead mines were worked not only by the Sauks and Foxes, but also by the Winnebagoes, Chippewas, and Potawatomis. The women worked the mines, using primitive methods that left much foreign matter in the metal, and the men floated the pigs or plaques of lead downriver to be traded for goods at the factory. Before the destruction of Fort Madison, the factory transshipped lead weighing 29,900 pounds to St. Louis in the fall of 1811.[21]

By the late 1820s, strong-willed white men were attempting to work the mines in defiance of the complaints of Indian agents and the orders of regional army commanders. About the only result was the lessening influence of the government Indian agents, once the Indians saw how powerless they were. It was reported in 1828 that the lead mines of the Sauks, Foxes, and other tribes in the area had been invaded by 10,000 illegal white miners. The solution was the old one: since the whites were there and would not leave, the only recourse was to extinguish the Indian title to the mines by treaty.[22]

If the history of Indian-white relations can be stated in terms of presidential policy, then the final years of the Sauks and Foxes as a free people might be expressed this way:

Under Thomas Jefferson (1801–9): The Indians gave up all claim to their homeland, but were beginning to receive some of the benefits promised by the treaty when the British intervened. By splitting the two tribes into factions, British traders involved them in the sparring between the United States and England.

Under James Madison (1809–17): The "British band" of Sauks and Foxes were directly involved in the War of 1812, causing the rest of the two tribes to suffer. The younger warriors, who could not be controlled by the older chiefs, brought about the destruction first of their factory and then of the entire post at Fort Madison. At the close of the war, the tribes signed treaties of peace in 1815 and 1816 in which they assented to the hated cession of 1804.

Under James Monroe (1817–25): The British band in 1817 refused to accept its annuities, saying their members would rather starve than part with their lands; eventually they accepted the annual payment. Pressure for the tribes to remove continued. There was intertribal warfare with the eastern Sioux. Whites were threatening the lead mines and encroaching on the land.

Under John Quincy Adams (1825–29): Evoking the terms of the 1804 treaty, under which the Indians had agreed to vacate when their lands were taken up by white settlers, the government ordered the Sauks and Foxes to move west of the river by the spring of 1829.

Under Andrew Jackson (1829–32): The Indians moved under protest. Then Black Hawk, an old Sauk war chief of the British band, led his followers back to the east side of the river in April 1832 to "plant corn." The band, including many women and children, was pursued and routed by Illinois volunteers and U. S. regulars; many were killed and Black Hawk was made a temporary prisoner. The affair is pretentiously called the Black Hawk War. In September 1832, under a new treaty, the Sauks and Foxes were permanently removed to the west side of the Mississippi. In his message to Congress the following year, Jackson said of Indians in general: "They have neither the intelligence, the industry, the moral habits, nor the desire of improvement which are essential to any favorable change in their condition . . . they must necessarily yield to the force of circumstances and erelong disappear."[23]

Jefferson, Madison, Monroe, Adams, Jackson: the details of their Indian policy differed, as did the degree of their compassion for the tribes, but the result was to be the same. There might be many presidents and presidential policies, but the American people had but one Indian policy—and it was nonnegotiable. Always the government caved in first, then the Indians.

NOTES

1. For the Cuivre River incident and events following, see Cottle to Bruff, 9 Sept. 1804, and Bruff to Wilkinson, 29 Sept. and 5 Nov. 1804, TERR. PAPERS, 13:62–63, 56–61, 76–80; and Pierre Chouteau to Dearborn, 7 Nov. 1804, Chouteau letterbook, Missouri Historical Society, St. Louis. For the truculent attitude of the Sauks and Foxes, see Stod-

dard to Dearborn, 3 June 1804, Missouri Historical Society, and Wherry to Stoddard, 14 Sept. 1804, TERR. PAPERS, 13:64.

2. Chouteau's message to the Sauks and his instructions to Honoré, both 18 Oct. 1804, are in his letterbook, Missouri Historical Society.

3. See sketchy references to Quashquame in Thomas Forsyth's narrative and Lyman C. Draper's annotations, *Wisconsin Historical Collections,* 6 (1827), 192; *Missouri Gazette* (St. Louis), 4 Oct. 1809; and GALLAND, 53.

4. Bruff to Dearborn, 5 Nov. 1804, TERR. PAPERS, 13:76–80. In a postscript he added: "Col. [de]Lassuss with the Spanish troops, arty. & stores are on the point of departure—his boats are loaded &c." Major James Bruff, of the First Artillerists and Engineers, was sent in the spring of 1804 to become both military and civil commandant of Upper Louisiana, but soon Captain Amos Stoddard assumed the duties of civil command while Bruff stayed on as military officer. See Dearborn to Stoddard, 16 May 1804, NARG 107, letters sent, 2:236.

5. TJ to Harrison, 27 Feb. 1803, LC.

6. Harrison to Dearborn, 15 July 1801 and 26 Feb. 1802, ESAREY, 1:41–46.

7. Harrison to TJ, 29 Oct. 1803, LC.

8. Dearborn to Harrison, 27 June 1804, ESAREY, 1:101. For the Sauk and Fox desire to have a trading house, see Stoddard to Dearborn, 22 June 1804, *Glimpses of the Past,* Missouri Historical Society, 2:114–15.

9. The treaty is in KAPPLER, 2:54–56. It directs that a meeting should occur between the Osages and the Sauks and Foxes "for the purpose of burying the tomahawk and renewing the friendly intercourse between themselves and the Osages" (art. 10). The treaty was the first to set a boundary for tribes claiming land in the Louisiana Purchase.

10. Wilkinson to Dearborn, 27 July 1805, TERR. PAPERS, 13:164.

11. Quashquame on Chouteau's offer: St. Vrain to William Clark, 28 May 1831, Clark Papers, vol. 6, Kansas State Historical Society, Topeka; Quashquame on the cession boundary: Thomas Forsyth's report, 1 Oct. 1832, Draper Manuscripts, 9T54–59, State Historical Society of Wisconsin, Madison.

12. GALLAND, 53. Of the more than $2,000 charged against the five signatories while they were in St. Louis, and which was made a part of the treaty terms, some may have gone for trade goods but certainly a share was spent for whiskey.

13. Harrison to Dearborn, 15 July 1801, ESAREY, 1:29. Harrison's genuine concern for the rights of Indians, and their sensitivity to liquor, is in contrast to his fervor to dispossess them of their lands by ostensibly legal means (PRUCHA, 157).

14. Harrison's missing letter is registered in NARG 107 as letters

received, H-236(2). Chouteau's comment on the treaty: Chouteau to
TJ, 31 Jan. 1805, Chouteau letterbook. TJ's comment to Dearborn, 16
Dec. 1804, LC. TJ's message to Congress, 31 Dec. 1804, AM. ST.
PAPERS, Indian Affairs, 1:693.

15 For the pardon, see Dearborn to Harrison, 12 Feb. 1805, NARG
107, letters sent. For the escape, Harrison to Dearborn, 27 May 1805,
ESAREY, 1:132.

16. The loss of annuity goods is discussed in Wilkinson to Dearborn,
8 Oct. 1805, TERR. PAPERS, 13:234, and John B. Treat to Dearborn, 15
Nov. 1805, TERR. PAPERS, 13:276. For the surveying of treaty lands, see
Jared Mansfield to Gallatin, 26 Nov. 1804, TERR. PAPERS, 7:239. See also
"Supplementary Act for Disposal of the Public Lands," 3 March 1805,
TERR. PAPERS, 7:264.

17. TJ to Harrison, 27 Feb. 1803, LC. Another portion of this
letter, basic to an understanding of TJ's Indian land policy, is quoted
earlier in this chapter.

18. TJ to Gallatin, 7 Jan. 1808, LC.

19. TJ to the Society of Friends in Pennsylvania, 13 Nov. 1807,
LC.

20. SHEEHAN is a thorough study of TJ's Indian policy. It is difficult
to state in a few words without doing TJ an injustice, as this statement by Nathan Schachner demonstrates: "While paying lip service to
peace, justice, and friendship, Jefferson's graduated steps for dealing
with the Indians envisaged a cynical and effective procedure for getting
rid of them that held little of these abstract principles and had only
expediency to commend it" (SCHACHNER, 731–32). For another sound
work on American Indian policy, see PRUCHA.

21. NARG 75, Fort Madison folder, drawer 43. The heavy lead was
tricky to ship because it occupied so little space in the hold of a keelboat.
If the boat were stove in, there would be no bulky cargo to hold back
the water until the craft could be beached.

22. The takeover of the lead mines is dealt with in PRUCHA, 178–82.
The interest of American citizens in the mines probably dates from a
six-column report in the *National Intelligencer,* 14 Nov. 1804, written by
Moses Austin and submitted—according to an editorial note in the
newspaper—at the request of Meriwether Lewis.

23. RICHARDSON, 3:1083.

CHAPTER ELEVEN

Exploring by Master Plan

So firmly have Lewis and Clark caught the nation's fancy that one often forgets to consider their expedition as part of a greater plan of exploration. What began as a response to Mackenzie became, with the achievement of the Louisiana Purchase, also the first step in Jefferson's larger scheme to examine and map the territory.

While Lewis and Clark were still staging near St. Louis, Jefferson was writing William Dunbar about his greater hopes. He said he would charge the surveyor-general north of the Ohio with the task of exploring the upper Mississippi, and that he expected Congress to authorize him to explore the rivers west of there. "In this case I should propose to send one party up the Panis river [Platte and North Platte], thence along the highlands to the source of the Padoucas river [South Platte] and down to its mouth. Another party up the Arcansa to it's source, thence along the highlands to the source of the Red river, & down that to it's mouth. . . . These surveys will enable us to prepare a map of La. which in its contour and main waters will be perfectly correct."[1]

His purpose in writing Dunbar was to ask him to direct the Arkansas–Red River expedition. He described it in terms much like the Lewis and Clark expedition, and said he assumed that Congress would authorize the funding. As he envisioned it, the exploration would be as vital to the national interest as was that of Lewis and Clark, for the Arkansas and Red rivers were thought to flow from the highlands near the southwestern boundaries of the Purchase.

"By locating the sources of these two affluents of the Mississippi," writes historian Isaac J. Cox, "his expedition would mark two important points on the 'undoubted' limits of Louisiana. Other similar points might later be located at leisure farther north. Meanwhile, the general public might become better informed regarding their new possession and the President and his advisers gain the necessary information to guide them in settling its boundaries with Spain."[2]

It was never Jefferson's intention that Dunbar should accompany the arduous expedition in person; his role was to be that of a home-based director. He was a fortunate choice in terms of his location, Natchez, and his interest in geography and other sciences. It would be necessary, however, to find a man to lead the expedition in person and a second observer to make scientific observations.

By mid-May, Dunbar had received no instructions from Jefferson other than his original letter of 13 March 1804. He had learned from Secretary of War Dearborn—who assumed Dunbar would accept the assignment—that he was expected to choose the men who would conduct the expedition, and that a military escort and suitable boat would be provided.

The rapport between Dunbar and Jefferson was such that plans were being made on the assumption that Dunbar would serve. Without awaiting further word from the President, he wrote him in May, "It will give me great pleasure to contribute every thing in my power to promote the proposed expedition on the Red & Arcansaw rivers." He sounded two perceptive warning notes. First, the Spanish ought to be applied to for consent, although "we might go up the Arcansaw river & come down the red river without any great probability of the Spaniards obtaining a knowledge of the expedition." This despite his own awareness that it might seem "improper condescension" to ask permission to explore "our own rivers." His second warning lay in his apprehension about the splinter band of Osages who had broken off from the main tribe and moved to the Arkansas. They were not understood to be friendly toward Americans. Dunbar knew that Pierre Chouteau had for some years enjoyed exclusive trading privileges with those Indians. It might be wise, Dunbar proposed, to let Chouteau suggest an appropriate guide and interpreter to ease the way through the Osage country.[3] Although he still had no further word from Jefferson, he wrote again in June, suggesting that the Red River, "being thought to be the most interesting of the two," ought to be ascended. His reasoning was that upriver travel, being slower, allowed more time for collecting and other scientific pursuits.[4]

Extensive preparation was going on in Washington as well as at Natchez. Jefferson had sent a set of instructions, leaving blank the name of the addressee, for the guidance of whoever would be chosen to lead the party. These were comparable to those given Michaux in 1793 and Lewis in 1803, even to the point of recommending birch bark as writing paper. Along with the five and a half pages of instructions, Jefferson had written Dunbar that Dr. George Hunter, of Philadelphia, had been appointed scientist to the expedition. He was not the botanist Dunbar had hoped for. "His fort is chemistry," Jefferson said, and he was qualified to take astronomical observations.[5]

Plans began to go awry in Washington upon the arrival of the Osage delegation sent from St. Louis by Lewis. From White Hairs, principal chief of the Osages who had not moved to the Arkansas, Jefferson learned of the schism in the tribe. As he wrote to Dunbar, the renegade Osages would undoubtedly oppose the passage of the expedition "and perhaps do worse." White Hairs had earnestly urged that the undertaking be suspended and that a mediator be sent to attempt a reconciliation of the two Osage groups. Jefferson said he was sending Pierre Chouteau to the Arkansas to "engage their consent to our mission and to furnish guides," as Dunbar had suggested, and that "on the whole therefore we conclude to suspend this expedition until the spring [of 1805]."

Something might be done immediately, however. Dunbar had written Jefferson about the interesting Ouachita River, and said he had thought of making his own investigation of that stream. Jefferson seized upon this notion as a way to keep the Red River party intact—after so much effort by the War Department to organize it—while negotiations were going on with the Arkansas Osages. The delay would also give Jefferson time "to remove Spanish impediments."[6]

• The Dunbar-Hunter Expedition •

Starting 16 October from a landing near Natchez, Dunbar and Hunter took their small expedition (without benefit of a commis-

sioned army officer) up the Red River to the mouth of the
Ouachita. Ascending this stream, the lower reaches of which
were then called the Black, they reached old Fort Miro by 9
November. That place was now called Ouachita Post, later to
become the site of Monroe, La. Dunbar wrote Jefferson from
here, complaining that the boat assigned him was too cumbersome
and that he was switching to another.[7] By 15 November the
party was crossing into present Arkansas, and by early December
the soldiers—a sergeant and twelve privates—were complaining
about the labor of portaging from the head of river navigation
across to the Hot Springs (at present Hot Springs, Ark.). The
party stayed at Hot Springs for a month, and were back at
Natchez by the end of January.

Dunbar had learned some practical things about exploration:
the need for a suitable river craft, the need for an officer to keep
the soldiers interested in their work, and, above all, he had plenty
of arguments against the plan of ascending one river and portaging to another. These thoughts he was to convey to Jefferson,
along with some data about the Red and Arkansas rivers. Both
Dunbar and Hunter had kept detailed journals which were sent to
Washington. It had been a minor expedition, as intended, but it
gave the principals an undisputed role in the history of western
exploration.[8]

· Planning for the Red River ·

After Congress added an additional $5,000 for exploration in
early 1805, Jefferson told Dunbar to go ahead with the Red River
arrangements.[9] Leaving the logistics to be worked out between
Dunbar and the War Department, Jefferson turned to two matters that concerned him personally as well as officially: the hiring
of suitable men to make astronomical observations and natural
history collections, and the removal of "Spanish impediments"
to passage of the party up the river.

Faulty communication hampered the staffing. Failure of the
mails was one problem, but in searching for an expedition leader
there was simply a failure of Dunbar and Jefferson to understand
each other. Jefferson had referred to a man he called Colonel
Freeman as eligible to head the expedition. The only "Colonel"

Freeman known to Dunbar was Lieutenant Colonel Constant Freeman, of the Artillerists, then commandant at New Orleans. Dunbar proceeded with his plans on the assumption that Constant Freeman was to become the military commander of the expedition and that he must be versed in the use of the sextant. When Dunbar saw the colonel and mentioned the expedition to him, Freeman said he knew nothing about it. Apparently Dunbar suspended, or at least slowed down, his arrangements while awaiting clarification from Jefferson.[10] When it developed that Jefferson was thinking of Thomas Freeman, a surveyor who had worked with Andrew Ellicott during the survey of the southern boundary between Spain and the United States in the late 1790s, Dunbar recognized the misunderstanding. He, too, had worked with *that* Freeman but had found him not too interested in the astronomical aspects of surveying. It was an awkward position for Dunbar, who probably would not have selected Freeman himself. Indeed, the whole planning process must have frustrated Dunbar, combining frequent lapses in understanding, delays in the mail, and decisions made by others which ran counter to steps he had already taken.

Jefferson was still looking for a naturalist. Apparently he had advanced beyond believing that a gifted amateur like Meriwether Lewis could both command an expedition and make satisfactory scientific observations. A versatile but eccentric botanist, Constantine Samuel Rafinesque, had met Jefferson briefly in the summer of 1804. In November he wrote that he had heard of the various western expeditions, wondered why no botanist had accompanied them, and himself volunteered to go along on such an expedition. Jefferson replied in December, explaining that the Red River expedition was forming and that Rafinesque was welcome to go but could not expect much remuneration except his expenses. But when the letter reached Philadelphia, Rafinesque (a French-German who was born in Turkey) had sailed for Europe.[11]

There was a more troubling failure of the mails in the case of Alexander Wilson. Wilson, a respected ornithologist known to Jefferson, wrote him in February 1806 and asked for a position as naturalist on the Red River expedition. He is said to have given the letter to William Bartram for seconding and forwarding to

Jefferson. It is likely the letter never reached Jefferson. Dismayed, Wilson wrote his nephew William Duncan: "I begin to think that either Mr. Jefferson expects a brush with the Spaniards or has not received our letters; otherwise, he would never act so impolitely to one for whom he has so much esteem as for Mr. Bartram." In later years, naturalist George Ord was to publish a tirade against Jefferson because of this episode, having overlooked Wilson's reasonable assumption that the President had not received his letter.[12]

The search for a naturalist was so unrewarding that Jefferson even offered the post to the venerable and infirm William Bartram, who declined with appreciation and regret. Finally Benjamin Smith Barton recommended a young medical student of his, Peter Custis. Although Jefferson must have been relieved to find a "scientist" at last, he may well have had misgivings about Custis. He was called a doctor in the correspondence, but was not to receive his medical degree from the University of Pennsylvania for another year. Born about 1781, on the Eastern Shore of Virginia, he had received a sound secondary education and had entered the Medical Department in 1804. He became Barton's friend and protégé, and learned from him the rudiments of botany and zoology.[13]

Until early in 1806 it had been mutually agreed that the Red River, more "interesting" than the Arkansas, would be explored first. Then Dunbar wrote Secretary Dearborn in February that he had decided to try the Arkansas, keeping the fact a secret and letting the Spaniards think he was going up the Red.[14] Unless there was another lapse in the mails, Jefferson must have known of Dunbar's decision when he wrote him on 28 March, leaving the decision to Dunbar as to which river was to be examined first. He did express a preference for the Red, however, and Dunbar then switched his plans. It was a fateful decision in view of Spanish opposition to the Red River expedition.

Jefferson had started negotiations with the Spanish early. Writing to Claiborne in May 1805, he asked the governor to apply to the Marqués de Casa Calvo for a passport. Claiborne was to explain that the mission was purely geographic, and that the United States was willing to allow two Spanish representatives to accompany the party. "As we have to settle a boundary with

Spain to the Westward, they cannot expect us to go blindfold into the business." Claiborne wrote the marqués in July, repeating what Jefferson had asked him to say, stressing the invitation to permit two Spanish persons chosen by Casa Calvo to go along at U.S. expense.[15]

Grudgingly the marqués consented, saying he might as well; the Americans would go anyway. He named among the Spanish observers Tómas Power, who had dealt in the past with General Wilkinson. But when Nemesio Salcedo, commandant-general in Chihuahua, learned of the passport he was outraged. In a sarcastic reply to Casa Calvo, Salcedo said he considered the expedition of "Mr. Guillermo Dumbar" both unnecessary and dangerous to Spanish interests. He not only withheld his permission for the passage of the party, but protested Casa Calvo's having given it. It could not have escaped Casa Calvo's fine wit, he said, that in case of hostilities the "scientific" information obtained could be put to dangerous use; that the expedition could do nothing to settle the boundary dispute; and that the expedition of Mr. Merri [Merriwether Lewis] was endeavoring to proselytize the Indians and turn them against Spain. "The Governors of the Provinces adjacent to the United States are ordered to Suspend the operations of any and all expeditions which may present themselves, and therefore it is to be expected that that [expedition] of Mr. Dumbar will be so treated by them."[16]

Long before the Red River expedition began, the cards were thoroughly stacked against it. Everyone seemed to sense its impending failure. Claiborne wrote Jefferson in March 1806 that Thomas Freeman had arrived and was preparing for the trip, but "I very much fear he will be interrupted in his excursion by our jealous and ill-disposed Spanish neighbors."[17] Aside from the friction aroused by the expedition, nothing seemed to be going right in relations between the two countries. Burr's suspicious activities in the lower Mississippi Valley, in 1805, had disturbed officials in both countries. Also, soon after several hundred Spanish troops had been sent to Pensacola, in West Florida, Jefferson had delivered his December 1806 message to Congress—laden with ominous statements about boundary questions and West Florida matters.

When Jefferson received Claiborne's letter expressing fears for the safety of the Red River venture, and describing Spanish developments in West Florida, he took immediate action. On the following day, the War Department ordered General Wilkinson to leave his location in St. Louis and go to the vicinity of New Orleans. "From recent information received from New Orleans and its vicinity," Secretary Dearborn wrote, "the hostile views of the Officers of his Catholic Majesty in that quarter, have become so evident, as to require the strictest precaution on the part of the United States."[18]

In this climate of moves and countermoves, enmity and misunderstandings, charges and countercharges, the Red River expedition prepared to move into a section of the continent claimed by both nations.

· An Exercise in Futility ·

On 19 April 1806 the expedition left Fort Adams, a few miles south of Natchez, heading for the nearby mouth of the Red in two flat-bottomed barges and a pirogue. The party contained twenty-four men, later augmented to forty persons in seven boats. Those who began the upriver trip, besides Freeman and Custis, included Captain Richard Sparks, of the Second Infantry, commanding; Lieutenant Enoch Humphreys, of the Regiment of Artillerists (who would help Freeman with the observations); two noncommissioned officers, seventeen privates, and a black servant.[19]

The plan was to find the approximate source of the Red, supposedly in the country of the Pawnees, then to go on horseback to the "top of the mountains" from which the river was thought to flow. They thought they would find this spot a few miles east of Santa Fe; actually the river rises in such a confusion of tributaries that its real source is difficult to define. The return trip was to retrace the route, profiting by Dunbar's observations about the difficulty of transferring to another stream. Thus the party would avoid not only the toilsome job of transporting their equipment overland, but also the need to build new boats.

The country below Natchitoches had been extensively described by Dr. John Sibley in several letters to Jefferson. The explorers were content with minimal observations until they passed Natchitoches, where they took on additional supplies and were reinforced by nine more men. By 7 June they had reached a small white settlement about forty-five miles above Natchitoches, the farthest American outpost, and on the next day they received the first word of a Spanish presence. An express from Sibley brought them the news that a Spanish force had departed from Nacogdoches, in Texas, to intercept them. No big surprise. Later that day, Sibley himself arrived to advise the leaders, and they proceeded.

The Great Raft, an impenetrable jumble of logs and brush in the river, was reached on 11 June. Detouring by way of creeks, lakes, and swamps, they were able to stick with their boats—to the amazement of local Indians and whites, who said that no one had done it before.

After reentering the main stream of the river below the Coashutta Indian village, an Indian guide sent by Sibley brought more word of the Spanish. A detachment of 300 Spanish soldiers was encamped ahead. Freeman and his associates counciled at the village with the Coashutta and Caddo tribes, and hired three Caddo warriors to serve as guides and scouts.

Freeman had been instructed to continue until he was halted by a superior force, an event soon to happen. An experienced Spanish officer, Francisco Viana, had left Nacogdoches on 12 July with a detachment of mounted soldiers and infantry. He was adjutant and inspector of the Internal Provinces under Salcedo and commanded the garrison at Nacogdoches. None too happy to reach the Caddo village and find an American flag flying, Viana cut it down. He then marched to a place near where the states of Texas, Oklahoma, and Arkansas come together, estimated at the time to be about 635 miles above the mouth of the Red, and waited for Freeman's expedition.

The confrontation occurred on 29 July. During the encounter, in which the Americans were menaced but not injured, Viana told Freeman that he must turn back to avoid being fired upon. Possibly the failure was a relief to Freeman and Captain Sparks, for other difficulties had developed. The boats had gone about as far as they could in the shallow water; Indian presents were running low and would have been needed to purchase horses for the exploration of the highlands and mountains. Although the

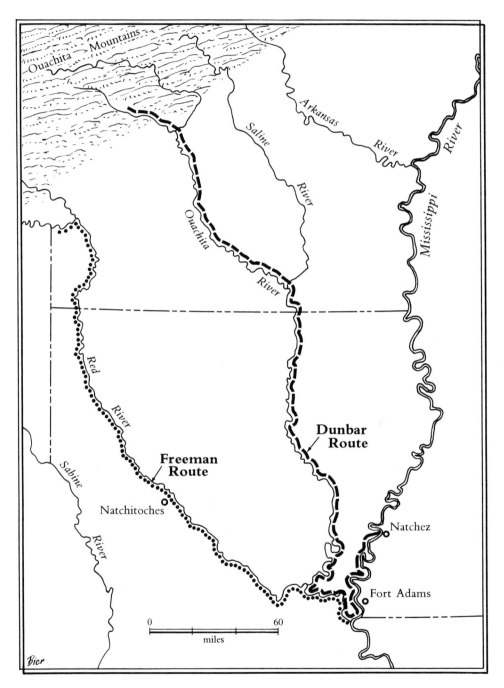

10. Routes of the Ouachita and Red River expeditions.

party had demonstrated the practicability of a Red River expedition, it was doomed to fall short; the Spanish only hastened the day. Freeman accepted Viana's ultimatum and began his downstream withdrawal. Three weeks later the tired explorers were back in Natchitoches and heading for Fort Adams.

The two civilian leaders collaborated in preparing a report of the expedition (FREEMAN & CUSTIS), which was published in a very small edition with no indication of the date of issue or the issuing agency. That small booklet, together with Freeman's map of the Red River compiled from his field notes by Nicholas King, and the largely unpublished correspondence of the principals, constitutes the meager record of the expedition.

An important aspect of the published account is the section on natural history, based on Custis's observations. Since the making of such observations was his main assignment, and considering that he was on the river for more than three months, his performance was not outstanding. He had a good grasp of scientific plant and animal names—though in the published report some are garbled—but he was no match for Meriwether Lewis as a student of natural history. His shortcomings were inexperience and an inadequate knowledge of botanical literature. In his defense, it must be said that the expedition was turned back before it had reached an area where previously unreported plants were to be found in significant numbers. Custis must not be dismissed as an unimpressive figure in the scientific investigation of the West, especially in the field of botany, until a detailed analysis of his work can be made. He listed or described forty-four trees and shrubs and nearly a hundred smaller plants, and made a collection of twenty-six dried plant specimens which he sent to the War Department. When that collection is located, and when his catalog of plants and animals is rendered into modern binomial names and studied, his work may take on a greater importance and he may have some claim to priority of discovery in a few instances.[20]

· The Expedition in Context ·

Jefferson habitually returned to Monticello each year, soon after Congress adjourned, to spend the "sickly season" away from the tidewater miasmas of Washington. He arrived home on 26 July, anxious about his crops—it was a bad year—and the success of a grist mill which was producing forty bushels a day. Soon he hurried on to Poplar Forest, the little country house he was building near Lynchburg. He had two expeditions in the field that he knew of; and another, Zebulon Pike's, of which he still had little or no information, was just setting out.

During the week of Jefferson's homecoming, Meriwether Lewis and a few of his men who were investigating the Marias River country had a confrontation with Indian horse thieves, killing two. Clark's detachment, floating down the Yellowstone, was passing the mouths of rivers such as the Rosebud and the Tongue. Having received no direct word of Lewis and Clark since their dispatches of April 1805, Jefferson justifiably suspected that they might have met disaster.

It is difficult to say when Jefferson learned that the Red River expedition had failed. Claiborne wrote Dearborn on 28 August and enclosed a letter from Freeman which undoubtedly dealt with the Spanish confrontation.[21] Dearborn would have received the letter within four or five weeks, at a time when Jefferson was in Virginia. Like Claiborne, Dunbar, and others who followed the progress of the expedition, Jefferson could not have been surprised at its abrupt return. Viewed leniently, his action in dispatching Freeman can be seen as an acceptable diplomatic tactic—a show of defiance in a climate of rising tension. It can also be viewed as a headstrong decision that put in danger the lives of Americans pursuing an impossible goal.

• The Arkansas Fiasco •

In the fall of 1806, Wilkinson was sent orders to reach a boundary compromise with the Spanish troops then filtering ominously across the Sabine River. Jefferson hoped the Spanish could be persuaded to retain no ground east of the Sabine except a small post at Bayou Pierre where they had maintained a detachment since the Purchase. Wilkinson's instructions to reach a peaceful settlement were unnecessary, for he had already signed on 5 November an agreement with the Spanish to withdraw beyond the Sabine. He agreed to keep his own troops east of the

Arroyo Hondo, about seventeen miles west of Natchitoches, thus providing a "neutral ground" between the two rivers until the boundary could be decided at the conference table.[22]

At this time Jefferson was of course unaware that Wilkinson's son, Lieutenant James B. Wilkinson, had begun a descent of the Arkansas River from the site of Great Bend, Kan., with instructions from Zebulon Pike to map the river and make suitable observations.[23] The information would not have changed Jefferson's mind about the need for a scientific survey of that river, from mouth to headlands, and he was going ahead with plans for such an expedition.

The Arkansas voyage reentered Jefferson's correspondence in mid-February 1807, when he sent Dearborn a memorandum that he thought might be useful to "Col. Freeman and our future explorers."[24] In Natchez and vicinity, arrangements were going ahead. Young Wilkinson had been ordered to command the military escort, and Thomas Freeman was to head the civilian party, but Dunbar despaired of finding a person "of the most slender knowledge in Natural history" to accompany the party. Reporting to Dearborn, Dunbar said there was to be an escort of thirty-five men, and that he was apprehensive the expedition might be assuming too military an appearance. He hoped that proper steps had been taken to pacify the Arkansas River Osages.[25]

Incredibly, and again because of the age-old problem of mail delays, Dunbar and the participants in the proposed expedition were hard at work on it, and looking forward to it, six weeks after it had been canceled. On 30 March Dearborn had written Dunbar, informing him that Congress "by some mistake or inattention" had made no appropriation for the expedition. He said that Jefferson had directed him to inform the principals that it was necessary to suspend all plans for the present season.[26]

Unless additional correspondence is discovered, Jefferson must be charged with passing on a distasteful job to Dearborn and dropping Dunbar from his list of correspondents. He did not write Dunbar about the cancellation, and in fact had not written him since March 1806, when the Red River expedition was forming.

Perhaps Dearborn spoke truthfully in saying that Congress

was to blame for suspending the Arkansas expedition, but in earlier times Jefferson would not have permitted such a "mistake or inattention" without strong protest. The real answer may lie in a poignant line that Jefferson wrote to old John Dickinson, revered pamphleteer of the Revolution. At the beginning of 1807, with more than two years of his second term still remaining, he told Dickinson: "I am tired of an office where I can do no more good than many others who would be glad to be employed in it."[27]

The year 1807 was to be a bad one for Jefferson, with the Aaron Burr trial ahead, and the embargo against Britain that was to bring him under intense fire from critics. With so many other matters to plague him, he may simply have grown weary of concern for an expedition that probably would have been intercepted by the Spanish anyway.[28]

NOTES

1. TJ to Dunbar, 13 March 1804, LC. Later TJ would add the Des Moines and the St. Peter's (Minnesota) rivers to his list of desiderata.

2. cox [3], 74. The Cox article is a concise summary of Dunbar's work. See also DE ROSIER and DUNGAN, both biographical studies. Dunbar's papers, with many gaps and no annotation, were published in 1930 by ROWLAND.

3. Dunbar to TJ, 13 May 1804, ROWLAND, 130–33. Dunbar quoted Stephen Minor, a Natchez associate of Wilkinson's, as believing that Casa Calvo would be flattered if asked to consent to the expedition. But Dunbar added, "I however doubt it."

4. Dunbar to TJ, 9 June 1804, ROWLAND, 133–35. "I lament that no good practical botanist attends the party," he said.

5. TJ to Dunbar, 15 April 1804, LC. There are two copies of Jefferson's instructions for the expedition, a draft and a poor letterpress copy. See fols. 24152 ff. and 24236 ff.

6. TJ to Dunbar, 17 July 1804, LC. On the same day, Dearborn ordered Chouteau, who was with the Osage delegation and had been appointed agent of Indian affairs for Upper Louisiana, "You will take the necessary measures for obtaining permission of the Big-track and his party for the safe passage of any party which may be sent by the P of the US to explore the sources of the Arkansas river . . ." (TERR. PAPERS,

13:31–32). Big Track, Great Track, or Cashesagra was thought to be the chief of the dissident Osages, although Lieutenant James Wilkinson would later report that Clermont was the principal chief (PIKE, 2:154).

7. Dunbar to TJ, 9 Nov. 1804, LC. Like Lewis and Clark, Dunbar let his chronometer run down without harm to his observations. In his journal for 29 Oct. he wrote: "The watch having been suffered to run down last night, the times of the altitudes of this day have consequently no connection with the former."

8. Both journals are in the American Philosophical Society library, Philadelphia. The expedition was described by Jefferson in his 1806 message to Congress, and Dunbar's report received some contemporary attention, as in the *National Intelligencer* for 15, 27, and 31 Oct., and 10 and 12 Nov. 1806. A century later Dunbar's verbatim journal appeared in PURCHASE DOCS. A fine modern account of the expedition is MC DERMOTT [2], an annotated edition of Hunter's journal. "For the public of that day the substance of their reports as issued by Congress was significant news about a recently acquired section of frontier country" (MC DERMOTT [2], 18).

9. TJ to Dunbar, 8 Oct. 1805, LC. During the search for an astronomical observer, Jefferson mentioned "Mr. Wiley," a Washington professor, and Seth Pease, a Post Office employee who had been hired by the War Department to make a clean rendering of the first map Lewis and Clark had sent from St. Louis. For that map, see L & C LETTERS, 1:182n, 193–94.

10. Dunbar to TJ, 8 Oct. 1805, LC, asking TJ to clarify the Freeman misunderstanding, and 17 March 1806, LC, saying that Thomas Freeman had arrived in Natchez. Constant Freeman was a holdover from the Revolution, well along in years, whom Governor Claiborne would later declare unfit to command the troops in the Territory of Orleans. Thomas Freeman, an Irish civil engineer, may be the Thomas Davis Freeman who was surveyor and inspector of the port of Plymouth, Mass., in 1792 (Letters of the Commissioner of Revenue, NARG 58). In 1796, Andrew Ellicott was appointed commissioner to determine and mark the boundary dividing the United States from the Spanish colonies of East and West Florida. Freeman, who had been surveyor for the District of Columbia and the city of Washington, was hired as his assistant. Work was begun in 1798, but a personal quarrel with Ellicott became so bitter that federal officials, although suspecting that Freeman was in the right, sustained Ellicott's decision to discharge him (Secretary of State to Freeman, 29 May 1799, NARG 59). When Ellicott published a journey of his activities on the survey, in 1803, he deleted all references to Freeman. Apparently Freeman's next assign-

ment, given him by James Wilkinson, was to plan and superintend the building of Fort Adams (Freeman to Alexander Hamilton, 9 Jan. 1800, Hamilton Papers, LC). In 1802, while engaged in establishing a line between the states of North Carolina and Tennessee and the lands of the Cherokees, he was ordered into Indiana Territory to lay out the Vincennes Tract, an area recently acquired from Indian tribes of the area (Secretary of War to Freeman, 16 June 1802, NARG 107). He traveled up the Wabash with territorial governor Harrison in the spring of 1803, to council with Indian leaders at Fort Wayne. He was in Mississippi, and available, when the exploring team was chosen for the Red River expedition, and that territory was to become his home when the expedition ended. By 1810 he had been appointed surveyor of lands south of Tennessee, with headquarters in Washington, Miss. Territory (TERR. PAPERS, 6:95). He still held this post when he died in Huntsville, Ala., in 1821. It is worth noting that Freeman, who gained almost no recognition from his arduous and disappointing struggle on the Red River, played a part in events following the death of his famous peer, Meriwether Lewis. It was Freeman who journeyed to the East Coast with Lewis's journals and other effects, following Lewis's apparent suicide on the Natchez Trace in the fall of 1809 (L & C LETTERS, 2:470).

11. See the Rafinesque-Jefferson correspondence in BETTS. The scientist returned to join the staff of Transylvania University, Lexington, Ky., and had some contact with Jefferson in later years. When the University of Virginia was being established, Rafinesque applied for a position there. TJ wrote 7 Nov. 1819 that professors were not then being hired, but said he would lay the application before the board in due time (Catalogue 14, 1975, Current Company, Bristol, R.I.).

12. CANTWELL, 136, is the source of Wilson's comment to Duncan. Wilson's *American Ornithology* was issued in nine volumes, 1804–14. Writing a bibliographical sketch of Wilson for the final volume, George Ord quoted the letter of 6 Feb. 1806 and added: "To this manly and respectful application, Mr. Jefferson . . . *returned not one word of reply.*" In 1818, when the criticism came to TJ's attention, he wrote uneasily to James Wilkinson and Henry Dearborn, asking them to recall what they could of the matter. By that time, everyone seemed to recall that the expedition in question was Zebulon Pike's. Neither Wilkinson nor Dearborn could throw any light on the subject. Jefferson suggested to Dearborn that they might have considered Wilson for the 1807 expedition up the Arkansas, which was canceled. The depth of the indignation TJ felt is evident in his letter to Dearborn: "I never saw till lately the IXth vol. of Wilson's Ornithology. To this a life of the author is prefixed, by a Mr. Ord, in which he has indulged himself in great

personal asperity against myself. . . . He almost makes his heroe die of chagrin at my refusing to associate him with Pike in an expedition to the Arkansa, an expedition on which he says he had particularly set his heart." For the correspondence with Wilkinson and Dearborn, see PIKE, 2:388–92.

13. TJ to Bartram, 6 Feb. 1806, LC. TJ's request may be the source of the erroneous belief that Bartram was offered a place in the Lewis and Clark expedition (see KASTNER, 113). Custis was a descendant of Thomas, brother of the famed John Custis of Arlington, who founded the Virginia dynasty of that name. His father, Robinson Custis, was a landowner at Deep Creek on the Eastern Shore of Virginia, and in his late years operator of a mill there. According to Robinson's will, his son Peter was to receive a "latin education" and "be brought up to one of the learned professions." Details of his early life are as yet obscure, but because he wrote his college thesis on "Bilious Fever of Albemarle County [Va.]," it is interesting to speculate that he may have spent some time in Jefferson's home territory. After the expedition he returned to Philadelphia to finish his studies and obtain his degree, then went home to Accomack County, Va., and considered for a time the practice of medicine in Onancock. By 1808, however, he was established as a physician in New Bern, N.C., where he lived until his death in 1842. Until now, Custis has been a very minor figure in the annals of western scientific exploration. MC KELVEY, the standard work on botanical exploration in the West, does not even mention him, and sources of information on his career are still to be assembled. Much useful material has been provided by genealogist Nettie Lietch Major, of Bethesda, Md., and by F. J. Dallett, archivist of the University of Pennsylvania. Some New Bern data has been provided by Emily Miles. Family papers are scattered, some surviving at the University of North Carolina Library. Three of Custis's letters to Barton, dated 1 June 1806, 21 May 1807, and 29 Oct. 1808, are in the library of the American Philosophical Society. See also his last will and testament, in the records of the Craven County, N.C., Superior Court, Will Book D, pp. 54–55.

14. Dunbar to Dearborn, 25 Feb. 1806, ROWLAND, 329–30, and TJ to Dunbar, 28 March 1806, LC. Jefferson wrote: "As soon as we shall have actual surveys of the Mississippi, Missouri, Arcansas and Red River we propose to have an accurate map made."

15. TJ to Claiborne, 26 May 1805, and Claiborne to Casa Calvo, 11 July 1805, LC.

16. Casa Calvo to Claiborne, 15 July 1805, LC, and Salcedo to Casa Calvo, 8 Oct. 1805, PIKE, 2:111–12.

17. Claiborne to TJ, 26 Mar. 1806, LC.

18. Dearborn to Wilkinson, 6 May 1806, TERR. PAPERS, 13:505–6. On 14 March, Dearborn had ordered Wilkinson to send all troops except one company from St. Louis to Fort Adams to await further orders. "From existing circumstances, the reinforcement of our Posts on the Lower Mississippi is considered a proper measure" (TERR. PAPERS, 13:454). Wilkinson delayed most of the summer before acting on Dearborn's order to transfer his headquarters to the Territory of Orleans.

19. The main source for the occurrences on the expedition is FREEMAN & CUSTIS. The best secondary account, COX [1], relies primarily on this document. At Natchitoches, a detachment of additional soldiers would be added to the group, commanded by Lieutenant John J. Du Forest. The ranking officer on the expedition, Captain Richard Sparks, was a seasoned frontiersman and soldier. Captured in Pennsylvania as a youth and raised for several years by Shawnees, he later returned to white ways and wandered into Kentucky and Tennessee. He married Ruth Sevier, daughter of Indian fighter John Sevier, who would later become governor of Tennessee; and when Sevier challenged Andrew Jackson to a duel, Sparks served as his second. He had joined the army in 1791, and rose in rank through ability and an occasional boost from his father-in-law. He commanded various frontier posts, including Fort Adams, and served as a colonel in the War of 1812. Most accounts of his career are based on the recollections of George Washington Sevier, the governor's son, in the Draper Collection, State Historical Society of Wisconsin, Madison.

20. Dr. Paul R. Cutright concurs in the view that Custis was not very zealous as an observer of natural history, but that he was handicapped by inadequate preparation and the early termination of the expedition. An exchange of correspondence with Cutright has been very useful to the author.

21. Claiborne to Dearborn, CLAIBORNE, 3:386.

22. MALONE, 5:246–47. See also ABERNETHY, chap. 10. The agreement was to remain in effect until the Adams-Onís treaty of 1819.

23. For young Wilkinson's role in the Pike expedition, see especially PIKE, 1:287, 339, 340, and 2:3–19. He became ill, experienced a difficult descent of the Arkansas, and his findings were of little value.

24. TJ to Dearborn, 14 Feb. 1807, LC.

25. Dunbar to Dearborn, 10 May 1807, NARG 107, letters received, D-154. See also Dunbar to Dearborn, 31 March 1807, same file, D-140, and Dunbar to Wilkinson, 3 May 1807, ROWLAND, 354.

26. Dearborn to Dunbar, 30 March 1807, ROWLAND, 196.

27. TJ to Dickinson, 13 Jan. 1807, Historical Society of Pennsylvania, Philadelphia.

28. TJ indirectly acknowledged that Spanish opposition had delayed exploration of the West. In replying to a letter from Anthony G. Bettay, of Vincennes, who claimed to have found a silver mine about 1,700 miles up the Platte, TJ expressed interest and said: "I should be glad of a copy of any sketch or account you have made of the river Platte, or the passage from its head across the mountains, and of the river Cashecahingo [?] which you suppose to run into the Pacific. This would probably be among the first exploring journeys we undertake after a settlement with Spain, as we wish to become acquainted with all the advantageous water connections across our Continent" (18 Feb. 1808, LC).

CHAPTER TWELVE

Zebulon Pike's Damned Rascals

History has been stern with General James Wilkinson, but not unjust. Recent studies have partially rehabilitated him from the status of arch-rogue to common rogue, but his rating is unlikely to show further improvement.

Wilkinson might have become a small-town physician with comfortable business interests, happily married into an influential family. He attended medical school at the University of Pennsylvania while in his teens, met Ann Biddle, whom he later was to marry, and returned to practice medicine briefly in his home state of Maryland. Finding the call to arms fascinating, he volunteered as a soldier in the Revolution, became an aide to General Nathanael Greene, and was present at Bunker Hill. While rising to the rank of brevet brigadier and serving as clothier-general until coming under fire from George Washington, he exhibited all the traits that were to typify his career: he was querulous, litigious, and conniving.

After the Revolution he moved to Kentucky and became involved in growing business interests, establishing a liaison with Spanish elements along the Mississippi and scheming to separate Kentucky from the Union. When he returned to the army in 1791 as a lieutenant colonel, Wilkinson fought Indians and quarreled notoriously with his superior, General Anthony Wayne. Upon the reduction of the army at the end of the century, he became a brigadier general and the ranking officer in the service. Because his primary responsibilities lay on the frontier, he was destined to serve in the West for many years. He was officially named commanding general by the War Department in 1800.

An appraisal from one biography: "It was a peculiar turn of the wheel of fortune that had placed military and executive authority on behalf of the United States in the hands of the man who for almost ten years had been the leading conspirator with the Spanish authorities in their effort to separate the Western lands from the union."[1]

After the Purchase, Wilkinson hoped to become governor of the lower district containing New Orleans. When the post went to Claiborne he campaigned for the governorship of the upper region, the Territory of Louisiana. Jefferson pondered long over the appointment, hesitant to combine civil and military authority, but the general was confirmed by the Senate in March 1805 after three days of debate. Jefferson rationalized that the appointment was justified because St. Louis was a kind of military post. He called it "the center of our Western operations, whether respecting the Spaniards, Indians or English, and as the outwork which covers all that frontier, is too important to be left in a state of anarchy, or placed in nerveless hands."[2]

Even then, Jefferson's attitude toward Wilkinson was ambivalent. In a cabinet meeting of 9 March 1792 he had noted Washington's appraisal: "Wilkinson. Brave—enterprising to excess, but many unapprovable points in his character."[3] It was *enterprising to excess* that was to put Wilkinson in disfavor most often, even though there were other aspects of his personality that Jefferson could appreciate. He was a fellow member of the American Philosophical Society, a man interested in geography and natural history, who could chat easily with ornithologist Alexander Wilson about game birds and inform him that the rail, commonly thought to be a seacoast bird, was to be found in large flocks near Detroit. His letters were florid, pretentious, often fawning, but he was careful to nourish Jefferson's hunger for information from the Trans-Mississippi region. The President apparently felt he had no choice but to appoint him, although the Spanish affiliation was widely suspected not only in Kentucky but in the halls of Congress.[4]

· Fox in the Chicken House? ·

Before leaving New Orleans for his new assignment, Wilkinson had conferred with Vicente Folch, the Spanish governor of West Florida, about how Spain might remain strong in view of the Louisiana transfer. In February 1804 Wilkinson offered to write out his thoughts on the subject in return for back payments on his retainer or pension. The report, his notorious "Reflections on Louisiana," was translated into Spanish and signed by Folch himself. Wilkinson wanted $20,000 but received a little more than half that. Besides advising that Lewis and Clark be cut off and arrested, he had recommended that Spain hold onto both Floridas and occupy the west bank of the Mississippi, or at least trade the Floridas for the territory west of the river, thus making Mexico safe from "an army of adventurers." He warned the Spanish that the Americans would have a post on the Pacific within five years—a close guess, considering the establishment of Astoria in 1811. And in a small detail that might have represented a personal grudge, he suggested that the salt works of Daniel Boone and his son Nathan on Salt Creek, an affluent of the lower Missouri, be broken up.[5]

A year later, departing from Washington for his assignment, Wilkinson had descended the Ohio and was on the Mississippi before he realized he had neglected to take the oath of office. He wrote an apology to Jefferson, then stopped at Kaskaskia to be sworn in by John Edgar, of the court of common pleas. He was traveling with his family, including his son James, who served him as adjutant.[6]

According to Wilkinson, Jefferson had named three important objects to which attention must be given: the prevention of trade from Canada on the west side of the Mississippi; the depopulation of settlements below St. Louis; the transfer of "the Southern Indians" from the Territory of Orleans north to the Territory of Louisiana. There were, of course, many other desiderata including the orderly government of the territory and early attention to its exploration.[7]

Knowing the way his government worked, Wilkinson had developed the ability to arrange for his private ventures to overlap those of his country, so that they could easily be concealed and implemented. It was expected that government officials would engage in private business in those days; their pay scales seemed to be adjusted to that fact of life. Wilkinson simply did it covertly as well as openly.

"I have equipt a Perogue out of my Small private means," he

wrote the secretary of war, "not with any view to Self interest, to ascend the Missouri and enter the River Piere Jaune, or yellow stone, called by the natives, Unicorn River, the same by which Capt. Lewis I since find expects to return and which my informants tell me is filled with wonders. This Party will not get back before the Summer 1807—They are natives of this Town, and are just able to give us course and distance, with the names and populations of the Indian nations and to bring back with them Specimens of the natural products." What happened to this expedition, if it developed, is not known. There are fascinating reports of white men on the upper Missouri at this time, unaffiliated with Lewis and Clark.[8]

Among those in Wilkinson's entourage when he came west was Captain John McClallen, who then commanded a company. He brought with him about $2,500 in goods which he hoped to use in the Indian trade after resigning his commission. In the same letter in which he reported the Yellowstone expedition, Wilkinson told Dearborn that he had equipped "a bold adventurer, who served under me during the late Indian War, and is now a Pensioner of the U.S.(McClelan) to look at St. Afee in person pending the Winter—he will take his departure from the Panis Towns on the River Plate." Lewis and Clark met McClallen on the lower Missouri 17 September 1806, and he told them he was "on reather a speculative expedition to the confines of New Spain, with the view to entroduce a trade with those people."[9]

These two expeditions were private. Wilkinson also instigated two public ones, both sufficiently legitimate for him to report them fully to the War Department. One was predicated upon the value of a military base at the mouth of the Platte, originally suggested by James Bruff, Wilkinson's predecessor in St. Louis. In the fall of 1805 the Arikara chief, bound for Washington, grew ill and decided, together with an Oto chief, that he would like to go home. Lieutenant James Wilkinson was assigned to escort them home and then to take post at the mouth of the Platte. The Oto chief died during the trip, and the Arikara chief went on to Washington (and died also). Dearborn reprimanded Wilkinson for attempting to establish a military base without permission.[10]

To facilitate the assignment of Pierre Chouteau to council with the dissident Osages, Wilkinson sent a military detachment under Lieutenant George Peter, of the Corps of Artillerists, to the village of the traditional Osages on the Osage River. Peter reported by letter, in September 1805, that 1,500 souls under their chief, Great Track, came north from the Arkansas to meet with Chouteau, and they agreed to break up their village and return to the Osage River the following spring. "I have taken the courses by a magnetic needle, and computed the distances by time, taking into consideration the rapidity and velocity of the stream, and hope it will be in my power to furnish you a pretty accurate chart."[11] Mapping the Osage was hardly a novel undertaking; the French knew it well and it was depicted on the 1804 map sent to Jefferson by Lewis. Still, Peter's trip was the first official move in that direction, antedating Zebulon Pike's by a year.

· Pike's Mississippi River Expedition ·

His full name was Zebulon Montgomery Pike, and he signed himself Z. M. Pike to prevent confusion with his father, Major Zebulon Pike, an old and infirm officer still on active duty. Until now, the young New Jersey lieutenant had had an undistinguished career, marked only by his service as district paymaster in the First Infantry. Meriwether Lewis had taken note of him, writing in 1804 while Pike was stationed at Fort Massac that he was recommending him to lead an expedition. Therefore, Pike later stated, "on General Wilkinson's arriving at Massac, and informing me that I would have charge of one of those expeditions, I conceived it to be a continuance of the designs of the government as suggested to me by . . . Lewis."[12] Wilkinson may have chosen Pike to become an explorer because he had known and commanded his father for so many years, or because the young officer was married to Clarissa Brown, daughter of one of Wilkinson's associates in Kentucky.

Jefferson would have approved the orders that Wilkinson gave Pike for his trip up the Mississippi in the summer of 1805. In addition to geographical matters, such as charting the river and the adjoining countryside, he was to purchase sites from the

Indians for potential military posts, announce to Indians and to Canadian traders the new authority of the United States, and to bring an Indian delegation back to St. Louis for a parley. In no sense was Pike sent up the river primarily to find its source; he was to look for it if time permitted "before the waters are frozen up."[13]

Departing from St. Louis in August with twenty men, Pike took a keelboat to the vicinity of Little Falls, Minn., where he was overtaken by winter. Wilkinson's assumption that he could return before the river froze was too optimistic. The party built a small stockade where most of the men spent the winter while Pike went on by dogsled and foot, with a few men, to visit British traders. The farthest point he reached was Cass Lake in northern Minnesota. It was not quite the source of the Mississippi, which rises in little streams issuing from the Hauteurs des Terres, south of Lake Itasca, but it was close enough for a searcher traveling under wretched conditions, with all the watercourses heavily iced over, and who had already "stretched his orders," according to Wilkinson, by staying on to hunt for the source.

Pike was back in St. Louis in April with maps and reports. He had negotiated with the Indians for a site that would later become Fort Snelling, at the mouth of the Minnesota. He had carried the flag and news of the change in Great Fathers to the Indians on the upper river, and he had warned British fur traders—who did not take him very seriously—that they were now trespassers. While he brought back no chiefs for council, a delegation came down the river not far behind him for talks with Wilkinson.

Not yet a captain, Pike did not have a company of his own. His men were borrowed (the army term is "on command") from the companies of Captains Daniel and Russell Bissell, at Forts Massac and Kaskaskia. One was Private John Boley, who had been detailed to accompany Lewis and Clark to the Mandans and help return the keelboat. He had arrived back in St. Louis just in time to be assigned to Pike. Pike's men were not hand picked and tested volunteers like those of Lewis and Clark; they were simply soldiers following orders. Several would profit by their experience on the Mississippi when assigned to go west with Pike in the summer of 1806. Pike wrote of them, "Although they are a Dam'd set of Rascels yet in the Woods they are staunch fellows and very proper for such expeditions as I am engaged in."[14]

When Pike's Mississippi River journal and maps reached Washington, the expedition caught Jefferson's interest. It was not the scientific probe that he wanted but there was raw material aplenty upon which to build future investigations. Nicholas King, the cartographer who had recently redrawn William Clark's map, was assigned to condense Pike's journal into a narrative for the instruction of Congress. He reduced Pike's sectionalized field maps to a manageable size and combined them into one. Evidently King's work was finished by the end of 1806, and a strong effort was made to get both the narrative and map into print before Congress adjourned in March 1807. Dearborn told Jefferson on 11 February that the journal was already off the press, and "I have been in daily expectation of receiving the maps from Philadelphia."[15]

Congress had adjourned before the maps and brochures could reach the members, and Pike's accomplishment received less immediate attention than it deserved. Jefferson ordered the publication sent out to some members of Congress and others, and he personally forwarded a copy to the American Philosophical Society. The *National Intelligencer* printed three long extracts on 20, 22, and 25 May 1807, with a headnote: "This interesting tract was intended to be communicated to Congress at their last session; but was not printed for distribution till after they rose. — We are satisfied that we shall gratify the literary curiosity of the public by laying before them copious extracts of it."[16]

• The Burr-Wilkinson Conspiracy •

The activities of Aaron Burr in 1805 and 1806 are too well known to require a detailed recounting here, where we are primarily concerned with Jefferson, Wilkinson, and Pike. They must be touched upon, however, because all three men were involved in the story and their lives changed by it.

Failing in his bid for the presidency, Vice-President Burr turned to the West. He evolved a scheme or schemes still not well understood, which would satisfy his aims and which for a time appealed to many people. Interesting to Spanish minister Irujo was the prospect of restoring New Orleans to Spain, and along with it a nice chunk of the American West. Equally attractive to British minister Anthony Merry was the prospect of striking a blow against Spain, with which England was then at war. To ambitious men on the frontier, the appeal was to private gain, a filibuster against the Internal Provinces.

Whether Wilkinson was the mastermind, the co-conspirator, or simply the man who finally denounced Burr depends upon who is trying to sort out the vast body of evidence.[17] Burr had gone west in 1805 and conferred with Wilkinson. The general said and did several things at the time which in retrospect seemed incriminating. Coming west again in 1806, Burr gathered men of like mind as he descended the Ohio with the supposed intent of attacking New Orleans with some kind of armed force.

Wilkinson's association with Burr had begun as early as 1800, and by 1806 it had grown in the public mind into a plan that encompassed the separation of the West from the remainder of the United States. It was more likely aimed at an invasion of Mexico.

The supposed connivance was predicated upon a war between Spain and the United States—a prospect always in the forefront of Jefferson's thinking. The people also expected it. The *National Intelligencer* in 1804 was running articles headed "Spanish Aggressions." Dearborn in 1805 was advising agent John Sibley in Natchitoches to cultivate the tribes in his area because they would be useful in a rupture with Spain. Jefferson's public statements at the end of 1805 were menacing.

While maintaining his contacts and erratically earning his retainer from Spain, Wilkinson fed information to Jefferson and Dearborn which they wanted to hear. Dearborn was especially receptive, saying, "I am more fully convinced, by your communication, of the practicability, if necessary, of a military movement, either by the Platt, the Osage or the Arkansas, to the Eastern part of Mexico; —and I am not sure that a project of that kind may not become necessary."[18] To Wilkinson, words such as these were a carte blanche.

· Zebulon Pike's Second Expedition ·

When he set out on his second expedition in the summer of 1806, Pike was unaware that he might be an unwitting element in an unsavory plan. Having completed one rigorous voyage and received the flattering approbation of the commanding general, he was ready for the next.

Still a lieutenant, he left St. Louis with borrowed troops, two civilians, and Lieutenant Wilkinson as second in command. The civilians were Antoine F. Baronet Vasquez, who would serve as interpreter, and Dr. John Hamilton Robinson, a physician whose presence on the roster would add mystery to the experiences that lay ahead.

Jefferson did not authorize the expedition and had no need to; it was, as he said in later years, mainly a military reconnaissance. The War Department, however, was properly notified in clear terms.[19]

Pike's orders contained several objectives. He was to escort some Osage prisoners, taken from the Potawatomis, to their village. Because a party of Kansas Indians had asked for help in making peace with the Pawnees, he was to attempt a treaty. He was to reach the Comanches, if they could be found, and try to bring them into the Great Father's fold. Finally, in an order revealing the universal ignorance of the western rivers, he was told to explore the Arkansas, examine the headwaters of both the Arkansas and the Red rivers, and descend the Red to Natchitoches. (William Dunbar could have warned him against changing rivers in mid-voyage.) Wilkinson wrote him, "you must indeed be extremely guarded with respect to the Spaniards— neither alarm nor offend them unnecessarily." Later, Wilkinson would be charged with having sent word to the Spanish that Pike was on his way.[20]

Betraying further ignorance of the terrain and the distances, Wilkinson expected Pike to be in Natchitoches before winter arrived. In a mistake that could have been fatal, Pike's men left St. Louis on 15 July dressed in summer uniforms and carrying no winter ones.

The first leg of the journey, from St. Louis to the Osage villages in present southwest Missouri, was a retracing of

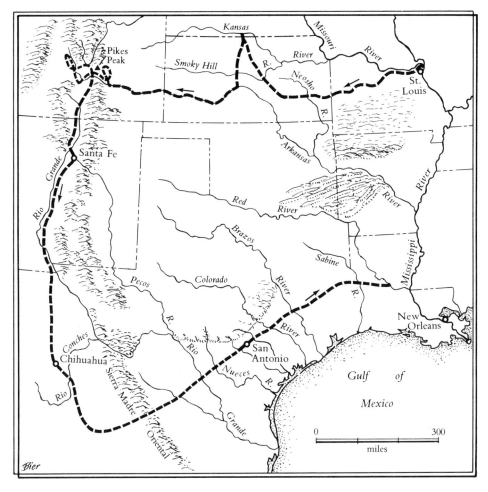

11. Route of Pike's western expedition, 1806–7.

Lieutenant Peter's route. From there the party angled northwest across Kansas to a site on the Republican River just inside the Nebraska boundary. The Pawnees were "Spanish" Indians, and Pike learned that a large body of Spanish troops had stopped at the village a few days earlier. Pike thought the soldiers, commanded by Lieutenant Facundo Melgares, were looking for him—and indeed they may have been. One historian suggests they may have been more interested in Lewis and Clark, who were at that time descending the Missouri and could conceivably have been intercepted.[21]

The Spanish horsemen returning to Santa Fe left a most convenient trail across the short grama grass that was the Kansas sod. After an encounter with the principal Pawnee chief, Sharitarish or White Wolf, who tried to discourage the expedition from continuing, Pike followed Melgares southward to the Great Bend of the Arkansas. By prearrangement, he ordered Lieutenant Wilkinson and a small detachment to descend the river. Although he complained about his food and equipment, would grow ill on the trip, and would see three of his five men desert, Wilkinson would complete the descent and provide sketchy information for his father and for Pike's published journals.

Pike and his fifteen remaining men proceeded up the Arkansas in late October and soon were beginning to look for the Rockies. The burned-out campfires of the Spanish and the chopped turf left by the hooves of their mounts promised to guide them to and even through the first range of mountains. In southeastern Colorado, near the confluence of the Purgatoire River and the Arkansas, Pike first saw the low, blue hulk of the Rockies on the horizon. Riding out with Dr. Robinson, he satisfied himself of the discovery, and when his men caught up with him "they with one accord gave three *cheers* to the *Mexican mountains.*"

It was mid-November and the mountains were not going to be friendly. At the site of Pueblo, where Fountain Creek flows in from the right, Pike became determined to examine the great peak rising in the northwest. It looked close enough, to an easterner, to be reached in a day. Directing his men to build a small, temporary stockade, he set out with Dr. Robinson and two men toward what was later to be known as Pikes Peak. After three days they had only reached the foothills, in deep snow, wearing those thin cotton uniforms. What he called the Grand Peak was still far away "and as high again as what we had ascended, and would have taken a whole day's march to have arrived at its base, when I believe no human being could have ascended to its pinnacal." He returned to his camp.

The next few weeks were to be a horror of cold and hunger, heightened by awful doubts as to their location on the uncharted terrain. They ascended the Arkansas a few more miles, turned up an affluent toward the right, wandered into South Park, then struck the main river again. Pike thought he had gone around the head of the Arkansas and was thus on the Red. But upon descending it he discovered familiar ground and decided he was back on the Arkansas. Abandoning that stream, ascending the Wet Mountain Valley and crossing the Sangre de Cristos at Medano Pass (leaving some frostbitten casualties to be regrouped later), he entered the San Luis Valley and found another stream that he thought was surely the Red. On the south side of a small branch called the Conejos, he built a stout little stockade of cottonwood logs and ran up the American flag. He was on the waters of the Rio Grande and in undisputed Spanish territory.

Historians as well as laymen who read Pike's account superficially, and who are aware of Wilkinson's capabilities as a conniver, often make wrong judgments about the expedition. The most prevalent one is the belief that Pike was never actually lost but only pretending to be. He had muddied the waters with a statement made to Wilkinson in advance. If he were apprehended by the Spanish, he said, he would tell them that he was "uncertain about the Head Waters of the Rivers over which we passed." In other words, he was going to *pretend* to be lost. When the time came, and he found himself in the hostile Rockies with no guide except a tracing of Alexander von Humboldt's highly misleading map of the region—compiled from secondary sources—Pike became really lost, not once but three times.[22]

Pike was not avoiding the Spanish. In fact, he apparently hoped to encounter Spanish troops and find out what he could about their strength and disposition, trusting in his ability to talk his way out of any situation. Dr. Robinson, who sometimes behaved as if he were a secret emissary of Wilkinson's and sometimes as a loner with private plans, left the stockade and set out to find Santa Fe, ostensibly to collect a bill from an American expatriate there.[23]

A patrol out of Santa Fe found the Pike stockade in late February 1807. He and his party (with the injured stragglers finally collected) were taken to Santa Fe, after he had explained that he thought he was on the Red River. Dr. Robinson was already there and, to continue the charade, Pike at first pretended not to recognize him.

The journals and maps were lost,[24] although Pike recalled enough, and could reconstruct enough from other papers, to produce a published account later. He was escorted to Chihuahua for a confrontation with General Salcedo, who treated him well and ordered him escorted back to the U.S. boundary between Nacogdoches and Natchitoches. Pike and a few of his followers were back on American soil by 30 June 1807, but five of the men were detained for two additional years. Sergeant William C. Meek, who killed Private Theodore Miller in a drunken affray, was imprisoned for fourteen years.

While in Mexico, Pike read of the Burr episode in a copy of the *Gacetas de Mexico*. He was soon to be involved in the repercussions, accused of complicity, and linked with Wilkinson in the conspiracy.

· Wilkinson Brings Burr Down ·

During the summer of 1806, perhaps even before Pike had started west from St. Louis, Wilkinson had decided to denounce Burr. Or *betray* Burr, as some would have it. The game was getting too dangerous to play, with certain elements of the press and many persons in high places aware of the plot. Wilkinson had gone to the Sabine to council with the Spanish and arrange the Neutral Ground agreement, but his puzzling delay in St. Louis before leaving astonished Jefferson and caused him to suppose it had something to do with Burr. It was not widely known that Mrs. Wilkinson was terminally ill (she died a few months later).

As historian Merrill D. Peterson has written: "Cautiously

suspending judgment on Wilkinson's complicity with Burr, he [Jefferson] grasped the opportunity to ease him out of the governorship of Louisiana. . . . He at once pressed the office on Monroe, and when Monroe was detained in England held it open for Meriwether Lewis, who came to his long journey's end in the fall."[25] Possibly Wilkinson dallied in St. Louis to take stock. He could ignite war on the southwestern border, on the one hand, or he could make peace on the Sabine, topple Burr, and come out a hero. At the time of the Neutral Ground arrangement, he sent an aide to the viceroy of Mexico with a bill of $120,000 for his services to Spain. And in October he sent a letter to Jefferson, exposing an enormous plot against the country. In Peterson's words, "He described the 'daring enterprise' and professed to be uninformed of its 'prime mover and ultimate objects,' but expecting a revolt in the territory, he had decided to make peace with the Spaniards and throw his army into the defense of New Orleans."[26]

Jefferson's actions during the ensuing months, during which Burr was arrested and brought to trial for treason, are perplexing in a twofold way. He was so determined to bring Burr to justice that he lost for a time his sense of proportion: Burr was completely guilty and Wilkinson was completely the innocent savior of the union. Leonard Levy, highly critical of Jefferson, says the Burr affair shows the "darker side" of the professed civil libertarian. Jefferson laid aside principles of justice, constitutionality, and even—for a lawyer—reasoned consideration of the evidence. He even announced publicly, through a special message to Congress, that Burr was guilty of attempting the "severance of the Union."[27]

To maintain Burr's guilt, Jefferson had to uphold Wilkinson during some outrageous actions in New Orleans. The general's despotic rule there soon had the city in a panic, anticipating a Burr invasion. There was gossip of plundering traitors and an uprising of slaves. Wilkinson tried to suspend the writ of habeas corpus and install martial law. When Governor Claiborne refused to go along, Wilkinson behaved as if martial law were in effect.[28] During dark days in New Orleans, Jefferson sent several letters to Wilkinson approving of his actions. Even when the Burr threat did not materialize, he told Wilkinson that his elaborate and highhanded measures for defense were nevertheless justified.[29]

Burr was acquitted of the charge of treason. The government, as Senator William Plumer wrote at the time, had staked its entire case on the shifting sands of Wilkinson's loyalty. Plumer was convinced that Burr had not contemplated treason, but that Wilkinson had himself created a reign of terror in New Orleans.[30]

Wilkinson weathered a court of inquiry in 1808, mainly because no convincing proof of his association with the Spanish could be generated. In 1811 he was court-martialed on several charges, principally his alleged mismanagement and graft in operations around New Orleans. He was acquitted.

When Jefferson addressed Wilkinson personally, his loyalty was absolute. After the Burr trial he wrote: "It is with pleasure that I perceive from all the expressions of public sentiment, that the virulence of those whose treasons you have defeated only place you on higher ground in the opinion of the nation. I salute you with esteem and respect." In 1811, while Wilkinson was undergoing court-martial, Jefferson said to him: "I look back with commiseration on those still buffeting the storm, and sincerely wish your argosy may ride out, unhurt, that in which it is engaged. My belief is that it will, and I found that belief on my own knowledge of Burr's transactions, on my view of your conduct in encountering them, & on the candour of your judges."

When he was discussing Wilkinson with others he tempered his praise. He told Monroe, not quite truthfully, that he had always restrained himself from expressing an opinion about Wilkinson, "except in the case of Burr's conspiracy, wherein, after he had got over his first agitations, we believe his decision firm, and his conduct zealous. . . . As to the rest of his life, I have left it to his friends, and his enemies, to whom it furnishes matter enough for disputation."

To Wilkinson personally he was affable to the end. Writing him in 1818 about the unsavory nature of his retirement from the army, Jefferson said: "A witness myself of the merit of your services while I was in a position to know and to feel their benefit, I made no enquiry into the circumstances which terminated them."[31]

Giving Wilkinson the benefit of the doubt in the puzzling Burr affair, and conceding that Jefferson could not know that positive proof would eventually confirm Wilkinson's Spanish dealings, it is still difficult to comprehend his continued loyalty to the general. Some of his kindly statements to Wilkinson may be attributed to politeness, as well as gratitude for the position Wilkinson took in the Burr matter. And yet a single sentence written by Wilkinson in 1804 could have changed the relationship forever. In a statement to the Spanish, previously quoted, Wilkinson had touched upon the project nearest Jefferson's heart. "An express ought immediately to be sent to the governor of Santa Fe, and another to the captain-general of Chihuaga, in order that they may detach a sufficient body of chasseurs to intercept Captain Lewis and his party, who are on the Missouri River, and force them to retire or take them prisoners." Had Jefferson seen that recommendation, Wilkinson's flamboyant public career would have been much, much shorter.

· The Futility of Gates ·

Once during the early years of Spanish resistance to crowding by the United States, the Spanish minister of state Manuel de Godoy had written a fatalistic comment in the margin of a report from the American provinces: "No es posible poner puertas al campo," he wrote. You cannot put gates on an open field.[32] With Pike successfully checked and some of his men still in custody, the Spanish were still half believing that it was possible. Their dealings with Jefferson and Madison, in the period after Pike's return, were angry ones.

As secretary of state, Madison first received a bill for money advanced to Pike by General Salcedo, along with an admonitory note from Valentín de Foronda, the current Spanish chargé d'affaires in the United States. Foronda pointed out that his government should have treated Pike and Dr. Robinson as spies, but "instead of punishing them according to all the rigor provided by Law, and making thus an example so that in future no one would dare to set foot on the territories belonging to the King my Sovereign without first asking his permission, he [Salcedo] has not only permitted Pike and his Soldiers to return to their Country, but, even more, he has advanced to them One Thousand Dollars for their expenses; for which amount he makes a claim."[33]

Jefferson authorized Madison to pay the bill, but not without a rebuttal: "Will it not be proper to rebut Foronda's charge of this government sending a spy in any case & that Pike's mission was to ascend the Arkansas & descend the Red river for the purpose of ascertaining their geography; that as far as we are yet informed, he entered the waters of the North river [Rio Grande], believing them to be those of the Red river: and that, however certain we are of a right extending to the North river, and participating of it's navigation with Spain, yet Pike's voyage was not intended as an exercise of that right, which we notice here merely because he has chosen to deny it, a question to be settled in another way."[34]

Madison paid the bill through Foronda, repeating Jefferson's statement in essence. Salcedo's gesture in releasing Pike was not appreciated by his home office. Pedro Cevallos, the foreign minister, ordered the general not to let such an incident recur "unless there is received first a request from the American Government, recognizing the excesses by its subjects and offering to punish them appropriately."[35]

Now, having received the money advanced to Pike, the Spanish tried to collect for their expenses in apprehending him. The amount was slightly more than 21,655 pesos. Foronda presented an itemized bill which included the cost of subsistence for the militiamen who, under Lieutenant D. Ignacio Sotelo, had gone out from Santa Fe to pick up the Pike detachment, the cost of escorting the party through Mexico, and items as small as "one iron piece for stirrup buckle," at two pesos.

Foronda wrote twice to Madison although, as he told Salcedo, he did not expect the American government to pay the bill. He wrote a third time, after telling Cevallos that he would "complain strongly of the lack of respect which he [Madison] has for my August Sovereign." After several more attempts, Foronda abandoned the effort. The Spanish sold what they could of Pike's captured effects, down to the last elk hide and broken carbine. One Spanish commandant along the trail where the Pike party had been escorted wrote that a roan horse left behind by the Americans had died, and he could not find on it "any horseshoe or anything else to take off it."[36]

· Pike's Last Years ·

Although Pike came home to a certain amount of acclaim, reactions to his expeditions were mixed. He had returned while Lewis and Clark were being feted in Washington. Instead of having Jefferson as a patron, he had a flawed general who was under fire. Instead of bringing back reams of journal entries and tales of a successful mission, he returned without his papers and with the knowledge that he had been escorted back under an armed Spanish guard. In his own mind he would always be considered runner-up to Lewis and Clark.

He wanted the praise that Jefferson had given Lewis and Clark; he wanted for himself and his damned rascals the land warrants and extra pay that Congress had voted to the Lewis and Clark party. He wanted acceptance into the Jefferson circle and it could never happen.

Pike had been in St. Louis in June 1805 when the Lewis and Clark keelboat had come down the Missouri laden with specimens. He felt he could bring gifts to the President more spectacular than a cowering prairie dog and a box of fluttering birds. While he was being marched home across Mexico, his party had met an Indian who had captured two grizzly cubs near the dividing line between Biscay and Sonora. As he later wrote Jefferson, "I conceived the Idea of bringing them to the United States for your Exclly. although then more than 1600 miles from our frontier post, (Natchitoches) purchased them of the Savage, and for three or four days made my men carry them on horse back." Later they were suspended in a cage on a pack mule "but always ordered . . . to be let oute the moment we halted, and not shut up again until we were prepared to march."

At the first opportunity, Pike shipped the bears off by water via New Orleans, sending Jefferson also a bow and arrows of the Apaches and promising other curiosities. Jefferson acknowledged the gift, then kept the bears at the presidential mansion in Washington for a while. Later he sent them to Charles Willson Peale in Philadelphia, and what happened to them is related by Peale's biographer: "The bears, from playful cubs, grew large and fierce. They would attack anyone, man or beast, who came within their reach. A teasing monkey had arm and shoulder blade torn off by a sweep of the great claws. They met their fate when one of them, one night, broke loose from his cage and stalked into the cellar of Philosophical Hall. The Peale family was in terror, and with reason. Peale closed the cellar door and window, and in the morning entered and shot the creature. The survivor was killed in its cage and mounted with its mate."[37]

The lively bears involved Pike in a brief flurry of correspondence with Jefferson, and gave the President some diversion, but did not decrease the social distance between the two men. There was no further correspondence. Jefferson spoke of Pike in a correctly polite way but gave him none of the accolades he craved. There was no invitation to membership in the American Philosophical Society; Pike had to be content with an invitation by the U.S. Military Philosophical Society, to whose members he dedicated his published journals.

Pike made a futile effort to obtain compensation, not merely for himself but for the men—some of whom were still detained in Mexico. He wrote Dearborn, pointing out that his interpreter Vasquez and seven men were still being held. "Several of those poor fellows have become cripples from their limbs being frozen, and are in a strange country amongst people whose language they cannot understand."[38] Three days later, Dearborn sent a copy of Pike's journal to Jefferson and asked whether it might not be well to consider extra compensation "or other notice." Pike himself kept in touch with a House committee and provided the documentation members might need to decide on the case. A bill was introduced in the House in March 1808, another in December. No action was taken, and the process was begun again in June 1809 under the direction of John Montgomery, of Maryland, who proposed that Pike should receive 640 acres of land; Lieutenant Wilkinson, 320; the enlisted men who served on both expeditions, 160; those on the western expedition only, 80.[39]

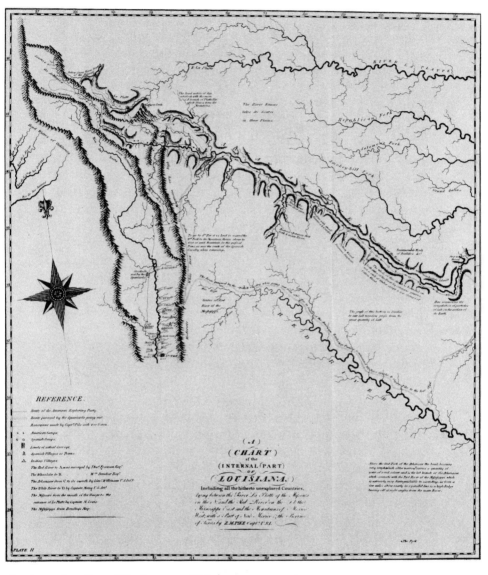

12. A section from Pike's map of his western travels.

No compensation was voted. The Congress may have felt that one more award such as that made to the Lewis and Clark party would set a cumbersome precedent, with the whole West waiting to be explored. Pike was bitter over the outcome. He had once pointed out to Wilkinson that he had executed *two* voyages "which I humbly conceive might be compared with the *one* performed by Captains Lewis & Clark."[40]

The need to release Pike's men from a Mexican prison in Carrizal gave Wilkinson still another opportunity to send an emissary to his Spanish friends. He proposed the mission to Dearborn in August 1808, suggesting that it could serve the dual purpose of freeing the men and determining the present state of conditions in Mexico. He told Dearborn that he understood "the Spanish are making some movement toward the Missouri," and brought the British into it also, saying he feared they might obtain a foothold in Mexico that would be a detriment to U.S. trade.

Dearborn complied, writing an authorization for Wilkinson to send an emissary. The man chosen was Wilkinson's former aide, Lieutenant Daniel Hughes. Among the letters carried by Hughes was one from Wilkinson to General Simon Herrera, with whom he had dealt in the Neutral Ground episode, asking for a testimonial to combat some of the charges that had been leveled at him. It was the period during which Wilkinson was undergoing a court of inquiry on charges of having dealt with Spain.

Hughes was successful in releasing Pike's men, except for Sergeant Meek, who was being held for murder—and the party reached Natchitoches 20 October 1809.[41]

Pike's career as a soldier flourished, thanks in part to Wilkinson's authority.[42] He spent a few years as a field officer serving in peacetime commands, and when the War of 1812 began he became a colonel commanding an infantry regiment. At the age of thirty-five, newly advanced to brigadier general, he was killed in the explosion of a powder magazine while leading an attack on Toronto.

Pike was uncomplicated, often childlike in his devotion to Wilkinson. His courage at times approached the foolhardy. He was aggressively patriotic, naively sentimental. When he came in sight of the U.S. flag at Natchitoches, at the end of his western expedition, he exclaimed (according to his journal): "All hail . . . the ever sacred name of country, in which is embraced that of kindred, friends, and every other tie which is dear to the soul of man."[43] No evidence connects him with Wilkinson's schemes or seriously challenges the documentary evidence that he was a loyal officer, happily spying for his country in the Southwest. Nothing that Pike ever tried to do was easy, and most of his luck was bad.

NOTES

1. HAY & WERNER, 157–58. This work is a generally accurate although unannotated biography; see also SHREVE and JACOBS. A new critical biography, and a selected edition of Wilkinson's papers, would be useful aids.

2. TJ to Joseph Anderson, 28 Dec. 1805, LC. For Wilkinson's appointment, see Wilkinson to Madison, 7 April 1805, TERR. PAPERS, 13:114–15, 421. For the debate over his appointment, PLUMER, 392, 393n.

3. ANAS, 61.

4. For the Wilson incident, see CANTWELL, 180. Wilkinson was one of the first subscribers to Wilson's *American Ornithology*. An example of his "natural history" letters is one to TJ, 6 Nov. 1805, LC, in which he introduces the President to the cottonwood tree, *Populus deltoides*. An anonymous letter from Kentucky warned Jefferson in 1801 that Wilkinson had been at the head of a plot to separate Kentucky from the Union (26 June 1801, LC).

5. See COX [2], 798. An ironic footnote to his recommendation about the Boones is his later report: "I am sorry to add that . . . the salt works of a son of old Danl. Boone, about hundred & fifty miles up the Missouri have been broken up [by the Sauk Indians]" (to Dearborn, 10 Dec. 1805, TERR. PAPERS, 13:298).

6. Wilkinson to TJ, 27 June 1805, LC. For the appointment of his son as adjutant, see his general orders for 11 May 1805, NARG 94. Upon his arrival in St. Louis, Wilkinson appointed a new adjutant, Lieutenant Daniel Hughes (general orders of 2 July 1805).

7. On the three objects, see Wilkinson to TJ, 6 Nov. 1805, LC. While there are no extant instructions regarding exploration, Wilkinson's actions upon arriving in St. Louis, and a letter he wrote many

years later mentioning verbal orders, make it clear that Jefferson had instructed him in this matter (see Wilkinson to TJ, 4 Aug. 1818, LC).

8. Wilkinson to Dearborn, 8 Sept. 1805, TERR. PAPERS, 13:199. There is fragmentary evidence of this expedition or another unidentified one, and its contacts with British travelers, in David Thompson's narrative regarding forty-two Americans on the affluents of the Columbia; for this and other articles on the subject, see *Oregon Historical Quarterly,* 26 (1925), 43; 38 (1937), 223–27, 391–97; 39 (1938), 425–31; 40 (1939), 188–89. JOSEPHY deals with the subject, 41–42, 652, 656–62.

9. L & C JOURNALS, 5:387.

10. Bruff to Wilkinson, 29 Sept. 1804, TERR. PAPERS, 13:56–61. Bruff thought that between the waters of the Platte and Rio Grande there was but a "short carrying place," where traders from Santa Fe met American traders. Wilkinson told Dearborn of this intention to establish a Platte post on 8 Oct. 1805, NARG 107, W-508. Dearborn scolded him for the move in a letter of 21 Nov. 1805, NARG 107, letters sent.

11. Peter to Wilkinson, 8 Sept. 1805, TERR. PAPERS, 13:231–32. Sometime during 1805, TJ wrote a note to himself: "Explore Osages river to source" (LC, microfilm reel 35, fol. 27110). There is no evidence that TJ ever saw Peter's map.

12. Deposition of Pike, 17 Nov. 1808, L & C LETTERS, 2:722. No recommendation of Pike by Lewis is known to exist.

13. Wilkinson to Pike, 30 July 1805, NARG 94, consolidated Pike file; also in PIKE, 1:3–4. While PIKE is now the definitive edition of his journals and letters, COUES is still valuable. A sound book-length biography is HOLLON, while two popular accounts of Pike's travels are JACKSON [2] and [3].

14. Pike to Daniel Bissell, 15 June 1806, PIKE, 2:113–14.

15. Dearborn to TJ, 11 Feb. 1807, LC. He enclosed a dozen copies of the brochure, which Jefferson had already seen in manuscript.

16. The King account is rare but not excessively so, being found in the Yale Collection of Western Americana, the Houghton Library at Harvard, the Newberry Library, American Antiquarian Society, Huntington Library, and Library of Congress. The LC copy is used as text for Jackson's reprint in PIKE, 1:134–89.

17. All biographies of T. J. deal with the Burr affair. Studies of Burr himself include ABERNETHY, SCHACHNER, MC CALEB [1] and [2]. For Wilkinson's involvement, see Abernethy's sources and PHILBRICK. A microfilm edition of Burr's papers is now available, prepared by Dr. Mary-Jo Kline under sponsorship of the New-York Historical Society,

and a letterpress edition of selected Burr papers, edited by Dr. Kline, is in preparation by Princeton University Press.

18. Dearborn to Wilkinson, 16 Oct. 1805, TERR. PAPERS, 13:240.

19. TJ to Dearborn, 27 Oct. 1818, LC: "If my memory is right, that was a military expedition, set on foot by General Wilkinson, on his arrival at St. Louis as Governor and Commanding officer, to reconnoitre the country, and to know the positions of his enemies, Spanish and Indian . . . and that it was unknown to us until it had departed."

20. Wilkinson to Pike, 24 June 1806, PIKE, 1:285–86, containing Pike's basic order, though he may have had verbal ones besides. Unlike Lewis and Clark, he carried among his instruments a telescope that would enable him to use the moons of Jupiter in navigation. His observations were erratic. His complete journal of both expeditions and all correspondence, including translations from Spanish documents, are in PIKE.

21. COOK [2], 460–90. See also p. 154. Cook's reasoning that Melgares was seeking Lewis and Clark is persuasive, but not documented.

22. Finding that he had mistaken the Arkansas for the Red River, while wandering lost and cold in the Rockies, he corrected his maps and tables. When his Spanish captors told him where he actually was, he crossed out the words "red River" on the map he was making, writing in "Rio del Nord."

23. Robinson had recently come west and signed on as a civilian physician at Cantonment Belle Fontaine, a new post a few miles above the mouth of the Missouri near St. Louis. He may have come at the invitation of Dr. Antoine Saugrain, the first doctor in St. Louis, who had carried a letter of recommendation from TJ (see p. 45); he married Saugrain's sister-in-law, Sophie Marie Michau, soon after arriving. Wilkinson failed to get him an army appointment as surgeon's mate, but assigned him to the Pike expedition. When he fell into Spanish hands by design, he asked permission to remain in Mexico— leaving a pregnant wife and the security of St. Louis behind. His request was denied. In later years he published a poor map of the West and tried vainly to organize a filibustering expedition into Mexico. About all that is known of him may be found by consulting the index to PIKE.

24. Historian Herbert E. Bolton located Pike's missing papers in the Archives of Mexico in 1907. See a brief account of the find in PIKE, 2:191n. Pike, with his journal of the Mississippi River expedition intact and with enough material on his second trip available from several sources, published *An Account of Expeditions to the Source of the Mississippi, and through the Western Parts of Louisiana* (Philadelphia, 1810).

The work was published the following year in London, then later in Paris and Amsterdam.

25. PETERSON [1], 848. After Wilkinson was relieved of the governorship, it was filled by acting governors until Lewis's appointment in March 1807.

26. PETERSON [1], 849. Two days after writing the decisive letter, Wilkinson marched to parley with the Spanish on the Sabine. A month later he was in New Orleans.

27. LEVY, 70.

28. Wilkinson to Claiborne, 7 Dec. 1806, MC CALEB [1], 145.

29. TJ to Wilkinson, 3 Feb. 1807 and 21 June 1807, and TJ to Claiborne, 3 Feb. 1807, LC.

30. PLUMER, 171. Plumer could never quite decide whether the Burr drama was burlesque, mystery, or Greek tragedy. His biographer, Lynn W. Turner, remarks that historians are in the same dilemma.

31. Quotations on Wilkinson's service and character are from TJ to Wilkinson, 20 Sept. 1807 and 10 March 1811, to Monroe, 11 Jan. 1812, and to Wilkinson, 25 Nov. 1818, LC. Wilkinson was court-martialed in 1815 on charges growing out of operations in the War of 1812—combined with charges of unofficerlike conduct, drunkenness on duty, and others. He was acquitted once more. Upon reduction of the army after the war, an attempt was made to find him a civilian post, but he rejected all offers and accepted a pension.

32. Quoted in COOK [2], 443, the occasion not identified.

33. Foronda to Madison, 22 Aug. 1807, PIKE, 2:226–27. Foronda had replaced Casa Irujo and would be the Spanish minister to the United States until 1809. TJ owned a copy of his *Lecciones ligeras de Chímica* (Madrid, 1791).

34. To Madison, 30 Aug. 1807, LC.

35. Madison to Foronda, 2 Sept. 1807, and Cevallos to Salcedo, 21 Nov. 1807, PIKE, 2:269, 279–80. Cevallos softened his censure of Salcedo by adding: "His Majesty does not fail to recognize the good desire to do right which motivated you, and the zeal with which you detained the above-mentioned American expedition."

36. For the itemized account and related documents, see PIKE, 291–92, 304–17, 347–49.

37. Pike to TJ, 29 Oct. 1807, TJ to Pike, 5 Nov. 1807, TJ to Peale, 6 Nov. 1807 and 6 Jan. 1808, Pike to TJ, 3 Feb. 1808, TJ to Peale, 6 Feb. 1808, and SELLERS, 2:228—all reprinted in PIKE, 2:275–94.

38. Pike to Dearborn, 26 Jan. 1808, PIKE, 2:288.

39. PIKE, 2:356–58.

40. Pike to Wilkinson, 24 Oct. 1806, PIKE, 2:157.

41. The related correspondence is in PIKE, 2:285–86, 324–30, 364–67. Hughes waited fourteen months to file a report of his journey with the secretary of war.

42. Claiborne recommended to Gallatin that Pike be appointed governor of West Florida if it were annexed (18 Feb. 1811, New-York Historical Society, New York City).

43. PIKE, 2:448.

CHAPTER THIRTEEN

End of the Lewis and Clark Era

The Lewis and Clark partnership ended tragically with the violent death of Lewis in the Tennessee wilderness. He and Clark were traveling to Washington by separate routes, in the fall of 1809, when he died. Learning the news while in Kentucky, Clark reacted in anguish and with a special knowledge of Lewis's situation. "I fear O! I fear the weight of his mind has overcome him." Clark's next thought was for the safety of the journals the two had compiled while crossing the continent. "What will be the Consequence? What will become of his papers?"[1]

Immediately after the expedition, Lewis and Clark, accompanied by the Mandan chief, had hurried off to Jefferson and an eager public. After the round of banquets replete with multiple toasts, and adulatory newspaper stories and meetings with high officials, they were looking to the future. Congress had promptly fulfilled Jefferson's promise that members of the expedition would be rewarded with land warrants and double pay.[2] Two matters remained: the timely publication of the journals, and the placement of Lewis and Clark in positions befitting their status as national heroes and symbols of a westering America.

The nation has always had a problem in knowing how to thank its heroes, particularly those who have achieved fame by feats of courage and endurance performed in the field. In later years, explorer John Charles Frémont was nominated for president—and his election would have been a political disaster. The hero of the Union, Ulysses S. Grant, was elected president and served with debatable success. There are other examples of men who were brought in from the battlefield or the wilderness and given desk jobs by grateful countrymen. William Clark turned his job into a rewarding career. Meriwether Lewis, whose assignment was entirely inappropriate, let it destroy him.

· Governor of the Territory ·

Lewis was appointed governor of the Territory of Louisiana; Clark became territorial agent for Indian affairs and brigadier general of the militia. Clark left Washington for St. Louis immediately after his confirmation in March 1807, stopping in Fincastle, Va., to become engaged to Julia Hancock.[3] Lewis stayed on the East Coast to make arrangements for publication of the journals and did not arrive in St. Louis for more than a year.

In Philadelphia, Lewis set about making plans for publication and renewed his acquaintance with members of the American Philosophical Society who had counseled him in 1803. He also reestablished his close friendship with Mahlon Dickerson and sat for a portrait by Charles Willson Peale. There was no time to lose in issuing a prospectus for the journals, as two of the enlisted men of the expedition already had announced books of their own. Lewis used the newspapers to minimize the effect of these announcements, declaring in a letter to the editor of the *National Intelligencer,* 18 March 1807, that only Robert Frazer had been given "permission" to publish anything, and that Frazer was "entirely unacquainted with celestial observations, mineralogy, botany, or zoology, and therefore cannot possibly give any accurate information on those subjects."[4]

Lewis's own announcement appeared as a separate brochure, to be circulated among postmasters for the signatures of subscribers, and as an advertisement in the *National Intelligencer* of 14 March. The Philadelphia publishing house of C. and A. Conrad and Co. announced the forthcoming set of two volumes, *Lewis and Clark's Tour to the Pacific Ocean through the Interior of the Continent of North America.* The first volume was to be a general account of the expedition. The second would be "confined exclusively to scientific research, and principally to the natural history of those hitherto unknown regions." Also announced was "Lewis & Clark's Map of North America," to be compiled from the observations made on the expedition and from the "collective information of the best informed travellers through the various portions of that region."[5]

When Lewis returned to St. Louis, he took over the leadership of the Territory of Louisiana from acting governor Joseph Browne. He was euphoric, anticipating not only a successful political career but also profitable ventures in land ownership. He hoped to bring his mother to St. Louis and to find, last, someone to marry. He was an ardent but unlucky suitor who, after several disappointments, wrote to Dickerson: "I feel all that restlesness, that inquietude, that certain indiscribable something common to old bachelors. . . . What may be my next adventure god knows, but on this I am determined, *to get a wife*."[6]

The pleasure soon went out of governing a rapidly changing frontier territory filling up with ambitious and quarrelsome men. Lewis governed ineptly and made powerful enemies, among whom was Frederick Bates, secretary of the territory. At some point he became a heavy user of alcohol. A curious fact that may indicate a personality change was his failure to reestablish a correspondence with Jefferson, who wrote him sternly: "Since I parted with you in Albemarle in Sep. last I have never had a line from you, nor I believe has the Secretary at War with whom you have much connection through the Indian Department."[7]

A matter that seemed simple enough was to become the final, exasperating problem of Lewis's governorship. The Mandan chief and his family must be returned to their village. The task was first assigned to Ensign Nathaniel Pryor, soon after Clark took over Indian affairs. As a veteran of the expedition, Pryor knew the territory but no longer knew the disposition of the Indians between St. Louis and the Mandans. The Arikaras fired on Pryor's party, injuring George Shannon—another Lewis and Clark alumnus—so badly that his leg was later amputated. Pryor retreated downstream, still chaperoning the Big White, who then took quarters at Belle Fontaine. Jefferson fretted over the failure. "We consider the good faith, & the reputation of the nation as pledged to accomplish this. We would wish indeed not to be obliged to undertake any considerable military expedition in the present uncertain state of our foreign concerns . . . but if it can be effected in any other way . . . we are disposed to meet it."[8]

The plan that finally worked was probably Clark's, but Lewis had the responsibility for it. The newly organized St. Louis Missouri Fur Company was mounting a trading expedition up the Missouri. Surely this party, strongly motivated to get past the Arikaras and on into the Yellowstone and Big Horn country, could safely escort the chief to his home. Clark was a member of the company, as was Lewis's brother Reuben and the two Chouteau brothers.

In the spring of 1809 the fur company successfully returned the Mandan chief and his family to their people. The pledge of the government had been fulfilled without, as Jefferson had stipulated, a disquieting military expedition. During the planning, however, Lewis had failed to await authorization for all his expenditures. The government had approved the sum of $7,000, but not the last-minute payment to Pierre Chouteau of two drafts totaling $940 to cover the cost of some ammunition, tobacco, and gifts for the Indians.

By this time Jefferson and Dearborn were both out of office. Madison was president and the secretary of war was William Eustis, who had no inclination to consider Lewis either a celebrity or a friend. Eustis declined to honor Lewis's drafts on the government for Chouteau's expenditures.

Lewis thus found himself out of favor with the new administration as well as with elements in the local government. His creditors quickly got the word that he was in financial trouble; he owed several thousand dollars for recent land purchases, and all were clamoring for payment. His chief detractor, Frederick Bates, wrote in the summer of 1809: "Gov. Lewis . . . has fallen from the Public esteem & almost into the public contempt. . . . How unfortunate for this man that he resigned his commission in the army: His habits are altogether military & he never can I think succeed in any other profession."[9] It was a cruel but accurate assessment.

Lewis departed for Washington soon thereafter, carrying not only his fiscal records but most of the journals and other records of the expedition. He had planned, when he left St. Louis, to go by way of New Orleans; en route he changed his mind and headed overland on horseback. At the same time, Clark left for Washington with his young wife and their tiny son, Meriwether Lewis Clark.

When Lewis reached Fort Pickering, where Memphis, Tenn., now stands, it seemed to the post commander that he was not in condition to travel. Captain Gilbert C. Russell, of the Fifth Infantry, detained him for a few days. Later he wrote to Jefferson, "The fact is which you may yet be ignorant of that his untimely death may be attributed solely to the free use he made of lequor which he acknowledged very candidly to me after his recovery & expressed a firm determination never to drink any more spirits. . . ."[10]

Lewis died at Grinder's Tavern on the Natchez Trace on 11 October 1809, under circumstances that can never be sorted out. The best assumption is that the gunshot wounds to the head and abdomen which killed him were self-inflicted. Clark believed it and so did Jefferson. Replying to Captain Russell, Jefferson said, "He was much afflicted & habitually so with hypocondria. This was probably increased by the habit into which he had fallen & the painful reflections that would necessarily produce in a mind like his."[11]

· Salvaging the Expedition's Findings ·

Clark stopped at Charlottesville, missing Lewis's mother because she was away from home, then spent a night at Monticello. He and Jefferson "spoke much on the af[fair]s of Gov. Lewis &c. &c. &c." Proceeding to Washington, he called on Secretary Eustis and "pointed out his [Lewis's] intentions & views for his protest." According to Clark's diary of the trip, Eustis declared that Lewis had not lost the confidence of the government.[12]

Lewis's journals were recovered and combined with those in Clark's possession. It might have been supposed that Lewis had made at least some progress in preparing the material for publication, but, as his publishers reported to Jefferson, "Govr. Lewis never furnished us with a line of the M.S. nor indeed could we ever hear any thing from him respecting it."[13]

Between them, Jefferson and Clark devised the idea of having a narrative of the expedition written by an experienced writer and the scientific material analyzed and published by a scientist. William Wirt, a Richmond attorney who would later become U.S. attorney general, declined an invitation to write the narrative. Clark traveled on to Philadelphia and persuaded Nicholas Biddle, a well-known literary figure, to prepare the report. Dr. Benjamin Smith Barton took possession of the scientific notes and specimens, promising to execute that aspect of the project.

Clark himself was to prepare the map. He returned to St. Louis to resume his duties as Indian agent and again take up his favorite avocation, cartography. It is likely that he already had spent much time on the map, which he was to compile from these sources:

(a) The base map that Nicholas King had prepared in 1803 and which he and Lewis had carried to the Pacific and back. From this he would take the Pacific coastline, as laid down by Vancouver and other mariners.

(b) His own 1805 map, sent back from the Mandans and redrawn by King.

(c) The small, detailed charts of the river courses between the Mandans and the Pacific, not yet compiled into a general map.

(d) Zebulon Pike's manuscript and published maps of his Mississippi River and western expeditions, the latter based in part on borrowings from Alexander Humboldt.

(e) Lieutenant James Wilkinson's map of the Arkansas River country.

(f) William Dunbar's map of the Ouachita expedition.

(g) Thomas Freeman's map of the Red River expedition.

(h) Information provided by John Colter about his trips to the Yellowstone country after the expedition.

(i) A map provided by George Drouillard, who had traveled less extensively than Colter but produced new data on the Big Horn River watershed.

In utilizing Pike's "The Internal Part of Louisiana," Clark was unwittingly perpetuating a plagiarism, for Pike had copied many of its features exactly from Humboldt's *Carte générale du Royaume de la Nouvelle Espagne.* Indeed, Pike was able to precede Humboldt in publishing the material, for he was using a copy that Wilkinson had taken from the manuscript version that Humboldt had made available to Washington officials in 1804. In a deposition made during Wilkinson's 1811 court-martial, General Henry Lee declared that Gallatin, after first declining on the ground that Humboldt wanted no copy made, permitted Wilkinson to have a tracing of the "northern provinces of Mexico." Undoubtedly the tracing passed from Wilkinson to Pike, and from Pike to his publisher.[14]

Humboldt's map was in itself a compilation, relying for its northern portion on the work of Bernardo Miera y Pacheco, who mapped the Domínguez-Escalante expedition of 1776 to the upper Colorado River basin and the Utah Valley. Miera, and then Humboldt, showed the Red River rising in the mountains east of Taos. Incredibly, Pike's map perpetuates the error, taking his Red River almost exactly from the Humboldt map although that map had led him disastrously astray when he was in the area. Pike may have had little to do with the final preparation of his map; possibly he turned all his data over to his publisher, John Conrad, and was not directly responsible for the misuse of the Humboldt map. Humboldt complained to Jefferson that not only Pike but also English cartographer Aaron Arrowsmith had borrowed from him without authorization. In his reply, Jefferson managed to condemn the British and defend Pike in the same breath. "That their [i.e., the British] Arrowsmith should have stolen your map of Mexico, was in the piratical spirit of his country. But I should be sincerely sorry if our Pike has made an ungenerous use of your candid communication here; and the more so as he died in the arms of victory gained over the enemies of this country. Whatever he did was on a principle of enlarging knolege and not for filthy shillings and pence of which he made none from that book."[15]

Clark made two or three copies of his great map, sending one he completed in December 1810 to Nicholas Biddle, who gave it to the publisher's engraver for use in the 1814 edition of the Lewis and Clark narrative. The published version—apparently the only one seen by Jefferson—excluded everything below the Kansas River and above the bend of Clark's river because of size limitations. Geographical historian John Logan Allen has called it "an item of superlative craftsmanship and analysis," and "a precise symbol of the nature of informed American geographical lore of the Northwest that began to take shape following the publication of the map and the [Biddle narrative]."[16]

After an unfortunate history during which the first publisher, Conrad, went bankrupt and turned the material over to Bradford and Inskeep, who also went bankrupt after publication, the Biddle narrative and map came off the press in 1814. Clark did not see a copy until 1816 and made no money from the work. Although the book was to become a classic, Jefferson was far from satisfied with it. To him only half the story had been told; the scientific portion entrusted to Dr. Barton was still unpublished, and Barton was dead.

Jefferson wrote Clark in 1816 that he still hoped to see publication of the astronomical observations, Indian vocabularies, and other papers. He proposed to ask the War Department to handle the astronomical part, reissuing the map with corrected longitudes, "and I should deliver the papers of Natural history & the Vocabularies to the Philos. society at Philadelphia, who would have them properly edited." He said he would also like to deposit the "travelling pocket journals" of the expedition with the society "to be recurred to on all interesting questions arising out of the published journal." Clark replied that he, too, desired further publication but that Biddle had all the material. "From the mortification of not having succeeded in giving to the world all the Results of that expedition, I feel relief & gratitude for the interest which you are willing to take, in effecting what has not been in my power to accomplish."[17]

A year later, Jefferson had made little progress in assembling the papers. He asked the American Philosophical Society to become "a depository of the papers generally," and he sent three volumes of Lewis and Clark journals he had in his library. He still hoped for publication:

With respect to the zoological, vegetable & mineralogical papers & subjects, it would perhaps be agreeable to the Philosophical society to have a digest of them made, and published in their transactions or otherwise. And if it should be within the views of the historical committee to have the Indian vocabularies digested and published, I would add to them the remains of my collection. I had thro' the course of my life availed myself of every opportunity of procuring vocabularies of the languages of every tribe which either myself or my friends could have access to. They amounted to about 40 more or less perfect. But in their passage from Washington to this place, the trunk in which they were was stolen and plundered, and some fragments only of the vocabularies were recovered. Still however they were such as would be

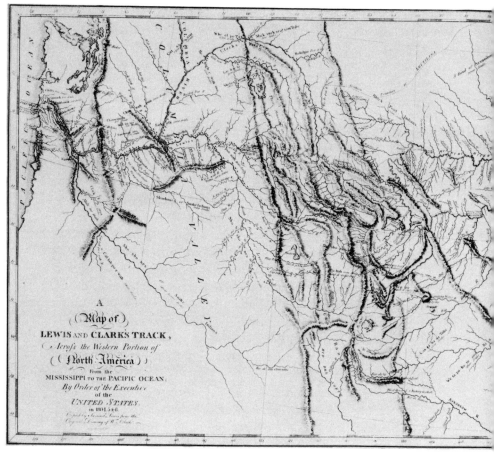

13. Map from the 1814 Lewis and Clark narrative. LIBRARY OF CONGRESS

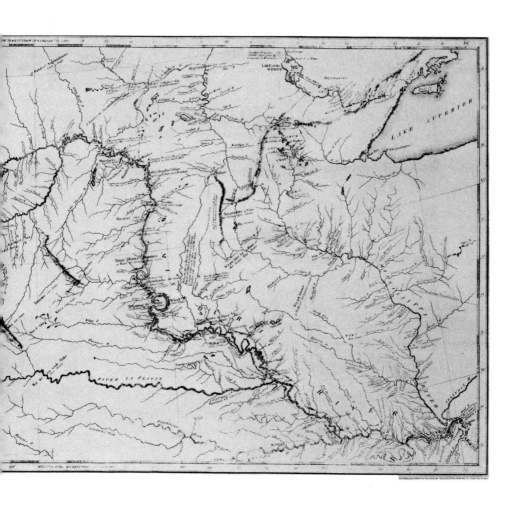

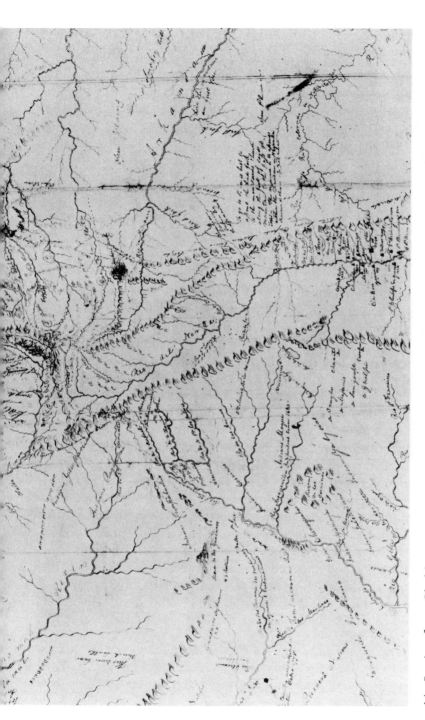

14. Section from Clark's manuscript map of 1810. BEINECKE RARE BOOK AND MANUSCRIPT LIBRARY, YALE UNIVERSITY

worth incorporation with a larger work, and shall be at the service of the historical committee, if they can make any use of them.[18]

The following spring, Biddle deposited with the society all the papers then available except the vocabularies about which Jefferson was so anxious. These were still in the hands of the Barton family and have not been found. Also missing were the many observations that might have made possible the calculation of correct longitudes. Although the vocabularies and celestial observations are sorely missed by students of ethnology and early exploration, the bulk of the Lewis and Clark journals are still safely on deposit with the American Philosophical Society.

· Second Response to Mackenzie: The Astorians ·

Dining with Samuel Latham Mitchill after returning from the Pacific, Lewis told him he thought the most important result of the expedition was the prospect of a trading house at the mouth of the Columbia.[19] Combined with James Wilkinson's prediction to the Spanish that the United States would be established on the Pacific within five years after 1804, it is strong evidence of the way thoughts about trade with Asia were moving.

Although American vessels already were engaged in the sea-otter trade between Canton and the Pacific Northwest, there was no established base of operations on land. The situation was the same for the British, and Alexander Mackenzie, whose recommendation for such a base in his *Voyages* had not been followed, was still urging an establishment at the mouth of the Columbia. In March 1808, Mackenzie submitted a memorandum to his government in which he once more pressed for British possession of the Northwest Coast. He declared that "the Fur Trade should be carried on from the Atlantic to the . . . mouth of the River Columbia . . . where a Commercial Colony might be planted." He cautioned that the Americans were fully determined to utilize the advantage the Lewis and Clark expedition had given them.[20]

At about the same time, Jefferson received a letter from John Jacob Astor, of New York, saying he wanted to engage in extensive Indian trade if two objectives could be attained. First, he needed "the countenance and good wishes" of the President; second, a charter from the state of New York. He said he intended to engage extensively in the fur trade, hoping to take over the greater part of such trade that now passed through Canada, and that he had already written New York governor Dewitt Clinton about the matter. If Jefferson would support his proposal he would apply to the New York legislature for a charter.[21]

Jefferson had never heard of this German immigrant, who had begun his American career by opening a small New York shop dealing in furs and musical instruments. When he received Astor's letter he asked Dearborn what information he had and Dearborn replied that Clinton spoke highly of him as a man well acquainted with the fur and felting business. Accordingly, Jefferson responded to Astor's request: "I learn with great satisfaction the disposition of our merchants to form into companies for undertaking the Indian trade within our own territories. . . . You may be assured that in order to get the whole of this business passed into the hands of our own citizens & to oust foreign traders who so much abuse their privileges by endeavoring to excite the Indians to war on us, every reasonable patronage & facility in the power of the Executive will be afforded."[22]

Perhaps because the New York legislature was soon to adjourn, or because he decided he did not need presidential endorsement, Astor went before the legislature before receiving Jefferson's encouraging reply. With Clinton's backing he received a charter on 6 April for an enterprise that was soon to dominate the American fur trade.

Jefferson's support proved to be only moral, but Astor found more material benefits in his friendship with the Albert Gallatin family. While the relationship was more personal than professional, Astor could not resist slipping into a friendly correspondence an occasional inquiry about official plans or actions that might affect his mercantile interests.[23]

Although the letter from Jefferson had mentioned trade "within our own territories," the Astor venture could not be confined. By 1810 the entrepreneur had organized the Pacific Fur

Company and combined it with his original organization, the American Fur Company. His destination was the mouth of the Columbia, which he planned to approach by land and sea.

His vessel, the *Tonquin,* set sail in September 1810 and—after a hazardous voyage—reached the Columbia in March 1811. In the first tumultuous weeks on the coast, a trading house was established, but the captain of the *Tonquin* was killed by Indians and the ship itself later destroyed by a white survivor of the Indian depredations.

Of greater interest geographically, to those concerned with overland exploration, was the party that set out from St. Louis in July 1811 under the leadership of Wilson Price Hunt. A businessman rather than an outdoorsman, Hunt was scheduled to become head of the Astor establishment after reaching the Columbia. He led his party from St. Louis to a point about 450 miles up the Missouri in the fall of 1810 to spend the winter, then continued upstream in April 1811. His party contained about sixty persons in four boats, including naturalists John Bradbury and Thomas Nuttall, who were going only part of the way. Choosing a more southerly route than that followed by Lewis and Clark (easier passage and safety from the hostile Blackfeet), Hunt left the river at the Arikara villages with a pack train of eighty-two horses. He moved by way of the Little Missouri and Powder rivers, the Big Horn and Wind River mountains, across the Continental Divide to the Snake River, then to the Columbia. He reached Astoria in February 1812.[24]

The Astor venture on the Columbia failed in the War of 1812 when an associate sympathetic to the British sold out to the North West Company. Astoria was not regained until the Treaty of Ghent, ending the war, restored it to U.S. hands.

Jefferson's next communication from Astor came in 1812 in the form of a summary of his Pacific operations. It was too early for Astor to know the full story—Hunt was still moving westward at last report—but Astor spoke of dispatching the *Tonquin,* whose captain was sent to find some Russian settlement with a proposal for friendly trade and mutual benefit. Astor said the *Tonquin* had made an amicable contact with the Russians, who referred its captain to the Russian government and the Russian-American Fur Company in St. Petersburg.

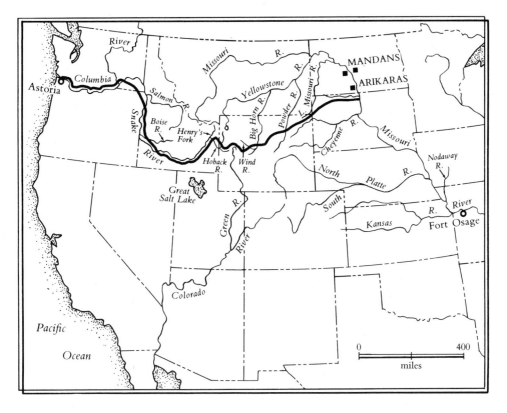

15. Overland route of the Astorians.

Replying, Jefferson erroneously recalled having invited Astor's proposal for a Pacific establishment. Then, in a statement that harked back to his old notion of a loose confederation of free nations on the continent, he spoke of his hope for "the establishment of an independent nation on the Pacific Coast, bound to the United States by ties of blood, language and friendship." Writing to Astor in the same vein the following year, he said, "I view it [Astoria] as the germ of a great, free and independent empire on that side of our continent, and that liberty and self-government spreading from that as well as this side, will ensure their complete establishment over the whole."[25]

Astoria seemed to Jefferson the realization of an idea he had nurtured since the return of Lewis and Clark. Senator Plumer, dining with the President in November 1806 while the explorers were still en route to the capital, heard Jefferson say he hoped that enterprising merchants would soon go to the Columbia and settle there. He doubted if the government itself was in a position to sponsor such a settlement.[26] Astor had taken that problem off the government's hands.

· The Sale of a Great Library ·

During the British invasion of Washington in 1814, the capitol building was burned, and with it about 3,000 volumes that had been assembled for the use of the House and Senate. A month later, Jefferson wrote President Madison to offer his own library for sale. "I have long been sensible that my library would be an interesting possession for the public, and the loss Congress has recently sustained, and the difficulty of replacing it, while our intercourse with Europe is so obstructed, renders this the proper moment for placing it at their service."[27] The offer represented a change of mind for Jefferson: he had meant his books to become the nucleus of a library at the proposed University of Virginia. Congress bought the books, but not without predictable rancor among the members. Some, the political enemies of Madison and Jefferson, assumed the collection would contain immoral and irreligious works. "The bill would put $23,900 into Jefferson's pocket for about 6,000 books, good, bad, and indifferent, old, new, and worthless, in languages which many can not read, and most ought not."[28]

Delivery of the books to Washington in 1815 did not mean the end of Jefferson's collecting; he had always said he could not live without books. It signified a kind of retrenchment, however, not surprising in a septuagenarian. Another act of his, soon after he offered the library for sale, was also symbolic of the fact that his interests were, if not waning, at least changing. His long affiliation with the American Philosophical Society, so important to him, began to change complexion. For years he had worried about his service as an absentee president of the society. Each time he was renominated he respectfully declined the office and was persuaded by the membership to continue. When he sent in his resignation on 23 November 1814, it was with special determination. "I shall consider myself sufficiently honored in remaining a private member of their body," he wrote Dr. Robert Patterson. Perhaps there was a reason beyond advancing age that prompted his move, one that he spoke of three years later in a letter to Caspar Wistar. He said he no longer had the urge to do research in the direction the society was moving. "The truth is that I have been drawn by the history of the times from Physical and mathematical sciences, which were my passion, to those of policies & government towards which I had naturally no inclination."[29] It was not quite true, for he still delighted in mathematics, geography, astronomy, and natural history. His earnest and successful effort to recover the Lewis and Clark records and deposit them with the society was continued after his resignation as its president.

· Fry-Jefferson *Redivivus* ·

Opposition by the Spanish, followed by the War of 1812, had stopped for a time the exploration and mapping of the West. No official western expedition had been proposed, purely for exploratory purposes, since the cancellation of the Arkansas River probe in 1807. The period immediately after the end of hostilities was to renew the government's interest in westward growth, but the aspect of geographical study that seemed to revive first was state-oriented. Internal improvement was flourishing. Work began afresh on the great National Road, which, beginning at Cumberland, Md., would reach Wheeling, on the Ohio, by 1818. Surveying of public lands was extensive as Indiana, Illinois, and Mississippi became states, and the territories of Michigan and Arkansas were formed. The so-called public-land states, formed after 1787, were being laid out in the rectilinear system of tiers and ranges, adapted from the plan that Jefferson had helped to devise in the land ordinance of 1785.

Certain geographical ideas had grown ahead of Jefferson's thinking. When he was queried by Thomas W. Maury about the idea of a map of the states showing a mineralogical survey and statistical tables, he confessed that the idea was new to him and he needed to think about it. Then, having pondered, he wrote a letter offering several practical suggestions for such an approach.[30] He was anxious as ever to promote geographical knowledge of the older areas as well as the new ones. "A great deal is yet wanting," he told Andrew Ellicott, "to ascertain the true geography of our country; more indeed as to its longitudes than latitudes. Towards this we have done too little for ourselves, & depended too long on the antient & inaccurate observations of other nations."[31]

By 1816 the commonwealth of Virginia was ready to undertake a comprehensive mapping program. Jefferson was consulted, and wrote Governor Wilson Cary Nicholas a remarkable twelve-page letter which, perhaps more than any other document, exhibits the technical side of his geographic and cartographic knowledge.[32]

The legislature had provided for topographic surveys of each county; a general survey of the outlines of the state and its most prominent rivers and mountains; an astronomical survey; and a mineralogical survey. Jefferson assumed there would be a general surveyor to supervise the whole project and county surveyors for the local work. He thought that each county candidate ought to be examined by the professor of mathematics at William and Mary, or some other expert, but he was doubtful about the supply of skilled men. "If one, competently qualified, can be found for every half dozen counties, it will be as much perhaps as can be expected." He hoped that in surveying rivers, the county surveyors would note which parts were navigable, record all confluences, and indicate towns, mills, ferries, bridges, crossings of roads, passages through mountains, mines, quarries, and other remarkable features.

He suggested the publication of a single-sheet map of each county on a scale of half an inch to the mile. "There are few house keepers who would not wish to possess a map of their own county. Many would purchase those of the circumadjacent counties." These county surveyors should be equipped with a circumferentor with cross spirit levels on its face, a graduated rim, and a double index, the one fixed, the other moveable, bearing a nonius. "The needle should never be depended on for an angle."

In comtemplating the general survey of the state, Jefferson thought of it as divided into two parts: the tidewater area, and the area above tidewater. He reminded Nicholas that the tidewater survey had already been done. "Some time before the war [of 1812], Congress authorised the Executive to have an accurate survey made of the whole sea-coast of the US. comprehending, as well as I remember, the principal bays and harbors. A Mr. Hassler, a mathematician of the first order from Geneva, was engaged in the execution and was sent to England to procure proper instruments." He was speaking of Ferdinand Rudolph Hassler, the man who had struggled vainly with the Lewis and Clark calculations for longitude and now headed the forerunner of the U.S. Coast and Geodetic Survey.[33]

In discussing the general survey, Jefferson's memory ran back to his boyhood, when his father, Peter, and Christopher Fry were producing their monumental map of Virginia. He referred to the great controversy between Lord Baltimore and Lord Fairfax, whose territories were divided by the Potomac. The question of which branch of the river above Harpers Ferry was the main branch caused an extensive survey to be made, and Lord Fairfax took advantage of the occasion to have his entire grant surveyed. "He furnished a copy of that survey to Col. Fry and my father, who entered it, on a reduced scale, into their map." Jefferson insisted that the longitudes of that survey could not be correct, as they were made before correction of the tables used to measure longitude by lunar distances.

The survey of mountains, Jefferson thought, should include

not only the principal continuous ridges, such as the Blue Ridge and the Alleghenies, but also isolated mountains such as the Peaks of Otter in Bedford County. As such promontories could be seen for great distances (the Peaks of Otter from twenty counties), they would offer distance and bearing to aid in the general survey. The heights of the gaps as well as the peaks were essential. Here he wrote a passage unusually detailed for a statesman who had done only casual surveying since his appointment as surveyor of Albemarle County in 1773:

But how are these heights to be taken, & from what base? I suppose from the plain on which they stand. But it is difficult to ascertain the precise horizontal line of that plain, or to say where the ascent above the general face of the country begins. Where there is a river or other considerable stream, or extensive meadow plains near the foot of a mountain, which is much the case in the vallies dividing the Western ridges, I suppose that may be fairly considered in the level of it's base, in the intendment of the law. Where there is no such term of commencement, the Survey may judge as well as he can from his view, what point is in the general line of the adjacent country. How are these heights to be taken, and with what instrument? Where a good base can be found, the geometrical admeasurement is the most satisfactory. For this a theodolite must be provided of the most perfect construction, by Ramsden or Troughton if possible, and for horizontal angles it will be the better of two telescopes. But such bases are rarely to be found. When none such, the height may still be measured geometrically, by ascending or descending the mountain, with the theodolite, measuring it's face from station to station, noting it's inclination between these stations, and the hypothenusal difference of that inclination, as indicated on the vertical ark of the theodolite. The sum of the perpendiculars corresponding with the hypothenusal measures, is the height of the mountain. But a barometrical admeasurement is preferable to this, since the late improvements in the theory they are to be depended upon nearly as much as the geometrical, and are much more convenient and expeditious. The barometer should have a sliding Nonius and a thermometer annexed, with a screw at the bottom to force up the column of mercury solidly. Without this precaution they cannot be transported at all, and even with it they are in danger from every severe jolt. They go more safely on a baggage horse than in a carriage. The heights should be measured on both sides, to shew the rise of the country at every ridge.

The measurement of elevations was still fresh in Jefferson's mind, for during the previous November he had measured both Peaks of Otter with a theodolite, finding the highest to be 3,203½ feet above tidewater level.[34] Although the use of the barometer for measuring elevations was well established, the fragility of the long glass tube of mercury had prevented its use on western explorations. None was carried by Lewis and Clark, who said little about elevations. Zebulon Pike used the theodolite, combined with an estimate of the base-line height determined from the rate of decline of the river levels.[35] A generation later, John Charles Frémont found glass barometers too fragile; when his last one broke, he resorted to measuring elevations by the boiling point of water.

Ten years were to elapse before the Virginia map could be issued in 1826. It was entitled *Map of the State of Virginia Constructed in Conformity to Law from the Late Surveys Authorized by the Legislature and Other Original and Authentic Documents by Herman Boye.* Drawn to a scale of one inch to five miles, it was engraved on nine separate sheets, and was generally termed the Nine-Sheet Map. When assembled, the sheets formed a map of Virginia measuring sixty by ninety-three inches.[36] It might have been much less a cartographic monument without Jefferson's encouragement and his suggestions to Governor Nicholas.

· The John Melish Map ·

After touring the seaboard states, Scottish geographer John Melish published *Travels in the United States of America, in the Years 1806 & 1807, and 1809* (Philadelphia, 1812). Jefferson, who had corresponded with Melish during and after publication of the work, subscribed in 1814 to a general atlas which Melish was offering by prospectus. By this time Melish had established himself in Philadelphia as a publisher of maps, charts, and geographic works, making him the first commercial cartographer in the United States.[37]

By 1816 Melish had produced a large *Map of the United States* in six sheets, covering the entire country. As it was printed from copper plates, the engraver could polish off portions of the plate and replace old information with new. As his compilation of cartographic data grew, Melish produced more than twenty states or "editions" of the map.[38]

Melish sent Jefferson a copy, declaring that it contained all that was known of Louisiana and expecting Jefferson to be especially interested in that aspect. The compilation embraced the work of Arrowsmith, Humboldt, Vancouver, Lewis and Clark, Dunbar and Freeman, Pike, and others. Although Jefferson's response was commendatory, he could not resist making a comment on Melish's southwestern boundary of the Louisiana Territory. The first edition of the map showed the boundary of the Purchase extending only to the Guadalupe River, a stream slightly northeast of the Nueces—which was the western limit of the old Spanish province of Texas. Jefferson said he was sure the Rio Grande should be the boundary. Accordingly, Melish corrected his copper plate and, in the 1818 edition, extended the United States to the Rio Grande.

The Melish map of 1818 was to be used in the forthcoming Adams-Onís Treaty establishing the line between Spanish possessions and the United States.[39] It was the first map that could be said to represent what Jefferson had wanted since the Purchase, a general delineation of the entire West.

With the publication of the Melish map, the era of Lewis and Clark could be considered closed. Lewis was gone, his journals preserved—some used as a source for published work, some only stored—and better trained geographers were soon to renew the study of the Trans-Mississippi region. Having sold his library, salvaged the records of Lewis and Clark, and resigned as president of the American Philosophical Society, Jefferson had himself come to the end of an era. His days of active interest in western exploration were done.

NOTES

1. Clark to Jonathan Clark, 28 Oct. 1809, typed transcript in the Bodley Papers, Filson Club Library, Louisville, Ky. The original has disappeared. Printed in L & C LETTERS, 2:726–27.

2. See "An Act making compensation to Messrs. Lewis and Clarke, and their companions," 3 March 1807, in L & C LETTERS, 2:377. The amount set aside for double pay was $11,000.

3. Clark's appointment as Indian agent excluded control of the Osages, who were to remain under the supervision of Pierre Chouteau. His commission as militia general was in lieu of a colonelcy in the regular army, blocked by the Senate because other candidates out-ranked him.

4. Although Frazer published no book, a copy of his map survives in LC. Sergeant Patrick Gass, however, had already joined forces with David M'Keehan, a Pittsburgh bookseller who would ghostwrite the first narrative of the expedition. See GASS.

5. The text of the prospectus is in L & C LETTERS, 2:394–97. CUTRIGHT [2] is a complete history of the Lewis and Clark journals and their publishing history down to the present day.

6. Lewis to Dickerson, 3 Nov. 1807, New Jersey Historical Society, Newark. The letter, reprinted in L & C LETTERS, 2:719–21, provides one of the few insights into Lewis's personal life that have survived.

7. TJ to Lewis, 17 July 1808, LC. From the time of his departure to assume the governorship to the day of his death in the fall of 1809, Lewis wrote Jefferson three, possibly four, letters—all official and containing only perfunctory expressions of esteem.

8. TJ to Lewis, 17 July 1808, LC.

9. Bates to Richard Bates, 14 July 1809, BATES, 2:68.

10. Russell to TJ, 31 Jan. 1810, LC.

11. TJ to Russell, 18 April 1810, LC. Those who write of Lewis's death are definitely of two schools. For the argument of those who believe he was murdered, see DILLON or FISHER. For an opposing view, see Jackson's annotations in L & C LETTERS, 2:574–75, 747–49.

12. Clark's diary of the trip, Sept. to Dec. 1809, is at the State Historical Society of Missouri, Columbia. Entries after 18 Dec. are missing, but his later movements and actions are well documented by correspondence. The diary is extracted in L & C LETTERS, 2:724–26. The journey is summarized in JACKSON [5].

13. C. & A. Conrad to TJ, 13 Nov. 1809, LC. Jefferson replied 23 Nov. that he was taking steps to recover the journals, and that Clark was the proper person to have them prepared for publication. Jefferson had not yet discussed the matter with Clark.

14. In his deposition, Lee also reported learning from Wilkinson that Aaron Burr had surreptitiously made another tracing for his own use. See PIKE, 2:368–69.

15. Humboldt to TJ, 21 Dec. 1811, DE TERRA, 792, and TJ to Hum-

boldt, 3 Dec. 1813, LC. Pike borrowed data for his description of Mexico as well as the cartographic data.

16. ALLEN [2], 375, 376. The manuscript map used in BIDDLE is in the Western Americana Collection of Yale University Library and was published in facsimile, in four large sheets, in 1950. Clark later retrieved the map and added new material to it. A notation that could not have appeared on the published version reads: "Mr. W. P. Hunts rout in 1811," a reference to the overland trek of the Astorians.

17. TJ to Clark, 8 Sept. 1816, Missouri Historical Society, St. Louis, and Clark to TJ, 10 Oct. 1816, American Philosophical Society, Philadelphia. Clark offered to make TJ a new map or send him the one he had, but there is no record of TJ's reply.

18. TJ to Peter S. Duponceau, 7 Nov. 1817, American Philosophical Society library. Duponceau replied 5 Dec. 1817, LC, saying that Biddle was helping the society to assemble the papers, and that TJ's vocabularies would be a welcome addition to the society's own collection. The American Philosophical Society library contains the remnants of Jefferson's collection, based on a printed list of more than 300 English words. Several copies with Indian equivalents are present, including a fragment with Pawnee words, the only survivor of the Lewis and Clark effort. The rest of their vocabularies were lost in the years immediately following Barton's death. A greater loss was the destruction of Jefferson's own collection, which he had been assembling—with the help of many volunteers in the field—for at least twenty-five years. His project is summarized in SHEEHAN, 54–58.

19. MITCHILL, 27–28. Mitchill said he looked upon Lewis "almost as a man arrived from another planet."

20. Mackenzie to Castlereagh, 10 March 1808, LAMB, 42.

21. Astor to TJ, 27 Feb. 1808, LC. TJ received the letter on 8 March, just ten days before Mackenzie wrote to Castlereagh. The standard work on Astor's business ventures is PORTER. The best edition of Washington Irving's *Astoria* is TODD.

22. TJ to Astor, 13 April 1808, LC. The exchange of notes between TJ and Dearborn occurred on 8 April (LC).

23. The Gallatins were hosts to Astor's daughter Dorothea for several months in 1812 (WALTERS, 215).

24. For Hunt and his overland passage, see BRANDON. Hunt is also a strong figure in Irving's *Astoria*. His route between the Snake and Columbia would later become an important section of the Oregon Trail. Returning home in 1812, his party may have become the first to cross South Pass.

25. Astor to TJ, 14 March 1812, TJ to Astor, 24 May 1812, and TJ to Astor, 9 Nov. 1813, LC. In his last letter Jefferson said, "It must be still more gratifying to yourself to foresee that your name will be handed down with that of Columbus & Raleigh, as the father of the establishment and the founder of such an empire." He was responding to Astor's letter of 18 Oct. 1813 (LC), reporting the return of the overland party under Robert Stuart and offering to let TJ read Stuart's journal. "You will see that there are large . . . Rivers in that part of the country of which we had no knowledge before." The Stuart journal is published in SPAULDING.

26. PLUMER, 520, in a diary entry of 2 Dec. 1806.

27. TJ to Madison, 24 Sept. 1814, LC.

28. Speech of Cyrus King, 26 Jan. 1815, quoted in BESTOR, 3. Correspondence involving the purchase is in JOHNSTON [2].

29. TJ to Patterson, 23 Nov. 1814, and TJ to Wistar, 10 June 1817, LC.

30. TJ to Maury, 3 Feb. 1816, LC. Perhaps without realizing it, he had fathered statistical presentation of American geographic data in his *Notes*. "Although the word had not yet entered the language, Jefferson commanded the idea and presented much of his data in statistical form" (PETERSON [3], 52).

31. TJ to Ellicott, 24 June 1812, LC.

32. TJ to Nicholas, 19 April 1816, LC. Care must be taken in using the microfilm copy of this letter, as the pages are out of order. The legislation authorizing the map was an act of 27 Feb. 1816 "to provide an accurate chart of each county and a general map of the Territory of this Commonwealth. County courts were directed to find suitable persons to make maps of the counties" (RISTOW [2]).

33. TJ had recommended the coastal survey and Congress had authorized it in 1807. Hassler went to Europe in 1811 to buy instruments and was delayed in returning until 1815. He was not made superintendent of the Survey of the Coast until 2 May 1816.

34. NOTES, 262–63. TJ also used the barometric method; among his papers is a long treatise on finding altitudes by this system, and a list of altitudes in the Blue Ridge and Allegheny mountains, by General Jonathan Williams (20 Aug. 1811, LC).

35. PIKE, 1:354n–55n. Pike's method led him to estimate the floor of the prairie east of Pikes Peak at 8,000 feet, when it was actually closer to 5,000. This, plus an error in using the theodolite, gave him an elevation of 18,581 for the peak. Its height today is considered to be 14,110 feet.

36. RISTOW [2], 238–39. TJ also arranged the hiring of John Wood to

supervise the county surveys and direct the compilation of the whole map.

37. TJ's papers contain a broadside of 18 July 1814, announcing that Melish was going into business. TJ had subscribed 21 Jan. 1814 to an atlas (LC).

38. RISTOW [1], 159. The article contains a reproduction of the map. Melish also was publisher of the nine-sheet map of Virginia in 1826.

39. BROOKS [1], 215–19.

CHAPTER FOURTEEN

Defining the Empire

It was incredible that until the summer of 1818 the old man had never been farther west than Staunton, Va., just beyond the Blue Ridge. The adventurer who had traveled in the Alps on muleback had never seen the Alleghenies. The sponsor of an exploration to the Pacific had never known the waters of the Ohio.

Inland trips had once seemed at least possible. During his last year as president, Jefferson had said wistfully, "I have never ceased to wish to descend the Ohio & Mississippi to New Orleans, and when I shall have put my home in order, I shall have the leisure, and so far I have health also, to amuse myself in seeing what I have not yet seen."[1] But getting his house in order was not Jefferson's style; the chance to see the wonders of inland America never came.

In August 1818 he journeyed to Warm Springs, about sixty miles west of Staunton near the present boundary of West Virginia. Because he had business at Rockfish Gap and Staunton, he decided to go the extra distance and take the waters. In a tavern at Rockfish Gap, a much-traveled pass across the Blue Ridge, he met with commissioners charged among other duties with choosing a site for the new University of Virginia.[2] From there, accompanied by Judge Archibald Stuart, who went as far as Staunton, and Colonel James Breckenridge of Botetourt County, who accompanied him all the way, he went on horseback to the famous spa.

Jefferson and Breckenridge topped Warm Springs Mountain on the first turnpike of the region, a road that dipped sharply down and edged the soothing waters of the pool. Their host, Colonel John Fry, could stand on the pillared portico of his inn and watch his guests appear in the gap on the eastern skyline.[3] A later gazetteer would report twenty-five cabins of brick, a hotel, and an octagonal bathhouse thirty-eight feet in diameter, housing water five feet deep at an average temperature of 98°. Chemists at William and Mary reported that the water contained nitrogen, muriate of lime, sulphate of magnesia, carbonate of lime, and sulphate of lime. It was recommended, said the gazetteer, as "a gentle aperient, diuretic, and sudorific." In other words, good for drinking and bathing.[4]

In letters that he wrote home to daughter Martha, Jefferson's experience at the springs declined from enthusiasm to misery. He first declared that he had tried the "delicious bath" and would bathe three times a day for a quarter-hour. There were plenty of vegetables and venison, but he regretted to find little "*gay* company" there at the time. Boredom had set in a week later. He had been advised to remain for three weeks, "but so dull a place, and so distressing an ennui I never before knew." All the interesting people seemed to have gone off to White Sulphur Springs, farther to the southwest, where a full and lively house was reported. In his third letter, even the venison had become scarce and all the ladies were invalids, "perfectly recluse in their cabins." Still worse, he had begun to develop boils. "A large swelling on my seat, increasing for several days past in size and hardness disables me from sitting but on the corner of a chair." So he proposed to return home by carriage at the end of his treatment.[5]

Standing in the pool for his thrice-daily immersion, or sitting on the edge of his chair in his cabin, the burdens of age must have felt heavy indeed. His peers were dying, and to those who remained he often found himself beginning his letters "My dear and antient friend." He could at least say with satisfaction at seventy-five what he had told the late George Rogers Clark, that he had "not occupied places in which others would have done more good."[6]

Aware that he was farther west than ever before, he might have spent a few minutes reflecting on the incredible changes that had been wrought—that *he* had wrought—in the vast lands beyond his hostel. Except for important negotiations with Spain and England, he was scantily informed of recent activities relating to the West: that a military post was in prospect for the upper Missouri; that an expedition to the Front Range was in the planning stage; that fur traders were breaching his Stony Mountains everywhere. But there was a long record of attention to western matters which he could review with pride, somewhat diminished by the realization that events had always run a pace or two ahead of his thinking. He had continually altered his policies to overtake reality, a fact of life he serenely accepted. "As new discoveries are made, new truths disclosed, and matters and opinions change with the change of circumstances, institutions must advance also, and keep pace with the times."[7]

· Three Levels of Empire ·

His vision may have been clouded here and there, and he may not have kept up with fast-moving events that swept the American people across the Mississippi, but throughout most of his life he had held three ideas about the hemisphere which had not wavered: (1) that the old confederacy of states east of the Mississippi should remain intact, possibly enlarging to embrace Canada and Cuba; (2) that the area west of the Mississippi ought to be developed by Americans, forming whatever free and independent principalities they wished, allied with but not a part of the United States; (3) that some day, in a future generation, the whole continent from the Arctic to the tip of South America would be peopled by free and independent allies.

The Old Confederacy. Jefferson was as jealous of the union of states in his day as Lincoln was to be in his. He opposed secession of the southern states from New England, and he feared that Kentucky—so remote, and with its trade route down the Mississippi interdicted by the Spanish—might break away. The thought that Aaron Burr's supposed revolt might carry the western states with it so frightened him that he set aside revered principles of orderly legal process.

With the approach of the War of 1812, he saw an opportunity for the "completion" of the confederacy by the addition of Canada, East Florida, and perhaps Cuba. He was out of power by then but watched the struggle with less than the detached view of the "peaceable farmer" he claimed to be. While the war

clouds swirled, he had written to Madison of Bonaparte's con-
senting, though with difficulty, to the transfer of Cuba. "We
should then have only to include the north [Canada] in our
Confederacy, which would be of course in the first war, and we
should have such an empire for liberty as she has never surveyed
since the Creation."[8] And when the war came, Canada was his
goal. It would mean the final expulsion of England from the
continent. He fired off strategic advice: "If we could but get
Canada to Trois rivieres in our hands we should have a set-off
against spoiliations to be treated of, & in the mean time seperate
the Indians from them and set the friendly to attack the hostile
part with our aid."[9] But Canada was not to fall, nor East Florida;
Cuba was not to acquiesce, and indeed the United States made no
territorial gains at all as a result of the war.

The New Confederacy. The Louisiana Purchase of 1803 had
forced Jefferson to remold his vision of the republic. Uncertain at
first about the very constitutionality of the Purchase, then unde-
cided about how it was to be developed, he soon had fit the new
acquisition into his scheme for the hemisphere. He and his Republican colleagues were not wholly in favor of forming new
states in the land between the Mississippi and the Rockies. The
distances were great and Jefferson had been wary of bigness. His
comment to John Breckinridge had been the key to his thinking:
"The future inhabitants of the Atlantic and Mississippi states will
be our sons. We leave them in distinct but bordering establishment . . ." (see p. 113). He had expressed a similar notion to
Joseph Priestley.[10]

As the consensus grew that the Trans-Mississippi would be
comprised of new U.S. territories, then states, the idea of bigness
did not daunt him any more. His successors in office had ac-
commodated their views to suit the will of the people: Monroe
now wanted everything east of the Rockies to become a part of
the Union. Later, John Quincy Adams would want it all, from
sea to shining sea. Louisiana already was a state and Missouri a
territory. Jefferson could write to Barbé-Marbois in 1817: "I
have much confidence that we shall proceed successfully for ages
to come; and that, contrary to the principles of Montesquieu, it
will be seen that the larger the content of country, the more from
it's republican structure, if founded, not on conquest, but [on]

principles of compact & equality, my hope of it's duration is built much on the enlargement of these resources of life going hand in hand with the enlargement of territory, and the belief men are disposed to live honestly, if the means of doing so are open to him."[11]

And the Hemisphere. If in his early years Jefferson felt that his beloved confederation could become ungovernable if too large, he placed no such restriction on the flourishing of American ideas and the advance of those who held them. "Our confederacy must be viewed as the nest from which all America, North and South, is to be peopled," he had told Archibald Stuart in 1786. Had Thomas Hart Benton made such a declaration a generation later it would have been considered a rank invocation of Manifest Destiny. Jefferson's comment was a private one, of course, made early in his career, and it was also pure rhetoric which would bear little analysis. The idea persisted, however, and during his first year as president he could say to James Monroe that he looked forward to "distant times" when his compatriots would expand to "cover the whole northern, if not the southern continent."[12]

In his Latin-American policy as in his Indian policy, he was to find that theoretical and rhetorical views could not stand against the hard realities of politics. During most of his lifetime, Spain was an implacable force. Besides the apprehension that was always with him—imminent war with Spain—there was the problem of the two Floridas. They were a natural part of the old confederacy, he believed, much more a part than Canada or Cuba. Surely his ardent and unflagging desire for the Floridas shaped not only his attitude toward Spain but, as an inevitable corollary, his stand on year-to-year Latin-American matters. His party and his nation shared these concerns.

As a result the United States stood by while monumental social revolt brewed in Venezuela and Colombia. When General Francisco de Miranda came to the United States in November 1805, equipped an American-owned vessel, and set sail for Caracas in an attempt to free his native Venezuela, Jefferson and his colleagues quickly disassociated themselves from the movement. Miranda's expedition was an illegal action, of course; but more than that, it endangered projected negotiations with Spain.

A more important figure in the South American movement for

freedom was Simon Bolívar, who led an epochal revolution without even an implied blessing from Jefferson. Born in Caracas, member of an affluent family, Bolívar became a disciple of Rousseau and a fanatical believer in South American freedom. Like Jefferson, he had witnessed the French Revolution. He had visited the United States during Jefferson's presidency but the two did not meet. It is ironic, if not incredible, that Bolívar waged a bitter revolution which was to unite for a time the nations of Colombia, Equador, and Venezuela; that he endorsed the principle of pan-Americanism—a unified North and South America—as Jefferson did; that he was making himself the most revered of Latin-American heroes; and that he did all this without receiving more than a perfunctory mention in Jefferson's private correspondence. There was no communication between the libertarian of the North and the *libertador* of the South.

In this matter, Jefferson lagged behind some of his friends and correspondents in their defense of a people struggling to rise. To the efforts of Du Pont de Nemours and Alexander von Humboldt to understand and encourage the revolutionists, Jefferson could only respond with nice phrases. His old friend Samuel Latham Mitchill was making a special effort to spread knowledge of Latin America in his *Medical Repository*. Most Americans, however, were as lethargic as Jefferson. By 1824, the Department of State finally had an employee who could translate Portuguese, the language of Brazil. Of the three men who were to play leading roles in Latin-American relations in the 1820s— James Monroe, John Quincy Adams, and Henry Clay—not one was specially qualified to do so (although Monroe spoke Spanish).[13]

Jefferson's real problem here was extreme constraint in his choice of nations qualified for freedom. United States citizens, certainly. But not the French, whom he believed during their Revolution were ready for nothing beyond a constitutional monarchy. Not the citizens of the region around New Orleans, at the time of the Louisiana Purchase, whom Jefferson believed incapable of handling too much republican elbow room for a while.[14] And finally, not the South Americans. To Du Pont de Nemours in 1811: "I fear the degrading ignorance into which their priests and kings have sunk them, has disqualified them from the maintenance or even knowledge of their rights, and that much blood may be shed for little improvement in their condition." To the same correspondent in 1816: "No mortal wishes them more success than I do, but if what I have heard of the ignorance and bigotry of the masses be true, I doubt their capacity to understand and to support a free government, and fear their emancipation from the foreign tyranny of Spain will result in a military despotism at home."[15]

Of Jefferson's views, it must be said that he was partly right about existing conditions and that his really optimistic statements about the future of the hemisphere were predicated on a long period of social change. When he said to Humboldt, "America has a hemisphere to itself," he did not mean right now. His full comment to Humboldt is more representative of his position: "In fifty years more the United States alone will contain fifty millions of inhabitants, and fifty years are soon gone over. The peace of 1763 is within that period. . . . And you will live to see the epoch now equally ahead of us; and the numbers which will then be spread over the other parts of the American hemisphere, catching long before that the principles of our portion of it, and concurring with us in the maintenance of the same system. . . . I am anticipating events of which you will be the bearer to me in the Elysian fields fifty years hence."[16]

Certainly Jefferson's timetable was wrong, and perhaps his very perception of the future; but later generations are learning not to pass judgment too quickly on Jefferson's dreams. They are careful to reflect that the man who said "we hold these truths to be self-evident" may yet surpass them all in the clarity of his vision.

· The Spanish Negotiations ·

While Jefferson soaked his body in the waters of the springs, two men were working hard to settle the differences between Spain and the United States. One was John Quincy Adams, secretary of state, the other Luis de Onís, Spanish minister in Washington. They had begun talks on the boundaries of Louisiana late in 1817, while a third of West Florida and all of East Florida were still Spanish, Texas was a source of contention, and the entire boundary between Spanish America and the United States was undetermined. As an unofficial advisor, Jefferson was holding out for Texas, but President Monroe was not anxious to press for it. Jefferson's interest in the proceedings was lively; he even protested against the habit of Onís in calling Monroe "His Excellency," a title that seemed to place Monroe on Onís's diplomatic level in European parlance.[17]

The Adams-Onís Treaty would be signed in Washington on 22 February 1819 and ratified in 1821. The United States would give up its claim to Texas and assume damage claims of Spain against American citizens. In return, Spain would cede all claim to the Floridas, and recognize a border that was drawn mainly along the east and west banks of the Sabine, Red, and Arkansas rivers, then cut directly west to the Pacific along the forty-second parallel. To many Americans, the most important part of the treaty was the foothold it gave them on Pacific shores—though they lamented the loss of Texas. The boundary lines had been drawn not on rights acquired by the United States in the Louisiana Purchase, but were set by "the comparative power of the two nations, the conditions of settlement on the frontiers, and the skill of the negotiators."[18]

· The Oregon Compromise ·

Another vital matter still pending while Jefferson was languishing and grousing at the springs was the settlement of the boundary between U.S. and British claims in the Northwest. The issue was being dealt with in London, where Richard Rush, minister to England, and Albert Gallatin, minister to France, were parleying with officials of the British crown. Signed on 20 October, the Convention of 1818 fixed the boundary between the two nations along the forty-ninth parallel as far west as the Continental Divide, and left the westernmost boundary undetermined. The two nations agreed that Oregon was to be open to both for ten years, jointly occupied with no prejudice to the claims of either. The agreement was to be renewed in 1827, and the permanent boundary line fixed at the forty-ninth parallel by treaty in 1846.

The United States had been lucky in the Northwest, as Jefferson knew. What if British seaman George Vancouver had not missed the mouth of the Columbia, when he sailed up the coast in 1792? Had he found it, American captain Robert Gray's "discovery" would have meant little. What if British explorer Mackenzie had found the Columbia River instead of the Fraser, which he only *thought* was the Columbia? What if Lewis and Clark had decided to ascend the Marias because it looked so much like the main branch of the Missouri? Or had chosen the wrong fork at the Three Forks? What if the Spanish had interdicted Lewis and Clark as they had Pike and the Red River expedition? And what if the Astorians had failed to reach the Columbia in 1811? David Thompson had arrived there from Canada only a few months later, intent upon building a British trading post. Upon such turns of circumstance do Manifest Destiny and the common destiny of nations devolve.

· Exploring Goes Professional ·

During Jefferson's sojourn at Warm Springs, a fundamental change occurred in the way the army looked at exploration. A topographical unit, which had been formed during the late war as an adjunct to the Corps of Engineers, was in August 1818 elevated to the status of a separate bureau under Secretary of War John Calhoun. Had it existed in 1804, William Clark might have had a genuine captain's commission instead of pretending to his men that he ranked equally with Lewis.

Successor to Lewis and Clark as the country's busiest explorer was Stephen H. Long, a Dartmouth man with a classical education and a flair for engineering, who had taught mathematics at West Point. At the moment he was the most experienced officer in the newly formed unit, having gone to Illinois in 1816 to establish a fort at Lake Peoria, to the Falls of St. Anthony (Minneapolis) on reconnaissance, and up the Arkansas to select the site of Fort Smith, both in 1817. Now he was preparing for a trip to the Front Range of the Rockies in 1819–20 that would represent the first official exploration of the area since Pike's unhappy tour. He would scout the headwaters of the South

Platte, Arkansas, and Canadian rivers, and members of his party would succeed, where Pike had not, in climbing what was yet to be called Pikes Peak.[19]

The American Philosophical Society, carrying on the tradition that Jefferson had helped to establish in 1793, would write a set of instructions for Long's western exploration and appoint a committee to monitor it. Among Jefferson's papers, however, there is no correspondence with Long or any indication that he knew the army had institutionalized the exploration of the West.

· Epilogue: The Jeffersonian Heritage ·

The trip home from the springs was extremely painful. Jefferson complained bitterly to his friends and relatives, who knew well his aversion to medical treatment. "I am lately returned from the warm springs with my health entirely prostrated by the use of the waters," he told Francis Wayles Eppes. "They produced an imposthume and eruptions which with the torment of the journey back reduced me to the last stage of weakness and exhaustion." He was ill for three months, he told Lafayette. And to John Adams he expounded a medical theory that might not have occurred to Hippocrates or Galen. "I was then in good health and it ought to have occurred to me that the medecine which makes the sick well, may make the well sick." Years later he would complain that since visiting the springs he had "never since had a moment of perfect health."[20]

Except for trips to Poplar Forest, which dwindled in frequency, he was done with travel. He had not been to Richmond since October 1809, perhaps because the place held unhappy memories of his governorship. He would go no more to the Natural Bridge, a beloved place in Rockbridge County that lay on a piece of his land, and which was his Royal Gorge, his Great Falls, his own sampling of the wonderlands of America.[21]

Though he was missing the day-to-day acceleration of western development, he was still consulted on large questions. Until his death he would have the satisfaction of seeing the government in the hands of men of like views: Madison followed by Monroe, then John Quincy Adams, who was a strong believer in exploration. "One hundred expeditions of circumnavigation like those of Cook and La Perouse," Adams told Congress, "would not burden the exchequer of the nation fitting them out so much as the ways and means of defraying a single campaign in war."[22]

Missouri Territory achieved statehood in 1821 under circumstances that evoked his lifelong equivocation about slavery. A national uproar preceded Missouri's admission for two years, while debate raged on the power of Congress to control slavery. The compromise was to admit Missouri as a slave state and Maine as a free one, preserving a sectional equilibrium in Congress. Jefferson opposed the decision, fearing "a division of parties by a geographical line," and rationalized his approval of slavery in Missouri in this way: "Of one thing I am certain, that as the passage of slaves from one State to another, would not make a slave of a single human being who would not be so without it, so their diffusion over a greater surface would make them individually happier, and proportionally facilitate the accomplishment of their emancipation, by dividing the burden on a greater number of coadjutors."[23]

His full approval of the Monroe Doctrine, which he participated in developing, was not a revival of his evanescent dream of hemispheric fraternity. It was a stern restatement of the anti-monarchical, isolationist stand he had always upheld. "Nothing is so important as that America shall separate herself from the systems of Europe, & establish one of her own," he wrote the Abbé Correa da Serra. "Our circumstances, our pursuits, our interests are distinct. The principles of our policy should be also."[24]

Daniel Webster, visiting Monticello in December 1824, found Jefferson alarmed at the prospect that Andrew Jackson might become president. Jackson was "one of the most unfit men I know for such a place." He had little respect for law, Jefferson declared, and was a man of such passionate rages that he often choked when speaking on a controversial subject. "He is a dangerous man," Jefferson said.[25] Jackson was not the sort that Jefferson could feel close to: a folk hero, war hero, tough and raw spokesman of expansionism and relentless Indian removal, a leader in whom the newly formed society on the frontier could see itself epitomized. That the Jeffersonian age was yielding to the Jacksonian the man of Monticello would never have grasped or accepted.

His remaining days were few now. No one can say how much he recognized or valued his contribution to the West. He had, after all, failed to list even the presidency of the United States in his self-composed epitaph. In western matters as in most others, he had not been an innovator but a reactor or responder. He was at his finest when responding brilliantly to unexpected events: to Mackenzie's startling voyage across Canada, or Napoleon's thunderbolt offer to sell Louisiana. He had another quality that always was evident: the strength to react stoically to disappointments and diminished expectations. There was no waterway across the continent, nor even a short portage. The Spanish were not going to let him complete his exploring program. The French in Upper Louisiana were not willing to uproot and come east across the Mississippi. The American people were unwilling to let the Indian problem resolve itself humanely. Some of these disappointments were burdensome to him; they were never shattering.

The recently formed University of Virginia, which he thought of as one of his supreme achievements, required much of his waning energy. In casting about for old friends who might help the university to extend its influence, he thought of William Clark. The companion of Lewis was now a settled figure on the frontier, a fair and earnest spokesman for the Indian affairs which he had managed for so long. He had been active as a militia general in the Mississippi Valley during the War of 1812, had served as governor of Missouri Territory, and still had many years of service ahead in St. Louis. A dinner companion in those days described him as "hale, of florid complexion, flaxen hair, stout pleasant countenance."[26]

Jefferson wrote Clark about his hope for the university, expressing a desire that young men from the West would choose to attend. Knowing Clark's penchant for collecting museum items, he asked that some might be sent for the university's museum. "Born, I believe, and raised, I am sure, within sight of our University, you must feel the double sympathies for the country and neighborhood of your birth." Jefferson asked for "curiosities in general of art or nature, and said that those of Indian manufacture "stand very near to nature itself."[27]

Clark replied that he had heard of the new school and that many of the young men in his area, including his own sons, had shown an interest in attending. He said he had little to contribute in the way of museum artifacts but would apply to his subagents for assistance. Then he turned to his unhappiness about the state of the Indians and his feeling of helplessness to stem the tide that ran against them:

In my present Situation of Superentendent of Indian Affairs, it would afford me pleasure to be enabled to meliorate the condition of those unfortunate people placed under my charge, knowing as I do their wretchedness, and their rapid decline. It is to be lamented that this deplorable Situation of the Indians do not Receive more of the humain feelings of this Nation. I find your answers to Indians who have visited you, and your advice to them treasured up by several of the Tribes, who refer to them for their course of future happiness. Those people begin to see their dependences upon Agriculture, and if proper aid was afforded them much could be affected in bettering their situation. As I feel some Solicitude for the Indians, It would afford me much pleasure to have your views on this subject, which would enable me to use the Small Means in my power to the foundation of more favourable results in their Condition.[28]

There was nothing that Jefferson could say or do. He did not reply.

On the day of Jefferson's birth in 1743, the Canadian La Vérendrye brothers had set out for home after a tantalizing view of a new western horizon. On the day he died in 1826, a young American traveler named Jedediah S. Smith was preparing to lead a party from his camp near Great Salt Lake to the uncharted regions of inland California.[29] The white spaces on the maps of Jefferson's West were filling in fast. An easier way across the Rockies, the South Pass, was beckoning the first of the wagon trains; it was the new generation's Cumberland Gap. Between the Cumberland and South Pass, and then reaching out another thousand miles to the Pacific, was Jefferson's remarkable monument: a land where the American people could do what they loved doing best. They could grow.

NOTES

1. TJ to Lucy Lewis, 19 April 1808, LC. Even his occasional trips to Staunton had been made while he was a young lawyer.

2. Reporting on the work of the commission, he wrote daughter Martha Randolph that Staunton had received two votes as the site of the university, Lexington three, and Charlottesville sixteen (4 Aug. 1818, BETTS & BEAR, 423–24).

3. RENIERS, 26–27, 104–5. Colonel Fry's hospitality was said to be the best of all the Warm Springs innkeepers; he provided dancing in the hotel ballroom and visited his infirm guests in their quarters.

4. MARTIN [1], 323–24. Long before he had seen the springs, Jefferson had written that they relieved rheumatism and that "other complaints also of very different natures have been removed or lessened by them" (NOTES, 35). Dr. A. Green of Philadelphia had written that the waters were almost incredible in their effect on rheumatism, gout, and "other local affections of the nervous system" (*Philadelphia Medical and Physical Journal*, 1 (1804), pt. 1, 24).

5. See TJ to Martha, 7 Aug., 14 Aug., and 21 Aug. 1818, BETTS & BEAR, 425–26.

6. TJ to Clark, 19 Dec. 1807, LC. An alcoholic invalid, Clark had died at Locust Hill a few miles north of Louisville on 13 Feb. 1818.

7. TJ to Samuel Kercheval, 12 July 1816, LC.

8. TJ to Madison, 27 April 1809, LC.

9. TJ to Madison, 6 Nov. 1812, LC. He was unhappy with the generalship of the time, declaring that Hull ought to be shot for cowardice and treachery, and Van Rensselaer should be broken for cowardice and incapacity.

10. "Whether we remain in one confederacy, or form into Atlantic and Mississippi confederacies, I believe not very important to the happiness of either part" (to Priestley, 29 Jan. 1804, LC).

11. TJ to Barbé-Marbois, 14 June 1817, LC.

12. To Monroe, 24 Nov. 1801, LC. His qualification, "distant times," is important, for he felt that the present interests of the country "may restrain us within our own limits."

13. WHITAKER, 147. Late in 1811 the United States, through a committee chaired by Mitchill, made a cautious approach to the cause of Spanish-American independence, welcoming the Latins as neighbors and voicing concern for their welfare, but taking care not to say anything that might encourage further rebellion against Spanish authority (WHITAKER, 82–83).

14. "We shall make [the government for the Territory of Orleans] as mild and free, as they are able to bear, all persons residing there concurring in the information that they are neither gratified, nor willing to exercise the rights of an elective government" (TJ to Du Pont de Nemours, 19 Jan. 1804, CHINARD [3], 81).

15. Letters of 15 April 1811 and 24 April 1816, LC. Jefferson's correspondence with Du Pont de Nemours, collected in CHINARD [3], presents the best material on his evolving attitude toward South America.

16. TJ to Humboldt, 6 Dec. 1813, LC. Bolívar had tried in vain to interest Humboldt in revolution, but the German savant had no desire for that kind of participation in the struggle.

17. Monroe to TJ, 28 April 1818, Papers of James Monroe, LC; TJ to Monroe, 19 Jan. 1819, LC.

18. BROOKS [1], v. This work is the standard study of the Adams-Onís negotiations.

19. For a biography of Long, an account of his western expedition, and editions of his northern journals respectively, see WOOD, JAMES, and LONG.

20. To Eppes, 11 Sept. 1818, and to Lafayette, 23 Nov. 1818, LC; to Adams, 7 Oct. 1818 and 18 Dec. 1825, CAPPON [2], 528, 612. In the 1825 letter to Adams he said the waters had destroyed his "internal organism."

21. Natural Bridge is a ninety-foot span of stone lying across a gorge cut by Cedar Creek in Rockbridge County, Va. Jefferson had owned it since 1774, but had seen it only twice in recent years, once in 1815 and again in 1817. On the last visit he had taken his granddaughters, Cornelia and Ellen Randolph, on a side trip from Poplar Forest. The countryside and bridge delighted the girls. Cornelia reported, "On looking down [from the bridge] it has very much the effect on your head that looking down a well has. We stood on the edge & look'd down with perfect safety . . ." (to Virginia Randolph, 30 Aug. 1817, Nicholas Trist Papers, University of North Carolina, Chapel Hill).

22. Adams's first annual message to Congress, RICHARDSON, 2:312.

23. TJ to John Holmes, 22 April 1820, LC. For a recent discussion of TJ on the Compromise, see MILLER, 221–52.

24. To Correa da Serra, 24 Oct. 1820, LC.

25. Memorandum of Dec. 1824, WEBSTER, 1:371. "His complexion, formerly light and freckled, now bears the marks of age and cutaneous affection. . . . His walk is not precise and military, but easy and

swinging. . . . His whole dress is very much neglected, but not slovenly. He wears a common round hat" (364–65).

26. An entry of 5 March 1826 from the diary of James Edward Calhoun, communicated by T. W. Baldwin.

27. TJ to Clark, 12 Sept. 1825, LC.

28. Clark to TJ, 15 Dec. 1825, LC.

29. Smith's account of his expedition is in BROOKS [2].

BIBLIOGRAPHY

ABERBACH   Aberbach, David Alan. "Samuel Latham Mitchill: A Romantic Nationalist in the Age of Jefferson." Ph.D. dissertation, University of Florida, Gainesville, 1962.

ABERNETHY   Abernethy, Thomas P. *The Burr Conspiracy*. New York: Oxford University Press, 1954.

ADAMS   Adams, John Quincy. *Memoirs*, ed. Charles Francis Adams. 12 vols. Philadelphia: Lippincott, 1874–77.

ALLEN [1]   Allen, John Logan. "The Geographical Images of the American Northwest." Ph.D. dissertation, Clark University, Worcester, Mass., 1969.

ALLEN [2]   ———. *Passage through the Garden: Lewis and Clark and the Image of the American Northwest*. Urbana: University of Illinois Press, 1975.

ALVORD &   Alvord, Clarence W., and Lee Bidgood. *First Explo-*
BIDGOOD   *rations of the Trans-Allegheny Region by the Virginians, 1650–1674*. Cleveland: Arthur H. Clark, 1912.

AM. ST.   *American State Papers*. Indian Affairs, 2 vols., Washing-
PAPERS   ton, 1832–34; Miscellaneous, 2 vols., Washington, 1834.

ANAS   Sawvel, Franklin B., ed. *The Complete Anas of Thomas Jefferson*. New York: Da Capo, 1970.

AUGUR   Augur, Helen. *Passage to Glory: John Ledyard's America*. New York: Doubleday, 1946.

AUTOBIOG-   Jefferson, Thomas. *Autobiography*. New York: Put-
RAPHY   nam, Capricorn paperback, 1959.

BAKELESS   Bakeless, John. *Lewis and Clark: Partners in Discovery*. New York: Morrow, 1947.

BATES   Marshall, Thomas Maitland, ed. *The Life and Papers of Frederick Bates*. 2 vols. St. Louis: Missouri Historical Society, 1926.

BEDINI   Bedini, Silvio A. *Thinkers and Tinkers: Early American Men of Science*. New York: Scribner's, 1975.

[311]

BESTOR   Bestor, Arthur. "Thomas Jefferson and the Freedom
                  of Books." In *Three Presidents and Their Books*. Urbana:
                  University of Illinois Press, 1955.

BETTS   Betts, Edwin M., ed. "The Correspondence between
                  Rafinesque and Thomas Jefferson." *Proceedings* of the
                  American Philosophical Society, 87 (May 1944), 368–
                  80.

BETTS & BEAR   ———, and James Bear, eds. *The Family Letters of
                  Thomas Jefferson*. Columbia: University of Missouri
                  Press, 1966.

BIDDLE   *History of the Expedition under the Command of Captains
                  Lewis and Clark, to the Sources of the Missouri, Thence
                  across the Rocky Mountains and down the River Columbia
                  to the Pacific Ocean. . . . Prepared for the Press by Paul
                  Allen, Esquire*. 2 vols. Philadelphia: Bradford & Ins-
                  keep, 1814.

BILLON   Billon, Frederic L. *Annals of St. Louis in Its Early Days
                  under the French and Spanish Dominations, 1764–1804*.
                  St. Louis: G. I. Jones, 1886.

BOORSTIN   Boorstin, Daniel J. *The Lost World of Thomas Jefferson*.
                  Boston: Beacon, 1948.

BOYD   Boyd, Julian P., ed. *The Papers of Thomas Jefferson*. 19
                  vols. to date. Princeton: Princeton University Press,
                  1950–.

BRADLEY   Bradley, Jared W. "Claiborne and Spain: Foreign Af-
                  fairs under Jefferson and Madison, 1801–11."
                  Louisiana History, 12 (Fall 1971), 297–314; 13 (Winter
                  1972), 5–28.

BRANDON   Brandon, William. "Wilson Price Hunt." In *The
                  Mountain Men and the Fur Trade*, ed. Leroy R. Hafen,
                  vol. 6. Glendale, Cal.: A. H. Clark, 1968.

BRODIE   Brodie, Fawn M. *Thomas Jefferson: An Intimate History*.
                  New York: Norton, 1974.

BROOKS [1]   Brooks, Philip C. *Diplomacy and the Borderlands: The
                  Adams-Onís Treaty of 1819*. University of California
                  Publications in History, vol. 24. Berkeley, 1937.

BROOKS [2]   Brooks, George R., ed. *The Southwestern Expedition of
                  Jedediah S. Smith*. Glendale, Cal.: A. H. Clark, 1977.

BURPEE [1]   Burpee, Lawrence J. *The Search for the Western Sea: The
                  Story of the Exploration of North-Western America*. Lon-
                  don: Alson Rivers, 1908.

BURPEE [2] ——, ed. *The Journals and Letters of Pierre Gualtier de Varennes de La Vérendrye and His Sons.* 2 vols. Toronto: Champlain Society, 1927.

BUTTERFIELD & RICE Butterfield, Lyman, and Howard C. Rice. "Jefferson's Earliest Note to Maria Cosway with Some New Facts and Conjectures on His Broken Wrist." *William and Mary Quarterly,* 5 (1948), 26–33, 620–21.

CALLAN Callan, John F., ed. *The Military Laws of the United States.* Philadelphia, 1863.

CANTWELL Cantwell, Robert. *Alexander Wilson: Naturalist and Pioneer.* Philadelphia: Lippincott, 1961.

CAPPON [1] Cappon, Lester J. "Geographers and Mapmakers, 1750–89." *Proceedings* of the American Antiquarian Society, 81 (Oct. 1971), 243–71.

CAPPON [2] ——, ed. *The Adams-Jefferson Letters: The Complete Correspondence between Thomas Jefferson and Abigail and John Adams.* 2 vols. Chapel Hill: University of North Carolina Press, 1959.

CAPPON [3] ——, ed. *Atlas of Early American History: The Revolutionary Era, 1760–1790.* Princeton: Princeton University Press, 1976.

CHINARD [1] Chinard, Gilbert. *Volney et l'Amérique d'après des documents inédits et sa correspondance avec Jefferson.* Baltimore: Johns Hopkins University Press, 1923.

CHINARD [2] ——, ed. *The Letters of Lafayette and Jefferson.* Baltimore: Johns Hopkins University Press, 1929.

CHINARD [3] ——, ed. *Correspondence of Jefferson and Du Pont de Nemours, with an Introduction on Jefferson and the Physiocrats.* Baltimore: Johns Hopkins University Press, 1931.

CHINARD [4] ——, ed. *Le Voyage de Láperouse sur les Côtes de l'Alaska et de la Californie.* Baltimore: Johns Hopkins University Press, 1937.

CHRISTMAS Boyd, Julian P. *The Spirit of Christmas at Monticello.* New York: Oxford University Press, 1964.

CLAIBORNE Rowland, Dunbar, ed. *Official Letter Books of William C. C. Claiborne.* 6 vols. Jackson, Miss.: Dept. of Archives and History, 1917.

CLARK Clark, Harry Hayden. "The Influence of Science on American Ideas, from 1775 to 1809." *Transactions* of the Wisconsin Academy of Sciences, Arts, and Letters, 35 (1944), 305–49.

COOK [1]   *A Voyage to the Pacific Ocean . . . Performed under the Direction of Captain Cook, Clerke and Gore, in the Years 1776, 1777, 1778, 1779, and 1780.* 4 vols. London, 1784.

COOK [2]   Cook, Warren L. *Flood Tide of Empire: Spain and the Pacific Northwest, 1543–1819.* New Haven: Yale University Press, 1973.

COUES   Coues, Elliott, ed. *The Expeditions of Zebulon Montgomery Pike, to Headwaters of the Mississippi River, through Louisiana Territory, and in New Spain, during the Years 1805–6–7.* 3 vols. New York: Francis Harper, 1895.

COX [1]   Cox, Isaac Joslin. *The Early Exploration of Louisiana.* Cincinnati: University Studies, 1906.

COX [2]   ———. "General Wilkinson and His Later Intrigues with the Spaniards." *American Historical Review,* 19 (July 1914), 794–812.

COX [3]   ———. "An Early Explorer of the Louisiana Purchase." *Library Bulletin,* American Philosophical Society, 90 (1946), 73–77.

COXE   Coxe, Daniel. *A Description of the English Province of Carolana.* London, 1722.

CUNNINGHAM   Cunningham, Noble E., Jr. *The Process of Government under Jefferson.* Princeton: Princeton University Press, 1978.

CUTRIGHT [1]   Cutright, Paul Russell. *Lewis and Clark: Pioneering Naturalists.* Urbana: University of Illinois Press, 1969.

CUTRIGHT [2]   ———. *A History of the Lewis and Clark Journals.* Norman: University of Oklahoma Press, 1976.

DARGO   Dargo, George. *Jefferson's Louisiana: Politics and the Clash of Legal Traditions.* Cambridge: Harvard University Press, 1975.

DARLINGTON   Darlington, William. *Memorials of John Bartram and Humphry Marshall, with Notices of Their Botanical Contemporaries.* Philadelphia: Lindsay & Blakiston, 1849.

DAVIS [1]   Davis, John W. "Thomas Jefferson, Attorney at Law." In *Jefferson Reader: A Treasury of Works about Thomas Jefferson,* ed. Francis C. Rosenberger. New York: Dutton, 1953.

DAVIS [2]   Davis, Richard Beale. *Intellectual Life in Jefferson's Virginia, 1790–1830.* Chapel Hill: University of North Carolina Press, 1964.

DE ROSIER   DeRosier, Arthur H., Jr. "William Dunbar, Explorer." *Journal of Mississippi History,* 25 (1963), 165–85.

DE TERRA   De Terra, Helmut. "Alexander von Humboldt's Correspondence with Jefferson, Madison, and Gallatin." *Proceedings* of the American Philosophical Society, 103 (1959), 783–806.

DE VOTO   De Voto, Bernard. *The Course of Empire.* Boston: Houghton Mifflin, 1952.

DILLER   Diller, Aubrey. "An Early Account of the Missouri River." *Missouri Historical Review,* 45 (Jan. 1951), 150–57.

DILLON   Dillon, Richard. *Meriwether Lewis: A Biography.* New York: Coward-McCann, 1965.

DOS PASSOS [1]   Dos Passos, John. *The Head and Heart of Thomas Jefferson.* Garden City, N.Y.: Doubleday, 1954.

DOS PASSOS [2]   ———. "A Portico Facing the Wilderness." In *Thomas Jefferson: A Profile,* ed. Merrill D. Peterson. New York: Hill and Wang, 1967.

DOUGHTY   Doughty, J. and T. *The Cabinet of Natural History and American Rural Sports.* 2 vols. Philadelphia, 1830–32.

DOUGHTY & MARTIN   Doughty, A. G., and Chester Martin, eds. *The Kelsey Papers.* Ottawa: Public Archives of Canada, 1929.

DUMBAULD   Dumbauld, Edward. *Thomas Jefferson: American Tourist.* Norman: University of Oklahoma Press, 1946.

DUNGAN   Dungan, James R. "Sir William Dunbar of Natchez: Planter, Explorer, and Scientist, 1792–1810." *Journal of Mississippi History,* 23 (1961), 211–28.

DUNMORE   Dunmore, John. *French Explorers in the Pacific.* London: Oxford University Press, 1965.

ECHEVERRIA   Echeverria, Durant. *Mirage in the West: A History of the French Image of American Society to 1815.* Princeton: Princeton University Press, 1957.

ESAREY   Esarey, Logan, ed. *Messages and Letters of William Henry Harrison.* 2 vols. Indianapolis: Indiana Historical Collections, 1922.

EWAN   Ewan, Joseph. "French Naturalists in the Mississippi Valley." In *The French in the Mississippi Valley,* ed. John Francis McDermott. Urbana: University of Illinois Press, 1965.

FARM BOOK   Betts, Edwin M., ed. *Thomas Jefferson's Farm Book.*

Princeton: Princeton University Press, 1953.

FELLOWS &
MILLIKEN
Fellows, Otis E., and Stephen F. Milliken. *Buffon.* New York: Twayne, 1972.

FIELD NOTES
Osgood, Ernest S., ed. *The Field Notes of Captain William Clark, 1803–1805.* New Haven: Yale University Press, 1964.

FISHER
Fisher, Vardis. *Suicide or Murder? The Strange Death of Governor Meriwether Lewis.* Denver: Swallow, 1962.

FOLEY
Foley, William E. "James A. Wilkinson: Territorial Governor." *Bulletin* of the Missouri Historical Society, 25 (Oct. 1968), 3–17.

FREEMAN &
CUSTIS
[Freeman, Thomas, and Peter Custis.] *An Account of the Red River, in Louisiana, Drawn Up from the Returns of Messrs. Freeman and Custis to the War Office of the United States. . . .* Washington, [1807].

FRICK &
STEARNS
Frick, George Frederick, and Raymond Phineas Stearns. *Mark Catesby: The Colonial Audubon.* Urbana: University of Illinois Press, 1961.

FRIIS
Friis, Herman R. "Baron Alexander von Humboldt's Visit to Washington." *Records* of the Columbia Historical Society, 1960–62 (1963), 1–35.

FRY & JEFFER-
SON
The Fry & Jefferson Map of Virginia and Maryland: Facsimiles of the 1754 and 1794 Printings. Charlottesville: University Press of Virginia, 1966.

GALLAND
Galland, Isaac. *Chronicles of the North American Savage,* 1 (May-Sept. 1835).

GARDEN BOOK
Betts, Edwin M., ed. *Thomas Jefferson's Garden Book.* Philadelphia: American Philosophical Society, 1944.

GARRETT
Garrett, Julia K. "Dr. John Sibley and the Louisiana-Texas Frontier, 1803–14." *Southwestern Historical Quarterly,* 45 (1942), 286–301, and six subsequent issues.

GASS
Gass, Patrick. *A Journal of the Voyages and Travels of a Corps of Discovery, under the command of Capt. Lewis and Capt. Clarke . . . from the Mouth of the River Missouri through the Interior Parts of North America to the Pacific Ocean, during the years 1804, 1805, & 1806.* Pittsburgh: M'Keehan, 1807.

GIBSON
Gibson, James R. *Imperial Russia in Frontier America.* New York: Oxford University Press, 1976.

GRISWOLD
Griswold, Bert J., ed. *Fort Wayne: Gateway of the West.* Indianapolis: Indiana Historical Society, 1927.

HATFIELD   Hatfield, Joseph T. *William Claiborne: Jeffersonian Centurion in the American Southwest.* Lafayette: University of Southwestern Louisiana, 1976.

HAY & WERNER Hay, Thomas Robson, and M. R. Werner. *The Admirable Trumpeter.* New York: Doubleday, 1941.

HEITMAN   Heitman, Francis B. *Historical Register and Dictionary of the United States Army.* 2 vols. Washington, 1903; reprinted, Urbana: University of Illinois Press, 1965.

HENDERSON   Henderson, Archibald. "Dr. Thomas Walker and the Loyal Land Company of Virginia." *Proceedings* of the American Antiquarian Society, 41 (1932), 77–178.

HINDLE   Hindle, Brooke. *The Pursuit of Science in Revolutionary America, 1735–1789.* Chapel Hill: University of North Carolina Press, 1956.

HOLLON   Hollon, W. Eugene. *The Lost Pathfinder: Zebulon Montgomery Pike.* Norman: University of Oklahoma Press, 1949.

JACKSON [1]   Jackson, Donald. "Some Books Carried by Lewis and Clark." *Bulletin* of the Missouri Historical Society, 16 (Oct. 1959), 3–13.

JACKSON [2]   ———. "How Lost Was Zebulon Pike?" *American Heritage,* 16 (Feb. 1965), 10–15, 75–80.

JACKSON [3]   ———. "Zebulon Pike 'Tours' Mexico." *American West,* 3 (Summer 1966), 89–93.

JACKSON [4]   ———. "Some Advice for the Next Editor of Lewis and Clark." *Bulletin* of the Missouri Historical Society, 24 (Oct. 1967), 52–62.

JACKSON [5]   ———. "A Footnote to the Lewis and Clark Expedition." *Manuscripts,* 24 (1972), 3–21.

JACKSON [6]   ———. "Ledyard and Lapérouse: A Contrast in Northwestern Exploration." *Western Historical Quarterly,* 9 (Oct. 1978), 495–508.

JACKSON [7]   ———. "Jefferson, Meriwether Lewis, and the Reduction of the United States Army." *Proceedings* of the American Philosophical Society, 124 (1980), 91–96.

JACKSON &   ———, and Dorothy Twohig, eds. *The Diaries of George Washington.* 6 vols. Charlottesville: University
TWOHIG   Press of Virginia, 1976–79.

JACOBS   Jacobs, James Ripley. *Tarnished Warrior.* New York: Macmillan, 1938.

JAMES   James, Edwin. *Account of an Expedition [with Long] from Pittsburgh to the Rocky Mountains.* 3 vols. In *Early West-*

ern *Travels,* ed. Reuben Gold Thwaites. Cleveland: A. H. Clark, 1905.

JAY   Johnston, Henry P., ed. *The Correspondence and Public Papers of John Jay.* 4 vols. New York: Putnam, 1890–93.

JOHNSTON [1]   Johnston, Josiah Stoddard, ed. *First Explorations of Kentucky.* Filson Club Publication no. 13. Louisville, Ky., 1898.

JOHNSTON [2]   Johnston, William D. *History of the Library of Congress.* Washington, 1904.

JONES   Jones, Anna C. "Antlers for Jefferson." *New England Quarterly,* 12 (June 1939), 333–48.

JOSEPHY   Josephy, Alvin M., Jr. *The Nez Perce Indians and the Opening of the Northwest.* New Haven: Yale University Press, 1965.

KAPPLER   Kappler, Charles J., ed. *Indian Affairs: Laws and Treaties.* 2 vols. Washington, 1904.

KASTNER   Kastner, Joseph. *A Species of Eternity.* New York: Knopf, 1977.

KELLNER   Kellner, Charlotte. *Alexander von Humboldt.* New York: Oxford University Press, 1963.

KNOLLENBERG   Knollenberg, Bernhard. *George Washington: The Virginia Period, 1732–1775.* Durham, N.C.: Duke University Press, 1964.

LAMB   Lamb, W. Kaye, ed. *The Journals and Letters of Sir Alexander Mackenzie.* London: Hakluyt Society, 1970.

LAPÉROUSE [1]   [Lapérouse, Jean François de.] *Voyage de la Pérouse autor du monde . . . rédigé par M. L. A. Milet-Mureau.* 4 vols. and atlas. Paris, 1797.

LAPÉROUSE [2]   ———. *A Voyage round the World, Performed in the Years 1785, 1786, 1787, and 1788, by the Boussole and Astrolabe.* 3 vols. and atlas. London, 1807.

L & C JOUR-   Thwaites, Reuben Gold, ed. *Original Journals of the*
NALS   *Lewis and Clark Expedition, 1804–1806, Printed from the Original Manuscripts in the Library of the American Philosophical Society.* 8 vols. New York: Dodd, Mead, 1904–5.

L & C LETTERS   Jackson, Donald, ed. *Letters of the Lewis and Clark Expedition, with Related Documents, 1783–1854.* Second ed., with additional documents and notes. 2 vols. Urbana: University of Illinois Press, 1978.

LEVY · Levy, Leonard. *Jefferson and Civil Liberties*. Cambridge, Mass.: Belknap Press, 1963.

LESSEPS · Lesseps, Jean-Baptiste Barthélemy. *Travels in Kamchatka, 1787 and 1788*. London, 1790.

LEWIS · Wayland, J. W., ed. *The Fairfax Line: Thomas Lewis's Journal of 1746*. New Market, Va.: privately printed, 1925.

LEWIS & ORDWAY · Quaife, Milo M., ed. *The Journals of Captain Meriwether Lewis and Sergeant John Ordway Kept on the Expedition of Western Exploration, 1803–1806*. Madison: State Historical Society of Wisconsin, 1916.

LONG · Kane, Lucile M., June D. Holmquist, and Carolyn Gilman, eds. *The Northern Expeditions of Stephen H. Long*. St. Paul: Minnesota Historical Society Press, 1978.

LONG & MARTIN · Long, Austin, and Paul S. Martin. "Death of American Ground Sloths." *Science*, 186 (Nov. 1974), 638–40.

LOOMIS · Loomis, Noel M. "Philip Nolan's Entry into Texas in 1800." In *The Spanish in the Mississippi Valley*, ed. John Francis McDermott. Urbana: University of Illinois Press, 1974.

LOVEJOY · Lovejoy, Arthur O. *The Great Chain of Being: A Study of the History of an Idea*. Cambridge: Harvard University Press, 1936.

MC ATEE · McAtee, W. E., ed. "Journal of Benjanin Smith Barton on a Visit to Virginia, 1802." *Castanea: Journal of the Southern Appalachian Botany Club*, 3 (1938), 85–117.

MC CALEB [1] · McCaleb, Walter. *The Aaron Burr Conspiracy*. New York: Dodd, Mead, 1903.

MC CALEB [2] · ———. *New Light on Aaron Burr*. Austin: Texas Quarterly Studies, 1963.

MC DERMOTT [1] · McDermott, John Francis. "William Clark's Struggle with Place Names in Upper Louisiana." *Bulletin* of the Missouri Historical Society, 34 (April 1978), 140–50.

MC DERMOTT [2] · ———, ed. "The Western Journals of Dr. George Hunter, 1796–1805." *Transactions* of the American Philosophical Society, 53 (1963).

MC GILLIVRAY · McGillivray, Duncan. "Account of the Wild North-American Sheep." *Medical Repository*, 6 (1803), 237–40.

MC KELVEY · McKelvey, Susan Delano. *Botanical Exploration*

of the Trans-Mississippi West, 1790–1850. Jamaica Plain, Mass.: Arnold Arboretum of Harvard University, 1955.

MACKENZIE   Mackenzie, Alexander. *Voyages from Montreal, on the River St. Lawrence, through the Continent of North America, to the Frozen and Pacific Ocean.* . . . 2 vols. London, 1801.

MALONE   Malone, Dumas. *Jefferson and His Time*. Vol. 1: *Jefferson the Virginian*. Vol. 2: *Jefferson and the Rights of Man*. Vol. 3: *Jefferson and the Ordeal of Liberty*. Vol. 4: *Jefferson the President, First Term, 1801–1805*. Vol. 5: *Jefferson the President, Second Term, 1805–1809*. Boston: Little, Brown, 1948–.

MANNING   Manning, William K. *The Nootka Sound Controversy*. American Historical Association Annual Report, 1904. Washington, 1905.

MARSHALL   Marshall, Thomas Maitland. *A History of the Western Boundaries of the Louisiana Purchase, 1819–1841*. University of California Publications in History, vol. 2. Berkeley, 1914.

MARTIN [1]   Martin, Joseph. *A New and Comprehensive Gazetteer of Virginia and the District of Columbia*. Charlottesville, Va.: Joseph Martin, 1835.

MARTIN [2]   Martin, Edwin T. *Thomas Jefferson, Scientist*. New York: Schuman, 1952.

MASSON   Masson, Louis François Redrigue. *Les bourgeois de la Compagnie du Nord-Ouest; recits de voyages, lettres et rapports inedits relatifs au Nord-Ouest canadien*. 2 vols. Quebec, 1889–90.

MAURY   Maury, Anne Fontaine. *Memoirs of a Huguenot Family*. New York, 1852.

MEDLIN   Medlin, Dorothy. "Thomas Jefferson, André Morellet, and the French Version of Notes on the State of Virginia." *William and Mary Quarterly*, 35 (Jan. 1978), 85–99.

MEGATHERIUM   Boyd, Julian P. "The Megalonyx, the Megatherium, and Thomas Jefferson's Lapse of Memory." *Proceedings of the American Philosophical Society*, 102 (1958), 420–35.

MESSAGE   [Jefferson, Thomas]. *Message From the President of the United States Communicating Discoveries Made in Exploring the Missouri, Red River and Washita, by Captains*

	Lewis and Clark, Doctor Sibley, and Mr. Dunbar. . . . Washington, 1806.
MILLER	Miller, John Chester. *The Wolf by the Ears: Thomas Jefferson and Slavery.* New York: Free Press, 1977.
MILLER & KEL-LOGG	Miller, Gerrit S., Jr., and Remington Kellogg. "List of North American Recent Mammals." *Bulletin* of the U.S. National Museum, no. 205, 1955.
MITCHILL	Mitchill, Samuel Latham. *A Discourse on the Character and Services of Thomas Jefferson.* New York, 1862.
MONTGOMERY	Montgomery, Franz. "Alexander Mackenzie's Literary Assistant." *Canadian Historical Review,* 18 (1937), 301–4.
MUNFORD	Munford, James Kenneth, ed. *John Ledyard's Journal of Captain Cook's Last Voyage.* Corvallis: Oregon State University Press, 1963.
NASATIR	Nasatir, A. P., ed. *Before Lewis and Clark.* 2 vols. St. Louis: St. Louis Historical Documents Foundation, 1954.
NIEMCEWICZ	Niemcewicz, Julian U. *Under Their Vine and Fig Tree.* Elizabeth, N. J.: Grassman, 1965.
NOTES	Jefferson, Thomas. *Notes on the State of Virginia,* ed. William Peden. Chapel Hill: University of North Carolina Press, 1955.
NYLAND	Nyland, Keith Ryan. "Doctor Thomas Walker (1715–1794), Explorer, Physician, Statesman, Surveyor and Planter of Virginia and Kentucky." Ph.D. dissertation, Ohio State University, Columbus, 1971.
PALUKA	Paluka, Frank. *The Three Voyages of Captain Cook.* Beta Phi Mu Chapbook, no. 10. Pittsburgh, 1974.
PASTON	Paston, George [pseud.]. *Little Memoires of the Eighteenth Century,* by Emily M. Symonds. New York: Dutton, 1901.
PEDEN	Peden, William Harwood. "Thomas Jefferson: Book-Collector." Ph.D. dissertation, University of Virginia, Charlottesville, 1942.
PENNANT	Pennant, Thomas. *Arctic Zoology.* 2 vols. London, 1784–87.
PETERSON [1]	Peterson, Merrill D. *Thomas Jefferson and the New Nation.* New York: Oxford University Press, 1970.
PETERSON [2]	———. *Adams and Jefferson: A Revolutionary Dialogue.* New York: Oxford University Press, 1978.
PETERSON [3]	———. "Thomas Jefferson's 'Notes on the State of

Virginia.' " In *Studies in Eighteenth-Century Culture*, vol. 7. Madison: University of Wisconsin Press, 1978.

PETERSON [4]   ———, ed. *Thomas Jefferson: A Profile.* New York: Hill and Wang, 1967.

PHILBRICK   Philbrick, Francis S. *The Rise of the West, 1754–1830.* New York: Harper & Row, 1965.

PIKE   Jackson, Donald, ed. *The Journals of Zebulon Montgomery Pike.* 2 vols. Norman: University of Oklahoma Press, 1966.

PLUMER   Brown, Everett Somerville. [*William Plumer's*] *Memorandum of Proceedings in the United States Senate, 1803–1807.* New York: Macmillan, 1923.

PORTER   Porter, Kenneth Wiggins. *John Jacob Astor, Business Man.* 2 vols. Cambridge: Harvard University Press, 1931.

PRUCHA   Prucha, Francis P. *American Indian Policy in the Formative Years.* Cambridge: Harvard University Press, 1962.

PRUSSING   Prussing, Eugene E. *The Estate of George Washington, Deceased.* Boston: Little, Brown, 1927.

PURCHASE DOCS.   *Documents Relating to the Purchase and Exploration of Louisiana.* Boston: Houghton Mifflin, 1904.

PURSH   Pursh, Frederick. *Flora Americae Septentrionalis.* 2 vols. London, 1814.

RANDALL   Randall, Henry S. *The Life of Thomas Jefferson.* 3 vols. New York, 1858.

RENIERS   Reniers, Perceval. *The Springs of Virginia.* Chapel Hill: University of North Carolina Press, 1941.

RICE   Rice, Howard C., Jr. *Thomas Jefferson's Paris.* Princeton: Princeton University Press, 1976.

RICHARDSON   Richardson, James D., ed. *A Compilation of the Messages and Papers of the Presidents.* 20 vols. New York, 1897–1922.

RICKETT   Rickett, H. W. "John Bradbury's Explorations in Missouri Territory." *Proceedings* of the American Philosophical Society, 94 (1950), 59–89.

RICKMAN   [Rickman, John.] *An Authentic Narrative of a Voyage to the Pacific Ocean. By an Officer on Board the Discovery.* Philadelphia: John Bell, 1783.

RISTOW [1]   Ristow, Walter W. "John Melish and His Map of the United States." Library of Congress *Quarterly Journal*, 19 (Sept. 1962), 159–69.

RISTOW [2]

———. "Maps." Library of Congress *Quarterly Journal*, 23 (July 1966), 231–42.

ROBBINS &
HOWSON

Robbins, William J., and Mary Christine Howson. "André Michaux's New Jersey Garden and Paul Saunier, Journeyman Gardener." *Proceedings* of the American Philosophical Society, 102 (Aug. 1958), 351–70.

ROBERTSON

Robertson, James A. *Louisiana under the Rule of the Spanish, French, and the United States.* 2 vols. Cleveland: A. H. Clark, 1911.

ROWLAND

Rowland, Mrs. Dunbar, ed. *Life, Letters and Papers of William Dunbar.* Jackson: Mississippi Historical Society, 1930.

SAUER

Sauer, Martin. *An Account of a Geographical and Astronomical Expedition to the Northern Parts of Russia.* London, 1802.

SCHACHNER

Schachner, Nathan. *Thomas Jefferson, a Biography.* New York: Yoseloff, 1937.

SELLERS

Sellers, Charles C. *Charles Willson Peale.* 2 vols. Philadelphia: American Philosophical Society, 1947.

SHEEHAN

Sheehan, Bernard W. *Seeds of Extinction: Jeffersonian Philanthropy and the American Indian.* Chapel Hill: University of North Carolina Press, 1973.

SHREVE

Shreve, Royal O. *The Finished Scoundrel.* Indianapolis: Bobbs-Merrill, 1933.

SIMPSON

Simpson, George Gaylord. "The Beginnings of Vertebrate Paleontology in the U.S." *Proceedings* of the American Philosophical Society, 86 (1942), 130–88.

SOWERBY

Sowerby, Millicent, comp. *Catalogue of the Library of Thomas Jefferson.* 5 vols. Washington: Library of Congress, 1952–59.

SPARKS

Sparks, Jared. *Life of John Ledyard, the American Traveller.* Boston: Little, Brown, 1847.

SPAULDING

Spaulding, Kenneth A., ed. *On the Oregon Trail: Robert Stuart's Journey of Discovery.* Norman: University of Oklahoma Press, 1953.

STILES

Dexter, Franklin B., ed. *The Literary Diary of Ezra Stiles.* 3 vols. New York: Scribner's, 1901.

TERR. PAPERS

Carter, Clarence C., and John Porter Bloom, eds. *Territorial Papers of the United States.* 25 vols. to date. Washington, 1934–.

TODD

Todd, Edgeley, W., ed. *Astoria: or Anecdotes of an*

Enterprise beyond the Rocky Mountains, by Washington Irving. Norman: University of Oklahoma Press, 1964.

VANCOUVER   Vancouver, George. *A Voyage of Discovery to the North Pacific Ocean.* 3 vols. London, 1798.

VENEGAS   Venegas, Miguel. *Noticia de la California.* . . . Madrid, [1757].

VERNER   Verner, Coolie. "Mr. Jefferson Makes a Map." *Imago Mundi,* 14 (1959), 96–108.

WALTERS   Walters, Raymond, Jr. *Albert Gallatin: Jeffersonian Financier and Diplomat.* New York: Macmillan, 1957.

WATROUS   Watrous, Stephen D., ed. *John Ledyard's Journey through Russia and Siberia, 1787–1788.* Madison: University of Wisconsin Press, 1966.

WEBSTER   Wiltse, Charles M., and Harold D. Moser, eds. *Papers of Daniel Webster.* 3 vols. to date. Hanover, N.H.: University Press of New England, 1974–.

WHITAKER   Whitaker, Arthur P. *The United States and the Independence of Latin America, 1800–1830.* Baltimore: Johns Hopkins University Press, 1941.

WHITTINGTON   Whittington, G. P. "Doctor John Sibley of Natchitoches." *Louisiana Historical Quarterly,* 20 (Oct. 1927), 467–73.

WOOD   Wood, Richard G. *Stephen Harriman Long, 1784–1864: Army Engineer, Explorer, Inventor.* Glendale, Cal.: A. H. Clark, 1966.

INDEX

DATE DUE